Typical and Atypical Development

For the children and parents I worked with
who inspired the writing of the book

Martin Herbert

Typical and Atypical Development

From Conception to Adolescence

BPS Blackwell

350 Main Street, Malden, MA 02148-5020, USA
9600 Garsington Road, Oxford OX4 2DQ, UK
550 Swanston Street, Carlton, Victoria 3053, Australia

First published 2003 by The British Psychological Association and
Blackwell Publishers Ltd,

5   2009

Library of Congress Cataloging-in-Publication Data
Herbert, Martin.
Typical and atypical development : from conception to adolescence /
Martin Herbert.
p. cm.
Includes bibliographical references and index.
ISBN 978–0–631–23465–4 (alk. paper) — ISBN 978–0–631–23467–8 (pbk. : alk. paper)
1. Child development.   2. Development disabilities.   I. Title.
RJ131 .H427 2002
612.6'5—dc21
2002006177

A catalogue record for this title is available from the British Library.

Set in $10^{1}/_{2}/13$pt Meridien
by Graphicraft Limited, Hong Kong

For further information on
Blackwell Publishing, visit our website:
www.blackwellpublishing.com

Contents

PART III: Typical development
Adaptation and learning

Preface

In planning this book I have had very much in mind the undergraduate and postgraduate students on abnormal and developmental psychology courses; also the trainee and qualified practitioners who work with children, adolescents and their families. The professionals come from various disciplines: clinical child psychology and psychiatry, paediatrics, social work, health visiting, nursing, education, speech and occupational therapy, and residential childcare. The knowledge base required by people entering as trainees, or working as qualified professionals in areas involving children with special needs, covers normal and abnormal child development, and also the life-experiences of able as well as disabled youngsters.

Having taught developmental and clinical courses for several years to undergraduate and postgraduate academic and professional students, as well as practitioners, I am conscious of how little cross-fertilization there has been between the developmental and clinical branches of psychology. Such mutual exclusiveness is particularly unfortunate when it comes to the assessment, understanding and rehabilitation or treatment of the physical and psychological problems of childhood. Much so-called 'abnormal' behaviour in children is not necessarily very different from normal activity in its development, persistence, and susceptibility to change. It seems fruitful to me to ask how a child develops behaviour in general, rather than limit the question to how he or she acquires abnormal or impaired behaviour as such.

Developmental psychopathology, a theoretical approach adopted in the book, is concerned with the description and explanation of changes in growth, emotional states and behaviour that are the outcome of maturational influences and life-experiences. A particular rationale, as a consequence, is the belief that work with the atypical problems of childhood (be they physical, psychological or a likely interaction of both) requires an understanding of what is typical in children's development; what they think, feel, do and say as they grow up. When there is a disability, an account of atypical development should help to explain how the normal developmental process is altered. As Vicky Lewis (1987) observes, an understanding of how a particular impairment may change the course of development in an individual child can also illuminate our understanding of what may be going on in the normal child. For example, it may alter the emphasis any explanation places on particular experiences.

Behavioural genetics, a further source of information for the book, focuses on why individuals within a species differ in behaviour (e.g. why children differ in rates of language acquisition). It also provides the evidence that in problem areas such as autism and reading disability there is a genetically influenced *continuum* between the normal and abnormal (Plomin, 2001a).

It is important to remember that not all children with disabling (atypical) conditions have atypical developmental patterns in all areas as they grow up. Five types of relationship between the development of disabled and non-disabled children are described in the literature:

1. Delayed development: This is development that is slower than in non-disabled (typical) children. The same stages are passed through and the same processes are involved, but atypical children may not ultimately reach the more advanced stages of development.
2. Abnormal development: This refers to circumstances where the processes of development are different from the normal. Consequently there are behaviours and developments not seen in children who are not impaired.
3. Compensatory development: In this category, disabled (atypical) children take a different route from that taken by typical children, although the end point is the same.
4. Absence of development: Here, children fail to develop in a particular aspect of development.
5. Normal behaviour displayed by disabled (atypical) children: In this category, aspects of the impaired child's development may be normal, developing within the range of variation reported for non-impaired children.

All of this, of course, begs an obvious, but awkward question: what is typical or normal? Kathleen Berger (2000) makes the wry comment that the typical (i.e. usual) patterns of growth and change are ones that everyone follows to some degree and that no one follows exactly. While, in an absolute sense, it is true that each person is 'an idiom unto himself, an apparent violation of the syntax of the species', as Gordon Allport (1937) put it, there are also important ways in which individuals resemble one another. Kluckhohn, Murray, and Schneider (1953) observed that 'every man is in certain respects like all other men, like some other man, like no other man'. We are like all other men and women, therefore some of the determinants of our personality are universal to our species. Personality will certainly figure as one of our developmental themes.

Children and their families with the kind of difficulties I will be describing, particularly in chapters 8 to 17, are likely to seek help from a wide range of professionals: geneticists, paediatricians, psychiatrists, general practitioners, clinical and educational psychologists, social workers, health visitors, speech and occupational therapists and physiotherapists. These practitioners work in a variety of agencies, and often (for developmentally impaired children) under the single roof of a multidisciplinary child development centre. Whatever the medical treatments or psychosocial interventions in use, the goal is usually to empower patients/clients so as to resolve problems and cope more effectively with day-to-day living and interpersonal relationships. These aspects of life, personal and familial, are frequently disrupted when parents are rearing a child or adolescent with physical and/or psychological disorders. The two often go together.

Having set out to describe some of the main aspects of typical and atypical child development, it would be ideal if there was the space to explore the extensive literature on treatment and rehabilitation. Such is the complexity and variety of these difficulties, and so vast the theoretical and practical knowledge required to inform the practice of the professionals, a book with an already wide remit, sadly, cannot do justice to the treatment methods and practical resources that are available. A selection of readings from the relevant literature is provided in the references and bibliography at the end of the book.

Organization of the Book

The book is divided into two halves, the first dealing with typical (normal) development, the second with atypical (abnormal) events. There are significant challenges, social, cognitive and emotional, faced by children at particular ages; and there are many difficulties associated with their efforts to master them. Despite the many variations, exceptions and anomalies, on the theme, my intention is to write about the normal (usual) patterns of growth and adaptation. These will be linked to equivalent chapters in the second half of the book (from part IV onwards) where I discuss atypical (abnormal) conditions. By cross-referencing, I aim to emphasize the continuities between, and similarities of, children with typical and untypical problems, and the fact that children may well fit into either 'category' when it comes to particular attributes. Thus, a child suffering from an autistic disorder may display above-average drawing, musical or numeracy skills. A child with normal developmental milestones, and high intellectual achievements, may suffer from a specific reading difficulty (dyslexia); another with Down's syndrome, a condition associated with intellectual disability, may be of near-average intelligence.

What has also guided my organization of the chapters, broadly speaking, is a consideration of the nature–nurture components of the child's amazing and sometimes hazardous journey to young adulthood, the period at which the book ends. These include influences stemming from the following 'forces' of nature:

- Genetically determined biological variables
- Non-genetic biological variables (e.g. anoxia during the birth process, malfunctioning of the pituitary gland, head injuries resulting from accidents, non-hereditary diseases).

The 'forces' of nurture (i.e. the influence of the environment) include:

- The child's past learning experiences
- His or her immediate social and psychological environment (e.g. parents, siblings, peers, other relatives, teachers)
- The general cultural, subcultural and social milieus.

There is nowadays a better appreciation of the significance of the last two forces listed in shaping the child's development. Urie Bronfenbrenner (1989) uses the term *social ecology* to describe the system of social influences impinging on the child and adolescent and their environment. These influences, as they affect the child or adolescent at different stages of development, will be a major theme of the book. As Bronfenbrenner conceptualizes them, they are:

- The microsystem, which comprises all relationships and transactions in a particular setting (e.g. the social and physical family environment)
- The mesosystem, which includes the interrelationships between the major settings such as home and school where children do their growing up
- The macrosystem, which contains the general beliefs, values and traditions of the culture or subculture that control the interactions between the various layers of the social system, and the tenets that reflect the meaning and value of life.

I shall describe physical and psychological problems that peak in their appearance or impact at particular ages. Some are transient but recur; others constitute the kinds of disability that engender special needs throughout the life-span. At times my choice of where best to place the discussion of particular physical and mental health problems is somewhat arbitrary, as they have their effect at various ages. Among the disabilities included are:

- Pervasive developmental disorders (e.g. autism, Asperger's disorder)
- Genetic disorders (e.g. Down's syndrome, Turner's syndrome, Tay-Sachs disease)
- Physical impairments (e.g. blindness, hearing impairment, cerebral palsy)
- Learning difficulties, moderate and severe
- Brain injury (e.g. anoxia, head injuries)
- Emotional and behavioural disorders (e.g. phobic anxiety, conduct disorder, obsessive–compulsive disorder, anorexia nervosa, delinquency)
- Psychiatric disorders (e.g. bipolar depression, schizophrenia)
- Personality disorders (e.g. psychopathy)
- Chronic/persistent illnesses (e.g. paediatric HIV, cancer, diabetes, bronchial asthma).

Kathleen Berger (2000), acknowledging the difficulties of organizing the vast interdisciplinary scope of contemporary human development studies, adopts the method of subdividing the subject into three domains:

1. Biosocial, which includes the brain and body and the influences that direct changes that take place in them
2. Cognitive, which includes thought processes, perceptual abilities and language acquisition
3. Psychosocial, which includes emotions, personality and interpersonal relationships with family, friends and the wider community.

Every aspect of human behaviour and personality reflects all three interactive domains, and all are important in different ways at every age. For example, Allport (1937) defines personality as the dynamic organization within the individual of these psychophysical systems. They determine the individual's unique adjustments to his or her environment. The definition emphasizes certain important features of personality: its changing (dynamic) nature, and the fact that it is less a finished product than a transitive process. Although it has stable characteristics, it is continually changing – a process of 'becoming'. The exegeses of intrapsychic life by psychoanalysts studying personality have delved into the individual's past. Yet people themselves are preoccupied most of the time in projecting their lives into the future.

   This preoccupation is also a feature of developmental science. Allport stresses the dynamic interrelatedness of different personal attributes; the individual is not simply a static aggregation of various qualities. He emphasizes the psychosocial and physical bases of human attitudes, habits, values, beliefs and motives. These in turn determine the unique adjustments each person will make to any situation, be it family, school, or community, in which they find themselves. There is a continuing two-way transaction and interaction between individuals and their milieu, one in which individuals are proactive agents of change, not merely reactive ciphers. Their self-direction, from the very beginning of life, constantly belies the seventeenth-century philosopher John Locke's proposition that the infant's mind is a *tabula rasa*, a blank sheet, passively receptive to all kinds of learning.

With regard to the psychosocial domain, it is the family that provides the basic setting for intimacy and growth. It has its own dynamic life-cycle and life-tasks that have a bearing on the way children are regarded and reared. Parents also have developmental dilemmas of their own to resolve, not infrequently agendas that can exacerbate the tensions with their youngster. What will also be considered within this domain, is the complexity of wider contexts, people, customs, institutions and beliefs. The historical ideas and contemporary fashions in childcare that make family life for parents and children such a varied and (for some theorists) contentious institution (e.g. Mount, 1983) provide additional themes for exploration. All of these strands will, I hope, make for an interesting and informative account of the child's journey from inside the mother's womb to the world outside, and to the childhood and adolescent experiences that lie ahead.

Parts I, II and III of the book deal with typical (normal) child and adolescent development, from conception to young adulthood. Part IV (chapters 8 to 12) introduces atypical aspects at the equivalent stages of development. Part V is about positive mental health and mental illness, dealing with child and adolescent antisocial activities and psychiatric disorders (in chapters 13 and 14 respectively). In chapters 15 and 16 of part VI there are reviews of the plight of children with special needs, such as those with pervasive developmental disorders (e.g. autism, learning disabilities) and children with serious, sometimes terminal, illnesses (e.g. cancer, HIV/AIDS). Chapter 17 considers the youngsters whose lives (at any of the ages or stages of development described in the book) are blighted by physical, emotional and sexual maltreatment. The two appendices deal with 'true and false beliefs' and the measurement of intelligence.

Acknowledgements

I am indebted to Joyce Collins, who shared with me the planning of the book; also to Paul Stringer for his expert and kindly editing. My gratitude also belongs to the many clinicians, authors and researchers, too numerous to name individually, for ideas and research data I found so useful.

Martin Herbert

The author and publishers gratefully acknowledge the following for permission to reproduce copyright material:

Extract from *The Secret Diary of Adrian Mole Aged 13¾* by Sue Townsend used by permission of The Random House Group Limited.

The publishers apologize for any errors or omissions in the above list and would be grateful to be notified of any corrections that should be incorporated in the next edition or reprint of this book.

Picture research for this book was done by Charlotte Morris.

Introduction

We must see the first images which the external world casts upon the dark mirror of his mind; or must hear the first words which awaken the sleeping powers of thought, and stand by his earliest efforts, if we would understand the prejudices, the habits, and the passions that will rule his life. The entire man is, so to speak, to be found in the cradle of the child.

Alexis de Tocqueville (1805–1859)

From Childhood to Adolescence

A book dealing with childhood and adolescence should have clear definitions of these concepts. The truth is that the questions 'What is childhood?' and 'What is adolescence?' have no easy answers, despite the fact that we have all been through these stages of development. 'To start with,' as Nicholas Orme, author of *Mediaeval Children*, observes, 'childhood lacks clear boundaries. In one sense it begins at birth, yet a baby takes a year or so to become a recognisable child that walks and talks. Its exit point is even less defined. The *Oxford English Dictionary* ends it at puberty, but puberty varies in age by gender and from child to child' (Orme, 2000, p. 3). (See chapter 7 on adolescence.)

Parenthood

The early intimations of being pregnant for the first time present the mother-to-be with changes and challenges that impact on her at various levels of her life – intrapsychic, interpersonal and social. Pregnancy, when accepted, is a unique and critical transition from independent single being, to one-half (eventually) of an irrevocable attachment that binds a mother to her child, and her child to her. It has been described as a crisis point, a point of no return, in a woman's search for a female identity (Etchegoyan, 2000). The father-to-child attachment should not be left out of this formulation, although it differs in certain important respects (Herbert, Sluckin and Sluckin, 1982). These are discussed later.

Parenting skills are complex, much of the time intuitive – a repertoire acquired by learning rather than instinct, and one that is shaped and reshaped, often painfully, on the anvil of first-hand experience. Parents (and teachers) observe the development of the children and adolescents in their care with a mixture of pleasure and bewilderment. Development, one is led to believe, is a progressive series of orderly, coherent changes, leading the youngster toward the goal of maturity. That may be the grand design, but as many parents and teachers know, their children's progress through life is often difficult, disorderly and incoherent, and the changes (when they are not being hindered by disability or resisted by emotional difficulties) are not always in the positive direction of self-sufficient adulthood. When this occurs such reactions are likely to be called 'problematic' and, at the extreme, thought of as 'abnormal'.

Concepts of Normality and Abnormality

The term abnormal is closely bound up with the concept of a deviation from some norm. The word norm, from its Latin root, means a standard, rule, or pattern. When physical or psychological development is designated as abnormal, it implies (with its prefix 'ab' meaning 'away from') a deviation from a physical, psychological or social standard. Behavioural difficulties in children provide an illustration of the uncertainty of where the threshold lies in labelling them as problematic. They are so common that they could be (and are) considered a normal part of development. Hewitt et al. (1989) found that 67 per cent of so-called 'normal' 2-year-olds were regarded as highly active by their parents; 78 per cent were reported to have tempers or irritability; 41 per cent night waking, and 23 per cent described as difficult to settle at night. In such populations it would seem to be the frequency and/or intensity of the particular behaviour (a matter of degree) that introduces the use of the term 'abnormal'.

I have preferred to reserve the term 'abnormality' for certain specifically defined conditions that have adverse effects (e.g. phenylketonuria, conduct disorder, autism or psychopathy), and to use the less stigmatizing description 'atypical' when referring to the children who suffer from such disorders. I do not think this choice is semantic hair-splitting. The term abnormal is burdened by many negative and emotive connotations. It has been used over the years to sort children into normal and abnormal categories, as if these distinctions are mutually exclusive, like the judgments strong and weak, good and bad. There is also something of a nihilistic tone to the word abnormal, conveying notions of pessimism and finality when applied to individuals, their situations, or their personality.

This form of categorizing is particularly susceptible to reification. The whole becomes less than the sum of its parts: the whole being the child as a handicapped entity; the parts being his or her individual strengths, which tend to be overlooked or not given due weight. It is a reductive rather than enhancing use of language. An added complication of 'either/or' distinctions applied to children is that they are inflexible. They do not lend themselves to finely tuned qualification. Those of their attributes that vary along continuous quantitative dimensions (e.g. intellectual ability), as well as those that represent qualitative individual differences within diagnostic categories (e.g. social skills), are at risk of being overlooked, ignored, or played down. It has been observed that perceptions of dependence and limited functioning are inadvertently reinforced by methods of assessment with age-equivalent values (mental age, social age) applied to describe a child's functioning. The danger is that an assigned functioning level in one area (e.g. cognition) will be generalized to all areas, producing stereotyped images and promoting invalid generalizations.

Some theorists question the value of the entire labelling or diagnostic exercise as it tends to be a by-product of *categorical* identification of children with disabilities. Others are not so radical, but wish for a more sophisticated dimensional elaboration of the assessment process, and seek alternatives to the more rigid categorical terms and classificatory systems. Several conceptual systems have emerged, promoting a dimensional approach (e.g. the *International Classification of Impairments, Disabilities, and Handicaps* (ICIDH2)) that includes descriptions of functioning and disability rather than persons. That last exclusion is important. Stigmatizing may not be the intention of professionals, but it is the perception of many of those who hear themselves being classified (and thereby diminished), with stigmatizing global terms such as 'mentally retarded', 'mentally defective', 'mentally ill' or 'emotionally disturbed'.

Terminology

Terminology in education and clinical practice is a complicated, sensitive and at times highly politicized issue. There is no wholly satisfactory resolution of the linguistic difficulties involved in describing deviations from the norm, be they physical or psychological. A good example of this is the rather meaningless although well-intentioned replacement of the term 'problematic', applied to unacceptable childhood behaviour, with the word 'challenging'. There are many who object to the word 'handicap' but it appears frequently in the literature, as does the description 'mentally subnormal' in the *Diagnostic and Statistical Manual of the Mental Disorders* (DSM-IV), the widely used classificatory system of the American Psychiatric Association (APA, 1994).

The use of the generic term 'atypical' may not be perfect, but nevertheless I feel that it is reasonably neutral, less pejorative than most alternatives. It is also more amenable to the sort of modulation that allows for degrees of handicap, and makes room for the many individual differences that are manifest in children with disabilities. The use of the terms handicap and disabled (and an additional one, impairment) requires an explanation. After much debate, the World Health Organization codified the terminology relating to abnormality, dysfunction and disadvantage (*World Health Organization International Classification of Impairments, Disabilities and Handicaps*, WHO, 1992). The WHO definition of impairment incorporates functional as well as structural components:

- Impairment is any loss of normal psychological, physiological or anatomical structure or function.
- Disability is the limitation of personal activity consequent upon impairment – any restriction or lack of ability (resulting from an impairment) to perform an activity in the manner or within the range considered normal for a human being.
- Handicap is the resulting personal and social disadvantage – a disadvantage for an individual resulting from an impairment or disability that limits or prevents the fulfilment of a role that is normal (depending on age, sex, social, and cultural factors) for that individual.

The following checklist indicates some of the disabilities dealt with in later chapters of the book:

Hearing

Moderate to severe: Hearing difficulties even with hearing aids; has or is likely to have persisting difficulty with language and communication sufficient to impair development.

Profound: Little or no hearing, with little or no benefit from hearing aids.

Vision

Moderate to severe: Partially sighted, visual difficulties sufficient to impair everyday activities and/or development despite the use of aids.

Profound: Blind, no useful vision.

Speech and/or language

Moderate to severe: Difficulties communicating through speech and language, and as a result unable to participate in the normal activities of a child of their age.

Profound: No meaningful speech or language, therefore unlikely to use speech as the primary means of communication.

Physical

Moderate to severe: Physical difficulty (e.g. motor) or chronic illness resulting in long-term impairment of health or development, even with the provision of drugs, diet or aids.

Profound: Difficulties with all basic functions, of such severity that assistance is likely to be required.

Learning

Moderate to severe: A permanent learning impairment sufficient to prevent the child from fulfilling roles or performing activities which are generally understood to be within the capacity of children of that age and cultural background.

Profound: Extreme or multiple learning difficulties.

Behavioural and emotional

Moderate to severe: Emotional and/or behavioural difficulties likely to be long-term, and be such as to impair the quality of the child's life, resulting in underachievement in normal social contexts (for example, school or workplace), with failure of social development and integration.

Profound: Emotional and/or behavioural difficulties likely to be so severe in the long-term that they seriously impair the quality of the child's life, resulting in inability to function in normal social contexts or constituting a risk to themselves or others.

Universal norms

There are universal norms, for example those relating to maturation, which have to do with the sequential unfolding of physical attributes such as the growth of organs of the body, the development of functions like walking and talking, or the production of hormones that trigger the onset of puberty. The genetic component in the heredity–environment equation is prepotent here, as a determinant of development. Nevertheless there is often room for some variation in the phenotype (i.e. all the individual's observable characteristics) due to the influence of the environment. Aspects of universality are contained in the word 'genetic', which refers to more than just the genes that make each person (except for identical twins) unique. It also applies to the genes that people have shared with all their fellow human beings for generation after generation, over hundreds of thousands of years. Not to be forgotten are the very many genes (well over 90 per cent) that humans share with other primates.

Individual development

When it comes to biosocial or psychosocial development (e.g. personality or moral development) the influence of the environment is powerful, and the range of individual and cultural differences, in both the goals to be attained and the timetable for achieving particular milestones, varies much more widely than maturational events. There are children who find it more difficult than most of their peers to meet certain developmental goals at the expected times, or for those with severe learning and other disabilities, to reach them at all. Not everyone agrees with the developmental milestones that are most often quoted in paediatric and psychological textbooks, or the many child-rearing guides written for caregivers. Parents from culturally diverse backgrounds hold differing beliefs about the ages at which their offspring can or should be able to perform life-tasks.

More fundamentally, they are concerned in different ways about the goals and values they wish to encourage in their children. Conflicts emerge when parents and older children disagree about the timing of milestones, such as assuming the degree of autonomy implicit in deciding to stay out late, or choosing friends of the opposite sex. These tend to be perennial preoccupations of immigrants from conservative Eastern communities who have settled in Western countries that have (as they may see it) undermining liberal views about the duties and obligations of the young. For developmental psychologists to overlook differences such as these, and others, in the educational and clinical fields is to perpetuate the kind of ethnocentric psychology which, with justice, has been so criticized (e.g. Durkin, 1995).

Bearing these matters in mind, I will attempt to address some of the issues arising from the diverse scripts that inform many parental actions, with an occasional backward glance at the ideologies and theories of previous generations. There has been an imbalance in the scientific past in the profuse attention paid to children's interpretations of events in social situations, their cognitive maturity and capacity to assimilate information, and the relatively sparse interest in the cognitions (e.g. theories) of parents on childhood problems and development. There was no parallel shortage of research (notably when it came to the mothers) into their allegedly 'pathogenic' motives and emotions.

Fortunately, developmental and clinical theory and research are more enlightened today, as exemplified by the interest in parental attributions. The internal models that parents develop about the nature of relationships are, to a large extent, based on their own childhood experiences. These schema are then carried forward in time and function as 'filters' through which the behaviour of their offspring are perceived, understood or mis-understood. To take one example, negative parental emotional reactions to their children's behaviour predict poor child and family outcomes, whereas positive emotions predict favourable outcomes (Patterson, 1982). Attribution theory contributes to our understanding of why some parents are more likely than others to react negatively. Whether or not a child's challenging activities elicit anger (as an emotional response) and aggression (as a behavioural reaction) depends on whether the youngster is judged to be *responsible* for his or her actions (see Weiner, 1995). A cross-cultural confirmation of this theory comes from a study of 149 Latina mothers of children with developmental disabilities who were interviewed about incidents involving behaviour problems. The researchers (Chavira et al., 2000) found that most of the mothers viewed their offspring as not responsible for the misdemeanours. Mothers who ascribed relatively high responsibility to the child were significantly more likely to report negative emotions (e.g. anger) than those who did not.

A further advantage of a cognitive perspective directed towards the attachments and attributions of parents and their children is that it helps to integrate theories (such as the 'cycles of disadvantage') that link the experience and actions of succeeding generations.

Belsky (1993) proposes (as does Bronfenbrenner) an ecological approach to the study of child development. This hypothesizes an integrated series of interactions between influences measured at various levels:

- The microsystem comprises the child's own characteristics and immediate environment.
- The exosystem includes social factors that impinge, for example, on the family at risk of abuse.
- The macrosystem is the larger cultural fabric that comprises broad societal attitudes to child-rearing and related matters.

At each level of this complex interacting system, influences known to be associated with particular styles of (for example) childcare and discipline, can be examined. The assumption underlying this model is that certain attributes of the caregiver may predispose him/her to indulge in a particular (e.g. physically abusive) activity. That person's style of parenting will in turn reflect his/her own developmental history, knowledge of child-rearing, mental state and social milieu.

In the light of all that has been said, it is plainly no easy task to pursue a coherent story about individual and systemic changes (typical and atypical) taking place over the first 16 or so years of the child's life-span, the time-span covered by this book. One of the other problems of such an ambitious endeavour is that there is no 'grand' unifying theory, to provide the kind of integrated conceptual framework that would make the task easier. Rather there are several theories (some overlapping) such as the social learning, cognitive-behavioural, psychodynamic, systemic, and epigenetic models that I shall draw on. These are slotted into a framework of developmental stages, notably those having a bearing on physical growth and personality development.

Stages of development

Stages of development are generally postulated when behavioural development appears to advance by means of a sequence of marked changes in complex patterns of activity. A stage is defined as a set of characteristics or components of behaviour that occur together and, as such, can be conveniently grouped. To be meaningful the description must have a theoretical basis. The proposed stages of development, as part of a process- and content-oriented sequence, provide a coherent framework for thinking about the course of development. They suggest the theoretical basis on which behaviour is conceptualized as both developing and segmented.

There is nothing new about this conception of development. Mediaeval people believed that human life progresses through a series of stages, each with its own characteristics. The Latin dictionary *Liber Etymologiarum* by Isidore of Seville (d. 636) included the terms *infantia*, *pueritia*, and *adolescentia*. Such divisions were to be found in English translation from around the year 1400. Orme (2000, p. 7), commenting on these historical facts, notes that childhood then '. . . was a concept – both as a single period from birth to puberty and as one divided into infancy and childhood, with adolescence as a further stage before adulthood.'

In order to consider typical and atypical child development in terms of stages, I have drawn on a literature with a long history. It soon becomes apparent that by no means all theorists have agreed on what constitute the most meaningful and fruitful dimensions for a division of childhood into segments. Some (e.g. Gesell et al., 1940) chose chronological or age-related stages as a framework for research. The Swiss psychologist Jean Piaget (1954) addressed himself to stages in the development of cognitive operations and structures. Sigmund Freud (1939/1974), the founder of psychoanalysis, postulated psychosexual phases in which different erogenous zones and associated needs predominate. Others (e.g. Sullivan, 1953) paid particular attention to stages in children's capacity to understand the interpersonal environment they inhabit. Theorists like Sears et al. (1957) emphasized critical and universal socialization tasks in the early life-span, such as feeding and weaning, and elimination, sex, aggression, and dependency training. Flavell (1992) elaborated the concept of stage-related changes to investigate sequences of development in broad content areas such as language acquisition, the use of memory strategies, and the emergence of gender identity.

Danziger (1971) observed that the practical problems of life have always suggested the choice of behavioural categories for study. The need to achieve has far exceeded studies of other human needs, a pointer perhaps to a concern with the ideology of entrepreneurship and economic under-development. The sheer volume of research into the antecedents of childhood aggression, conduct disorder and learned helplessness, reflects our concern with contemporary social problems such as violence, delinquency and over-dependency – all explored in the chapters to follow. Clearly developmental research does not take place in some rarified, socially and politically neutralized ethos called 'pure science' (Durkin, 1995).

Personality development

Erik Erikson (1965) describes early personality development in terms of stages in the development of patterns of reciprocity between the self and others. They involve, at each stage, a conflict between opposite poles of this relationship – one that has to be resolved in order to move on unburdened by emotional 'loose ends' to a mature adulthood. There is a series of *crises* to which Erikson gave names such as 'trust–mistrust', 'confidence–doubt', and 'initiative–guilt' (see table 1).

There seems to be a connection, according to Danziger (1971), between these bi-polar pairs and the concepts of assimilation and accommodation, postulated by Jean Piaget (1954). Assimilation occurs when children alter the environment to meet their own needs, play being at one extreme. Accommodation occurs when children modify their own behaviour in response to the demands of their milieu, imitation being at the other extreme. Danziger suggests that it is possible to understand the bi-polar pairs as a similar lack of balance or conflict in the development of social reciprocity. This conflict assumes qualitatively different forms at different stages of development. The model describes the child threading his/her way between opposing forces of ego and alter while trying to find, as they mature, a balance between self-centred individualism and a need to conform, with a degree of self-abnegation, to the rules and mores of family and community. The former tends to be encouraged somewhat ambivalently in the West. The latter, broadly speaking, is an Eastern priority (e.g. Roland, 1988; Sinha and Sinha, 1997; Wallach and Wallach, 1983; Whiting and Edwards, 1988).

The ideas described above indicate one aspect of the contrasting views of development, as something that occurs either to the individual or within him/her. Two important questions about the continuity or discontinuity of behavioural development, follow:

• Does the child's behaviour progress continuously by gradual accretions, without sudden or sharp shifts? or

Table 1 Developmental stages and crises

Approximate age periods	Characteristics to be achieved	Major hazard to achievement	Facilitative factors
Birth to 18 months or so	Sense of trust or security.	Neglect, abuse or deprivation of consistent and appropriate love in infancy; harsh or early weaning.	If parents meet the preponderance of the infant's needs, the child develops a strong sense of trust.
Around 18 months to about 3 years	Sense of autonomy – child viewing self as an individual in his/her own right, apart from parents although dependent on them.	Conditions which interfere with the child's achieving a feeling of adequacy or the learning of skills such as talking.	If parents reward the child's successful actions and do not shame his or her failures (say in bowel or bladder control) the child's sense of autonomy will outweigh self-doubt/shame/guilt.
3 to 5 years or so	Sense of initiative – period of vigorous reality testing, imagination, and imitation of adult behaviour.	Overly strict discipline, internalization of rigid ethical attitudes which interfere with the child's spontaneity and reality testing.	If parents accept the child's curiosity and do not put down the need to know and to question the child's sense of initiative will be enhanced.
5/6 to 11 years	Sense of duty and accomplishment – laying aside of fantasy and play; undertaking real tasks, developing academic and social competencies.	Excessive competition, personal limitations, or other conditions which lead to experiences of failure, resulting in feeling of inferiority and poor work.	If the child encounters more success than failure at home and at school he or she will have a greater sense of industry than of inferiority.
12 to 15 years	Sense of identity – clarification in adolescence of who one is, and what one's role is.	Failure of society to provide clearly defined roles and standards; formation of cliques which provide clear but not always desirable roles and standards.	If the young person can reconcile diverse roles, abilities, and values and see their continuity with past and future, a sense of personal identity will be developed and consolidated.

Based on Erikson's theorizing

- Does the course of development progress step-like, divided into stages or levels, with dramatic changes of behaviour from one stage to the next, the stages following each other in an orderly sequence?

The answer is not necessarily a dichotomous 'either/or' one. In many theoretical contexts the notion of stages seems useful; in others (as we shall see) it does not.

Age- and Stage-related Tasks

Ciccetti, Toth and Bush (1983) have extended the exploration of stage theory, suggesting that the developmental tasks (or issues) that emerge at particular phases during the children's progress through life remain critical to their continuing adaptation even when their centrality has been superseded by new agendas. This is somewhat different from the construction of the ontogenetic process (by theorists like Erikson) as a series of unfolding tasks that must be accomplished, but which then decrease in importance. Each developmental task has to be coordinated and integrated, as a continuing process, into the overall scheme of the child's adaptation to his/her environment.

Competence and maturity

Among such tasks to be discussed later in the book are the following:

- Becoming attached to caregivers
- Learning to talk
- Learning control over elimination
- Developing self-control (e.g. over aggressive outbursts)
- Restraining sexual inclinations
- Developing moral attitudes
- Mastering social and other life-skills
- Adjusting to school
- Mastering academic competencies
- Becoming increasingly independent, self-directed.

The issue of competence is common to all ten stage-related tasks and, as the child gets older, to his or her self-esteem. This idea makes for a creative conceptual bridge between clinicians and developmental experimentalists. Failure to develop skills and social competence, and this is particularly salient in the case of children suffering from failure-to-thrive, attention deficit hyperactivity disorder (ADHD), and other clinical disorders, engenders a sense of inadequacy with escalating disruptive ramifications. There are corresponding roles for caregivers which, if benign, increase the probability that their children will successfully negotiate the tasks. There is evidence in this transactional model that parents can facilitate or impede their offspring's development, depending on their child-management skills or lack of them.

The thrust of development is toward the goal of independence and the sort of maturity that will make that autonomy viable. Maturity is a value judgement and therefore impossible to define in absolute terms. However, mature individuals in Western culture are generally thought to be capable (relative to their age) of:

- being flexible in the face of new situations and able to change when it becomes necessary
- developing a point of view (their own outlook on things), being themselves and capable of independent action and thought
- showing a sense of humour
- accepting reality
- accepting themselves – showing respect and liking (as opposed to narcissistic love) for themselves, plus self-awareness
- enjoying human relationships (lasting affectionate, altruistic, responsible emotional attachments to other people)
- being able to tolerate a certain amount of solitude
- respecting other people's views and rights
- working out for themselves many of their own values; not passively accepting conventional wisdom at all times, and
- knowing when to say no, when to resist unacceptable 'diktats' from authority.

High-risk groups, among them depressed and abused children have special difficulties surmounting the developmental tasks associated with the early and middle years of childhood, tasks that require (as stepping-stones on the path toward maturity) a successful resolution (see chapters 14 and 17).

Crises of Development

According to Ausubel and Sullivan (1970), what they refer to as 'transitional phases' or 'developmental crises' are brought about by significant and relatively rapid shifts in the child's biosocial status. These are periods in which qualitatively new and discontinuous (inter-stage) changes in personality formation are being formulated. The individual is in the marginal position of having lost an established and accustomed status, for example being an only child. Or s/he may not yet have acquired the new status toward which the factors impelling developmental change are impelling them. A typical example is not yet being sufficiently independent to separate from mother for the first time so as to attend a nursery group. At a later stage it may be the difficulty of adapting to the bodily changes that indicate entry into young adulthood (see chapter 7).

Ausubel and Sullivan (ibid.) postulate two major categories of precipitant to these developmental crises:

1. An urgent need within the culture for a fundamental modification of the social and personality adjustment of an entire group of children who are in a given stage of developmental equilibrium
2. The occurrence of marked changes within individuals such as developmental advances in physical attributes (e.g. puberty), basic drives (e.g. sexual) and competencies (e.g. conceptual sophistication) which are so crucial that the present status or modes of adaptation are incompatible with their current presentation of self.

Formal psychologists are not the only ones to think of child development in terms of stages. Parents also tend to divide the years of childhood and beyond (also parenting itself) into segments. Thus, children progress from being infants, to being toddlers, pre-schoolers, school-goers, teenagers, and eventually young adults. Parents have a notion of a child being 'ready' or 'unready' to move on to a new stage of development, one that requires a novel set of responses from both the child and the caregiver (Goodnow and Collins, 1990).

Other theorists, such as Freud and Erikson, have also recognized that crises in dealing with life-tasks can hinder the adaptive capacities of the child or adolescent. Paul Baltes and his associates (Baltes, Reese and Lipsitt, 1980) have played an important part in emphasizing the life-span nature of development and the importance of historical factors. Baltes is at pains to stress that age-related trends constitute only one of the three major influences operating on development throughout the person's life. These are described in table 2.

The point was made earlier that there is no general integrated or conceptually coherent theory of childhood development to provide a touchstone for understanding and assessing clinical and/or developmental problems. There is simply no single or agreed explanation of the processes of typical (i.e. normal) growth and development. Cultural diversity adds to the multiplicity and variety of influences that make the search for universally typical patterns of development something of a chimera.

The Developmental History

Any discussion of a child's developmental history requires an examination of several systems: her/his physical and social systems (family and school) and the wider community system (sometimes a minority ethnic group). Like the

Table 2 Life-span developmental influences

Influence	Description
Normative age-graded influences	These are powerfully correlated with age and are influenced (like the other two categories) by an interaction of biological and environmental forces, varying in their predominance. For example, puberty (which is age-related) has a sequence of biological components; entry into British schools at 5 years of age has not.
Non-normative history-graded influences	These are historical events (e.g. mass movements of people as refugees or immigrants, wars, famine; one-child families in China; the advent of television or computer games) which affect most members of a particular generation or cohort of children.
Non-normative life-events	These are those events that occur outside the range (for most people) of the influences described above: for example, head injuries sustained in a car crash – in such a case there would be powerful biological repercussions, as compared with what would be the predominance of the psychological reverberations of a messy divorce. Mind you, this may no longer be a good example of a trauma outside the range of most Western children.

child, these systems change and develop over time. Within them physical capabilities, social and psychological skills and strategies are acquired as s/he grows up. They result from a complex interaction of two basic processes: *learning* and *maturation*.

- Learning is usually defined as any enduring change in behaviour that results from instruction or experience. The influence of children's environment will depend to a large extent on their capacity to learn, and the presence of significant people to 'teach' them.
- Maturation is the term applied to those developments that are canalized; they are pre-programmed and occur in a predictable sequence.

The needless polarization of these influences has led to a perennial debate between so-called 'nativists' and 'empiricists' among philosophers and psychologists. Do pre-programmed (i.e. in-built) structures allow babies to make sense of the stimuli impacting on their sense organs? Or is the essential requirement that they experience the world they have entered, and learn to make sense of it by trial and error? These issues have featured in the debates about the development of the child's mind and selfhood.

Mental development

There have been huge strides in research and new ideas about this critical aspect of development. Before the 1970s (broadly speaking) researchers saw *object awareness* rather than *person awareness* as the central issue in the early development of the mind. Trevarthen and Aitken (2001) argue that evidence now suggests that even newborn infants, with their very immature though elaborate brains and limited cognitions, are motivated (beyond the instinctive behaviours that attract parental care for immediate biological needs) to communicate intricately with the expressive forms and feelings displayed by other humans. This evidence of an initial purposeful psychosocial state, referred to as *intersubjectivity*, is thought to be fundamental for our understanding of human mental development. The authors also believe that it will be crucial for accurate interpretations of the influences of nature and nurture in the 'baffling spectrum' of psychosocial pathologies in children, and for the development of effective educational and therapeutic interventions. We return to this topic in part II. (The measurement of intelligence – one aspect of mental development – is discussed in appendix II.)

An important question for a book dealing with atypical as well as typical children is: 'What happens to the development of blind and deaf children who, because of physical and sensory impairments, are restricted in their access to the physical or verbal cues which make up the non-disabled child's world?' This gives us our cue for examining, in the following chapters, how the *nativist* and *empiricist* views, and the two processes (maturation and learning), operate during the children's life-journey, particularly if they are disabled.

part i

Typical Development
Where the Journey Begins
The Intrauterine Stages and
Perinatal Period

The history of man for nine months preceding his birth would,
probably, be far more interesting, and contain events of greater
moment than all three score and ten years that follow it.
Samuel Taylor Coleridge (1772–1834)

The child's first home, the mother's uterus, is almost always hospitable; nevertheless the 38 weeks (266 days or so) between conception and birth present more risks (notably during the first 8 weeks of life) than any similar span up to the ninth decade. They begin with fertilization. Despite the potential risks most babies arrive in the world outside their mother's body, on time and in a healthy state. The particular hazards that faced them are detailed in chapters 8 and 9.

The major milestones during pregnancy are the three trimesters that are defined by the physiology of fetal growth, dated from presumed conception:

- the first, encompassing the first 12 weeks
- the second, ending at 28 weeks, and
- the third, covering the remainder of the pregnancy.

Biologists and embryologists divide the period of gestation into three unequal sub-periods: the germinal, embryonic and fetal stages of prenatal development. These stages in the unborn child's journey and the birth are the subject of chapters 1 and 2.

chapter one

The First Steps

And the first step, as you know, is always what matters most,
particularly when we are dealing with those who are young and
tender.

Plato (428–348 BC)

Conception: The Beginning of Life

We all set out on life's journey as a barely visible particle of matter, no more
than a single fertilized cell, but one that contains in its 46 chromosomes an
unimaginably vast store of information for shaping that life. The Chinese
reckon the person's age not from the moment of birth (as we do) but from
conception, adding on a full year for convenience. In fact, development
begins about 266 days before birth when the spermatozoon (a male germ
cell from the father) enters and fuses with an egg (ovum) from the mother.
A newborn female has some two million eggs stored in her ovaries. Only a
few hundred will be called upon during her life. Unlike normal body cells,
the nucleus of an ovum contains only half of the genetic material, or chromosomes, required for full development. After puberty, an ovum ripens
once every month in one of the woman's two ovaries, typically around the
middle of the menstrual cycle. It is discharged into the corresponding Fallopian
tube (oviduct), and begins its slow 15 cm journey toward the uterus, pro-
pelled by small hair-like cilia that line the tube. An unfertilized egg is the
largest cell in the body.

The male equivalent of the ovum is produced in vast numbers by the
testis. A sperm cell has a head containing the nucleus, and half the normal
number of chromosomes. Attached to the head is a tail that propels the
sperm (tadpole-like) towards the ovum. An estimated 500 million sperms
are released by the male on ejaculation. One of the sperms that make their
way into the oviduct during the time the ovum is making its descent may
unite with the ovum resulting in the conception of a new individual. Only
one sperm head can penetrate the ovum wall and fertilize the ovum. If not

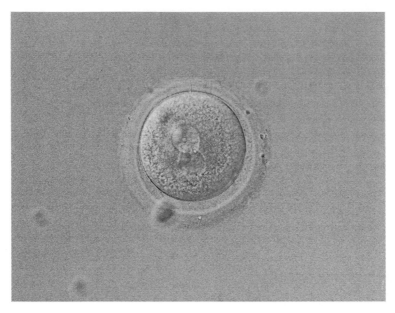

Figure 1 The moment of conception: the ovum is about to become a zygote following its penetration by a single sperm (CC Studio/Science Photo Library)

fertilized within 24 hours, the ovum dies and disintegrates in the uterus after a few days.

When fertilization is successful the sperm cell begins to disintegrate within a few hours, releasing its genetic content. The ovum also releases its genetic material, and a new cell nucleus forms around the hereditary information contributed by both parents. The new cell is referred to as a zygote. A biochemical reaction repels other sperm, thus preventing them from repeating the fertilization process. The process in which the two cells approach, unite, and re-form into a fertilized egg takes about 24 hours. This new cell nucleus contains 46 elongated thread-like bodies (chromosomes), each of which consists of thousands of genes, the basic units of heredity. According to the Genome Projects published in *Science* and *Nature* (see below) there are some 40,000 genes which, they estimate, can make 250,000 proteins available to the estimated 100 million million cells in any adult human.

As the zygote (one-twentieth the size of a pinhead) sets out on its 3 to 4 day journey through the Fallopian tube toward its prenatal home in the uterus it begins to reproduce itself. There are two forms of cell division, as described below.

1. Somatic cell division (mitosis)

All somatic cells in humans and in most other species are diploid. They possess matching (homologous) chromosomes arranged in pairs and they

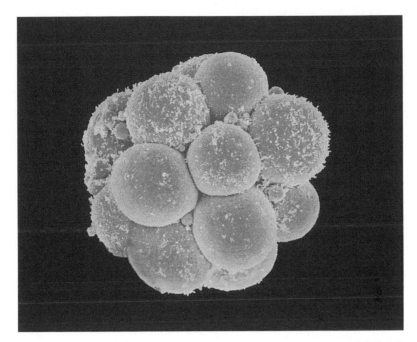

Figure 2 The human embryo at the 16-cell stage, some 3 days after fertilization: known as a morula, this cluster of large rounded cells, called blastomeres, is in the process of subdividing to form a hollow ball of cells (the blastocyst) on its journey to implantation in the wall of the uterus (Dr Yorgas Nikas/Science Photo Library)

proliferate through mitotic division. Mitosis occurs during tissue growth and now proceeds apace for the new being. At first the zygote, which contains 46 chromosomes, divides to form two new cells. Before it does this each of its 46 chromosomes doubles; then each doubled chromosome divides in half by separating lengthwise down its centre. The chromosomes next go to the opposite side of the cell. Thus when the cell itself divides down the centre, the new cells will each contain 46 chromosomes, as did the original cell. This process is repeated again and again: the two cells become four, four become eight, eight become sixteen, and so on and on.

By the time the infant is born s/he consists of billions of cells that make up bones, muscle, organs and other body structures. The human baby-to-be will undergo the equivalent of 42 successive divisions in progressing from a fertilized ovum to a full-term neonate. Gradually, as this process continues, the resulting cells begin to assume special functions, as part of the nervous, skeletal, muscular and circulatory systems. Not only do cells differentiate, many of them move from one place in the embryo to another along very specific pathways, by mechanisms that are poorly understood.

2. Germ cell division (meiosis)

In addition to body cells, human beings possess germ cells that have the specialized function of producing gametes: the sperms in males and ova in females. The germ cells are haploid. They possess half the number of chromosomes (one of each homologous pair). When the male germ cells in the testes and female germ cells in the ovaries produce sperm and ova respectively, they do so through the process referred to as meiosis. Meiotic cell division produces ova and spermatozoa by reducing the number of chromosomes from the diploid 46 (22 pairs of chromosomes plus the sex chromosomes) to the haploid number 23 chromosomes. When fertilization takes place the set of 23 chromosomes from each parent combines to make up the 46 chromosome-carrying zygote.

Genetic Variation and Influence

Genetic determinants

Variation in the genetic makeup of the chromosomes takes place during meiotic cell division by means of a process termed crossing over or recombination. This occurs before the stage of cell division, when the chromosome pairs are pulled apart to the poles of the cell. It leads to genetic material from one chromosome exchanging with the other member of the pair, and results in a completely independent assortment of genes. Each member of a pair corresponds to the other in size, shape and the hereditary functions it serves. The genes on each chromosome also function as pairs, the two members of each gene pair being located at the same sites on their corresponding chromosomes. From the moment of conception the child-to-be, an entirely novel combination of the parental genes, carries forward in her or his cells the blueprint that determines the genetic aspects of growth and development through life.

Male and female heredity

Twenty-three pairs of the elongated thread-like chromosomes are present within the nucleus of every cell, except the egg and sperm cells, which consist of 22 matched pairs: the non-sex autosomes and one pair of sex chromosomes. In the male, the sex chromosomes consist of an X and Y chromosome; in the female there are two X chromosomes. The genes on the chromosomes in the sex cells are the ones that are transmitted to successive generations. As we saw, they also work in pairs, each gene being paired with a gene on the corresponding chromosome, one member of the gene pair coming from the father, the other from the mother. Each child thus inherits half of each parent's genes.

A major aspect of genetic determination is the child's sex (his or her gender identity is a matter we shall return to). It is the father (one half of whose sperm contains a Y chromosome, the other half an X chromosome) who determines, by fertilizing the ovum of the mother (who has two X chromosomes), the sex of their offspring. A child's sex is 'decided' by whether an X-bearing or Y-bearing sperm fertilizes the ovum. And the awful irony is that throughout history, as Shaffer (1999) points out, mothers have been belittled, tortured, divorced and even beheaded for failing to bear their husbands a male heir!

Even before the female baby is born she will have the ova which, when fertilized at the time of her sexual maturity, will constitute her contribution of genetic material to the next generation. The processes by which spermatozoa and ova are formed are named spermatogenesis and oogenesis respectively. One of the distinctions between spermatogenesis and oogenesis relates to the timing of meiosis in the life of the individual. Oogenesis begins in late fetal life or at about the time of the female's birth. The process is arrested, however, before the first meiotic division is completed. By, or before the end of the female's life as a fetus, all the ova she is ever going to have are already produced and have reached the so called dictyotene stage of meiosis. They remain in this state until puberty, and from puberty onwards will ripen at the rate of one a month (or more, since some pregnancies are multiple) until the menopause.

The ovum fertilized in a woman of 40 is 20 years older than one fertilized in a woman of 20. Sperms, on the other hand, are produced throughout male adult life from puberty onwards. As a result, the spermatozoon of a man of 40 that fertilizes an ovum is of recent production, no older in that sense than that of a man of 20.

Development, which is about the increasing complexity, differentiation and specialization of the cells, is under the direction of genes that function like minute chemical factories from their home base on the chromosomes. They modify the activity and development of entire cells in keeping with the environment in which they are located. From conception onwards, the child's environment and inherited capacities (the genes in that original cell turn up in all the millions of cells that eventually constitute the adult) interact to produce a complete individual, the emphasis being on that word 'individual'. More than a million genetic differences between humans have been found so far. The observable result of the highly complex nature–nurture interaction is referred to as the phenotype.

Developmental psychology is essentially about the emergence of individual differences. This individualism begins with the 'lottery' described earlier, whereby we receive our genetic makeup. It continues as such by being shaped by the child's personal life-events, and her/his idiosyncratic construction of their world (Kelly, 1955). Even siblings, given the figurative personal 'goggles' through which they view life do not, in a sense, inhabit the same environment, despite living in the same home.

Multiple births

MONOZYGOTIC (MZ) TWINS

Perhaps to a somewhat lesser extent the same applies to monozygotic (identical) twins despite the fact that they share the same set of genes (genotype). This comes about because they have developed from a single zygote. In the

Figure 3 Monozygotic (identical) twins: these children share identical genes (PhotoDisc)

Figure 4 Monozygotic (identical) quadruplets: they too share identical genes, unlike dizygotic (fraternal) twins. Triplets, quads etc. are commonly born to parents who have had fertility treatment (© Associated Press)

zygote stage of cell division, the cells split off into two (or more) separate organisms. A majority of MZ twins result from division of the inner mass at the blastocyst stage, when the organism is implanting into the uterine wall and the embryonic membranes are beginning to develop. These twins share one placenta and chorion but generally have two umbilical cords and amniotic sacs. In some 20–30 per cent of cases the split takes place before the zygote stage, during so-called cleavage divisions. The two organisms implant separately, and have two placentas and chorions (O'Brien and Hay, 1987). Identical twins occur in approximately one in every 250 births around the world. They are always of the same sex.

The splitting of an embryo into two sections fails, in rare circumstances, to result in complete separation. Such twins were widely exhibited in side-shows in the nineteenth century. Their origins in Siam gave the name Siamese Twins to this atypical form of twinning, a title best replaced by the words 'conjoined twins'.

FRATERNAL (DIZYGOTIC, DZ) TWINS

The statistics for the birth of fraternal (dizygotic) twins are one in every 125 births. They share no more of their genotype than any other pair of siblings, as they result from the fertilization of two different ova by two different sperms. The twins may be of different sexes. The sharing of genetic make-up makes MZ twins ideal for investigating the contribution of heredity and environment in disorders like autism and schizophrenia. Fraternal twins and non-twins provide excellent contrast and control groups in such studies. There appear to be advantages for first-born and heavier twins in terms of their well-being and development.

The Genotype

The genetic constitution of the child, referred to as the genotype, is the total set of genes. The genes are present in every cell of the body, but not all of them are active. It is the site and functions of the cell that determine which of them are active. Particular sets of genes, for example, are active in bone cells. Genes influence and direct the development and functioning of all of the organs and body systems, and account, inter alia, for variations in height, hair and eye colour, body shape and intelligence.

The Human Genome Project

This is a monumental global effort to read the entire human genome – the master blueprint that gives instructions to the person's many billions of cells. The deciphering of the human genetic code, an awesome number of letters making up the linear sequence of DNA (deoxyribose nucleic acid), reached a watershed with the publication of two decades of painstaking research in the February 2001 editions of *Nature* and *Science*. The two research groups have virtually managed to 'map' the many thousands of genes stored on these DNA threads. These have been referred to rather dramatically as the first clear words from the 'book of life'. The use of the word 'first' is apt, as this most promising and exciting journey of discovery has barely begun.

To the surprise of many researchers the number of genes is fewer than the fifty to one hundred thousand expected. There are, in fact, around forty thousand genes, some two times as many as the fruit fly and only three hundred more than a mouse. Although the number seems limited compared with expectations, there is a vast number yet to explore and understand. Much of the complexity arises from the combining of these genes. They work together (along with interacting environmental influences) to create or influence complex patterns of human behaviour.

Our genomes come packaged in tightly coiled threads of DNA which if unwound and tied together, would probably stretch more than one-and-a-half metres. A DNA molecule is a long chain of 'building blocks' called nucleotides. Genes are made up of two chains of DNA, the sides of which are sugar-phosphate molecules. This edifice spirals upon itself and is referred to as the double helix (Watson and Crick, 1953).

The regular structure of DNA enables the genes to be accurately interpreted and reproduced. The nucleotide building blocks come in only four different kinds: adenine, thymine, cytosine and guanine (shortened to A, T, C, and G). These are the same in all animals and plants; what is different is the order in which they are strung together. They are arranged in different combinations on different parts of the chromosome. The sequence of building blocks in a human being is not only different from insects and animals, but it also differs, although less so, from the sequence in every other human individual. The DNA is distributed among the multitude of cells making up the human body. It represents a set of instructions on how to make a body, written in the A, T, C, G alphabet of the nucleotides.

The coded message of the DNA is translated into another alphabet. This is the alphabet of amino acids that spell out the vital protein molecules. Genes only specify the sequence of amino acids that are linked together in the manufacture of a molecule called a polypeptide, which folds up in many different ways to make different proteins. These proteins not only constitute much of the physical fabric of the body, they also exert sensitive control over all the chemical processes inside the cell, selectively turning them on and off at precise times and in precise places.

The genome map sets out to find out where different pieces of information are on the chromosome. The exploration of the map is far from complete and the sorting out of what is, and what is not relevant to function, will take many years of research. The reason why geneticists refer to a genetic 'map' is that information is arranged in a line along each of the chromosomes. As we have seen, each chromosome is a very long string of letters that contains a defined, ordered sequence of information. Each combination of bases provides coded instructions that regulate the various activities of the body, and indeed its development. Only 3 per cent of the three billion letters in our DNA code (the As, Ts, Cs and Gs) that actually encode the genes that make up the human genome, and thus make us what we are, appear in the genes. This 3 per cent is very similar in other mammals, and even in insects.

Plomin (2001b) states that mutations are quickly weeded out from these bits of DNA because these are so crucial for development. When they are not weeded out, they often cause the severe single-gene disorders. The remaining 97 per cent has been described as 'junk', 'litter' or 'rubbish'. He does not believe that this large remainder is 'just along for the ride'. There is increasing evidence that most genetic influence on complex traits involves this 97 per cent of the genome, not the 3 per cent that codes for classic genes. Variations in this 97 per cent have a regulatory activity that is responsible for the widespread influence of genes on complex medical disorders such as heart disease and psychiatric disorders such as schizophrenia.

Plomin (ibid.) makes the point that such conditions are genetically *influenced* but not genetically *determined*, unlike single-gene disorders such as phenylketonuria (PKU). As he describes it, genes work like risk factors, slightly increasing or decreasing risk for a disorder. They do not work like a 'master puppeteer pulling our strings'. A large proportion of the disorders dealt with later in the book are influenced by many as opposed to single genes, and therefore it is the discovery of human gene sequences that will be particularly important. By sequencing the genome for many people's DNA, we are rapidly finding all the bits of DNA that differ between them.

Among the many interesting findings to fuel the genetic modification debate, has been the discovery of bacterial genes in our genomes, a phenomenon referred to as 'horizontal transfer'. The implications are that it is possible for 'intrusive' DNA from other outside organisms, to get into our genomes.

Similarities and Differences in Individuals and Groups

As every ovum and sperm contains a different assortment of genes, every child inherits a mix of genetic information that differs from the siblings. The exceptions are, as we saw earlier, monozygotic twins who inherit the same selection of genes. Ashley Montagu (1964) estimated that in a single mating the possible combinations between the 23 male and 23 female chromosomes amount to 8,388,608 and the chance of any such combination being precisely repeated more than once, approximately one in 70 million.

Although there can be wide variations within a family group, a child is still somewhat more similar to his or her blood relations than to anyone else. After all, their genes are drawn from a gene pool provided by the same two parents. Although each sibling inherits half of each parent's genes, they never inherit the same half owing to the random distribution of chromosomes (and genes) into the sperm and ovum gametes that unite to generate new life.

Researchers on the Genome Project have so far collected almost a million tiny variations in the genetic code – single nucleotide polymorphisms or SNPs – that might explain why humans differ from one another. The variation between any two individuals in the same population could be greater than that between two different groups. Craig Venter, head of one of the genome research groups (quoted by Tim Redford, science editor, *The Guardian*, 12 February 2001) found no way of telling which of some African-American, Asian-American and Hispanic-American individuals, was which. He stated that no serious scholar in this field considers race to be a scientific concept. We all evolved out of the same three or four groups in Africa. Different populations were fixed with immigrations. Venter considers that there is more diversity within Africans than there is between Africans and Caucasians; we are part of a continuum because we evolved from the same set of people over a relatively short period of time.

Inherited characteristics

Genes are sometimes identical in a pair (homozygous), sometimes different (heterozygous). Those that are dominant (e.g. brown eyes) determine which characteristics will emerge when paired with recessive genes (e.g. blue eyes). The implications of this for the inheritance of abnormal physical or mental disorders are highly significant, and are discussed later. Genes may show their effects early in life (e.g. gender differences or a condition such as Down's syndrome); they may appear later in life (e.g. schizophrenia), or they may be delayed until late in life (e.g. the dementias). Genetic influences contribute to cognitive abilities, an issue that has given rise to heated debates within psychology and sociology (Plomin, 1990, 2001b). Plomin (2001b), in a review of the behavioural genetic literature, states that many studies, adding up to more than 8000 parent offspring pairs, 25,000 pairs of siblings, 10,000 twin pairs, and hundreds of adoptive families, converge in concluding that genetic factors contribute substantially to general intelligence ('g'). Estimates of the effect size (heritability) vary from 40 to 80 per cent. Estimates based on the entire body of data are about 50 per cent, indicating that genes account for about half of the variance in g.

The term heritability is sometimes misunderstood. It is not a synonym for 'inherited'. Heritability estimates, which may vary widely across populations and environments, are not informative about the development of individuals. Although heritability estimates are useful in determining whether there is any hereditary basis for the *differences* people display on one or another attribute, they tell us nothing about children's capacity for change. They should therefore not be used to formulate public policy of the kind that could put constraints on children's development, or in some other way adversely affect their welfare.

Genetic material inherited at conception normally remains unaltered throughout life, and is transmitted to the offspring in the same form. It may change (mutate) in exceptional circumstances, but the mechanism of heredity is remarkably reliable, and the vast majority of infants is born within the normal range of variation. The basic chemical structure of the chromosomes appears to be very stable. Genetic errors do sometimes occur and they take different forms, the subject matter of part IV.

Many characteristics in which there is quantitative variation, notably complex ones like intelligence, temperament, stature, longevity and athletic ability, depend on the action, called polygenic inheritance, of many genes. Polygenic mechanisms are thought to produce attributes that are approximately normally distributed (e.g. height, weight, blood pressure and IQ). The physical capabilities, social and psychological skills, and strategies acquired by the individual, plus all the developmental changes that occur as the child grows up, result from an interaction of maturational and learning processes.

Maturation and learning

Maturation is the term applied to those developments in the child such as beginning to walk and talk, becoming pubescent, and others which are canalized, which is to say that they occur in a predictable sequence, as a function of time or age. It is an orderly process that progresses in fetal development from the simple to the complex. The direction is cephalocordal (i.e. from top to bottom – brain forming before legs) and proximodistal (i.e. from the centre to the periphery – the spinal cord forming before the arms). Maturation also refers to the various neurophysiological and biochemical changes that take place from conception to death. Among these will be the hormonal changes of puberty which contribute to the shaping (via bodily changes) of male and female identity (see chapter 7). The environmental influences, which are so critical, depend in large part – as with so many other human attributes – on learning (i.e. instruction and/or experience).

Progress from Conception to Birth

The germinal stage: the first 14 days

The baby-to-be's first journey following the fertilization, which took place in one of the mother's two Fallopian tubes, is as a cluster of dividing cells moving down her oviduct and uterine lumen. Cell division begins 24 to 36 hours following conception. During the process of so-called cleavage division, from 0 to 40 hours, all cells are identical. By the time the zygote has reached the uterus – a journey taking 3 to 4 days – cleavage has proceeded to the point where the zygote has 12 to 16 cells. By 4 days of age (the number of days counted from conception) the egg mass at around 16 cells is called a morula. After approximately 4 days the multiplying cells separate into two distinct masses: the outer cells of the bilaminar disk forming a protective cocoon around the embryo, a cocoon that will create the rudiments of the all-important placenta – the embyro's life support system, and the shelter within which it will grow.

The inner layers of cells called the embryonic disk will form a nucleus of cells to become the embryo. Further differentiation takes place in the Fallopian

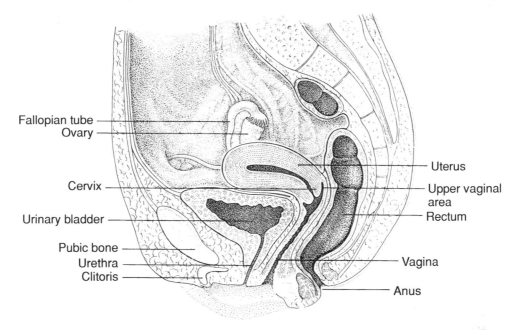

Figure 5 The female reproductive system

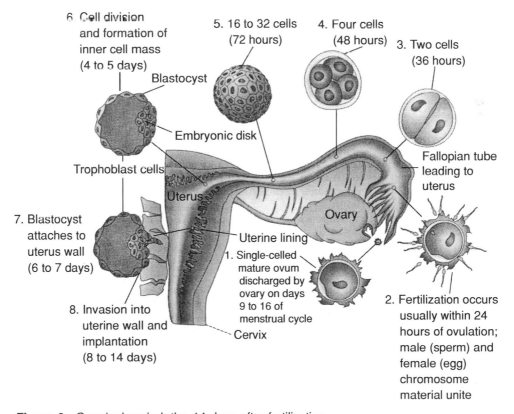

Figure 6 Germinal period: the 14 days after fertilization

tube resulting in the so-called blastocyst. As it approaches the uterus small burr-like tendrils (villi) emerge from its outer surface, and after entry into the womb they burrow into its lining (the endometrium). This process is known as implantation and, at around 10 to 14 days, marks the end of the germinal period and the beginning of the embryonic stage of development.

> **Comment:** Close to 60 per cent of all developing blastocysts fail to implant properly and therefore do not survive the germinal period. Most of them were grossly abnormal.

The embryonic stage: the third to the eighth week

The first stage of development of the conceptus (the product of conception) itself, is the embryonic stage. The embryo, as one of its major tasks, secretes chemicals that suppress the mother's immune system so that the embryo will not be rejected as an alien intruder, but allowed to grow. They have a second task of producing the chorionic gonadotrophin which stops the embryo being carried away by a menstrual period. The ovulation cycle now ceases. Pregnancy induces a higher metabolic rate (10–25 per cent higher than normal) in the expectant mother, and results in her body accelerating all of its functions. Cardiac output rises steeply and is maintained almost to the maximum level throughout the rest of the pregnancy. Breathing becomes more rapid as the mother sends more oxygen to the baby and exhales more carbon dioxide.

From the third week following conception, the embryo enters a highly sensitive period of growth. The first trimester of human development is a period of morphogenesis in which a differentiated fetus will eventually emerge from a homogenous embryo. The major organs and basic tissues are laid down. Development proceeds in an orderly manner and at a regular rate, with specific changes occurring at specific times. Every organ and every tissue – in fact, every cell – has its own timetable for coming into existence, for developing, for taking its place in the machinery of the body, and for beginning to carry out its function. And every small timetable is meshed with every other timetable. At no time in the future will this baby-to-be change as much as during these early prenatal months. Montagu (1964) makes the point that during this so-called *critical period* the development of the human body exhibits the most perfect timing and the most elaborate correlation that we display in our entire lives. He uses as an analogy the building and launching of a satellite, involving thousands of people and hundreds of electronic devices which, he says, is not nearly so complex an operation as the building and launching of a human being.

During the first phase of embryonic differentiation there are a number of spontaneous abortions, often of embryos with major chromosomal defects. They are not absorbed earlier because this is the first stage of development that is governed by the genetic material (DNA) of the embryonic cell nucleus. Earlier cleavage division is governed by the ribonucleic acid (RNA) that still survives from the original (i.e. the unfertilized) ovum.

Disturbances in the uterus can also produce calamitous effects on their growth and development. Only one out of every six embryos gets beyond 8 weeks in the womb. It is during periods of rapid change that an organism is most vulnerable to deleterious influences; so it is no wonder that mothers have to be careful about their health, which in essence means their baby's health and well-being. After this phase of development it is difficult, if not impossible, to affect the morphology of the organism in any fundamental manner. At 3 weeks, the embryo is already 10,000 times the size of the zygote from which it developed. However, this is not the time of maximal growth velocity. In the case of body weight that achievement occurs at approximately 20 weeks. The rate of growth thereafter slows down until term. Maternal factors such as uterine volume now confine the fetus.

From roughly the beginning of the third week after conception the hitherto formless mass of cells becomes a distinct being. A perceptible sign of body formation is the development of a three layered (trilaminer) disk. A portion of the outer layer of cells folds into a neural tube that soon becomes the brain and spinal cord. The disk becomes attached to the uterine wall by the short, thick umbilical cord, and the placenta develops rapidly. The organism is now made up of three layers:

- The ectoderm (to become the nervous system, skin, hair and teeth)
- The mesoderm (to develop into the circulatory system, muscle and bone tissue)
- The endoderm (which will become the digestive system, and various internal organs).

There is a rudimentary heart that begins to beat by the end of the fourth week, and the eyes begin to form. The neural tube closes; if not the result is a hare lip or spina bifida. Growth rate is about 1 mm per day. The support systems for the embryo develop, namely:

- The amniotic sac and fluid in which the embryo will float. This is a watertight membrane that develops from the trophoblast and surrounds the developing embryo, regulating its temperature and cushioning it against injuries.
- The chorion, which is a membrane that develops from the trophoblast and becomes attached to the uterine tissues to gather nourishment for the embryo. It acts as a safety cushion around the amniotic sac.
- The yolk sac, which manufactures blood.

The placenta, which is formed from the lining of the uterus and the chorion, provides for respiration and nourishment for the unborn baby, also for the elimination of its metabolic wastes. It pumps out hormones such as chorionic gonadotrophin, which help to support a healthy pregnancy. The umbilical cord, a soft tube containing blood vessels, connects the embryo to the placenta. The villi of the growing placenta intermingle with maternal blood vessels of the uterine wall so that they eventually constitute spaces surrounded by 'pools' of blood. The mother's blood flows in and around these spaces and an exchange of materials can take place within them. Small blood vessels from both mother and embryo intertwine, but they do not join. Although she and her baby do not share blood-streams, there is an interchange of certain substances – nutrients and waste – between their circulatory systems by way of the placental barrier; they include vitamins, antigens, antibodies, blood proteins, amino acids, drugs and viruses. Small molecules (oxygen, food, salts from maternal blood and carbon dioxide plus digestive wastes from infant blood) can pass to and from the mother's and the embryonic blood vessels. Large molecules such as red blood cells, most bacteria and various toxins, hormones and maternal wastes that could harm the developing conceptus cannot do so.

The late embryonic stage

Ultrasound can detect the presence of the embryo. By 5 weeks after conception arm and leg buds form. Until now female and male embryos look alike. At the fifth to sixth week of gestation the rudimentary testes and ovaries can be distinguished by microscopic examination. The first primordial structure to differentiate sexually is the bipotential gonad; and it is the male who manifests the first sexual difference. The male derives from the more basic female form, contrary to ancient received wisdom. If fetal androgen (a male hormone similar to the testosterone produced by adult male testes) is not present, or removed from an embryo with XY chromosomes (carrying the male genes that were imposed from the moment of fertilization), it will develop internal female sexual structures. If male hormones are present, the embryo develops male internal sexual characteristics. At 5 to 6 weeks of life part of the genital gland (the medulla) begins to proliferate and the surface portion (the cortex) regresses. When the genital gland differentiates into the primitive testes, these organs secrete fetal androgen. Low levels of androgen in a female embryo (conceived with XX chromosomes and female genes) allow the normal development of female sex organs.

Although a rare event, an imbalance in this system of hormone secretion can occur during fetal development. If there is insufficient androgen in a male embryo or an excess of androgen in a female embryo, the result is an individual with both male and female sex organs – an intersex phenomenon or hermaphrodite. (See Calapinto, 2000 and Money, 1993 on these atypical developments.)

It is hypothesized that sexual differentiation does not end with the completion of the formation of the physical sexual structures (at 12 weeks for the female ovaries; 16 weeks for male organs). Appropriate sexual behaviours (for example, controversially: aggression, spatial reasoning, rough and tumble play) are thought to become encoded physiologically in the brain. One can hear the cries of protest and sceptical requests for proof at this suggestion.

By 7 weeks, facial structures fuse (otherwise facial defects such as cleft palate occur). By 8 weeks, crown–rump length is 3 cm (slightly over 1 in) and weight is 1 g (about 0.03 oz). The major development of body organs and most structures is now complete.

Nerve cells that will form the brain will travel along pathways that are being laid down by glial cells which enable the neurons to move towards each other, connect and become active. The all-important nerve cells, as Pinker (1997) observes, are born in appropriate numbers at the right times, migrate to their resting places, send out connections to their targets and hook up to the appropriate cell types in the right general regions. All this is achieved under the guidance of chemical trails and molecular locks and keys. What is missing, as he points out, is an answer to the mystery as to how precisely this happens.

The fetal stage: the ninth week up to birth

Despite a mother's responsibility as host in protecting her baby-to-be, and the intimate emotional bond she may feel toward her unborn child (see the following chapter), courts of law have given recognition to the fact that the fetus is only a temporary lodger, always a distinct individual. The fetus has its own unique pattern of genes, and possesses its own nervous system and blood stream. As we have seen, there is no more direct blood tie between a mother and child than between a father and child. Despite its tenancy of the womb the fetus has rights of its own. There are passionate debates about the extent and balance of the rights of the mother and her unborn baby, arguments that are too complex for a brief and adequate discussion, and therefore not pursued in this text.

By the second trimester that begins on week 13, the pregnancy is well established and 'shows'. Many women report a surge of energy and a sense of well-being, earning the trimester (which lasts until the end of week 27) the soubriquet 'golden period of pregnancy'. Most of the baby's external features that are observed at birth are now apparent. The body begins to straighten and elongate. The head is large in comparison to the body. The heart beats at 140–150 per minute. All of the structures that will be present

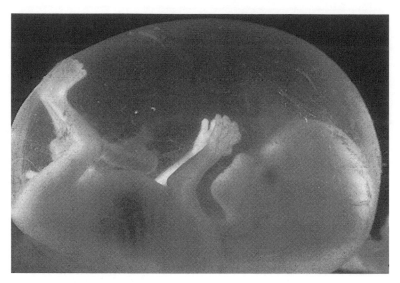

Figure 7   At 14 weeks, surrounded by its amniotic sac, the fetus is recognizably the infant it will become, with discernible facial features, limbs and sexual differentiation (Petit Format/Nestlé/Science Photo Library)

when the baby is born, in 7 more months, have already formed, at least in their beginning stages.

Apgar and Beck (1974) observe that medically, the unborn organism is no longer an embryo, but a fetus; not an it, but a he or she; not an indistinct cluster of cells, but an increasingly recognizable, unique human being in the making. It seems somehow miraculous after this highly sensitive period of development just how much (and how often) things go right despite the potential hazards. The vast majority of babies emerge into the world as reasonably intact beings.

The placenta now takes over the production of pregnancy hormones, the mother's hormone levels begin to resume a balance making for enhancements in appearance and in mood (sometimes a sense of elation) for many. The fetus not only looks more human; it is possible by 12 weeks to discern its gender. It now contains nearly the same number of neurons as an adult, and the nerves from the brain begin to be coated in myelin, a layer of protective fat. This is a crucial stage in their maturation as it facilitates the passage of messages to and from the brain.

THE FINAL MONTHS

These months find the baby growing bigger in her mother's abdomen; it is during this final period that the body parts and organ systems are enlarged and refined. Some of the milestones of fetal development are the announcing of his or her presence by kicking (by 16 weeks), sucking their thumbs and

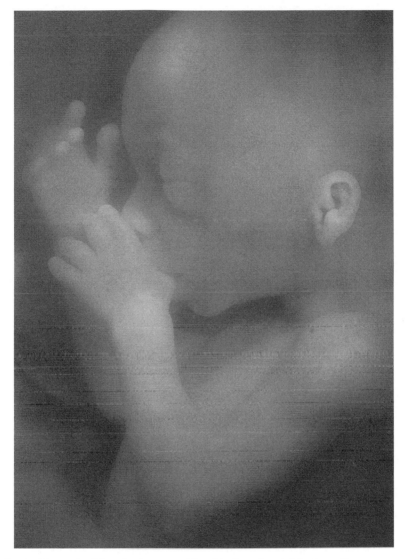

Figure 8   A 19-week-old male fetus sucking his thumb: at this time, the crown–rump length is around 18 cm and the fingers and toes have formed; the mother will have noticed the fetus's movement (Neil Bromhall/Science Photo Library)

displaying the beginning of hair growth (by 20 weeks). By the seventh month the fetus is able to breathe, cry, digest, and excrete, and is in a good position to survive premature birth. The final months of fetal development are primarily concerned with length and weight-gain. At the end of the fifth month the fetus is around 20–30 cm (8–12 in) long and weighs about 225–450 g (0.5–1 lb); at the sixth month it is 28–35 cm (11–14 in) in length and its weight is 680 g (1.5 lb).

During the final 3 months *in utero* the fetus is reported to be capable of learning from the events in its environment. Despite the protective roles of amniotic fluid, embryonic membranes, uterus, and maternal abdomen, it is not entirely cut off from what is going on in the world outside. The uterine environment is a stimulating, interactive home for a now ceaselessly active – kicking, hiccuping, face-pulling, crying, hitting out – inhabitant. Certainly, the fetus with the use of its rudimentary access to the fundamentals of experience and communication – touch, taste, smell, hearing, and vision – is preparing for life outside the womb.

Several experiments have revealed the following about the fetus:

- Listening begins at 16 weeks.
- It actively processes and responds to sounds that are filtered through the amniotic fluid that surrounds it, distinguishing, it is claimed, between music, language, intonation, rhythm, and other auditory stimuli. Researchers state that prior to any *ex utero* experience, newborns show that they have already extracted information about some of the important abstract features of mother's voice during their period in the womb. It is claimed that congenital deafness may be diagnosed during the prenatal period because of possible access to the fetus while it is in the womb (see Shahidullah and Hepper, 1993, and chapter 2).
- It shows sensitivity to light, responding to it with accelerated heart rate.
- It shows skin sensitivity to a hair stroke to a growing number of areas of the embryonic/fetal body.

Eventually, at around 266 days after conception, the baby usually rotates into a downward position with its head settling into the bony part of the mother's pelvis, relieving the pressure on her abdomen. This so-called engagement (the 'drop') is one of the first signs that labour is approaching. There may be different intervals of time before its actual onset. In the weeks preceding delivery the uterus may have 'practice' contractions (first described in 1872) which are usually brief and relatively painless. They tone up the delivery system for the 'real thing', while helping adjust the baby's position. By the time true labour begins, the cervix will probably have already started to dilate and thin (efface), initiated often by the pre-labour contractions.

No one can predict what will happen during labour; fortunately most births go without a hitch. The typical birth and the exceptions are described in chapters 2 and 9 respectively.

Comment: About 5 per cent of all fetuses are aborted spontaneously before possible viability at 22 weeks, or are stillborn after 22 weeks.

The chronology of events in the child's first journey is summarized below.

Summary of Prenatal Events: Times After Conception

The germinal stage

Week 1
- A single-cell mature ovum is discharged by an ovary between days 9 and 16 of the mother-to-be's menstrual cycle.
- Fertilization takes place in one of the woman's Fallopian tubes: a male sperm cell penetrates the wall of the ovum.
- 0–24 hours: ovum and sperm (gametes) unite to form a fertilized egg (zygote) with 46 chromosomes (23 + 23).
- The one-cell zygote begins to float down the Fallopian tube toward the uterus, a journey that will take about a week.
- Cell division (mitosis) begins 24–36 hours after conception. Each of the cells is identical during the cleavage divisions, until the third doubling.
- At 36 hours there are two cells; at 48 hours four cells, 16 to 32 cells at 72 hours, and so on and on.
- 3–4 days the egg mass is called a morula and is made up of 12 to 16 cells.
- At about 4 days following conception, the mass of cells, now called a blastocyst, is a ball-shaped group of cells consisting of 16 to 64 cells. It is now about the size of a pinhead. Each cell is about the size of a normal cell, much reduced from the original zygote.
- At the eight-cell division stage, cell differentiation begins. The cells take on, for the first time, distinct characteristics, and they gravitate towards particular locations that foreshadow the types of cells they will become.
- Around the end of the first week or the beginning of the second week a hollow sphere forms, as the blastocyst undergoes further differentiation. It has an inner layer (the embryonic disc) that forms a nucleus – the future embryo; and also an outer layer of tissues to protect and nourish the embryo – the future placenta.

Week 2
- After 6–10 days following conception the blastocyst approaches the uterus and enters it. The blastocyst now has some 150 cells.
- Implantation is completed usually 12–14 days after conception. The blastocyst has some 250 cells. Tendrils on the cell mass burrow into the wall of the uterus thus attaching itself. Its outer layer forms four major support structures: placenta, amnion, chorion and umbilical cord.
- At about 14 days a mature placenta begins to develop.

The embryonic period: the third to the eighth week

Week 3
- The mother-to-be misses her menstrual period. A pregnancy test is now positive. The embryo secretes chemicals that suppress the mother's immune system so that it will not be rejected; also gonadotrophin which stops its evacuation by a menstrual period. During the first weeks the mother's body produces oestrogen and progesterone which make the uterus enlarge, and cause the muscle fibres to thicken.
- The neural tube begins to form 20–22 days approximately after conception. This will become the brain and spinal cord.
- The embryonic (trilaminar) disk is rapidly differentiating into 3 cell layers: ectoderm, mesoderm and endoderm.
- 21–28 days: the eyes begin to form.

Week 4
- The neural tube closes. The head begins to take shape. A blood vessel that will become the heart begins to pulsate.
- The placenta is fully formed, and the maternal–placental circulation begins to function.
- The two bloodstreams are separated by a membrane that allows substances to be diffused from one bloodstream to the other; they never mix.

Week 5
- A tail-like appendage extends from the spine.
- Buds that will form arms and legs appear. Eyes, ears and nose and mouth are forming and by the middle of the week the eyes have corneas and lenses.
- The brain divides into three main sections: forebrain, midbrain and hindbrain.
- Peripheral nerves are appearing.

Week 6
- Primitive nose and ears develop. Facial structures fuse.
- A cluster of cells appears that will develop in male or female sex organs.
- Males and females are still virtually identical. Later, a gene on the Y chromosome sends a chemical signal that initiates the development of male sex organs. Indifferent gonad begins to develop on female sex organs (Koopman et al., 1991).

Week 7
- The ears are well formed. The embryo has a rudimentary skeleton. Limbs are developing from the body outwards. Sexual development begins on the seventh and eighth week.

Week 8
- The circulatory system functions on its own. The liver and spleen produce the blood cells.
- Ovaries and testes are distinguishable. The first muscular contractions take place, directed by the embryonic brain.
- The body begins to straighten and elongate. The head is more rounded. Features of the face are formed. All the basic organs and body parts of a human being (except sex organs) are present. The embryo is now more human in appearance. The tail is no longer visible having been incorporated into the lower spine.
- The mouth has 20 buds that will become baby teeth.
- The gross structure of the nervous system is established. The brain develops rapidly from this time.

The fetal period: ninth week until birth

12 weeks after conception
- By the end of the third month the fetus can move every part of her/his body. It changes position, sucks its thumb, kicks, frowns, squints, swallows amniotic fluid and urinates.
- Startle and sucking reflexes, facial expressions, finger prints and lanugo, are all present.
- The external genital organs are fully formed.
- Simple abortion by curettage is no longer possible.
- The *first trimester* ends.

13 to 16 weeks
- The umbilical cord continues to grow and thicken in order to carry sufficient nourishment from mother to fetus.
- Skin and true hair have developed.
- The skeleton becomes bony.
- The fetal heart is growing stronger and can be heard with a stethoscope.
- Movements of the fetus become obvious to the mother ('quickening').

17 to 24 weeks
- Digestive and excretory systems develop more fully. Fingernails, teeth buds, toenails, hair and eyelashes grow.
- The most impressive growth is in the brain which begins to react to stimuli (Carlson, 1994).

22 to 25 weeks
- Viability begins around 25 weeks (Moore and Persaud, 1993); the baby has a good chance of survival if born prematurely.

- By the end of the second trimester, the fetus's visual and auditory senses are clearly functional.

25 to 27 weeks
- Weight-gain, particularly fat, accelerates and continues over the final 10 weeks.
- There is a leap forward in brain development. Brain wave patterns change.
- Terminals of lung and associated blood vessels develop.
- The *second trimester* ends.

28 to 32 weeks
- The heart rate is regulated by bodily movement.
- The nervous system is well organized for survival. The odds of premature survival after 28 weeks (previously thought of as the 'time of viability') are much improved. Currently, neonatologists generally put this threshold at 25 weeks. Babies born earlier than this are still in the second trimester zone; they have a daunting, unfinished developmental journey to complete outside an all-providing womb.
- A range of tests – such as ultrasound, fetal monitoring, fetal acoustical stimulation – is available to check on both normal and risky pregnancies, at this time.

35 to 38 weeks
- The final trimester sees the maturing of the respiratory system and cardio-vascular system. All the organ systems mature rapidly.
- The lungs begin to expand and contract.
- The fetus takes in fluid through the mouth and nose and then exhales it.

38 weeks
- The baby weighs 3400 g (7.5 lb) on average.
- The *third trimester* ends

Unanswered Questions

A very small sample of such issues includes the following:

1. Is the fetus in any sense, a conscious being? And if so, at what stage of its prenatal existence did consciousness emerge?
If the baby is a conscious being surely its conscious awareness is not suddenly 'switched on' at birth. If not, how far back do we have to go to its onset? At birth four of the five senses are fairly well developed. Vision lags behind. The fetus possesses the following:

- Touch: from about 8 weeks into the pregnancy.
- Hearing: unfocused from 20–22 weeks; certainly focused enough by 24 weeks to startle and register an increased heart rate in response to a very loud sound.
- Vision: from 26–28 weeks.
- Smell and taste. These are both less capable of being pinpointed in time, but seem to emerge somewhere between 8 and 20 weeks.

In neurobiological terms, awareness requires a cortex capable of receiving and processing adequate stimuli from outside and within it, a condition that effectively rules out awareness before 20 weeks of prenatal life. It is not possible to go beyond this statement that there is a period when presumably consciousness cannot emerge.

2. Does the fetus experience pain?
Given the increasing ability to intervene surgically before birth, this becomes an important question. Pain is subjective and the fetus is in no position to tell us how he or she feels. What is undeniable is that they do show stress responses indicated by increases in noradrenaline levels.

3. Does the fetus have a memory?
This question relates, in part, to the mystery of consciousness. It is not possible to comment meaningfully about the concept of a conscious memory, although there are many anecdotal accounts, notably of personal prenatal experiences recovered as 'memories' in psychotherapeutic sessions. These amount to evidence on a par with data associated with a belief in UFOs. One either believes or disbelieves the 'evidence', or one adopts a cautious agnostic position.

   With regard to memory as a product of conditioning, there is research on animals indicating that prenatal experimental conditions elicit conditioned physical responses (stress reactions) that are replicated in postnatal situations of a similar kind. We know that human mothers who suffer domestic violence experience an increased heart rate that is also registered in her fetus. After birth the baby responds to recordings of the mother's increased (stressed) heart rate with an increase in its own heart rate.

> **Note:** Chapters 8 and 9 continue the account of the child's first journey in its atypical (abnormal) manifestations.

chapter two

The Perinatal Period

When the child can no longer be contained in so small a place,
being and requiring more nourishment, it kicks and breaks the
membranes and ligaments that held it and the womb by expelling
faculty, sends it forth with great straining, and this is called travel.
Nicholas Culpeper: *Book of Life* (1651)

The perinatal period of development extends from the final stages of pregnancy and delivery, to the early days following the baby's birth. The perinatal environment includes influences such as drugs prescribed for the mother to relieve pain during the birth, delivery methods, and the immediate physical and social environment into which the neonate enters.

Anticipation of the Birth

The baby-to-be

The last 3 months of fetal life in the womb is not only a period of growth, but also a time to learn. The fetus is readying itself for birth. The relatively simple learning involved is possible because of its ability to respond to the world outside. It reacts by moving suddenly if a powerful torch is shone over the womb. It also responds to changes in pressure on the mother's stomach by pushing against it with shoulders, knees or elbows. It practises some of the actions (e.g. thumb sucking, opening and closing its eyes) that will facilitate later reflexes such as feeding and blinking. The fetus is also developing preferences (e.g. his or her mother's voice). By the time the perinatal stage begins, the fetus is extraordinarily well prepared for the rigours of the world outside the mother's body.

The mother

The mother is faced with various decisions as she anticipates the birth of her child, one of the first being the location for the delivery. Much concern has been expressed about the actual place of birth. Is it to be home or hospital? The physical safety of mother and baby is a vital consideration. From that point of view the hospital provides some advantages. A variety of professional services in some parts of the world are at hand if or when required. Experts are available before, during, and after birth: the family doctor, antenatal classes instructor, midwife, obstetrician, and paediatrician. In the UK a community midwife monitors the baby's first 10 days of life after which a health visitor takes on a statutory health promoting and illness prevention role, a responsibility lasting 5 years.

All of this represents a very medically orientated set of birth and after-care procedures. They would be regarded as unnecessary in many cultures, and indeed surplus to requirement for a growing number of expectant mothers in industrialized countries. Natural childbirth is making a comeback, and research indicates that there are many benefits to the demystification, which means the 'de-medicalizing' of childbirth (see Brockington, 1996). Nowadays it is often said that for healthy women, the home is the best place for a psychologically relaxed confinement. There are other advantages: labour is less extended in time, and medication is not so often required (Beard and Chapple, 1995). There is an increase in the numbers who wish to have their babies, assisted by midwives, at home. The issue of receiving medicated pain relief causes parents worry about the effects of the drugs on the vulnerable baby. Once a mother has an intravenous drug, it enters the infant's bloodstream at 70 per cent of its concentration in her blood. Obstetricians and anaesthetists claim to be supported by research for their assertion that the drugs used to prevent or relieve pain during labour and delivery are not harmful to mother or child.

Fads and Fashions

What emerges from historical and cross-cultural studies of a variety of perinatal practices, is the remarkable adaptability of human beings. It is this adaptability that has enabled the human species to survive and thrive in all manner of situations. Sadly, there are exceptions. Among the upper classes in Western cultures, women called 'wet nurses' were often hired to breast-feed babies. The fate of many of their own infants is discussed in a 1978 book *Infanticide: Past and Present* by Maria Piers.

At one time there was a widespread belief that labour pains were conducive to the growth of motherly love; a possible reason for a long-enduring, maybe extant, opposition to the administration of pain-killing drugs during labour. The seventeenth-century physician Nicholas Culpeper wrote in his *Book of Birth*:

> Though child-bearing since Eve's sin is ordained to be painful as a punishment thereof, yet sometimes it is more painful than ordinary.

Small wonder though, that fear lingers on when so many of the old beliefs take so long to die. Marie Stopes, writing a long way forward in time (1920), in a book entitled *Radiant Motherhood*, refers to the 'gossipy opinion that women who are spared the full torture of childbirth do not have equally passionate love for the child'.

In the nineteenth century well-to-do ladies were often advised to stay in bed and rest for several weeks after giving birth. It may well be that this practice helped to reduce the high incidence of illness then prevalent in women during confinement. As perinatal morbidity and mortality in women and infants declined at the turn of the century, lengthy confinements to bed ceased to be customary. Not everyone thought highly of this change in custom. Marie Stopes expressed bitter regret in 1920 that the long, postpartum stays in bed were no longer practised (Stopes, 1920/2001). This is a good example of how fashions change over the years.

Fashions may impact adversely on deeply held cultural and/or religious beliefs. Let us take two examples, one from Asia, another from Africa. They illustrate how Western infant-care doctrines and 'bonding' procedures, popular in the 1970s and 1980s, and still applied by doctors and nurses in some maternity wards today, can have disturbing repercussions for women from some ethnic groups (Sluckin, Herbert and Sluckin, 1983). In some Asian communities, mothers are considered unclean for the first 3 days after birth and close physical contact with the baby is avoided. The infant is managed, depending on local custom, by a close relative of the mother or father. Some immigrant parents could feel intense conflict over skin-to-skin 'bonding procedures' (see below). Then again, women from certain parts of Ghana are said to 'lie between life and death' when in labour. The period of confinement is regarded as an anxious time because it is widely believed that a newborn baby may in fact be a spirit child and not a human child at all. If it is a spirit child, it will return to the spirits before a week is out: thus for the first 7 days (in some areas, 3 days for a boy or 4 for a girl) mother and child are confined to the room in which the birth took place. The parents are not allowed to mourn its loss but should show signs of joy at being rid of such an unwelcome guest. It is possible to see the *adaptive* element in such cultural beliefs; they may help parents to come to terms with death, especially in areas where there are high infant mortality rates. This is speculative; what is more certain is that when it comes to making decisions about arrangements for birth, possible bereavement, and early childcare, the primary consideration should be a sensitivity to the personal and cultural values, and thus, the well-being of parents.

The Birth: Labour and Delivery

The newborn infant

Many 'childcare philosophers', well-meaning friends, parents, and grand-mothers have influenced the way in which women approach birth and the care of their young infant.

Throughout history until relatively recent times, infant mortality was very high indeed. Childcare of the newborn has tended to be primarily directed towards the preservation of life, although various misguided practices have sometimes rendered ineffective the efforts of all those attending childbirth. An important contemporary helping role – that of a midwife to childbirth – goes a very long way back, being mentioned in *Genesis* and *Exodus* in the Bible. Midwives held respected roles in ancient Greece and Rome. Coming closer to present times birth mothers, very broadly speaking, would sooner or later hold and suckle the baby after giving birth. At some stage mother and baby would be washed clean. In Europe and in many other parts of the world, but certainly not everywhere, young babies were traditionally swaddled. This provided some protection for the helpless infant, and therefore, by and large, probably did more good than harm. At various times these basic early routines, giving the baby to the mother, washing the baby, putting it into swaddling clothes and so on, were a matter of debate and to some degree subject to fashion.

New styles of care continue, generally, to be an integral part of economic and ideological developments in society, and they encompass a broad front. In the 1940s, Grantley Dick-Read, in his book *Childbirth Without Fear*, introduced ideas about natural childbirth, about educating expectant mothers (by means of antenatal classes) and about other features of preparation, which might counter women's fears of giving birth – major causes of pain during labour. The French obstetrician Frederick Leboyer (1975) was most concerned about the trauma of birth for the baby, an event he called 'the torture of the innocents'. The assumption seemed to be that a baby was suddenly and unceremoniously thrust out into a cold, bright world, experiencing an immense shock after its previous warm, calm residence in the womb. He recommended various methods in his book *Birth Without Violence* (e.g. a quiet relaxing birthing room, skin-to-skin contact with the mother, and bathing in warm water) to stay close, as he believed, to the ambience of the uterine environment.

Some practitioners are sceptical about these assumptions and the effectiveness of the procedures. Michel Odent (1984) rejected the traditional method in which the mother's feet were held in stirrups, the delivery taking place against the force of gravity, thus requiring stronger contractions. He promoted a more natural, instinctive procedure and presentation, in which interference is kept to a minimum. This approach resonates with the practices in many non-Western cultures. A majority of babies in such societies are born at home, compared with the massive majority (nearly 99 per cent) in the USA whose delivery takes place in a hospital (Philpott, 1995). Those present, family members and female assistants, the delivery position adopted (e.g. squatting) and other features of the birth process, tend to be naturalistic. In Kenya the cultural rituals of the Pokot people support the mother's coming birth, celebrating the imminent delivery, while the father forgoes hunting to be available to help his wife. A midwife, assisted by female relatives, delivers the baby, following which the placenta is buried ceremoniously in the goat enclosure. The baby receives a tribal potion for its health. Mothers are given 3 months to recover in seclusion, free of domestic chores, and free to devote themselves to the care of their infants (Jeffery and Jeffery, 1993; O'Dempsey, 1988). In Uttar Pradesh in Northern India attendants who deliver babies offer little support and discourage a mother's cries of pain. These procedures, as we can see, are worlds apart – a reminder to us of the cultural variations in the initial stages of children's journey in the outside world.

The availability of social support and antenatal preparation for mothers, and the opportunity to experience natural childbirth, appear to benefit them and their infants (Brockington, 1996). Advocates of parental freedom of choice criticize the practice of treating pregnant women (and their partners) as if they are patients awaiting an illness called birth, rather than as thinking adults who have the right to contribute to decisions about the delivery of their baby. Birth plans are designed to ensure just such active involvement on the part of the parents who draw them up themselves, often with their GP's assistance.

Birth position

Before the eighteenth century women laboured vertically, using birthing stools and holding bars, squatting to ease the labour pains. As with so many fashions these simple methods in similar form have come full circle, and are the choice of many women today, although lying the expectant mother on her back for the delivery continues to be advocated in hospitals. Other methods such as going 'back' to uncomplicated nature, as practised by some African cultures are also gaining more widespread interest and acceptance.

Contemporary practice

Gradually, scientific advancement and a better understanding of human physiology and the causes of disease have brought about an era of relative enlightenment, the emphasis being on the word 'relative'. 'Normal' labour and delivery proceed in three stages that overlap somewhat with each other, taking about 12 to 14 hours in total for first-time mothers and around 7 hours for subsequent babies. The process of giving birth is as follows (see Biswas and Craigo, 1994):

• The labour begins: As the baby's head descends, pushing down on the cervix, the mucous plug at its entry (a protection against infection) discharges through the vagina. This is a sure sign labour contractions are likely to begin within a matter of a few days. However, as seems so often the case with human development, there is a good deal of variability in the timing of the preliminary stages leading to the baby's first appearance. In the first stage of labour, preparing the mother for delivery, the opening at the bottom of the uterus (the cervix) dilates to allow the moulding of the baby's head to the birth canal. A widening to 10 cm (4 in) is necessary to allow the passage of the baby. In addition, the pelvic bones spread out (effacement), a process that usually begins, as we saw earlier, some weeks before delivery. In this early phase, the contractions are relatively far apart and the mother's discomfort relatively unintense. There is an early, active and transitional phase during which the contractions become more frequent and intense, accompanied by a growing sense of discomfort. The most reliable sign of 'real' labour is contractions that occur at regular and increasingly shorter intervals. This is the time (intervals 5 to 15 minutes apart) mothers are usually advised to call for the professionals. If the 'bag of waters', the baby's protective amniotic pool, breaks during the course of labour, the baby is assuredly on its way – the birth is imminent. The cervix dilation increases throughout. The contracting uterus helps to push the baby's head further down into the pelvis. In the transitional phase the contractions are powerful and the discomfort intense. The cervical dilation is 10–11 cm. This stage usually takes 8 to 10 hours in first pregnancies.
• The second stage sees the baby's head (about 97 per cent of babies are born in the head-first position) pushing through the birth canal. This stage normally lasts 1 to 2 hours in first pregnancies; 30 minutes or less with later ones. The powerful contractions tend to be around 2 to 3 minutes apart and last about a minute. During this period the baby secretes high levels of vital hormones (the catecholamines adrenaline and noradrenaline) which help to open up the lungs, dry out the bronchi, and mitigate the intermittent deprivation of oxygen. At last, as an exhausted mother must

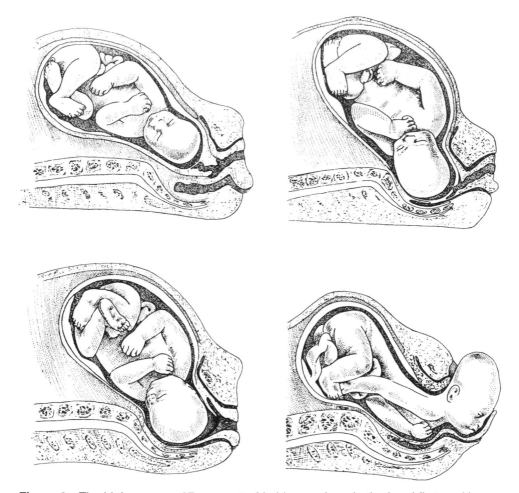

Figure 9   The birth process: 97 per cent of babies are born in the head-first position

think of it, the baby becomes visible at the vaginal opening and is born. His or her birth completes a truly extraordinary journey.

• In the third stage the placenta (afterbirth) is expelled, a process normally taking 15 or 20 minutes. The placenta is examined carefully for intactness.

Both too much and too little speed in the delivery of the newborn can have negative consequences. Such eventualities in the second stage of delivery are of most significance. It is referred to as *precipitate labour* if it takes less than 10 minutes for the baby to pass through the birth canal. Potential dangers arise from the prevention, due to the contractions, of normal blood flow (and thus adequate oxygen) to the neonate, or intolerable pressure to the head resulting in brain hemorrhaging. A prolonged labour may result in anoxia (see chapter 9).

We should not forget a baby's own adaptive capacities while expressing our concern for the parents. Fetuses doubtless are stressed by the rigours of delivery, but their own production of activating stress hormones is protective, assisting them to withstand oxygen deprivation by increasing their heart rate and the flow of oxygenated blood to the brain. It could also be said that the stresses endured by babies ensure that they emerge wide-awake and prepared to breathe. Most infants begin to adjust to the outside environment and quieten down within minutes of their first loud cry (MacFarlane, 1977).

In the United States, 90 per cent of babies are born between the 37th and 42nd weeks of pregnancy and are considered 'timely'. The average timely or 'full-term' baby weighs about 3500 grams (7½ lbs). The 'premature' baby is considered in chapter 9.

Dworetzky (1981) contrasts the 'newborn baby' of the old Hollywood movies – in which the delivery-room nurse handed the mother a 40 pound 'newborn' possessing a crewcut and a full set of teeth – with the real thing. As he describes it, in reality newborn infants have skin that is soft, dry, and wrinkled; they typically weigh between 6 and 9 pounds and are almost 20 inches in length. The newborn's head may seem huge in proportion to the rest of its body, and it is responsible for fully one quarter of the baby's length. The neonate may appear chinless, its forehead is high, its nose is flat, and when it cries, its body turns crimson. He adds that although the baby's eyes may eventually be brown, their eyes are usually steely blue.

During infants' first hours of life they are more wide-eyed and alert than they will be for days to come, in part due to the heightened levels of adrenaline and noradrenaline flowing through their systems during the trauma of birth. These physiological changes help them to cope with the considerable strain of passing through a narrow birth canal. They also assist babies in their mobilization of the heart, liver, and lungs now working on their own. Neonates are also in a highly alert state so as to cope with the impact of a myriad of new experiences. For the newborn baby, birth means a transition from an aquatic life in the womb, supported with an umbilical life-support system, to an independent air-breathing, temperature-regulating, and nutrient-absorbing existence. The latter is aided by the infant's rooting (orienting) to the nipple when the side of his or her mouth is stimulated, and by their active sucking reflex that allows them to derive nourishment from the breast or bottle.

The Mother and Postnatal Infant Care

The first hours

The 'postpartum period' is the period lasting for about 6 weeks after childbirth – a time when the mother's body adjusts both physically and psychologically to the process of childbearing (Richards and Bernal, 1971). Psychologically the event is momentous; with the birth of the first child the parents have created a new family. The tasks of the parents, the roles they occupy, and their orientation toward the future all change profoundly. This apparently simple step into parenthood can provide them with a severe test. The first hours after the baby's arrival can be a memorably happy time for the mother to enjoy her child, if she is given, as we saw above, the care and emotional support she needs.

Physically, the after-effects of childbearing are also momentous. After delivery the mother's body experiences sudden changes in hormone production. After a steep drop in oestrogen and progesterone following the delivery of the placenta ('afterbirth') the levels recover as the ovaries begin producing hormones. The woman will begin menstruating again in about 4 to 8 weeks if she is not breastfeeding. Emotional lability around this time is not uncommon. It is quite normal, in the statistical sense of not being unusual, for what are called the 'baby blues' to distress the mother about 3 to 5 days after she has given birth. They last between 1 week and 10 days and affect some 80 per cent of mothers.

A woman is not a 'blank page' on which the experience of mothering will be etched. In general her previous experience of having infants is a potent influence on her actions with a new baby. Multiparous women appear more efficient than primiparous ones in managing their children, and are less likely to be influenced by outside disturbances. They respond more quickly to their babies' crying and are more likely, subsequently, to feed them. They are less likely than primiparae to feel an initial indifference to the newborn baby, a not uncommon but disconcerting experience for first-time mothers.

Proximity of mother and baby

To fall in love or, more prosaically, become bonded, mother and baby have to get to know each other, which means getting together – a particular advantage of the hopefully relaxed feeding situation. Feeding the baby (breast-feeding being the preferred option because of its many health-promoting properties) is initiated as soon as possible in order to provide the infant with the benefits of colostrum. It is highly nutritious, contains antibodies (secretory immunoglobulin A), high concentrations of leukocytes (white cells that destroy bacteria and viruses), and also has a useful laxative effect.

In the 1970s Beekman published *The Mechanical Baby*, citing the writings over the last five hundred years about the theories and practices of childcare, including the care of newborn infants (Beekman, 1977). From time to time new thoughts on the handling of neonates and new practices (reflecting current ideologies and social attitudes) have emerged. Yet with the passing of time, novel ideas become old-fashioned; they fade away, perhaps to reappear later in new guises, they undergo re-formulations, they alter in their emphases, they re-emerge, they go out of fashion again. No wonder some mothers become confused, even distressed, by the conflicting advice they receive about the 'correct' way to manage their infants. (Aries' *Centuries of Childhood* and Sally Crawford's *Childhood in Anglo-Saxon England*, provide a fascinating historical background to these childcare issues.)

Views as to how near a newborn infant should be to its mother have been of particular interest to theorists, midwives, nurses and social workers. Dick-Read (1942) advocated, among other things, the practice of 'rooming-in'; that is, of keeping the newborn baby in the same room as its mother. The aim was to enable the mother to see her baby at all times and to get her to attend to the baby's needs. The desire to allow mothers to nurse their babies was part of the impetus for the movement in the 1940s to have newborns rooming-in with their mother in the hospital. The sooner and more frequently a baby nurses after birth, the sooner the mother's milk is available. If the breast is not stimulated in the first few days after she gives birth, her milk production system will turn off.

The rooming-in practice had been standard in American hospitals up to the turn of the last century. However, epidemics of diarrhoea, respiratory infections and the like among newborn infants led subsequently to stricter isolation arrangements of babies in separate wards. Special units for premature babies were also being set up. All these new arrangements reduced contact between mothers and their babies to a minimum.

On both sides of the Atlantic this restrictive tradition prevailed until a reaction against it began to set in, in the 1930s, when, among other things, rooming-in became respectable once again. One feature of this reaction was hostility towards hospital nurseries. Dick-Read considered them undesirable because they were thought to hinder a healthy development of mother–infant relationships. The practice of keeping the mother and her newborn baby together, it was said, should be re-adopted not only in private homes but also in maternity hospitals.

A very influential voice in America was that of Benjamin Spock. In his manual published in 1945 he strongly favoured the 'rooming-in plan'. He argued that under this arrangement the mother would learn a great deal about her baby's hunger patterns and other rhythms, such as sleep and bowel movements. Instead of regular fixed-hour feeds, 'self-demand' breast- or bottle-feeding was now considered to be best for the baby. A baby nursed on demand will nurse every 2 or 3 hours. The idea of rooming-in seemed at that time in the United States to be quite revolutionary; in fact (as we have seen) it only meant a return to what had been commonly done before the restrictive practices became firmly established. Spock freely acknowledged that his teaching would be difficult to put into practice in hospitals; it certainly required a departure from the then customary attitudes and administrative arrangements. He was a proponent of the view that fathers should be allowed, indeed expected, to participate in all baby-care activities.

Maternal Bonding Theory

What emerged in the 1970s was a stark 'critical period' hypothesis applied to mother-to-child attachments, the so-called 'maternal bonding' theory. What is this theory that proved so controversial? Put briefly, it was proposed that in some mammalian species, including our own, mothers become bonded to their infants through close contact very soon after birth. During the hours following birth, tactile, visual and olfactory stimulation of the mother by her baby was thought to be critical (i.e. time-limited) to her becoming attached to it. Where the mother's initial responsiveness was disrupted by separation from the baby having to go into intensive care (to take one example) there was a risk, it was feared, of long-term adverse consequences for the mother–child relationship.

Although past its heyday, it is worth commenting on the maternal bonding doctrine. Any reports of its demise (despite undermining evidence) are premature, as it continues to figure in formulations at case conferences, read about in magazine articles, and discussed on TV programmes. Every so often a psychological theory escapes the confines of sober academic debate associated with professional conferences or learned journals, and enters the wider public arena (and consciousness) by way of extensive publicity in the mass media. This was the fate of the maternal bonding doctrine which enjoyed (or suffered) the somewhat unrestrained discussion afforded to new fashions. Its meteoric rise and lingering fall (at least in its most extreme form) from grace, provide a salutary lesson on how initially liberalizing ideas from developmental psychology and the field of childcare, can become oppressive when a cautionary 'ought' becomes a dogmatic 'must'.

A particularly worrying aspect of the maternal bonding doctrine for mothers-to-be or mothers separated from their babies at birth was the warning of dire consequences. As Vesterdal (1976), one of many proponents of the pessimistic prognoses, claimed, the mother–child interaction may be stopped at the very beginning by separation of the child from the mother. This, it was suggested, would happen if the child had to be taken to a special care baby unit (SCBU) of the hospital immediately after birth, because of prematurity or some serious illness. There would be enormous difficulties in establishing contact between mother and child with the result that she might feel alienated from it, and a normal bonding would not be able to develop. Therefore, immediately after the birth of her baby, the mother (according to the doctrine) must be made to hold and fondle it, in order to become emotionally tied to the baby. It was even postulated that if the attachment to the child proved to be inadequate, the harmful long-lasting consequences could lead to child abuse (e.g. Lynch, Roberts and Gordon, 1976).

At the theoretical level the premise of a critical period for maternal bonding was an awesome claim, considering that no other adult human actions of great complexity had ever been explained causally in terms of ethological, and essentially reductionist concepts, such as *imprinting*. It certainly could not explain the origins of fatherly love or the committed attachments of adoptive and long-term foster parents, not to mention the loving bonds of siblings. At the applied level these ideas influenced day-to-day practice in maternity hospitals, homes and nurseries. They influenced decisions made in courts of law (e.g. whether a child was to be taken away from its parents, or which of the contesting parents was to be given custody). They influenced the advice given to young mothers by doctors, nurses and social workers; and they influenced what young mothers think, do, and feel.

Clearly, what was needed was empirical evidence. The close-contact, critical-period bonding theory was justified on two grounds. One was rooted in studies of animal imprinting behaviour. The other had to do with observations of human mothers, comparing those who had had little or no contact with their newborn babies with those who had extended contact time (see Klaus and Kennell, 1976). The animal work on which some of the theorizing was based did not stand up to critical analysis. There is insufficient space here for a detailed review of the human evidence on bonding. Durkin (1995) and Herbert, Sluckin and Sluckin (1982) have analysed the methodological weaknesses in those studies that led to overconfident childcare prescriptions. The ideological certitude that made so many professionals cling so tenaciously to a flawed doctrine is part of a broader issue of what has been called the 'professionocentric' bias of developmental psychology.

To summarize: the most rigorously controlled studies indicated that close contact soon after birth makes no difference to mothering effectiveness or to mother-love, either as reported by mothers or as inferred from their behaviour. There seems to be no reliable evidence that skin-to-skin contact is necessary for the development of mother-love; and, what is more significant, mother-to-infant attachment does not depend on such contact occurring during a sensitive period of short duration after the birth of the baby. With regard to the risk of child abuse, it is worth quoting a study, unusual for its large numbers, by Gaines et al. (1978). They investigated the circumstances of 240 mothers, drawn from known abuse, neglect and normal control populations. The multivariate analysis included 12 variables. Six of them discriminated between the abusing, neglecting and normal mothers at a high level of significance. Infant risk, determined on the basis of neonatal complications requiring hospitalization, was not a successful discriminator. According to the authors, the hypothesized relationship between mother–neonate bonding and maltreatment was not supported. (Child maltreatment is dealt with in chapter 17.)

Bonding to the Unborn Baby

Despite the fragility of the evidence, physicians began to ask themselves whether parental viewing of the early fetus (before 'quickening') by means of ultrasound imagery would accelerate bonding with the fetus (Fletcher and Evans, 1983). The issue may sound unrealistic, even fanciful; but this is not to say that it does not raise important issues. It is a moot point whether the positive feelings that many mothers-to-be experience during the months of pregnancy represent an 'attachment' or can legitimately be called 'love' although surveys indicate that that is what they feel toward the unborn child. If there were to be a sensitive period for bond formation, should doctors try, in any event, to extend it back in time to fetal existence?

There do seem to be important moral implications in the attempts to bond mothers to their unborn babies (Fletcher and Evans, 1983). Stillbirth after 24 weeks' gestation accounts for 0.5 per cent of births in England and Wales (Office for National Statistics, 1998). Parents tend to suffer traumatic grief for many months after the loss. There is speculation that the following child may be at risk as a 'vulnerable', 'replacement' child, engendering anxious, over-protective parenting. There is indeed some evidence that siblings of stillborn infants are more vulnerable to psychological and behavioural problems later in life (Hughes et al., 2001). In a study of 53 infants next-born after a stillbirth, and 53 control infants of primigravid mothers (ibid.), the former group showed a significant increase in disorganization of attachment to their mothers.

It would make sense in adaptational terms if problems were not heightened by special time-limited sensitization (with long-term sequelae) to an unborn child or a neonate. It would be strange, in survival terms, if critical sensitivities (with irreversible consequences) in a mother's relationship to her infant occurred when she is particularly vulnerable – exhausted, sometimes ill, and not uncommonly depressed. Dunn (1975), on the basis of a 30-week longitudinal study of 70 mother–baby pairs concluded 'that the post-partum period, rather than being a sensitive period may be a time when the relationship between the mother and baby is buffered against difficulties of adjustment'. Almost half of primiparae (first-time mothers) studied by Robson and Kumar (1980) felt an initial indifference to their newborn babies.

Ideological 'coercion'

It is sad to think that the eminently realistic, sensible, and humane idea of allowing a mother and her new baby to get to know one another early on, by means of frequent and intimate social interaction, becomes intrusive and unrealistic. The trouble is that when medical and other 'authorities' give their support to a particular theory or favour some child-rearing practice, it is nigh impossible for the general public to demur. This is what seems to happen when the permissive encouragement of physical contact becomes an authoritarian diktat, and more so when it is reinforced by an 'expert' warning of a malign fate if ignored.

Old wives' tales and quasi-psychological theories as to what is, or is not, best for mother and child, still abound today. However, there is no need, generally speaking, for mothers to feel anxious lest this or that practice will have dire psychological effects on the child, for years to come. Hilde Bruch (1954) is concerned that dogmatic advice creates a false illusion of omnipotence in the area of parent education. She believes that modern parent education has substituted 'scientific knowledge' for the tradition of the 'good old days'. She complains that an unrelieved picture of modern parental behaviour, a contrived image of artificial perfection and happiness, is held up before parents who try valiantly to reach the ever-receding ideal of 'good parenthood' like dogs after a mechanical rabbit. Her conclusion is that the new teaching implies that parents are all-responsible and must assume the role of playing 'preventive fate' for their children.

The Competent Infant

The neonate is not the somewhat amorphous incompetent, coming ill-prepared into the 'booming and buzzing' world early psychologists like William James (1890) imagined it to be. Right up to the 1950s the newborn was considered by many to be a helpless creature, a *tabula rasa*, to be 'written on' and thus shaped and moulded by the environment. Babies in general were considered to be helpless and passive. They cry, sleep, display some simple reflexes, and do little else. We now know, through innovative experimentation (e.g. Slater, 1990), that babies enter the world outside and begin their daunting journey through life 'wired up' with several already existing or imminent competencies that have survival value. This repertoire is biologically adaptive for its own species and its particular needs, as it would be for other primates and less phylogenetically evolved neonates. Research suggests that the infant's world, although blurred, is not that different from the adult's world. The equipment for visual interpretations is part of the human brain potential at birth; of course the function and meaning of objects awaits later learning.

The upsurge of exciting research on infant capabilities in the 1960s and 1970s probably caused the pendulum to swing too far in the direction of a 'look what this incredible baby can do' notion of 'competence'. There is perhaps a more balanced view today. Although human babies are socially pro-active and mobilize an impressive repertoire of competent behaviours, they are completely dependent on the caregiving of others, and for much longer than other species. They are at an intermediate level between two extremes:

- they are not as immature as those of the altricial species such as mice and rats, whose young have eyes closed and ears sealed; however
- they lag behind the young of precocial species, such as lambs, ducklings and calves.

Human babies are precocious in sensory development and can make a surprising degree of sense of their world at birth and before delivery. The premature infant born 3 or 4 weeks early is not a completely different individual from one who is full-term. Its eyes are open, and in many other ways it is not that much less mature in awareness of the world than the infant born at term.

Parenting

Our small nuclear families in the West provide fewer opportunities for boys and girls to learn the craft of parenting, an omission not suffered in many other cultures. Among the pre-existing factors which can influence the way the Western mother behaves and relates to her offspring are her own cultural and social background, her own experience of being parented, her personality, her previous experience with babies, and her experiences during pregnancy and birth. Mutual attachments between a baby and her mother develop in the context or continual mother–infant interactions. Many authors, notably Robert Hinde (1979), emphasize this point. Whatever the mother does in relation to her baby affects the baby; and the baby's behaviour thus affected, in turn, influences the mother's next action, and so on. Even in the case of very young infants, these interactions are of considerable complexity. This makes each sequence of interactions for a given mother–infant pair quite unique.

It has been shown that the same mother's sensitivity to her offspring's needs, and provision of stimulation for them, may differ from one child to the other. A variety of conditions may influence childcare practice, within the same mother, or as between different mothers. For example:

- Breast-fed infants, it seems, are fed for longer periods than bottle-fed babies during the first 10 days of life. They spend less time in the cot and cry more, all of which may have possible consequences for the subsequent mother–child relationship and the child's development. (Richards and Bernal, 1971).
- Mothers who are highly anxious during the pregnancy have been evaluated as having a less satisfactory interaction with their babies at 8 months

than mothers who had been low in anxiety (Davids, DeVault and Talmadge, 1963).

- A study conducted by Hubert (1974) found that whether the baby was intended or wanted was related to the decision whether or not to breast-feed. These findings suggest that the mother's attitudes during, or even before, pregnancy, may have some consequences for the mother–child interaction.

Although maternal attitudes before the child's birth probably do have some effects that are measurable in the early months of the child's life, these should not be overemphasized. Attitudes do tend to change in a positive direction during pregnancy, even when the baby is initially unwanted (Hubert, 1974). It is not simply that maternal attitudes determine the mother's beha-viour with her child; the actual experiences with the child may also lead to more positive attitudes later. However, as we indicate in chapter 11, it is also possible for mothers who began with very positive attitudes to the child, to react to his or her difficult temperament with resentment and even hatred.

There does seem to be a genetic factor that may have an effect on childcare practice. Plomin and Bergaman (1991) indicate that parental warmth to children (measured in a variety of ways) shows substantial genetic influence, while parental control does not. The environment is not influenced directly by genetic factors. Part of a genetic effect might operate, for example, through genetically influenced susceptibility to high-risk environments. Child abuse is likely to be one of the areas where gene–environment interactions require investigation (see chapter 17). There is an important moderating variable to be considered in later chapters when we look at problem development: the resilience or vulnerability of children that results in similar environments having very different consequences for youngsters with different attributes (Horowitz, 1990).

Siblings

Sibling rivalry is quite likely to occur in families which have just experienced the birth of a second child (Dunn and Kendrick, 1982): older children tend to resent the amount of attention given to the new baby. They usually adapt fairly soon and come to play an increasing caregiving role in the family. This role is a continuing and important one in many cultures. A survey by Weisner and Gallimore (1977) found that older children were the principal caregivers for infants in 57 per cent of the 186 societies they studied. In the inappro-priate (i.e. culturally atypical) category of childcare, the *duty* of care is put upon or assumed (often in distressed home circumstances) by children. The term 'parental child' is used to describe a child who, by virtue of having a cross-generation coalition with one parent, is permitted to have parental authority over siblings. The term 'parentification' has been used to describe the expectation that one or more children will fulfil the parental role in the family system.

A child who assumes, unprompted sometimes, many of the adult responsibilities and worries of family life and attempts to provide emotional support to his or her single (frequently abandoned) parent, is in a role-reversal that amounts in most cases to deprivation, perhaps even abuse. Clearly these are generally unsatisfactory burdens for a child, although sometimes invaluable to parents with another child who is disabled, a restrictive mental health problem such as agoraphobia, or an unresolved bereavement. Barnett and Parker (1998) point out that it is not surprising that the professional literature tends to emphasize the pathological aspects of parentification. But they suggest that the issue is not wholly clear-cut. For some individuals (depending on a host of mediating variables), parentification experiences may involve some advantageous compensatory adaptation, positively enhancing their competence for coping with life.

Environmental Influences

Environmental influences can determine whether individuals achieve all their genetic potential. Thus a child who is well endowed with inherited intellectual potential, may fail to achieve it if s/he is deprived of opportunities to learn. The opposite is also true; an unusually facilitative environment may enhance limited genetic potential. There is another possibility: the child's environment can be affected by her or his hereditary make-up. This is an example of the use of genetic research to help us understand the environments and has been called 'the nature of nurture'. Twin and adoption studies have shown that genetic factors can have effects on the environment itself and that such effects can be found on aspects of the environment measured in psychological research. Parents of high intelligence, for example, not only transmit the advantages of their genetic pool to their offspring but also transmit an ethos (in the form of a home environment) that is stimulating, challenging and enriching. Children who are easy in temperament and sociable make parenting a rewarding activity and thus influence the interactions of their parents in a positive direction. This raises the issue of what is called gene–environment correlation.

Gene–environment correlations (GrE)

The term gene–environment correlation refers to a non-random association between the genotype of the individual and the environment. Three types can be distinguished:

1. Passive gene–environment correlation refers to the environment that is imposed on the child by parents. In families of biologically related individuals this will be a positive correlation because of the shared genes of parents and child. For example, the athletic parent is not only more likely to expose the child to a sporting environment but is also more likely, as a sports person of prowess, to produce a child whose genotype predisposes her or him to be athletic.

2. Reactive gene–environment correlation refers to alterations in the environment caused by the reactions of others to the phenotype (and therefore to the genotype) of the individual. Thus, the parents who attend to their child's athletic activities will spontaneously arrange coaching for him or her, thereby promoting their talent.

3. Active gene–environment correlation, in which case the individual seeks out certain environments. The athletic child is likely to spend more time training and entering competitions, thus enhancing his or her skills.

GrEs can also be negative, as is the case with special school programmes which are below standard, and which stigmatize children with lower ability, undermining their self-esteem, their motivation and, in all likelihood, their accomplishments in life. Rutter et al. (1999a, b) provide another example of adverse gene–environment associations. Antisocial individuals are much more likely than other people to provide negative rearing environments. When one or both parents exhibit antisocial behaviour, there is a marked increased rate of marital discord, marital breakdown, and dysfunctional parent–child interactions and relationships. Antisocial activity is genetically influenced and represents part of the mediating mechanism. Because the genes that influence susceptibilities to antisocial activities in the parents also affect their parenting qualities, this means that the genetic risk will be associated with an increased environmental risk.

Rutter and his colleagues (ibid., p.33) describe how 'active' or 'evocative' GrE comes about. Genetically influenced antisocial behaviour such as disruptive classroom activities and delinquency during school-going years, with worse to come after leaving school, induces negative responses from other people (e.g. conflict with teachers and, later in life, partners, neighbours, friends, and employers). Such an antisocial life-style leads to people's withdrawal of social support and other environmental 'costs' (e.g. educational underachievement, unemployment, unsatisfying menial jobs, family tensions, and incarceration for committing crimes). These effects are the result of people's actions irrespective of whether or not such behaviour is genetically or environmentally influenced. However, the consequences will in part reflect GrE.

Representational Models of the Infant

There are other influences on caregiving relationships that are cognitive rather than affective in origin; perceptions of the infant that Bowlby (1988) referred to as mothers' 'representational models'. He suggested that these internal working models have a propensity for stability within individuals, and that they guide behaviour in caregiving relationships. What, perhaps, is surprising is that they influence parental interpretations of the infant's characteristics and behaviours not only after birth, but also prenatally. The descriptions by 96 expectant mothers of their offspring before birth predicted their security of attachment over a year later (Benoit, Parker and Zeanah, 1997). We return to this topic in the next chapter.

> **Note:** Atypical perinatal events are described in chapter 9.

part ii

Typical Development Infancy

Things do not change,
We do.

Henry David Thoreau (1817–1862)

The First Relationship (Stern, 1977)

The major developmental task of this phase of life according to Erikson (1985) is the baby's willingness to let her or his mother out of sight without undue anxiety or rage, because she has become an inner certainty as well as an outer predictability. The infant needs to develop a sense of trust, and later a growing autonomy. A lasting sense of trust, security, confidence or optimism (as opposed to distrust, insecurity, inadequacy or pessimism) are thought to be based upon affection, continuity of caring and the reasonably prompt satisfaction of the infant's needs. We all need relationships that provide a safe haven, emotional support and a sense of security.

These basic needs are made possible by the fact that children develop attachments to their mothers and other significant people – adults and children. Howe (1995) observes that 'in our development, what is on the social outside eventually establishes itself on the psychological inside. In this sense, relationships with others become internalized. It is in our relationships with others that our self forms, the personality takes on many of its characteristics, and we develop mental models that seek to make sense of people and social situations' (p. 24).

Attachment theorists claim that human babies are biologically programmed to attach themselves to their parents, or to other significant caregivers. And parents are biologically predisposed to bond with their infants. The development of childhood attachments begins with the child's entry into social life.

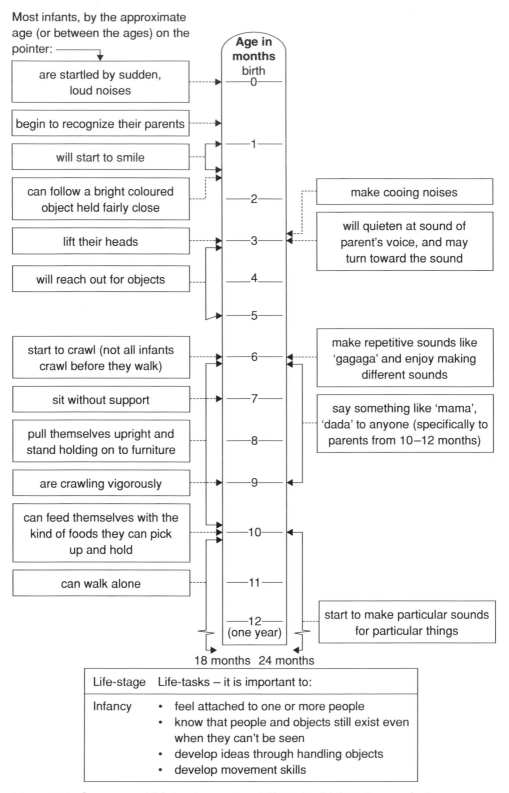

Most infants, by the approximate age (or between the ages) on the pointer:

Age in months
birth
—0—

are startled by sudden, loud noises

begin to recognize their parents

—1—

will start to smile

can follow a bright coloured object held fairly close

—2—

make cooing noises

lift their heads

—3—

will quieten at sound of parent's voice, and may turn toward the sound

will reach out for objects

—4—

—5—

start to crawl (not all infants crawl before they walk)

—6—

make repetitive sounds like 'gagaga' and enjoy making different sounds

sit without support

—7—

say something like 'mama', 'dada' to anyone (specifically to parents from 10–12 months)

pull themselves upright and stand holding on to furniture

—8—

are crawling vigorously

—9—

can feed themselves with the kind of foods they can pick up and hold

—10—

can walk alone

—11—

—12—
(one year)

start to make particular sounds for particular things

18 months 24 months

Life-stage	Life-tasks – it is important to:
Infancy	• feel attached to one or more people • know that people and objects still exist even when they can't be seen • develop ideas through handling objects • develop movement skills

Figure 10 Summary: child development and life-tasks (birth to 1 year plus)

The Development of Sociability

Social life for the newborn baby means a gradually widening circle of significant people, initially family members, notably parents (increasingly in the UK and USA a single parent), but most crucially, a mother or mother-substitute. In many ways, as we saw earlier, infants are socially competent. Particularly important are those of their actions that function primarily in social situations, notably their attraction to the kind of auditory and visual stimuli provided by caregivers to babies. It is highly advantageous that infants show signs of being sociable – seeking attention and smiling for example – at a very early age. And this is what they do so well. They turn their heads to patterned sounds rather than monotonic stimuli, particularly those sounds within the frequency range of human speech. They lock onto face-like patterns, but not onto other complex and symmetrical arrangements, when they are only 30 minutes old.

Sociability is plainly important for infants' ongoing development. Being able to recognize mother at 2 days of age (Bushnell, Sai and Mullin, 1989) and to produce winning smiles at an early age (Durkin, 1995) demonstrate this attribute. They also tend to protest if an adult leaves them on their own from as early as 6 weeks old. Newborns can usually focus their eyes to a distance of 20 cm, a distance well suited to engage in eye contact with the mother from the first feeding experience, a crucial step in the process of mutual attraction. They can discriminate all four tastes, with a distinct preference for something sweet, and they are able to differentiate their mother's milk odour from others (MacFarlane, 1977). Babies can suck, grasp, cling and reach, all responses that underlie feeding, proximity seeking and maintaining behaviour. They possess other pro-active behaviours that are designed to give them an early orientation to the social world. Smiling and cooing (comfort sounds) are observed within a few weeks or months. For the all-important human need to communicate, the very young infant's signalling repertoire – crying, cooing, smiling and arm movements – is effective in eliciting nurturing behaviour from the mother or mother-surrogate. These and other activities that have the effect of 'locking in' mutually affectionate responses, are soon in place.

Harry Harlow (1971) is of the opinion that mother-love in humans is often absent at the outset. Specific love – the bond to the child – tends to develop slowly but surely, gradually growing stronger and stronger. Very much later it may weaken, but it probably never vanishes. The course of the growth of paternal love appears to be essentially similar, a matter we return to.

Crying and Smiling as 'Social Communication'

The basic function of the infant's cry is to signal some need, notably to ensure attention and proximity from caregivers he or she is unable to approach physically. The baby's cries and arm movements are heard and seen shortly after birth. Infants have different cries for hunger, pain and anger, and spend up to 11 per cent of their time in crying. Such signals of, *inter alia*, distress elicit the mother's comforting response. The crying, and the maternal response to it, are thought to serve as constituents of a biological system of behaviour binding child and mother closely together. The summoning cry of the newborn child generally leads to the prompt and consistent presence of carers when discomfort, pain, hunger, or boredom require attention. Studies indicate that maternal attitudes, measured before the child's birth, can affect the mother's interactions with her child. Positive attitudes toward infants are related to the mother's responsiveness to the baby's crying, and to her social behaviour in the early months of life (e.g. Moss, 1967).

The pain cry has an abrupt and loud onset. The intensity of the cry, rather than its acoustic properties, appears to guide the parent as to the nature of the baby's need (Gustafson and Harris, 1990). Typical neonates cry for between 2 and 11 per cent of the time, a frequency that increases over the first few weeks. It peaks at 6 weeks of age when babies cry for 2 to 3 hours per day. This figure reduces to less than an hour a day by 3 months (Needleman, 1996). It is a fairly common view that the constant close-contact mother–infant rearing found in many cultures makes crying relatively redundant as a means of indicating need. However, the same peak with regard to frequency of crying has been found in close contact and non-close contact cultures (St James-Roberts, Bowyer et al., 1994). A particularly trying ordeal for parents is the daily bout of intense (seemingly inconsolable) crying associated with *colic*, a puzzling condition aetiologically, affecting 15 to 20 per cent of children between the ages of 2 weeks and 3 or 4 months of age.

Babies, at first, do most of their crying in the evening, but the pattern changes later and the most intense crying occurs just before feeding. Crying patterns vary from infant to infant, which means that parents have to learn how to differentiate between hunger, anger and pain cries (St James-Roberts and Plewis, 1996). Mothers can discriminate between taped episodes of anger and pain cries in their own 5-month-old babies, a skill not available to fathers. Neither can reliably discriminate between the taped cries of someone else's baby. Newborns seem to be able to discriminate between the sound of another infant's cry and their own. Tape recordings of another infant's cry cause newborns to cry, while the sound of their own cry calms them (Martin and Clark, 1982). Caregivers generally smile and talk to the baby if it smiles, and they tend to pick up an infant if he is crying, talk to him, and feel rewarded by the fact that the crying usually stops. It is the many encounters of this kind that gradually attach *social meaning* to infants' behaviour as they learn the reinforcing consequences of their signals (Seligman, 1975).

The Nature of Attachment

All infants need to become attached to a parent (or parent substitute) in order to survive. In the child-to-mother relationship the central notion in attachment theory has been that of proximity maintenance and the gaining of maternal protection from possible harm. The child's attachment relationship(s) have been viewed as a biopsychological 'solution' or strategy for coping with life-threatening circumstances such as predation, danger and illness during the lengthy period of human developmental immaturity. A child's fear or discomfort elicits proximity-seeking to a parent, and is usually responded to with parental retrieval and physical comforting (Herbert, Sluckin and Sluckin, 1982; Howe, 1995; Howe et al., 1999).

The specific attachment of a young animal to a particular adult or adult-substitute is known as *infantile attachment*. Ducklings, goslings and chicks, although normally attached to their natural mother, can easily become attached (if exposed very early in their life) to a foster parent, or, in the laboratory, to a moving inanimate object. This type of early learning is known as *imprinting*. The newborn of mammalian species, capable of locomotion soon after birth (as are most herbivores such as horses, cattle or deer) also appear to form attachments by exposure to figures in their immediate environment, normally their mothers. The existence of an attachment is inferred from behaviour. The presence of three elements is essential to define a child's attachment activity:

1. The child seeks closeness to parents or surrogate caregivers (*proximity-seeking*).
2. When the attachment figure is present, a child can explore the world around him or her without anxiety (*secure base effect*). The attachment figure fosters a sense of security in the child.
3. Any threat to the continued presence of the attachment figure initiates protests from the child (*separation protest*).

Children engage in attachment behaviour in situations such as hunger, pain, fatigue, threat, or anxiety, which engender distress. The child's attachment relationship is the primary social context within which crucial infant homeostatic functions such as temperature regulation, feeding and protection from the elements occur.

The child's exploration of the environment is seen as proceeding from the 'secure base' of a physically and emotionally available parent. Given this premise, attachment theorists argue that the nature of a child's attachment will have a significant impact on a wide variety of crucial physiological and psychological developmental functions.

Progress of child-to-parent attachment

By about 4 months old, infants generally behave in much the same friendly way towards people as they did earlier, but will react more markedly to their mother. They will smile and coo and follow her with their eyes more than they will other people. But although they may be able to recognize her, the bond has not yet developed which makes them behave in such a way as to maintain close proximity *to* her in particular – the real meaning of attachment. Attachment behaviour is best demonstrated (see Ainsworth's experiment below) when the mother leaves the room and the baby cries or tries to follow her. It is also evident when not just anyone can placate the infant. At 6 months about two-thirds of babies appear to have a close attachment to their mothers, indicated by separation protests of a fairly consistent sort. Three-quarters of babies are attached by 9 months. This first attachment is usually directed at the mother, and only very occasionally towards some other familiar figures.

During the months after children first show evidence of emotional bonds, one-quarter of them will show attachment to other members of the family, and by the time they are a year and a half old all but a few children will be attached to at least one other person (usually the father), and often to several others (usually older children). The formation of additional attachments progresses so rapidly in some infants that multiple attachments occur at about the same time. By one year of age the majority of children will show no preference for either parent, and only a few retain their mother-centredness.

Schaffer (1977) writes that by their first birthday children have learned to distinguish familiar people from strangers. He or she has developed a repertoire of signalling abilities that can be used in a discriminating manner in relation to particular situations and individuals. They are also about to acquire such social skills as language and imitation. He adds that, above all, they have formed their first love relationship: a relationship which many believe to be the prototype of all subsequent ones, providing them with that basic security which is an essential ingredient of personality. Unfortunately, this attribute is sometimes absent or fragile (see p. 293).

The other side of the attachment equation – the parents' commitment to their offspring – is a relationship implying unconditional love, self-sacrifice and nurturant attitudes that are quite likely to last a lifetime. This type of attachment is known as *maternal* or *paternal bonding*. Obviously a great deal is at stake in the success of attachment processes – be they child-to-parent or parent-to-child (see the checklist below for some of the key factors involved in successful bonding).

Children's growing bonds of love and loyalty are a great source of joy to parents, but such ties of affection also serve a utilitarian function. The accompanying respect and goodwill enhances all the adults' efforts to teach them (this applies to teachers as well). The fact that children identify with

Does the parent do any of the following:
- Initiate positive interactions with the infant?
- Respond to the infant's vocalizations?
- Change voice tone when talking to the infant?
- Show interest in face-to-face contact with the infant?
- Show the ability to console or comfort the infant?
- Enjoy close physical contact with the infant?
- Respond to the infant's indications of distress?
- Respond promptly to the infant's needs?
- Respond appropriately to his or her needs?
- Respond consistently?
- Interact smoothly and sensitively with the infant?

Prompt responding: Infants have very limited abilities to appreciate the contingencies (association) of events to their own behaviour; an interval of only 3 seconds is required to disrupt the contingency learning of 6-month-old infants. Where the adult takes appreciably longer to answer the infant's signals there will be no opportunity for the child to learn that his or her behaviour can affect his or her environment and, in particular, the behaviour of other people.

Appropriate responding: This means the ability to recognize the particular messages the infant is trying to communicate, and to interpret and react to them correctly.

Consistency: A child's environment must be predictable; he or she must be able to learn that his or her behaviour will produce particular consequences under particular conditions.

Interacting smoothly: Parents can mesh their interactions with the infant's in a manner that is facilitative and pleasurable as opposed to intrusive and disruptive.

their parents and are 'on their side', so to speak, makes the task of teaching, and learning, much easier.

Attachment theory (see Thompson, 1991)

Attachment theory, as developed in John Bowlby's seminal writings (1969, 1973, 1988), integrates ethology, psychoanalysis, psychobiology, sociobiology, cognitive development, and the cybergenetic theory of control systems. The attachment bond is thought of not in terms of particular discrete behaviours, but rather as belonging to a *behaviour system* which represents an underlying organization mediating a variety of observable discrete actions. What appears to be essential in the formation of that special bond between parents and infants is the opportunity for them to develop a mutual, interlocking pattern of attachment behaviours, a smooth synchronous 'dance' (as Seligman, 1975, calls it) of interaction. It is the outcome of this dance that determines their helplessness or mastery (Isabella, et al., 1989). When they make some response, it can either produce a change in the environment or be independent of what changes occur. At some primitive level, the infant calculates the correlation between response and outcome. If the correlation is zero, helplessness develops. If the correlation is highly positive or highly negative, this means the response is working and the infant learns either to perform that response more frequently or to refrain from performing it, depending on whether the correlated outcome is good or bad.

Essentially, he or she learns that responding works and that, in general, there is synchrony between responses and outcomes. When there is little or no synchrony, they are helpless; they stop performing the response, and further, they learn that in general responding does not matter. Such learning experiences, if repeated over and over, have the same consequences that helplessness has in adults. There is an absence of response initiation, a negative cognitive set, and anxiety and depression. All of this is likely to be more disastrous for the infant because what is developing is foundational. It is at the base of the infant's 'pyramid' of emotional and motivational structures. At the opposite end from this failure of parent–infant interactions are the kinds of responsive care and playful, game-like interactions parents and babies enjoy. These are especially suitable for providing rapid contingent responses to infants, thus eliciting from them in turn, positive social responses.

For John Bowlby and Mary Ainsworth, the ability to use an attachment figure as a secure base affords a haven of safety and also provides the confidence necessary to explore and master ordinary environments. Ainsworth and her colleagues (1978) developed a test of infants' responses to a situation that was strange to them, the aptly named 'strange situation'. In this experimental method a mother enters a room with her infant. Some minutes later a stranger enters too. After a few minutes the mother departs unobtrusively, leaving her baby alone with the stranger. The mother then returns and the stranger leaves the room. Using this method, Ainsworth and her colleagues were able to identify three distinct styles of attachment:

1. The 'securely attached' infant reacted positively to the stranger when the mother was present, but was visibly fearful and cried when the mother left. When the mother returned, the upset infant went to her and was quickly comforted.
2. The 'insecure/avoidant' infants were somewhat indifferent to their mother when she was in the room, and they may or may not have expressed distress when she left. When she returned, they made no move to interact with her, stiffened or looked away.
3. The 'insecure/ambivalent' infants were distressed on entering the room and showed little exploration. They were very upset when the mother left. When she returned they wished to be near her, but resisted all her efforts to comfort them. They struggled if picked up, and showed a great deal of angry behaviour.

A fourth category was added later:

4. The 'disorganized' infant showed incomplete, interrupted movements, and freezing. There was fear of the parent. The main feature is a lack of a coherent attachment strategy.

Each attachment style is based on a specific pattern of emotionality. Bowlby always emphasized that secure attachment relationships fostered independence and curiosity, and formed the basis for competent problem solving. Sroufe (1990) makes the point that if early attachment to a caregiver is indeed a significant aspect of a child's development it should relate to his or her social behaviour at a later stage of life. Certainly, the evidence is that securely attached infants at 2 years of age are less frustrated and happier than insecurely attached infants. Later they are more socially competent and obtain better results in third grade.

Clearly, secure attachments are not the only pathway to competence in life. There is a diversity of socializing agents and contexts other than parents and family life in the infant's world. Some infants have attachments to many people. In Hausa society both the grandmothers and siblings provide a significant amount of care to infants (Super, 1980). There is also the recipient of care – the infant him/herself – to consider when assessing the developmental course of competence and other attributes. Jerome Kagan (1989) believes that infants are highly resilient and adaptive, equipped by evolution to stay on a developmental track even in the face of wide variations in parenting style.

Some scholars feel that investigations should now place more emphasis on the role of attachment relationships in actively fostering the child's exploratory activities, promoting emotional regulation during exploration, and organizing and interpreting novel and curious information. The 'strange situation' test, as we saw, emphasizes the central proximity-maintenance function of attachment behaviour, whereas in more natural circumstances, the child and parents will be frequently monitoring and managing a balance between attachment and exploration, a far from easy task. The parental role involves both a protective and limiting condition for child and adolescent exploration. (See chapter 13 for a discussion of risky 'exploratory' behaviour in adolescence.)

Internal Representations and Selfhood

How do children begin to conceptualize these core experiences of proximity to a beloved parent, regulation of safety, and gradual exploration of the outside world? During the second year of life, children begin to symbolize or represent experience, and develop a concept of self. Alfred Lord Tennyson

(1809–1892), in his poem *In Memoriam*, anticipated the interest of psychologists in a uniquely human aspect of development:

> *The baby new to earth and sky,*
> *What time his tender palm is prest*
> *Against the circle of the breast,*
> *Has never thought that 'this is I'.*
>
> *But as he grows he gathers much*
> *And learns the use of 'I' and 'me',*
> *And finds 'I am not what I see,*
> *And other than the things I touch.'*
>
> *So rounds he to a separate mind*
> *From whence clear memory may begin,*
> *As thru' the frame that binds him in*
> *His isolation grows defined.*

Piaget (1954) contrasts explicit cognitive symbols (such as names of objects, which invite correction, clarification and cultural generalization, and may have denotative meaning) with affective symbols. The latter are less conscious and explicit. They are highly individual, more bodily experience oriented, and may be connotative in meaning. It is suggested that affective symbols or representations originate from repeated 'intersubjective' experiences, that is to say: representations of interactions that have been generalized which already form part of a knowledge base developed during the first year of life.

Along very similar lines Bowlby (1969, 1973) proposed that young children represent their experience and expectations of proximity-seeking, and availability of a secure base, in an internal working model that helps them manage aspects of their unique family environment that are attachment-related. Remarkable continuities have been demonstrated between infant attachment strategies and internal working model characteristics at 6 years of age.

Development of Self–Other Awareness

We can only speak of a child as a person when s/he becomes aware of her/himself as a separate individual, and others as separate social beings. Trevarthen and Aitken (2001) have provided a review of the evidence supporting the theory of innate 'intersubjectivity', the notion that the infant is born with awareness specifically receptive to subjective states in other persons. The progression and timing of this awareness (abstracted from their paper) is as follows:

- 2 months: There is evidence of 'primary intersubjectivity'; the infant possesses an active and immediately responsive conscious appreciation of the adult's communicative intentions. Babies and their mothers, while looking and listening to each other, are mutually regulating one another's interests and feelings in intricate, rhythmic patterns, exchanging multi-modal signals and imitations of vocal, facial, and gestural expression.

• 2 to 3 months (perturbation tests): The infant shows emotional awareness of his or her mother's contingent and emotionally appropriate behaviour, and actively engages with it.

• Around 6 months there is an orderly age-related transformation of the infant's motives; the infant shows increasingly intricate, precise, and select-ive coordination with his or her mother's richly reflected, rhythmically patterned, and repetitive expressions of communication and dramatic actions of play.

• Towards the end of the first year there is evidence of 'secondary intersubjectivity' (person–person–object awareness). This means that there is joint interest of infant and mother in their surroundings. This is trig-gered by the infant's emerging curiosity about the timing and direction and focus of attentions and intentions of his or her mother. Trevarthen and Aitken (ibid.) suggest that this change in infants' experience and acceptance of joint attention to the world clearly has momentous con-sequences in subsequent learning, and profound effect on the ways mothers act with and speak to their infants.

At the very foundation of normal development is the child's emotional tie to his or her parents and their bonding, in turn, to their offspring. The one presumes the other (see Stern, 1977). To become a person in their own right, children must gradually detach themselves, at least in part, from their mother's protective cocoon and develop a point of view of their own. Like a spaceship which has to force itself out of the earth's gravitational pull in order to make its journey, children must move out of safe orbit around their mothers and strike out to find their own place in the world. By the child's first birthday the most dramatic development and growth have taken place, in just 12 months since his or her birth. Figure 10 on page 64 is a reminder of some of the extraordinary tasks and achievements of the infant.

Note: The implications of insecure attachments are discussed in chap-ter 12.

chapter three

Early Childhood:
The Pre-School Stage
Infant Growth and Development

'Do you know who made you?'
'Nobody as I know of,'
said the child with a short laugh . . .
'I 'spect I growed.'
                    Harriet Beecher Stowe (1811–1896): *Uncle Tom's Cabin*

Infant growth and development are so rapid parents sometimes feel that
they cannot keep up with the changes. This dramatic growth becomes a
major part of the important health checks carried out in the UK by regular
visits from the health visitor. Growth is not necessarily a smooth, continuous
process. In the early months of life weight and height increase rapidly,
followed by a constant rate of increase until puberty, when there is another
growth surge. Body proportions also change considerably from birth to
adulthood.

Physical Development

At birth the average baby weighs around 3.2 kg (7 lb) and measures around
51 cm (20 in) in length. Most neonates lose 5 to 10 per cent of their birth
weight in the first days of life. They eliminate more body wastes than they
take in by way of nourishment. By the fourth month they have doubled
their birthweight, by the end of the first year, tripled it. In each month of the
first year they add almost 2.5 cm (1 in) to their length. While every part of
the child's body grows, some areas grow more than others, and more quickly,
particularly the parts that grew most slowly during prenatal development. A
newborn infant has a large head that reflects the early development of the
brain as compared with other body tissues.

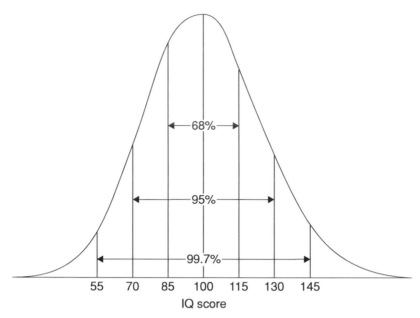

Figure 11   The normal distribution curve is a method of representing the way in which many human characteristics are spread amongst the population: most people are around average and therefore account for the central part of the bell-shaped curve

Measurement

Caution is required when measurements of growth and development are interpreted. It is important that they are looked at with reference to a normal range so that reliable deductions about the individual's well-being can be made. This means distinguishing between *normal* and *average*.

Growth is monitored from serial measurements, a single measurement only being useful if it is clearly atypical/abnormal. It is useful to know the average weight of a 1-year-old or the average age at which a child walks unaided. However it is also vital to know how far from the average a measurement can deviate and yet remain within what is considered the range of what is normal.

On the Wechsler Intelligence Scale for Children (WISC), for example, the average score is 100 and the standard deviation (SD) is 15. This means that a child with an IQ that falls between +1 and −1 SD is in the area between IQs 115 and 85. Such a score is within the broadly 'normal' range of IQ, as this range of scores encompasses some two-thirds of the population of children of the same age. A score of 55 (3 SDs below the mean/average) would lie at the outer extremes of IQ and indicate a learning disability. A child with an IQ of 145 at 3 SDs above the mean would have an exceptionally high level of intellectual functioning. (See appendix II for a discussion of the measurement of intelligence.)

Influences on growth

It is generally considered that the potential for physical growth after birth is determined largely by genetic factors, i.e. maturational changes occurring regardless of practice or training. Nutrition, disease and emotional factors also influence the extent to which this potential is achieved. For example, a change in physical size may be due to dietary change rather than simply a maturational effect of muscle and bone growth. Several decades of international research seem to have settled a long-standing debate about the advantages and disadvantages of breast- and bottle-feeding. Clearly breast-feeding is nutritionally superior to bottle-feeding (see Berger, 2000). It helps the mother's body to recover and it provides the infant with vital antibodies that give it a resistance to several disorders. Human milk has special ingredients like DHA (decosohexaenoic acid) and AA (arachidonic acid) that contribute to brain and retinal development, and also lactoferrin and lipases which protect the digestive system.

Parental responsiveness is also important in something as basic as providing growth-enhancing sustenance to a baby. Typically, feeding times have to be adapted to the cycles of hunger and satisfaction expressed by the infant. The caregiver needs to be alert to changing needs for nourishment as the child matures, by altering his/her diet.

Differences in early physical and temperamental development

Cultural observations, ethnocentric assumptions and prejudices influence our ideas as to what constitutes 'normal' infant behaviour. For example, there are some ethnic or racial variations in the rate of early physical development, a matter we shall return to. Asian infants are reported to be somewhat slower than their Euro-American counterparts in achieving certain motor milestones; African and other black babies develop somewhat faster, before and after birth (see Tanner, 1990). Do such differences arise from differences in rates of maturation, or do they reflect certain ethnic differences in level of activity or placidity? Some babies are much more active from early infancy onward than other infants. (See chapters 10 and 12 for accounts of atypical aspects of motility.)

Even in the period toward the end of feeding, when most babies are quiet and sleepy, they move their arms, lift their heads, kick, or – if they are on their backs – move their whole bodies till the covers are off. This goes on right up to the moment their eyes shut. Even when asleep they frequently move from spot to spot in the crib. Their mothers can never turn away for a moment when their babies are high up on, say, the bed, for fear they will squirm off. In contrast, the quiet babies tend to lie where they are placed and move both little and slowly. Sometimes they are almost as still when

awake as when asleep. Often only their eyes move. Cross-cultural observations of newborns – as such, not yet exposed to parental 'shaping' – revealed
the following differences in temperament:

- Chinese babies were relatively placid.
- Navaho babies were relatively placid, less excitable or irritable than Euro-
American infants, and better able to quieten themselves.
- Euro-American babies were the most active and irritable, and most diffi-
cult to console.
- Japanese babies were vigorous in responding but easier to quieten than
the Euro-American infants.

The Nervous System

An aspect of growth that is of incalculable significance for the countless
physical and psychological systems on which the child depends for normal
functioning is the integrity of the nervous system (see chapter 10). The
human nervous system is divided into two basic parts:

1. The central nervous system (CNS), which consists of the brain and the
spinal cord.
2. The peripheral nervous system, which consists of the collection of nuclei
that regulate bodily functions (autonomic nervous system), and the
extensive network of nerve fibre bundles that carry *sensory* (incoming)
and *motor* (outgoing) information between the brain and the entire body.

The Brain Growth Spurt

No aspect of growth in the baby is more crucial than the rapid development
of the brain. At birth the infant has already reached about 25 per cent of its
adult brain weight as compared with less than 5 per cent of its adult body
weight. By the age of 2 the child has attained about 75 per cent of its adult
brain weight and only 20 per cent of its adult body weight. The logic of this
weight advantage is that it is imperative for the brain to be ahead if it is to
make all the other infant developments possible. The last 3 prenatal months
and the first 2 years after birth have been called the period of the 'brain
growth spurt'.

How the genes control brain development is still unknown. However, a
reasonable summary of what we know so far is that brain nodules assume
their identity by a combination of what kind of tissue they start out as,
where they are in the brain, and what patterns of triggering input they get
during critical periods in development. The neurons, influenced by the sites

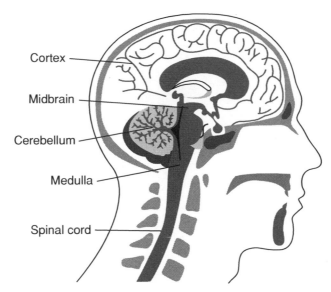

Figure 12 The development of the brain: the medulla and midbrain are largely developed at birth; in the first 2 years after birth it is primarily the cortex that develops, although increases in the dendrites and in synapses also occur throughout the nervous system

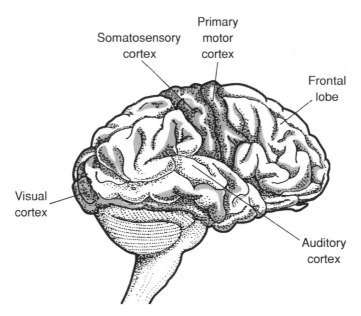

Figure 13 Specialization of the brain: areas of the brain are specialized for the reception and transmission of different types of information

to which they migrate, assume specialized functions, such as cells of the visual or auditory areas of the brain.

In view of the importance of the brain it is understandably the most protected organ in the body – by the skull and the blood/brain barrier, which prevents several toxic or poisonous substances in the blood from gaining access to the brain. The least developed part of the brain at birth is the cortex. This is the convoluted grey matter that wraps around the midbrain which, with the medulla, is the most fully developed part of the newborn's central nervous system. The midbrain and medulla regulate attention and habituation.

The Brain and Communication

What is emerging at this stage in the relatively large head of the neonate, is an immensely complex communication system. The brain's communication system consists primarily of neurons (nerve cells) connected by networks of axons and dendrites (nerve fibres). Each neuron has a single axon and numerous dendrites, the former meeting the latter at intersections called synapses. Dendrites have many spines along their many branches, which increase their surface area so they can interconnect more effectively. Children with Down's syndrome have dendritic spines that are quite sparse and small (Purpura, 1974). After birth, axons begin developing a fatty coating, known as myelin, which aids in the faster conduction of impulses.

Dendrites and axons are both found in sensory, CNS, and motor neurons. Collections of these two projection fibres make up the white matter in the CNS. The cell bodies in the CNS make up the grey matter that constitutes the outer layer of the brain. In essence neurons are cells that are specialized to conduct electrical impulses. The neurons communicate by transmitting impulses through the axons to the dendrites of other nerve cells, without them actually making direct contact with each other. Synapses are the very small gaps that exist between adjacent neurons. The electrical impulses trigger brain chemicals (neurotransmitters) to carry information about the impulses from the axon of the transmitting neuron across the synaptic gap, to the dendrites of the receiving neurons. The average neuron transmits signals to about 1000 other ones.

There are three kinds of nerve cell:

1. Sensory neurons: Sensory or afferent neurons transmit signals from receptors that detect events inside or outside the body.
2. Motor neurons: Motor or efferent neurons transmit signals from the brain to the body's musculature or glands.
3. Interneurons: These connect the neurons with each other. Most interneurons are located in the CNS.

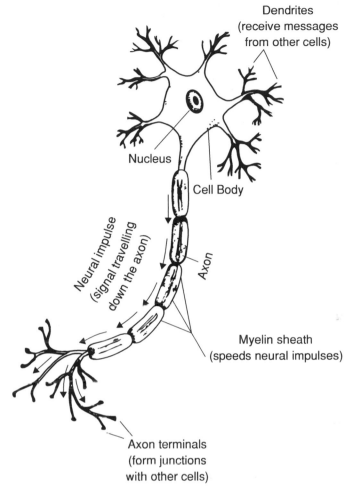

Figure 14 An isolated neuron: within the brain, nerve fibres increase in size and number over the first 2 years of life, thereby greatly increasing the number of neuronal connections and enabling impressive advances in cognition and the control of actions

Growth of the Brain

The volume of the brain quadruples between birth and adulthood. Thus a major aspect of brain development consists of adding connections to the neurons, all of which are in place around the time of birth. In fact at birth, the neonate brain contains a surplus of neurons in its complement of over 100 billion nerve cells. The axons and dendrites that make up the neural networks are somewhat rudimentary, with relatively few synapses (connections). In the months and years to come there are major spurts of growth and refinement in these networks, most notably in the cortical region that controls thinking and perception.

During the first months there are dramatic increases in the dendrites and axons (conducting fibres that emanate from neurons) and in the number of synapses. An estimated fivefold increase in the density of dendrites in the cortex (as many as 15,000 connections per neuron) is established in the first 2 years (Diamond, 1990).

Neurophysiologists have discovered the following:

• Following the initial burst of synapse formation in the first months after birth there is a pruning of synapses in all areas of the brain. This process seems essential because initially there are many more connections than necessary, and this abundance creates many redundant pathways.
• Experience seems to erase some of these connections and strengthen the necessary ones in the circuitry.
• The maximum density of synapses in the areas of the brain responsible for language comprehension and production occurs at about 3 years.
• The cortical cells responsible for vision are maximally dense at 4 months of age, with rapid pruning thereafter (Huttenlocher, 1991).
• Pruning continues throughout early childhood, into adolescence.
• The same developmental pattern of 'rise and fall' is observable in the complexity of dendrites, and in measures of energy used by the brain (glucose uptake). A major contributor to the brain growth spurt is the development of a second type of nerve cell, called glia, which nourish the neurons and eventually encase them in insulating sheaths of a waxy substance called myelin. They continue to form throughout life, ensuring good conductivity along the fibres (Tanner, 1990).

Perhaps the most obvious change to be seen through a microscope is the increase in size and complexity of the dendrites of neurons. Often, the pattern of connections of a nerve cell appears to become more specific and specialized. In addition, large increases in the density of synapses can be observed through more powerful electron microscopes. Investigations have revealed something quite unexpected. Using a variety of different methods, and looking at a number of measures, researchers have reported that later in infancy and childhood there are sometimes regressive or subtractive events during brain development. For example, in most regions of the cerebral cortex studied, the density of synapses increases until it is even greater than in adults (usually around 150 per cent); pruning of the surplus is essential.

The development of the brain early in life is not entirely the result of the unfolding of maturation, but rather a combination of a biological programme and early experience. For example, myelination of the nerve fibres leading from the visual cortex of the brain will not proceed normally unless the baby has had sufficient visual experience in a lighted environment.

Plasticity

Plasticity refers to the fact that the immature brain's organization is relatively fluid, and that it may recover in early development from injury that would not ordinarily be possible in the later years. Indeed, the adaptive powers of the young brain and its ability to utilize functional compensation in the face of acquired damage are impressive, although not quite as amazing ('one hemisphere can do the job for two') as once thought. Much depends upon the particular brain functions that have been damaged, a subject we return to in chapter 10.

The autonomic nervous system (ANS)

The control system responsible in large part for so-called psychophysiological reactions is the autonomic nervous system. This network of motor nerve cells plays a large part, not only in maintaining the individual's internal environment and homeostasis, but also in determining his or her level of arousal, particularly their emotional state. It regulates the work of:

- the glands
- the blood vessels
- heart muscle
- stomach muscles
- intestines
- bladder, and
- lungs.

The autonomic nervous system not only controls the day-to-day 'vegetative' functions of the body, but also operates to change the economy of the body when the person is faced with stress. Disturbance of this function sometimes leads to pathological conditions referred to as psychophysiological or psychosomatic illnesses, bronchial asthma (see chapter 10) being a good example.

Biological Basis of Personality

Undoubtedly genetic influences contribute to normal variations in personality (Loehlin, 1992; Plomin, 2001a), although establishing the degree of influence is far from easy. Nevertheless, the genes responsible for the heritability of personality are now being identified (Hamer and Copeland, 1998). Most personality traits show moderate genetic influence.

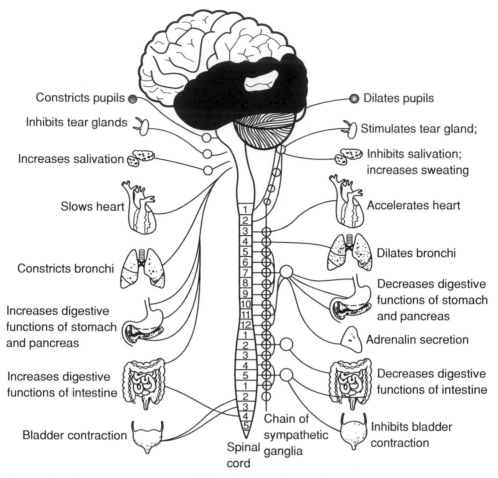

Figure 15 The parasympathetic (left) and sympathetic divisions of the autonomic nervous system

Cuddliness

Rudolph Schaffer (1977) discusses a range of intrinsic patterns in babies in his book *Mothering*, and he suggests that the quality of 'cuddliness' in infants may be such a characteristic. It might be thought of as a very early personality or temperamental attribute. Schaffer found that some babies are 'non-cuddlers'. They resist close physical contact, and he observed that this characteristic appeared not to stem from the mother's behaviour toward her child. Such a quality may have unfortunate emotional consequences if the mother interprets this trait as rejection of her overtures.

Neuroticism

Individuals who score high on the dimension of personality called neuroticism are thought to have inherited the properties of an excessively reactive ANS, one that is biased toward sympathetic nervous system predominance (Eysenck, 1967). This bias is thought to contribute to the acquisition of emotional problems. The integrating processes which regulate the balance between the sympathetic and parasympathetic divisions of the autonomic nervous system are located in the brain. This theory is reviewed critically in Herbert (1974).

The sympathetic and parasympathetic nervous system

The nerves from the spinal cord have branches to the sympathetic ganglia, which they control. The parasympathetic ganglia are controlled by branch nerves at the lower end of the spinal cord and by a nerve from the medulla known as the *vagus* ('wandering') nerve because it connects with most of the organs of the body. They include the heart, lungs, liver, stomach and much of the digestive tract.

The sympathetic and parasympathetic systems tend to have opposed actions. The sympathetic nervous system acts to adjust the body to states of alarm or emergency, and the main role of the parasympathetic nervous system is to organize the normal activity of the body's organs. The two systems are not simply opposed; in many instances they act in a coordinated pattern. For example, if a corrosive poison is swallowed, there is sympathetic arousal, with dilation of the pupils and sweating, together with vomiting, which is organized by the parasympathetic system.

Interest in the relationships between the psychology of the person (e.g. attitudes, traits and stress-proneness), a variety of illnesses (e.g. ulcers, asthma) and ANS activity has led to a number of correlational studies. Indices of ANS activity can be measured quite readily: heart rate (speeded by the sympathetic system, slowed by vagal activity); the electrical resistance of the skin; the temperature of the skin; and blood pressure. Unfortunately many of the psychophysiological studies make simplistic assumptions about the unitary nature of ANS reactions, as in the construct 'arousability'.

Sleeping Patterns (see Horne, 1988, 2001)

An infant's pattern of sleeping is as individual as the uniqueness of his or her developing personality. This basic 'sleep cycle', as it is known, is programmed – a biological given (not learned) and, as such, cannot be altered by the parents or their baby. It is biologically regulated by a system of neurons situated in the core of the brain.

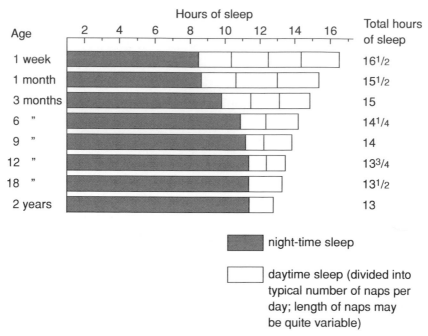

Figure 16   Typical sleep requirements in childhood

Typical ('normal') sleep patterns

Going back to the very beginning, the fetus in the womb is thought not to be truly awake, but alternating between *active* sleep and *quiet* sleep. Newborn (full-term) babies spend some 75 per cent of each 24-hour period asleep. They usually have, on average, about eight periods of sleep a day, often in snatches, and the length of period varies from baby to baby. Newborns typically sleep for 2 to 4 hours at a time (note the wide range). Their need for sleep also varies widely, from 11 to 21 hours in any 24-hour period. By 6 months of age, babies are spending some 60 per cent of each 24-hour period asleep. Typical sleep requirements of the young child are illustrated in figure 16.

Night waking

Brief periods of night waking are quite usual in infancy; by the end of the first month most babies are waking up twice a night to eat. Two-month-old infants spend, on average, some 9 per cent of the night's sleeping time actually awake; by 9 months of age the time awake reduces to about 6 per cent. Infants usually settle themselves and go back to sleep again, although sometimes they cry out. The extent to which parents are conscious of infants' waking depends on whether s/he sleeps with them, how often they monitor whether the child is asleep, and their sensitivity to crying.

Types of sleep

Sleep is not a *single* state distinguishable from the waking state; it is *two* very different states.

1. REM or rapid eye movement sleep, which is an active period of sleep when we do our dreaming.
2. Non-REM sleep, which is the kind we usually think of as 'sleep'; a quiet, deeper kind of sleeping without body or eye movements. Most of the restorative functions of sleep occur in this phase; there is little, if any, dreaming and there is a regular pattern of breathing and heart rate.

REM sleep appears in the fetus at about 6 or 7 months' gestation, and non-REM sleep between 7 and 8 months. At birth, a full-term baby will have 50 per cent of its sleep in REM state (premature babies 80 per cent); 35 per cent by age 3; and 25 per cent for late childhood, adolescence and adulthood. REM sleep thus seems most important in the early months as the fetus and baby develop. Babies make frequent transitions between the two states and during the periods of light/active sleep a baby is easily awakened. About half of a newborn baby's sleep (as we have seen) is spent in each of these active v. quiet states. As children mature they develop at their own pace the ability to pass through periods of light sleep more rapidly.

Nursing and rocking help a baby enter the deeper, quiet phase of sleeping. Some babies sleep relatively little; many need more sleep, but they will get all the sleep they need provided they are not left hungry, are not in pain, or not constantly interrupted. The 2-month-old, on average, may need 27 minutes to drop off.

Sleepless nights

According to a survey of 2000 first-time mothers carried out by *Mother and Baby* magazine in 2001, just settling their infant to sleep at the beginning of the night took 25 minutes on average. After that mothers reported getting up an average of three times a night to feed, change and comfort their child. The average mother was only able to get 4 hours of sleep a night during her baby's first 4 months rising to 5 hours at around 18 months of age. They bore the brunt of the child's sleeping (or non-sleeping) habits as only 17 per cent of fathers regularly got out of bed at night to attend to the infant; one in five never got up to help. A majority of the women reported feeling resentment amounting (in conjunction with their exhaustion) to extremely strained relationships with their partners.

Daytime napping

The move from round-the-clock sleeping to a daytime napping schedule happens largely on its own. By the second month, infants are awake more during the day. By the third to sixth month, parents' lives are enjoying some regularity again, as the baby may have developed a routine of two longer daytime sleeping periods. Many babies don't sleep through the night until they are 6 months old; at this age a minority do so.

One can encourage the transition to a daytime napping schedule by putting a baby down between 8 and 10 a.m. and 1 or 2 p.m. Some time during the second year there is a transition to a single afternoon sleep, and by 4 years of age children may not feel the need for a nap.

Sleeping arrangements

By far the majority of the world's cultures (including Western cultures prior to about 1800) have the infant sleeping in the same bed as his or her parents. This so-called 'co-sleeping' typically tends to continue until babies are weaned. The values of collectivist cultures, which place more emphasis on interdependence rather than separateness, play a large part in the choice of this practice (see Harkness and Super, 1995). Indeed, Mayan mothers consider separate beds and rooms as tantamount to child neglect (Morelli et al., 1992). By way of contrast, Western parents are likely to be advised that co-sleeping may lead potentially to bad habits, dependency, and 'unhealthy' attitudes.

The older child

Night waking is still common in the older child; only about 50 per cent of all toddlers sleep through the night at the age of 2. By this age, most children are taking just one nap a day, usually after lunch. Going to bed may become a problem with a wilful toddler, and keeping him or her there may be an added ingredient of misery for parents. Some children simply aren't sleepy when their parents think they should be, while others fight sleepiness as if it is the enemy.

One cannot legislate for when a child falls asleep, but one can establish (early on, preferably) a pleasant routine for when s/he goes to bed. The bedtime ritual is a particularly powerful habit; a regular routine of meal, bath and then a story before bed makes the child's world seem well-ordered, safe and comfortable. It is not trivializing to set up these routines. Psychologists and social workers who visit chaotic homes where there is no certainty, regularity and routine know how disturbing this is to young children. It is also not helpful to older ones when they enter the relatively orderly life demanded at school.

Feeding Behaviour

During the early weeks after birth, many of an infant's waking hours are taken up with feeding. At such times mothers need to be calm, and sensitive enough to respond from moment to moment to changes in the baby's behaviour. For example, they commonly respond to pauses in the child's sucking at the breast by nudging the baby; they gaze and talk to it. Personality theorists (notably the Freudians) have emphasized the importance of satisfying feeding experiences in the early development of personality traits (e.g. oral optimism v. pessimism), although these notions are contentious (see Lee and Herbert, 1970).

Problems surrounding food and feeding can arise out of difficulties in early parent–infant relationships (Iwaniec, Herbert and Sluckin, 1988). Likewise stresses and strains in these relationships may stem from feeding problems, some of which may have originated in, and become superimposed on, the pain associated with organic disorders such as oesophageal stricture and pyloric stenosis, early in the child's life. Children's temperaments may also lead to clashes with the parent, the mealtime disruptions taking place in the context of other behaviour-management problems (see chapters 5 and 15). Failure of normal physical growth is usually detected in infants through their unsatisfactory weight gain, a condition called *failure-to-thrive* when extreme.

Attachment theorists, as we shall see, also stress the importance of feeding among other early social activities. Eating is a social activity even at this age. The mother's mere exposure to her baby makes a contribution towards the development of a bond to and from the baby; in fact it may be a central factor. This is a view that emerges from studies of 'exposure learning'. There is evidence that liking for anybody or anything is initially a direct function of *familiarity* (Herbert, Sluckin and Sluckin, 1982), certainly a feature of the mother and baby feeding experience.

Note: The implications of insecure attachments are discussed in chapter 12.

chapter four

Perceptual, Motor and Language Development

Credulity is the man's weakness,
But the child's strength

Charles Lamb (1775–1834)

Perceptual Development

Infancy is the period when most basic perceptual capabilities emerge (Aslin, 1981a,b). So, how do newborn infants learn to make sense of the world around them? Many ingenious experiments have been created to explore the many facets of perception. Perception has been defined as the means by which information acquired from the environment, via the sense organs, is transformed into experiences of objects, events, sounds, tastes, etc. They include:

- perceptual organization
- space or depth perception
- visual constancies
- pattern recognition
- theories of perception, and
- individual and cultural differences in perceiving.

Perceptual learning occurs when we actively explore objects in our environment and detect their distinctive (or invariant) features. William James, in his *Principles of Psychology* (1890/1950) described the world of the newborn baby as extreme confusion (see page 57). This view of an infant bombarded by chaotic information in all sense modalities underestimated the capabilities of infants, their competence as observers of their new environment. Steven Pinker (1997) comments that it was the psychologists of those times who were confused, but it should be remembered that they did not have the experimental equipment and knowledge, plus the vast storehouse of painstakingly obtained data, that we have today.

Psychologists generally make use of three basic research methods to study infants' perceptual abilities:

1. *The preference technique*: the duration and number of times babies look at (and from) two stimuli presented side by side.
2. *The habituation–dishabituation paradigm*: used to test infants' abilities to discriminate between two stimuli by habituating the infant to one (i.e. diminished responding) then presenting the other. If the second stimulus is perceived as different, they will dishabituate and again respond.
3. *Classical conditioning* (see p. 122): establishes the degree to which stimuli are perceived to be similar to the training stimulus.

Despite extensive research we do not know in detail how discriminated and preferred stimuli are perceived and interpreted.

Crucial developments in the child's perceptual repertoire take place in three stages in the 12 months after his or her birth – see table 3.

Table 3 Three stages of perceptual development during the first year of life

Period	Stage	Infant can:
0–2 months	Stimulus seeking	discriminate between visual stimuli
2–6 months	Form constructing	perceive numerous forms and shapes
6–12 months	Form interpretation	make sense of what they perceive

After Shaffer (1999).

Vision and Fine Motor Movement

Vision

A child's ability to explore her or his environment relies heavily on visual acuity, yet it is the least mature of their senses when they are born. Nevertheless, the retina and the rods and cones are fairly well developed at birth. The neonates are sensitive to light. They can detect and track a slowly moving stimulus, preferably faces or face-like stimuli in which they are particularly interested (Johnson, Dziurawiec et al., 1991). The world is seen in colour. However, vision in newly born infants is blurred (about 20/400); normal vision is 20/20. What they do have is effective focus to the distance of around 20 to 30 cm, which gives the clear vision of their mother when being fed; otherwise their field of vision is restricted.

Newborn infants can turn their eyes with approximate accuracy towards a sound source presented to the left or right of them. Studies of eye movements

(Aslin, 1981a,b) have shown that infants fixate specific features of the environment from birth. Babies prefer to look at things that are somewhat novel. They tend to be attracted to areas of greater contrast or discontinuity in visual stimuli, for example, patterns. As they get older, scanning becomes broader in scope and progressively larger amounts of information are sought. The baby advances from a single-feature selection (restricted exploration) to a broad and detailed examination of complex visual stimuli, notably, in the first 2 months of life, the human face.

By 3 months of age the progress made is extraordinary, the baby now being able to focus on objects at varying distances as well as an adult can. Progress from saccadic (shifting) eye movements to the smoother tracking of moving objects is apparent by 6 months of age (Hainline, 1985). Binocular depth cues are perceived and responded to in babies over 3 months of age (Yonas and Owsley, 1987). The fovea (centrally located cells on the retina), which are responsible for receiving the sharpest and clearest images, become fully functional before the first birthday, bringing about 20/100 visual acuity at 6 months, and about 20/20 vision by 12 months (Haith, 1990). In other words, at this early age children can see as well as adults.

What is worth commenting on here, as it is nicely illustrated with regard to vision, is the way babies help to build their own brains while still at a fetal stage of development. The rhythmical waves of firing of groups of cells in the retina (there is no visual input as the eyes are closed at this stage of development) play an important role in helping to structure parts of the brain later involved in vision. It would appear that one part of the nervous system is creating what has been referred to as a kind of virtual environment specifically to aid the development of other later developing parts. Brain development, it would seem, is not the passive unfolding of a genetic plan, but more of an activity-dependent process.

Other aspects of perceptual development are size and shape constancy.

SIZE CONSTANCY

Some size constancy is found in infants between the ages of 75 and 85 days (Bower, 1966). The full skill emerges between 6 and 8 months (McKenzie, Tootell and Day, 1980).

SHAPE CONSTANCY

Shape constancy has been displayed in 3-month-old infants (Caron and Carlson, 1979). It makes sense, in evolutionary terms, for infants to display size and shape constancy – where a given object is perceived as having the same size/shape regardless of its distance from them – because this helps them to perceive the environment 'as it really is', rather than inaccurately.

Three- to four-month-old infants remember objects and expect them to obey the laws of continuity, cohesion, and contact as they move. They have quite a remarkable understanding of there being a stable and lawful world. As 3-month-olds can barely orient, see, touch, and reach, let alone walk, talk, and manipulate objects, they could not have learned anything by the standard techniques of interaction, feedback and language.

Face recognition

Experiments indicate that newborn infants (under an hour old) have a tendency to turn their head and eyes to look at faces more often than to most other complex patterns they have encountered. This is a reflex-like response controlled by some of the older subcortical parts of the brain. This bias toward staring, particularly at faces over the first days and weeks of life, serves a critical purpose. It provides the necessary input for training some of the developing 'higher' parts of the neonate's brain, within the cerebral cortex.

By 2 months the ability to recognize faces allows the infant to select the mother's face. The baby also shows a preference for a human face over scrambled versions of the face (Maurer, 1985). By 4 months, infants show a marked preference for looking at faces to the point of being able to 'identify' the human face and discriminate between different people on the basis of facial information.

By 5 months of age, babies respond differently to faces displaying different emotions, such as anger, sadness, surprise, and happiness (Balaban, 1995).

After 3 months the baby's smile is selective, mostly directed to people s/he knows well.

Depth perception

Some evidence of rudimentary depth perception is found in infants before 2 weeks of age (Bower, Broughton and Moore, 1970). With further experience the infant will acquire knowledge about the sizes of different objects and more precise depth perception will emerge. The increased mobility (and consequent exploration) of infants helps them to gain a better appreciation of the spatial characteristics of the environment.

The perception of movement

By 6 or 7 months babies distinguish between how hands act upon objects and how other objects act upon objects. They have opposite expectations about what makes people move and what makes objects move: objects launch each other by collisions; people start and stop on their own. By 12 months, babies interpret cartoons of moving dots as if the dots were seeking goals. For example, they are not surprised when a dot that hops over a barrier on its way to another dot, makes a beeline to it after the barrier is removed.

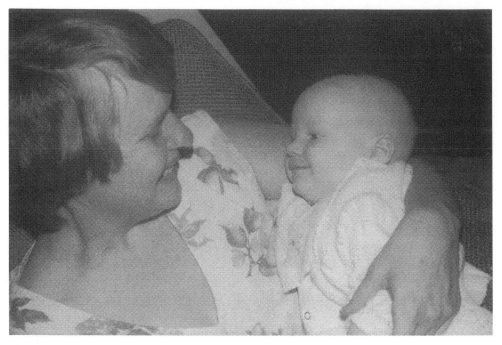

Figure 17 Reciprocal communication between mother and child: eye contact and smiling

Three-year-olds describe dot cartoons much as we do, and have no trouble distinguishing things that move on their own, like animals, from things that don't, like dolls, statues and life-like animal figurines.

Perceptual-motor skills

There is now a wealth of fascinating research that makes use of film to analyse the function of intricate and intricately related perceptual-motor skills in infants, as they strive to make sense of, and master, their environment. As both vision and motor skills improve, hand–eye coordination develops. At 6 months of age infants use a clumsy palmar grasp; by 9 months a scissor grasp is used to pick up objects; and at 12 months they will pick objects up precisely between the ends of the thumb and index finger in a pincer grasp (Sheridan, 1989).

Motor Development

Motor development is the most readily observable domain in the first year. There is considerable individual variability in the emergence of motor

Table 4 Ages when motor skills are achieved

Motor skill	Average age (and range)
Holds head steady when held upright	3 weeks (1 week–4 months)
Lying on tummy, lifts self by arms	2 months (3 weeks–5 months)
Rolls from side to back	2 months (3 weeks–5 months)
Rolls from back to side	4.5 months (2–7 months)
Grasps cube	3 months, 3 weeks (2–7 months)
Sits alone with coordination	7 months (5–9 months)
Crawls	7 months (5–11 months)
Pulls to a standing position	8 months (5–12 months)
Uses a pincer grasp	9 months (7–10 months)
Stands independently	11 months (9–16 months)
Walks alone	13 months (8–18 months)

milestones, as well as some cultural differences that affect their development. Many milestones are achieved earlier today, compared with the turn of the century, probably because of better healthcare and changing child-rearing practices.

Gross motor skills

Gross motor skills are the large bodily movements that emerge directly from reflexes, a good example being the swimming movements of arms and legs, and the attempts to lift their heads, when newborns are placed on their stomach. Eventually, after much practice, by wriggling and pushing forward, using friction with the surfaces they are put down on, they inch forward, and at around 6 months manage a 'belly-crawl'. At between 8 and 10 months of age, most babies can crawl (or creep) on all fours, i.e. coordinating hands and knees as their means of propulsion. It is not long before they have learned to climb up onto furniture as well as other (sometimes risky) 'challenges'. There are other non-crawling means of travel adopted by some 10-month-old infants, e.g. dragging themselves along on their bottoms, or rolling over and over. The ability to stand up seems to emerge quite suddenly. Table 4 provides a checklist of the approximate ages when particular motor skills are achieved.

Walking also progresses from reflexive newborn stepping to a hand-held walk, then to a speedy coordinated gait, or more accurately a sometimes somewhat unsteady toddle, at around 12 or 13 months (Thelen and Ulrich, 1991). For all the mastery of self-directed movement, they do tend to wobble a bit from side-to-side as well as forwards – hence the sobriquet 'toddlers'.

Their relatively large and heavy heads and stomachs, plus short little legs, make them spread their legs out to maintain balance. This is not always successfully achieved. A further observation of the curiosity of children, at this age, has earned them another name: 'the great explorers'. Any form of mobility offers exciting new opportunities and challenges for infants.

Motor development is effectively completed in infancy. When pulled to sitting, the head comes up in a line with the trunk by 3 months, and is then held steady as the child is supported sitting. The child will sit unsupported for a minute or so at 7 months and for 10 minutes by 9 months. At 6 months a child will start to take weight on his or her legs and at 9 months s/he bounces or stamps when supported. By 11 months a child will stand unsupported. Thus in infancy the sequences from lying, to sitting, to standing, to walking all take place.

Of course there are variations between infants, an important fact to convey to parents, in the timing of particular changes. For example, 50 per cent of children can walk unaided at 13 months, but a few can do this at 8 months, and others do not achieve this skill until 18 months. The changes in motor ability that follow walking tend to be consolidation and refinements of existing abilities rather than the emergence of completely new skills. Walking gradually becomes more competent and running becomes fluent and controlled.

By 18–24 months the child runs stiffly, walks really well, climbs stairs with both feet on each step, unscrews the lid on a jar, stacks four to six blocks, turns pages one at a time, and picks things up without overbalancing. This is an impressive (and by no means complete) set of achievements when one considers how few locomotor skills were available to the neonate 2 years before.

Cultural variations

Parenting practices undoubtedly influence motor milestones, a claim substantiated in cross-cultural studies. Hopkins (1991) compared the motor development of white English babies with that of black infants of immigrant Jamaican parents. The findings confirmed similar studies in demonstrating that the black infants sat, crawled and walked earlier than their white counterparts. This acceleration only occurred if the mothers had followed traditional routines that they used to promote early motor development. These included massaging infants, stretching their limbs, and holding them by the arms while gently shaking them up and down.

There is evidence that American infants aged 2 to 8 weeks can be helped to walk at an earlier stage than controls if they are regularly held in an upright posture and encouraged to practise their stepping reflex. The use of 'training' to promote motor skills is practised (before children are 8 weeks old) by the *Kipsigis* of Kenya. They 'walk' children by grasping them by the armpits and propelling them forward. Throughout their first months of life they are seated in shallow holes designed to support their backs and maintain an upright posture. Given the pressured acceleration of muscular growth and the practice involved (maturation and experiencing combining) it is perhaps not surprising that the *Kipsigi* babies sit unassisted some 5 weeks earlier, and walk unaided about a month earlier than Western infants (citation from Shaffer, 1999).

Werner (1972, 1979) studied the physical cognitive and social development of children who lived in African, Asian and Latin American countries to determine the applicability of many common Western theories and concepts of development to other non-Western cultures. Werner found that children reared in traditional and pre-industrial communities showed a marked acceleration in psychomotor development in the first year of life compared to children raised in Western, industrialized societies. It was apparent that the children exhibiting an accelerated rate of psychomotor development shared a number of commonalities in their first year of life:

- Membership of an extended family with multiple caregivers
- Breast-feeding on demand
- Constant body contact with adult caretakers
- Lack of segregation from adult activities
- Lack of a set routine for feeding, sleeping, and toileting
- Lack of restrictive clothing.

The 'clumsy' child

The problem of clumsiness or poor motor coordination involves a discrepancy between the mind's intention and the body's execution. It is mentioned in this section because it is not all that an untypical phenomenon in childhood. Clumsy children are often of average or above average intelligence, but sometimes their intelligence is focused into very narrow and specific activities, and it has been observed that they may develop rigid and stereotyped ways of getting things done. They generally improve considerably in late childhood and adolescence, but a majority still remains somewhat awkward. Some boys with this handicap are inclined to so-called 'girlish' games because they find gymnastics and sport an ordeal. Exclusion from such 'manly' pursuits may also bring problems in its wake. Because, to their peers they seem different, even odd, clumsy children tend to become outsiders – left out of social group activities. It is not difficult to imagine the frustrations suffered by clumsy children in a bustling, overcrowded classroom – they are the proverbial bull in a china shop. The more severe cases of clumsiness and poor motor coordination (dyspraxia) are discussed in chapter 10.

Fine motor skills

These are the skills that involve small body movements (usually of the hands and fingers) and they are more difficult to master than the gross motor skills, requiring as they do the precise coordination of complex muscle groups. These skills develop step-by-step. Grabbing is a good example of this, progressing from staring and waving arms at a dangling object within reach (during first 2 months); touching it only (by 3 months); sometimes able to grab but timing the grasping poorly (by 4 months). Finally, by 6 months of age, with a concentrated stare and much deliberation, they are able to grab at and hold onto almost any object of the right size, including an illuminated object that is moving in a dark room. Other fine motor skills follow. By about 6 months of age infants can hold an object in one hand and finger it with the other, and turn it around while examining it. This is the ideal way to learn about the distinctive features of an object and the multitude of features of the world in which the child is journeying.

Research by Phatak (1969) on a sample of Indian and American infants, indicates that irrespective of class differentials, traditionally reared infants displayed higher levels of psychomotor development compared with American infants. Once a baby is able to sit upright for long periods and to reach inward across the midline of his or her body (at around 4 to 5 months) s/he begins to explore interesting objects by grasping them with both hands. They can be transferred from hand to hand and fingered with the spare hand. The next major acquisition of manual skills occurs when, near the end of the first year, babies use the pincer grasp (thumb and forefingers) to lift and explore objects. Such newly available manipulative skills can be put to all sorts of interesting tasks: picking up bits and pieces on the floor, twiddling knobs or pushing switches. Nothing is sacred, especially when the child can crawl or walk.

In Down's syndrome motor development is typically slower than normal; nevertheless it moves through the sequence from sitting, to standing, to walking, in the normal order. However, with the use of intervention programmes specifically aimed at giving large amounts of practice in sensory-motor tasks, it is possible to accelerate motor development to almost normal levels.

Note: A chart published by Mary Sheridan illustrating the detailed development progress of infants and young children (1 month to 5 years of age) in posture and large movements, vision and fine movements, hearing and speech, social behaviour and play, is available from the Department of Health (*Protecting Children: A Guide for Social Workers Undertaking a Comprehensive Assessment*: HMSO, 1989). The guide provides information for every 3 months of age from 1 month to 18 months of age; thereafter 6 monthly descriptions up to the age of 5 years.

The Proactive Brain

Theorists make the point that infants' brains have been viewed as passively shaped by their environment because, in part, babies are unable to walk or reach out accurately during the first few months of life. It is not until later in their first year that they are capable of much more than the newborn's few positive eye movements, eventually becoming capable of the complex and accurate eye movements of adulthood. But infants are capable from birth, as we have seen, of directing their eyes towards faces and other things that interest them. They also have sufficient ability to allow them to practise assiduously, thus developing new brain circuits in the cerebral cortex. They become capable of integrating the visual and motor information required for skilled eye movements. In this sense, it appears that babies actively contribute to their own future brain development.

The enwrapping of nerve cells in myelin – which allows them to conduct nerve impulses rapidly and continuously – is nearly complete only when the child reaches 4 years of age. The fibres that link the cerebellum to the cerebral cortex – necessary to the fine control of movement – do not have their full complement of myelin until age 4. For all that, it is still possible for specific environmental influences to alter the rate at which change takes place. Some practice is necessary for the child to develop motor skills. Dennis (1960) demonstrated that when opportunities for exercise and movement are greatly restricted there is some retardation in motor development. An adequate diet and good health are also critical.

This is the time to 'childproof' the room. Such restrictions contrast dramatically with the freedom of movement in traditional Indian practice. Parents follow a permissive and indulgent child-rearing philosophy within an extended family environment. The presence of multiple caretakers permits a greater opportunity for exploration, while simultaneously allowing for the continuation of dependence on adults (Phatak, 1969). The relationship between the infant and the mother in the Indian culture is characterized by close physical contact and security. Children are free to roam around the home rather than be confined to a playroom.

More complex skills such as skipping, riding a bike and throwing a ball and catching tend not to develop until around the school-going age. In general children cannot reach a particular milestone without achieving the previous ones (e.g. they do not run until they can walk or walk until they can stand).

Because of the regularity and predominantly self-contained nature of motor development, it is usually assumed that it involves a genetically programmed sequence. Although the rate of development varies, the sequence is virtually the same for all children, even those with marked physical or intellectual impairments.

Speech and Language Development

Language development is a critical component of social development as so much teaching and learning is facilitated by verbal communication. The advent of speech and language enhances the child's ability to solve problems without acting them out concretely on objects in his or her environment.

The auditory system

The process whereby human infants develop language usage is one of the most fascinating and complex of their attainments. The acquisition of speech and language depends on the ability to hear sounds, a modality that newborns arrive with at a level of readiness far in advance of vision. The auditory system of the human fetus is functional at around 10 weeks before birth. Babies become used to sounds such as the mother's heartbeat. Neonates can discriminate between their own mother's voice and other mothers' voices while not yet 24 hours of age. The research evidence indicates the match (in-built) between auditory skill and the range of the human voice. Infants have auditory acuity comparable to adults within the general range of pitch and loudness of the human voice, although there is greater facility with high-pitched sounds (Weisner and Gillenwater, 1990).

- By 6 months of age babies have mastered the skill of associating a parental voice with its owner (Spelke and Owsley, 1979). We saw earlier that newborns can discriminate between their mother's voice and another female voice (De Casper and Fifer, 1980).
- By 3 months babies can discriminate speech sounds in all languages (Polka and Werker, 1994).
- After 6 months, discrimination becomes more specialized (the previous ability is lost) and the infant can only distinguish successfully in the language that is inputted (ibid.). Hearing impairments are dealt with in chapter 10.

Speech production

In order to master the developmental task of producing speech sounds in their mother tongues, the language spoken to them, children require intact anatomical equipment that allows them to produce speech and classify sounds. To learn to speak, infants need to hear the speech they produce and at the same time receive feedback from the movements of their vocal tracts. This necessitates a special anatomical link between the auditory (hearing) system and speech production system, which includes the lungs, trachea (windpipe), larynx (which contains the vocal chords), pharynx or throat, mouth (including tongue, teeth, and lips) and the nose. These speech production organs form a tube (the upper part of the vocal tract) extending from the lungs to the lips. Speech sounds come from constricting the larynx and vocal tract in various ways.

Language and brain function

In most human beings the language areas are on the left side of the brain, although some left-handed people have them in the right hemisphere. As the baby's brain develops, the two hemispheres of the brain become specialized for certain functions: music and other serial-ordered phenomena along with language on the left side; spatial organization and spatial pattern recognition (e.g. face recognition) on the right. This process is called lateralization. If some language function is lost due to an injury, it may be lost for good unless other nerve centres can take it over. Dead cells are not replaced but there is a degree of plasticity in functioning of the immature brain. We are born with *all* the nerve cells of the central nervous system (CNS) we will ever possess – some million million of them. The circuitry in the brain has fixed pathways that are thought to be modifiable by enriched environmental influences as children mature. The circuitry for word knowledge may be dependent on the amount of input the baby receives. The vocabulary size of babies with highly conversant mothers is reported to be considerably larger than of those with taciturn mothers, the gap being wider at 24 months than at 20 months (Huttenlocher, 1991).

The pre-linguistic period (see Pinker, 1994)

The development of language passes through distinct stages beginning with the infant who demonstrates an ability to distinguish between different speech sounds (Mussen, Conger and Kagan, 1984). The average 8-month-old child is unable to use words. At 10 months s/he probably will have one word; at 12 months about three words. At a year and a half his or her vocabulary may be 20 words. During the next 3 months it will jump to over 100, and at 2 years it may contain as many as 250 words. By the age of 3 the child is using sentences to describe past and present happenings.

Developments that underlie human communicative behaviour during the pre-verbal stage involve several component elements taking place simultaneously. These are:

- the perception of speech sounds (an innate capacity) and phonological development (learning to produce speech sounds)

- the development of gestures, and
- the development of conversational competencies.

Children need to learn four types of knowledge about language (Shaffer, 1999):

1. Phonology: the sound system of a language.
2. Semantics: the meanings conveyed by words and sentences.
3. Syntax: the collection of grammatical rules indicating how words may and may not be combined to construct sentences.
4. Pragmatics: the principles determining how language should be modified to suit the context in which it is being used (e.g. simplifying the speech used with a child as compared with an adult).

Children usually learn about language in the sequence described above. They reach certain linguistic milestones, the world over, at about the same age, despite cultural differences in the structure of their language. Language is species specific; animals have no linguistic system.

Nativist theory

According to nativist theory (e.g. Chomsky, 1968, 1976) human beings are biologically programmed to acquire language. Noam Chomsky proposed that human infants come into the world with a *language acquisition device* (LAD) which contains a 'universal grammar', a knowledge of rules that are common to all languages. He argues that the structure of language is far too elaborate to be either taught by parents (as was suggested by Skinner) or discovered by trial-and-error processes. The LAD allows children who have acquired sufficient vocabulary to string words together in novel, rule-based utterances, and to comprehend much of what they hear.

Slobin (1985) allows for the existence of an inborn language-making capacity, but not an innate knowledge of grammar. Rather, she sees it as an inherited set of cognitive and perceptual abilities that are highly specialized for language learning. Holzman (1997) proposes that not only is the human infant innately predisposed to acquire language, but competent speakers (and perhaps mothers especially) are innately predisposed to use language in talking to very young children in a way that *teaches* them to use language. As she comments, it looks as though the behaviour of the baby, who is fostering his or her language development, elicits language behaviour from the mother that is appropriate to the stage of development of the infant's language skills. It also appears that mothers' linguistic behaviour provides feedback that elicits responses from the infants that help them gain linguistic competence.

And it appears that mothers respond to their infants as though the infant's arm and body movements and babbles, cries, and vegetative noises were intended to be meaningful and to communicate meaning. Human babies, like other species in infancy, have innate signals that are informative but not intentional. Eventually the human baby learns from its mother's responses what their particular acts and vocalizations mean. Infants between the ages of 3 and 5 weeks start to coo, which involves producing vowel-like sounds over and over again.

- Between 4 and 6 months of age infants begin to babble, consisting of combinations of vowels and consonants, typically, 'bababa' and 'dadada', that do not seem to have any meaning for the infants. The babbling displayed by babies up to the age of 6 months is somewhat similar in all parts of the world. It appears to be pre-programmed, as it is produced by congenitally deaf children who have no experience of hearing sounds produced by themselves or by others (see chapter 10).
- Progression to the next stage occurs 'naturally' only in hearing infants. Throughout the following stages, children's understanding of language is far ahead of their ability to express themselves, which is not infrequently the source of frustration and outbursts of temper.
- Between 9 and 11 months the infant will begin to inhibit an activity in response to the word 'no', although he or she will not generally be using the word himself or herself (Sheridan, 1989).
- The first recognizable spoken word appears at about 1 year, and from this, single word labels are used for familiar objects and people (Nelson, 1973).

In the single-word stage the meaning attached to words may differ markedly from the conventions of adulthood, e.g. 'cat' may mean any four-legged furry animal, an over-extension of meaning (Mussen, Conger and Kagan, 1984). The single-word stage lasts several months, speech being used increasingly for specific effects, and as more words are added, used with increasingly precise and adult-like meaning. Sentence development comprises the next stage.

The infant's pre-linguistic communication reaches a peak at about 16 to 20 months. Meaningful words appear towards the end of the first year or the beginning of the second year of life. At first they constitute a very small proportion of the infant's vocalization, but during the later part of the second year they become prominent. Thereafter as his or her spoken language improves, non-verbal communication tends to decline, although s/he continues to use it.

The ultimate language problem for growing children is to relate words into meaningful sentences. Their first sentence may be a single word; for instance, they will use the word 'do' to obtain many of their demands. From a single word grows a variety of longer sentences. At approximately 18 months, when children have some 50 words in their speaking vocabularies, words begin to be combined in pairs to convey ideas (e.g. 'Dadad gone'), and not long after there is a steady increase in sentence length and complexity. At 2 years the average length of their sentences is one to seven words. At 5 it has expanded to four to six words. The eight words most often used in constructing the first sentence are: 'I', 'is', 'it', 'do', 'a', 'this', 'not' and 'the'. Nouns and verbs are used at first more frequently than adjectives and connectives. Even those first two-word sentences show systematic regularity of word order, and from the very beginning express the basic grammatical relationships of subject, predicate, and object.

Children from different nations with different languages express essentially the same range of meanings in their earliest sentences, including such basic semantic relations as identification, location, negation, attribution, agent-action and agent-object. By this stage infancy has come to an end but language-development continues apace. By the time they begin to form word patterns, some sex differences begin to manifest themselves. At 18 months, girls exceed boys in the ability to use consonants at the beginning, in the middle and at the end of a word. The mean number of consonants used by girls in the initial position is 8.7 as against 7.7 for boys. For the medial position, the mean for girls is 7.9 and for boys 6.9. In the final position, girls use 2.9 consonants while boys use 2.4.

From 3 years, sentences are used to describe past and present happenings. The average adult length of sentence (six to seven words) is achieved by school-going age, reflecting important changes in the development of grammatical ability, which appear to be closely linked with the development of cognitive and intellectual capacities. As these increase in capacity and sophistication, children can learn more complicated grammatical rules. By the age of 5 or 6 years, children can use several thousand words in complex adult-like sentences and are able to understand complex meanings. Their speech is fluent with few remaining infantile substitutions (Sheridan, 1989). Improved verbal ability often facilitates cognitive functions such as memory, thinking, reasoning and problem solving. (Problems of speech and language are dealt with in chapter 10.)

To take one example from day-to-day childcare of how sensitive parenting facilitates the youngster's development, it has been shown that maternal speech occurring in the context of joint attention to pictures and books is particularly rich in those features that are important in rapid language development. In such a situation the mother's speech is likely to be especially closely tied to the child's interests, and to what he or she is trying to communicate. The extent to which such situations occur in the daily lives of mothers and children may well have considerable implications for the child's mastery of linguistic skills. These come on apace in our next stage of development. But this is not the case for children with Down's syndrome. Linguistic delays become apparent by the first birthday. Most of them reach the concrete operations stage, and possess the communication skills of a school-aged child. The abstract reasoning and hypothetical thinking characteristic of formal operations is not evident.

Note: Atypical aspects of growth and development are discussed in chapter 10.

part iii

Typical Development Adaptation and Learning

All our lives long every day and every hour, we are engaged in
the process of accommodating our changed and unchanged selves
to changed and unchanged surroundings; living in fact, is nothing
else than the process of accommodation . . . when we suspend it
temporarily we sleep, when we give up the attempt altogether
we die.

Samuel Butler (1835–1902): *The Way of All Flesh*

Adjustment and Adaptation

Throughout their lives, and notably during the period of social learning referred to as socialization, children are required to adjust to a never-ending stream of changing physical events, social situations and people – young and old. Failure by children to adapt to social norms, at home or school, was termed 'maladjustment' in the past. Adjustment is biologically and psychologically vital to life. Living creatures can only exist physically within rather narrow limits of pressure and temperature, and under a limited variety of chemical conditions. As beings that consume energy, they must at all times adjust their energy intake to their output. They live in communities with other creatures, some aiding and some threatening – or competing – in their effort at survival. Adaptation is a notion central to Charles Darwin's theory of evolution. Darwin (1859) proposed that over aeons of time, new species appeared and flourished because genetic mutations allowed some forms of life to adjust to their circumstances better than others. This effort, with its particular and often precise demands, is the process of adaptation. There is an inexorable progression in which the fittest members survive the hazards of living and propagate themselves.

Even in the psychological realm, the basic evolutionary law, 'adapt or perish', holds true. Scientists from many disciplines have long been interested in studying the adaptive processes used by different species (and cultures) to enable them to function effectively in different, sometimes harsh, environments. Clearly, humans have evolved, and owe the design of their bodies and minds to evolutionary processes. Evolutionary psychology, a discipline that has aroused much controversy, has attempted to unravel the ways in which natural selection and genetic drift have shaped the psychological mechanisms that make us think and behave in the way we do today. It may have failed to do this with any precision; but it has added an important dimension to the way in which we study human behaviour (see Krebs and Davies, 1993; Ridley, 1995).

Individuals whose adaptive systems are impaired (e.g. those with profound intellectual disabilities and mental illnesses) or deviant (e.g. recidivists who persistently break the law) may be cared for in specialized institutions or secured in prisons. They cannot (or will not) survive in the outside world on society's terms. Of course, the question of the discriminatory nature of 'society's terms' raises moral issues about the rights of its 'less able' citizens. Contemporary theoreticians and practitioners advocate that society should itself adapt in ways that allow individuals who are intellectually disabled to lead lives that are as 'normal' as possible. The policy of 'normalization' has given rise to many, though insufficient, changes in the direction of more humane attitudes and practices. The reality, of course, is that there are countless people who cannot make the necessary adjustments to life's vicissitudes, and who opt out of it by committing suicide. Among them, sadly, are rising numbers of adolescents (see chapter 14). There are others who survive, but whose survival is tenuous. Many can be seen sleeping rough in our cities. Feeling alienated, ill, unwanted or aimless, their existence appears marginal – far removed from their fellow citizens who can be said to be 'living life to the full'.

Human beings have attained their mastery because of the flexibility of their intellectual equipment, their ability to deal in abstract and divergent thinking, and to engage in complex problem solving. If they cannot accommodate themselves to their environment they alter the environment to suit their needs. Of all their many gifts the human brain represents the zenith, in both intricacy and reliability of all the 'systems' that have evolved to coordinate the millions of adjustments, internal and external, necessary to life. Not to be forgotten are those achievements described in chapter 4: infants of the genus *homo sapiens* developing deft motor skills and hand-movements that have their parallel in *homo erectus'* growing mastery of the environment by adopting, *inter alia*, an upright posture, and by using marvellously flexible fingers and hands for tool-making. The ability to learn from experience is yet another evolutionary achievement that has served the human species well. This is our cue to examine the means by which society passes on skills and values to the next generation. This issue will dominate much of our discussion in later chapters on the development of atypical behaviour.

Cultural Influences

In the wake of thinkers like Margaret Mead, Sigmund Freud, Ivan Pavlov and John Watson, there has been a psychological preoccupation with the influence of the environment in the acquisition of behaviour, often to the neglect of biological and, notably, genetic factors. Margaret Mead (1901–1978) was a dominant figure in the field of anthropology for many decades, and known particularly for her seminal research in Samoa, a group of islands in Polynesia. Mead highlighted her theory of cultural relativism in her reports (e.g. Mead, 1928, 1935, 1949). She asserted that adolescence in Samoa was made easy because of sexual freedom allowed to pubescent youngsters. She also compared the child-rearing practices of two different groups of the South Sea Islanders, the Arapesh and Mundugumor. Children of the Arapesh tribe were trained in a manner that produced broadly peaceful, non-aggressive citizens. The Mundugumor parents inculcated aggressive, warrior attitudes in their children, in much the same spirit as the citizens of the city state Sparta, in ancient Greece. Mead's observations of these cultural differences were a major basis of her view that *nurture* supersedes *nature* in shaping human individuality. Her original data, and her conclusions, have been both criticized and defended with great passion, but remain influential to this day.

The environmentalist point of view has always been particularly strong in America. It is reflected in the optimistic philosophy that, 'any child, given the right circumstances, can become president of the USA'. John B. Watson, a behaviourist psychologist at Johns Hopkins University during the first decades of the last century, gave an impetus to this piece of folklore (Watson, 1928). He believed that planned habit training could mould the child in any desired shape. As he put it:

> Give me a dozen healthy infants, well-formed, and my own specified world to bring them up in, and I'll guarantee to take any one at random and train him to become any type of specialist I might select – doctor, lawyer, artist, merchant-chief, and yes, even beggarman and thief, regardless of his talents, penchants, tendencies, abilities, vocations, and race of his ancestors.

Watson underrated the influence of individual differences in temperament, and failed to take into account the power of inborn characteristics to modify the environment itself (Bell, 1968). As a biosocial organism the child's development can be influenced powerfully by inherited constitutional traits as well as by psychosocial experiences. The impact of the child's temperament, for example, can be a delight, or lead to the despair of parents, the subject matter of chapter 11.

The Family Environment

The family is the crucial early conduit for ideas and practices of the type described above. The durability and universality of the family (family groupings have been traced back some 500,000 years to the Pleistocene period) suggest that it has proved itself as an organization of critical value to the survival of the individual and the human species. There have been many sociological, anthropological and psychological theories in scholarly books and doctoral theses, 'explaining' how the family has managed to adapt and survive for so long. Ferdinand Mount, author of *The Subversive Family: An Alternative History of Love and Marriage* (1983), asserts that despite all official efforts to downgrade the family, to reduce its role and even to stamp it out, men and women obstinately continue to mate and produce children. They persist in living in pairs together with their children, in developing strong affections for them and in placing family concerns above other social obligations. The family's impressive longevity does not mean that it is a monolithic entity or has remained unchanged. It has been, and continues to be, susceptible to the impact of social, economic, and historical forces, providing a dynamic, changing environment in which succeeding generations of children are reared. Decreasing fertility and increasingly long lives have profoundly modified the family life-cycle. Both the structure of the family and dynamics of family life have changed significantly in a relatively short time. Families in industrial societies have given way (with relatively few exceptions) to small units of parent and offspring. Childcare practices are a good example of the way in which advice to parents is subject to fashions and fads.

Childcare Practices

It is generally assumed today that it matters a great deal how the infant is cared for. His or her future could well be blighted unless they are reared 'correctly'. But was this concern for childhood as a special and vulnerable period of life, always the case? According to some historians, childhood in mediaeval time was (in conceptual terms) non-existent. Children who survived their early years were, it is said, dressed like 'little adults', put to work at a tender age, and beaten if they showed the weaknesses of their years (see p. 136). The historian Nicholas Orme (2000) has challenged this interpretation. He illustrates how mediaeval parents (or presumably those from a better-off section of society) saw childhood as a distinct phase of life, one in which children played games, enjoyed a variety of toys and books, clothes, and sometimes being thoroughly spoiled. Birth took place in a darkened room so that the babies would not squint; they were fed pap, shod in soft slippers, given badges to chew, provided with bibs, swaddle-bands, petticoats and the equivalent of nappies ('tail-clouts'). Later there were wooden frames to help the child learn to walk. They were baptized at birth – a hedge against the risk of an early unchristian death and a hellish fate. If children were respected as individuals, the privilege belonged mainly to boys. Girls were virtually ignored.

Notwithstanding variations in family pattern and style of parenting through the ages, and in contemporary times, all societies seem to be broadly success-ful in the task of transforming helpless, self-centred infants into more or less self-supporting, responsible members of their particular form of community. Indeed, as we have seen, there is a basic 'preparedness' on the part of most infants to be trained – that is, an in-built bias toward all things social (Stayton, Hogan and Ainsworth, 1971). During the first year of life mother and baby enjoy a host of mutually rewarding interactions (proactive and reactive) in the course of which they develop all-important emotional attachments. But how 'all-important' is the presence of maternal as opposed to non-maternal care in this first year or so of the infant's life? Like so many theoretical pro-positions in developmental psychology, this is a highly contentious issue.

Maternal Privation and Deprivation

'The day-care wars'

Jay Belsky, in his Emanuel Miller lecture, comments that 'in the decade and a half since the advent of what have (rightly) been called "the day care wars" a substantial amount of research has appeared on the effects of non-maternal care initiated in the first year of life' (Belsky, 2001, p. 846). (See references to the NICHD study of early childcare.) A brief account of the origins of the controversy surrounding this topic is necessary to understand how ideological and political doctrines become entangled with developmental theorizing. Much has been made of the young child's need for maternal care during what is thought of as the earliest 'sensitive' (the term 'critical' has also been used) stage of its life.

From the late 1940s and 1950s, empirical evidence of the deleterious effects of absence or insufficiency of maternal care for babies and young children was reported and widely disseminated. John Bowlby's seminal work on maternal deprivation was published by the World Health Organization in 1951. He concluded that children who had been separated from their *mothers*, or otherwise deprived of their *mother's* love and care, for even a short period of time, were at risk of suffering deficits in their emotional, social, psycholo-gical, and even physical development (see chapter 11 on 'failure to thrive'). In the wake of these important findings, there have been passionate debates about whether the child's mother is the person who should devote herself to this task. Are fathers and other caregivers acceptable, or 'good enough', for a responsibility that has such short- and long-term implications for the child's well-being? Some of the more heated reactions to this work and its ramifications arose from the dogmatic insistence that mothers should take complete and uninterrupted care of their young children – an ideological or economic confidence trick in the view of certain critics. This is a matter we return to below.

Bowlby eventually modified his views as new evidence emerged (see reviews by Bowlby, 1969; Rutter, 1972). Research indicated that children remaining for a prolonged period in very disturbed unbroken homes were more likely to have problems in development than those losing a relationship when a home breaks up. Mounting evidence seemed to suggest that substitute care, when excellent and consistent, could mitigate the adverse effects on young children of periods of separation from their parents (Shaw, 1986). Some of the early work in this field appeared to confuse *privation* (i.e. children who had never known a close relationship with a mother) with *deprivation* (i.e. children who had enjoyed a relationship with a mother, and then lost it). The effects of the latter are much more complicated and difficult to anticipate than the former, as is the type of deprivation that does not involve actual physical separation from the mother. The work of Mary Ainsworth and her colleagues (1978) illustrated how a mother can be physically present but 'emotionally distant'. A child in this situation is quite likely to be insecure in his or her attachment and subject, in that sense, to maternal deprivation.

Childminding

When childminding is required, the choice for parents is usually between babysitters, day care centres, and willing grandparents. It may require, in the now old-fashioned sense of the term, a 'role reversal' in which the father stays at home to look after the home and the children. In the inappropriate category of childcare (where it amounts, in some instances, to 'surrogate' parenting) is the duty of care put upon, or assumed (often in distressed home circumstances) by children.

In the late 1980s, an analysis of the research literature by Belsky (1988) on infant day care disturbed a figurative 'hornet's nest' by questioning the received wisdom about substitute care then (and to this day) prevalent. He concluded that early and extensive non-maternal care carries risks in terms of increasing the probability of insecure infant–parent bonding and promoting aggression and non-compliance during the toddler, pre-school and early primary school years (see Belsky, 2001). If correct, the 'comfort' afforded to many parents who felt they and the infant were safe if 'quality' substitute care (a major problem in itself) could be arranged, is seriously undermined.

Looking toward fathers for help in this respect is not forthcoming. Data linking quality of fathering with maternal employment and/or childcare is generally inconsistent; however, there is convincing evidence that father–son attachments are at risk for insecurity when non-maternal care, full- or near full-time, is initiated in the infant's first year of life (ibid.). Belsky concluded his critical review by stating that 'no longer is it tenable for developmental scholars and child-care advocates to deride the notion that early and extensive non-maternal care of the kind available in most communities poses risks for young children and perhaps the larger society as well. . . . Appreciation is growing that child-care quality may not have as substantial an impact on child development as was often presumed to be the case' (ibid., p. 855).

The worry about the risks of day care, of whatever kind, may cause agonizing choices for those who have freedom to decide what to do about the 'job v. baby' dilemma. But countless women have no freedom to choose because they have to earn a living, or a career they wish to follow. In the UK 49 per cent, and in the USA 55 per cent, of mothers with infants below 1 year of age, were in employment in the 1990s. In America, most mothers with young children, despite the reassuring opinions of professionals, would prefer, if possible, to be able to do what they regard as being best for their babies, namely caring for them themselves, no matter what first-rate substitute care is available.

The Father's Role

Prior to the 1970s researchers and clinicians appeared to be uninterested in fathers. It went without saying, at that time, that mothers had a far greater influence on the development of children than fathers. As we have seen, it was particularly the absence of the mother (maternal privation and deprivation) that was inculpated in disturbances of this development. Feminists, and other sociologist critics, rejected these assumptions as facile and discriminatory. They suggested that both the maternal deprivation and maternal bonding concepts served to legitimize the social arrangement whereby mothers are expected to provide the predominant care for their offspring. The father, in Western society, tended to be presented as peripheral – always appearing in the unfolding drama of the child's development in a role (conveniently, when it came to the chores and unremitting attention required of childcare) *subsidiary* to that of the mother's role and relationship with their infant. He was accorded the status of genitor and external economic provider; also, 'at best', in the role of a 'super dad' who was good at playing with the children and taking them on outings.

Such views contrasted markedly with the dominance of the social stereotype of motherhood as being natural, biologically designed, and the font of the child's emotional support (see Richman and Goldthorp, 1978). Freud suggested that a woman's anatomy is her 'fate'. As we noted above, developmental psychology has a close relationship with social policy and it has provided ideological reinforcement for this stereotype of motherhood. The relationship between ideas and social structure is a highly complex, speculative and polemical subject; it is not our task to explore it in detail here. However, it is as well to remember how conventional theories of child-rearing imply that the contemporary nuclear family with its clear sex-role divisions, and ascribed tasks, its emphasis on privacy and somewhat intense emotional attachments, is natural, unchangeable and functional for members of the family and society alike. These assumptions cannot be taken for granted. Paradoxically these same theories are pervaded by a preoccupation by family therapists and analysts with the family's and the mother's inadequacy, when it comes to performing their 'natural' functions.

And it is precisely here that the male–female dichotomy has additionally disadvantageous sexist connotations. When men are portrayed as economic providers, operating mainly *outside* the home to sustain the family unit, and mothers are presented as the providers of emotional support *within* the home: it is mothers who are scapegoated when the children develop problems. This sexist bias is buttressed intellectually by psychiatric and psychodynamic theories. It is ironic that where the mother's absence is blamed for much childhood psychopathology, aspects of her very presence are also put forward as determinants of psychiatric problems in children. Stella Chess (1964), a child psychiatrist, refers to the phenomenon as *'mal de mere'* – the tendency to blame childhood psychopathology on mothers, who, at best, are incompetent, and, at worse, cruel and neglectful. The clinical literature until fairly recently presented a litany of solipsistic descriptions of allegedly pathological mothers as schizophrenogenic, asthmagenic, intrusive, double-binding, overprotective or rejecting. Fathers somehow (perhaps because they rarely attended the clinic with the child) tended to be described as passive and in the background. They largely escaped censure in the 1950s and 1960s.

Paternal attachments

Earlier chapters referred repeatedly to *parental attachment*, implying that adult-to-infant bonding is not uniquely the role of the mother. Attachment was described as a matter of degree whose strength depends on many factors, one of them being the degree of exposure of the adult to the infant, or familiarity of the adult with the infant. Now is the time to be more explicit, and suggest that father-to-infant attachment is not so different in kind from maternal attachment. Certainly paternal behaviour soon after the birth of a baby very often resembles in many details maternal behaviour. Paternal attachment, however, often (but not invariably) appears to be less strong than maternal attachment. There are some good reasons for this. In the first place, general responsiveness of the human male to infants tends to be less marked. It would not be altogether surprising if there were genetic factors responsible for this. In many, but not all, species of primates males are less nurturing to the young than females, although males tend to be protective both towards the females and their offspring. Undoubtedly, however, the role of the human male in relation to the young is enormously influenced by culture, custom and convention. Until relatively recent times in western and central Europe men were not expected to perform certain domestic duties, including the feeding of young infants, changing nappies, etc. The situation in this regard is at present changing rapidly. It may be that without the conventional cultural overlay, men's feelings and responses towards babies would not be all that different from women's. If, for whatever reason, the responsiveness of males to babies is on the whole less strong than that of females, then specific paternal attachments would be initially somewhat handicapped in their development. In the end they would not perhaps reach the intensity of maternal attachments. The fact cannot be ignored that it is usually the father, not the mother, who abandons their offspring.

Secondly, in the usual Western family the extent of contact between father and baby is less than that between mother and baby. This may be regrettable, but it is a fact that cannot be overlooked. In these circumstances, paternal attachments have less opportunity to grow at the same rate as maternal attachments. Exposure learning, classical conditioning, operant learning, imitation and the rest of the bonding influences have less time to operate. Perhaps this is a major reason why paternal attachments often seem less emotional than maternal attachments, and dominate men's lives less than they do women's lives. What perhaps is surprising is that, despite everything, the attachments of fathers to their offspring are, for the most part, extremely strong. To say, however, that paternal attachment is essentially of the same kind as maternal attachment does not imply that the father's role in our society is basically no different from that of the mother's. The interested reader may pursue further the topic of the father's role by referring to a volume edited by Lamb (1981) and on the subject of comparative parenting in a text edited by Sluckin and Herbert (1986).

The specifics of parenting

Reviews of the literature repeatedly point to the conclusion that there is little evidence of a connection between *specific* parenting practices and later characteristics of the child. Despite extensive research, there is much doubt as to how different methods of child-rearing influence the development of the child's personality. Thus, we do not really know whether the psychological development of children is affected by feeding methods (breast-feeding v. bottle-feeding, or fixed-interval feeding v. on-demand feeding) or by early or late weaning, and so on. The available evidence suggests negligible effects for these early events (e.g. Caldwell, 1964; Crain, 1985; Garbarino and Binn, 1992; Kagan, 1984; Yarrow, Campbell and Burton, 1968). But it also suggests that what is important in child-rearing is the general social climate in the home: for example, the attitudes and feelings of the parents, which form a background to the application of specific methods and interactions of child-rearing. The mother who does best, for example, does (with a sense of confidence) what she and the community to which she belongs believe is right for the child. If mothers get confused it is hardly surprising given the rapid – indeed, radical – changes in family life.

Society can facilitate mothers' self-efficacy with policies that support their parenting and family life. Belsky (2001) discusses how helpful tax arrangements and meaningful periods of maternal leave are appropriate structural responses to the plight of mothers who do not have the luxury of choice when it comes to giving up their jobs. Our next subject highlights some of the dilemmas described above.

Divorce

Motives for family dissolution have changed, resulting in more situations of divorce and reconstituted families. In the early 1960s, around 90 per cent of children spent their childhood and teenage years in homes with two married biological/birth parents. Today the figures are around 59 per cent in the UK, and 40 per cent in the USA. The reasons for the dramatic fall in numbers are the increase in divorce and separations due to breakdowns in cohabitation arrangements – a rapidly increasing choice for couples. In 1993, according to the US Bureau of the Census, about four out of ten first marriages ended in divorce. Reconstituted families, in which one or both partners have been married before and are combining two families into one, are a very common phenomenon. In about one out of every three marriages, one or both parents have been married before. Following divorce most children (84 per cent) reside with their mother in a single-parent home. This tends to be a temporary arrangement as re-marriages are popular, and rates of cohabitation high for those who do not choose to re-marry. Adjustment for the child is not necessarily made any easier as divorce rates are higher in re-marriages than first marriages. Figures from the Office for National Statistics (ONS) indicate that one in eight children in the UK will live at some stage in a family in which their birth parent had either re-married or formed a new partnership before they were 16 if current trends continue. The adjustment of children in divorced single-parent families and in stepfamilies is very similar. (See Hetherington and Stanley-Hagan, 1999, for a review of the literature.)

What this means is that increasing numbers of children spend periods of their childhood with divorced, re-married, single or step-parents, and with step- or half-siblings. It is likely that many of today's young children are unwillingly involved in the precipitating events and aftermath of a divorce. Children who are exposed to multiple marital transitions experience the most adverse outcomes in psychological adjustment (Capaldi and Patterson, 1991). A self-perpetuating element is at work here. There is a long-term correlation between parental divorce (separation) and divorce and depression in adulthood – to mention only a few of the risk factors (O'Connor et al., 1999). Most children do not want their parents to separate, and they may feel that their father and mother have not taken their interests into account. A majority of them are bewildered at the time because they get little or no explanation of the reasons for the breakdown of the relationship. This may not be the end of disruption of the child's life, as broken homes frequently involve reduced social and economic circumstances for the single mother (Edelstein and Herbert, 1998).

Psychological consequences of the break-up of families

Children are generally the losers when their parents' marriages end in divorce or their partnerships (long-term cohabiting) are terminated. Boys and girls are equally vulnerable. Divorce is a lengthy process, not simply a single incident in children's lives. A 20 year study (2000 couples and 200 of their children who had reached 19 years of age) by Paul Amato at Pennsylvania State University, revealed that 40 per cent had divorced by the previous year. A small majority were 'very good' marriages. Children were more harmed by parents who argue rarely and then divorce unexpectedly than those whose parents confronted each other bitterly and frequently prior to breaking up. Forty per cent of divorces involved marriages in which the child's parents were in constant and violent conflict, but did not separate. Theirs was the worst plight of all. (Research described by Alexandra Frean, social affairs correspondent of *The Times* newspaper, 16 July 2001.) As with other investigations there was evidence that children benefit from the break-up of violent, disharmonious partnerships although they suffer grave disadvantages from the actual sound and fury of the break-up itself. Children report a sense of relief when the conflict between the parents ends. Perhaps one of the worst aspects of their predicament is their powerlessness to act on their own behalf.

Adolescents do not get off more 'lightly' than children when enduring their parents' divorce. The results of a 2 year study of more than 10,000 American adolescents by Yongmin Sun revealed that negative effects on every indicator of academic progress (psychological well-being, attendance, behaviour and drug and alcohol abuse) were evident at least 1 year before the marriage ended. These consequences were accompanied by a decline in parental interest in, and commitment to, their offspring. (Reported by Tracy McVeigh in *The Observer*, 5 August 2001, p. 10.)

Wallerstein and Blakeslee (1989, p. 60) comment in the conclusion to their review as follows:

> We wanted to believe that time would lessen the feelings of hurt and anger, that time itself heals all wounds and that people by nature are resilient. But there is no evidence that time automatically diminishes feelings or memories; that hurt and depression are overcome; that jealousy, anger and outrage will vanish. Some experiences are just as painful ten years later; some memories haunt us for a lifetime.

Hetherington and Stanley-Hagan (1999) conclude, at the end of an important review of the literature (p. 137), that divorce can have a lifelong impact, but the consequences are not always negative or regressive ones. Many children who grow up in the aftermath of a divorce overcome the trauma and go on to contribute to, rather than rebel against, society. Although children in divorced families, in comparison to those in non-divorced families, are at risk of developing more social, emotional, behavioural, and academic problems, most eventually emerge as competent, well-functioning individuals.

Protective factors

The great diversity in response to divorce is related to the interaction of risk and protective factors associated with individual characteristics of the child and the family and extrafamilial environment. The parental role – authoritative and secure – is crucial. In the case of the separated couple it should be as free of conflict as possible, and as supportive (in the parental sharing) as can be negotiated. It may be possible to have a 'good' divorce even if it was a 'bad' marriage. Children's reactions to divorce and separation reflect their particular coping abilities, which are associated with their age and stage of psychosocial development. For some, becoming someone's stepchild – a likely consequence of divorce and re-marriage – is not always a welcome life event, or an easy adaptation. The difficulties are legendary, as are the dilemmas concerning even the most well-intentioned step-parent's role in a reconstituted family.

A study of over 450 children (aged 5 to 16) of separating parents, conducted by researchers at King's College (London) for the Joseph Rowntree Trust, found that they were less likely to display anxiety, aggression, poor personal relationships, problems at school, or longer term difficulties, if their grandparents supported them through the break-up. Closeness to the mother's parents was particularly protective. Listening to children's views is also critical to their long-term well-being. Research has repeatedly highlighted the importance of wise custody decisions and good relationships post-divorce between the child/ren and the custodial parent (see follow-up studies by Wallerstein and Kelly, 1980; Hetherington, Cox and Cox, 1982; and Hetherington and Stanley-Hagan, 1999). Here again, knowing the children's point of view is critical in making these arrangements.

A great deal of research (admittedly, worryingly ethnocentric) has addressed itself to these complex issues by investigating the consequences of family dissolution as indexed by divorce and (given the massive increase in cohabitation) 'separation'. Whatever the research problems (undoubtedly a methodological minefield) Hetherington and Stanley-Hagan (ibid., p. 137) are quite unambiguous in asserting that the family environment with the fewest risks when it comes to socializing children is 'a happy, intact, two-parent family. Children are at risk for developing problems in adjustment when they grow up in either a *conflicted* two-parent home or in a single-parent home.'

Adoption

Adoptive children must be our concern if we are considering the impact of different environments. They are likely to have two sets of parents: the birth parents and the adoptive parents. The latter combines the legal and parenting roles. The nature of adoption has provided developmental and clinical researchers with a quasi-experimental design. Family members normally share both heredity (first-degree relatives correlate 0.50 genetically) and environment (they share the same family). Thus, familial correlations cannot tell us about the relative extent to which genetic and environmental factors contribute to observed resemblance between family members. The adoption method separates the effects of nature and nurture by studying adopted-apart genetic relatives (to assess the role of genetics) and by studying genetically unrelated individuals brought together by adoption (to assess the role of family environment).

The Egyptians, Romans, and Greeks all sanctioned adoption. In earlier periods, adoption was utilized primarily to serve adult ends – particularly to acquire heirs in order to provide continuity for a family line. Views on adoption have changed markedly over the years. The attitude of some people to adoption in the eighteenth and early nineteenth centuries was very different from the one shared by most of us today. George Eliot indicated, in her novel *Silas Marner*, the religious belief that to adopt a child because children of your own had been denied you was to try and choose your lot in spite of Providence. The adopted child would never turn out well, and would be a curse to those who had wilfully and rebelliously sought what it was clear that, for some high reason, they were better without. Adoption was only permissible and likely to succeed if it came about by chance, not intent. George Eliot made the point that the 'blood bond' is less important than the bonds forged by long-term tenderness and affection. And she has been shown to be correct. In fact, researchers provide evidence that adoption is notable for its high success rate both in absolute terms and relative to other forms of substitute care (Shaw, 1986). Like other parents, adopters will have their share of difficult children, an issue discussed in the chapters on atypical behaviour.

Surrogate Parenting

Foster care

There is a widely held opinion that family foster care is the preferred option for children in need of out-of-home care, providing as it generally does a better opportunity for them to develop into well-functioning adults (see Barber, Delfabbro, and Cooper, 2001). Unfortunately, there is a significant exception to this optimistic view. Children entering permanent care at an older age (notably adolescents with mental health and behaviour problems), and after the breakdown of a succession of placements, tend to have negative developmental outcomes.

Parentification

The term 'parentification' has been used to describe the expectation that one or more children will fulfil the parental role in the family system. A child who assumes, unprompted often, many of the adult responsibilities and worries of family life and attempts to provide emotional support to his or her single (frequently abandoned) parent, is in a role-reversal that amounts in most cases to deprivation, perhaps even abuse. Clearly these are generally unsatisfactory burdens for a child, although sometimes invaluable to parents with another child who is disabled, a restrictive mental health problem such as agoraphobia, or an unresolved bereavement. It is not surprising that the professional literature tends to emphasize the pathological aspects of parentification. But the issue is not wholly clear-cut. For some individuals (depending on a host of mediating variables), parentification experiences may involve some advantageous compensatory adaptation, positively enhancing their competence for coping with life.

Learning Theory

Environmental influences are mediated by learning processes (Herbert, 1994, 2002). The vast majority of childhood behaviours are learned and this includes the problematic ones that adults (and sometimes peers) find so disturbing. Children have to be taught how to behave appropriately. This involves teaching them to conduct themselves in a socially 'normal' manner. Two persons are involved: a learner and a teacher. Parents as teachers do not have the 'benefit' (if such it is) of a formal training in parenthood. If fortunate, they may have the advantage of having had an informal induction into parenthood based on observing, helping and learning from good parents of their own.

What is learned, be it at home or at school, or anywhere else, is a central concern of developmental and clinical psychology. A core theoretical assumption of clinically applied learning theory is that much atypical (dysfunctional) behaviour and cognition in children is on a continuum with normal (functional, non-problematic) activity and thought. These phenomena do not differ in general (although there are important exceptions as we shall see) from their normal counterparts in their development, their persistence, and the way in which they can be modified.

Unfortunately, and it is the case with all forms of learning, the very processes that help the child adapt to life can, under certain circumstances, contribute to maladaptation. An immature child who learns by imitating an adult does not necessarily comprehend when it is undesirable (deviant) behaviour or distorted thinking that is being modelled. The youngster who learns adaptively on the basis of classical and instrumental conditioning processes (discussed below) to avoid or escape from dangerous situations can also learn in the same way (maladaptively) to avoid school or social gatherings. A caregiver may unwittingly reinforce antisocial coercive behaviour by attending, or giving in, to it.

The nature of learning

When experience leads to a relatively permanent modification of behaviour, attitude or knowledge, we say that learning has occurred. Memorizing a formula, recognizing a face, reading music, and becoming fearful of doing maths or going to parties, are all examples of learning. It is necessary to distinguish between *learning* an action and actually *performing* it. Basically, as far as the developing child is concerned, there are three preliminary questions to be answered:

1. Does s/he know *what* to do?
2. Does s/he know *how* to do it?
3. Does s/he know *when* to do it?

The child may know the appropriate behaviour or skill and when to produce it, but still does not perform it. So there are four more questions:

1. How can I get him to do what I want him to do?
2. Now that he does it, how can I encourage him to continue doing it?
3. How can I get her to stop doing what I don't want her to do?

4. Now that she has stopped doing it, how can I encourage her to desist from doing it?

The stimulus control of behaviour

The basic assumption of a stimulus-response (or stimulus control) analysis of behaviour is the proposition that the most fruitful way of understanding how a child's actions have come about is to analyse them in terms of four basic components:

1. Prior stimulation (S)
2. Organismic variables (which include motives and the biological and psychological states of the individual) (O)
3. Responses (R)
4. Reinforcement consequences (C)

The complete description of any behavioural sequence requires the specification of each of these elements and their interaction with each other. The 'formula' for a particular pattern of behaviour can be written as follows: $S \rightarrow O \rightarrow R \rightarrow C$. Stimuli are vital because they direct behaviour. Or to put this another way, it is crucial for the individual's survival that s/he learns to respond appropriately to stimuli. We know that learning of the most basic kind – conditioning – is possible for the fetus in the mother's womb and for newly born babies. It is necessary to examine this form of learning in some detail because atypical mental health problems such as phobias, depressions, obsessions and compulsions are thought by many to be largely acquired by a process of learning. Atypical physical disorders may acquire an overlay of learned behaviours of a dysfunctional kind. For example, the learned behavioural, cognitive or affective overlay may be predisposing to organic conditions such as epilepsy, and the Lesch-Nyhan syndrome, or an adverse constitutional temperamental disposition.

Models of Learning

There are five major types of learning: classical and operant conditioning; observational and cognitive learning; and social learning.

1. Classical (respondent) conditioning

Classical conditioning provides one explanation of how our behaviours come to be elicited by such a wide variety of stimuli. Ivan Pavlov (1849–1936) was the Russian scientist whose genius led to the exploration of this form of learning. Some of them don't always serve a useful purpose. What precisely is the conditioning process that can be 'subverted' to produce problem behaviour? In a typical experiment from Pavlov's laboratory, a dog was given food while viewing a stimulus of circular shape. After a few such combinations, the presentation of the circle alone, in the absence of the food, would excite the feeding centres in the dog's brain; it would lick its chops, look into its bowl, and secrete saliva which could be measured. This salivary reaction to a visual stimulus, a response that does not occur naturally, is an example of conditioning.

The stimulus (the circle) which the dog had to learn to respond to is called the *conditioned stimulus* (CS). The stimulus (the food) which *initially* elicited the response (salivation) is called the *unconditioned stimulus* (UCS). The natural, untrained response (the salivating response to food) is called the *unconditioned response* (UCR). When it is transferred to another object (the circle) it is called the *conditioned response* (CR).

Conditioning model (paradigm)

Food (UCS)	–	Salivation (UCR)
Circle	–	?
Circle + food	–	Salivation
Circle + food	–	Salivation
Circle (CS)	–	Salivation (CR)

This is all very well, but isn't such low-level learning too trivial to bother with? In humans (and we trace these developments in the following chapters), insight and language make symbolic and abstract thinking possible. These things in turn make human learning much richer, more complex and more flexible than would be possible on the basis of conditioning alone. Nevertheless, basic conditioning is still very important in humans, as well as in the animal kingdom, where it is crucial.

Higher order conditioning occurs when a response that has come to be elicited by one stimulus through conditioning is transferred to a new stimulus. This process is greatly extended in human learning, especially when it comes to verbal behaviour (language). It has been shown that if names of different nations, names of other persons, even nonsense syllables, are paired with words having a negative tone, such as 'bitter', 'ugly', 'failure', and so on, they subsequently tend to be viewed in an unpleasant light. In such higher order conditioning, a stimulus once learned (a word gaining unpleasant connotations) serves as the basis for further conditioning of negative feeling to other stimuli. Higher order conditioning is possible through the association of many conditioned responses until a complex hierarchy of behaviour is developed.

2. Operant conditioning

In essence, operant behaviour (mainly under voluntary control) is defined by the manner in which it changes the environment; it is behaviour that is maintained by its consequences. Actions are increased or strengthened (and thus shaped) by having consequences that are rewarding (positive reinforcement), or that lead to the avoidance of, or escape from, punishment (negative reinforcement). They are reduced or eliminated by punitive sanctions (fines, penalties, etc.) which follow, contingently, their unwanted performance.

The term *operant* refers also to a class of behaviours, all of which have an identical effect on the environment. A child, for example, may find that s/he can get his or her parent to forgo an unwelcome command to go to bed (a rewarding outcome) by a variety of operants – screaming, crying or pleading. The parent, by giving in, escapes the aversive behaviour (also a rewarding outcome). The repeated consequence of such behaviours reinforces them; in other words, increases the probability of their performance in future situations of a similar kind – both for parent and child.

This learning principle is illustrated by an experiment conducted by Yvonne Brackbill on the smiling responses (the so-called 'operants') of eight normal infants ranging in age from $3\frac{1}{2}$ to $4\frac{1}{2}$ months (Brackbill, 1958). Brackbill studied her experimental participants for two or three sessions a day over several days. After securing a 'base level' of smiling in her infant subjects (i.e. after she had measured how much smiling the babies normally displayed), she carried out the conditioning sessions. During these sessions she stood motionless and expressionless 15 inches above the subject. As soon as the baby smiled, she smiled in return, began to speak softly and picked it up. After holding, jostling, patting, and talking to the baby for 30 seconds, Brackbill put it back in its crib. In the next phase of the study, she stopped giving attention altogether, in order to see whether the cessation of reinforcement would extinguish the expected increase in smiling responses.

The experimenter measured the frequency of smiling throughout, plotting on a graph the child's acquisition of smiling responses. The resultant cumulative curve showed a steep increase in the rate of smiling for the infants subjected to conditioning. By contrast, a control participant, put through the same situations as the experimental babies (but without reinforcement), showed no increase in smiling. In other words, the smiling responses of eight normal infants were modified and brought under experimental control. Infants can be conditioned to increase the frequency of their smiling. By removing the rewards, their newly acquired behaviour (increased smiling) can be extinguished.

The terms positive or negative reinforcement refer to a *procedure*, whereas the terms positive or negative reinforcer refer to an *event* which, presented in conjunction with a targeted behaviour, increases the likelihood of that behaviour occurring. A careful observation-based analysis of the positive and negative reinforcing stimuli that produce or maintain fearful, antisocial or other unwanted behaviours, is referred to as a functional analysis. All children, given their different learning experiences and training histories, possess a unique reinforcement profile. An event that functions as a reinforcer for one child may not do so for another; an event that functions as a reinforcer in one situation may not do so for the same individual in another. (See Herbert, 1987b, 1998a, 2002, for detailed accounts of the theoretical and practical aspects of behavioural analysis.)

3. Observational learning (vicarious conditioning)

Stimulus-response theories of learning and their various clinical applications continue to be acknowledged for their undoubted usefulness; however, learning theory has moved on. Albert Bandura's concept of vicarious conditioning, learning by observation, is central to the child's rapid acquisition of many complex and novel skills, notably social behaviour. As Bandura (1969, 1977) explains, one can acquire intricate response patterns merely by observing the performance of appropriate models; emotional responses can be conditioned observationally by witnessing the affective reactions of others undergoing painful or pleasurable experiences; fearful and avoidance behaviour can similarly be extinguished.

Imitation begins early in life. Infants between 12 and 21 days of age showed rudimentary visual imitation ability when they replicated the facial expressions and tongue protrusion of the adult facing them (Meltzoff and Moore, 1977). Deferred imitation, a more advanced strategy, does not emerge until the second year, around 12 months. It has significant repercussions for infant–caregiver attachment. Infants demonstrate productive memory capacity in being able to imitate ritualistic games and remember the location of objects. This ability is important in the development of representational and language skills.

Watching and imitating the behaviour of exemplary models, is considered by social learning theorists to be the cornerstone of learning for socialization. Of course, not all models of social behaviour (notably the significant ones for young children – their parents) are appropriate people to imitate. Many may be socially deviant or mentally disturbed. Experiments and observations have convincingly illustrated how children imitate, not only desirable behaviour, but also inappropriate actions. In one study, the nursery-children who observed aggressive models displayed a great number of precisely imitated aggressive responses, which rarely occurred in the other ('control') group which observed non-aggressive models. In addition, the results indicated that models observed on film were as effective as real-life models in transmitting hostile patterns of behaviour.

The example given above is a very simple one, but even such apparently simple patterns of learning are difficult to analyse. Psychologists are not certain why some models have an almost irresistible influence over children while others are ignored. Deficiencies in imitation may be due to:

- inadequate attention to the modelled activities (one thinks here of the hyperactive child)
- inadequate retention of the stimuli ('I keep forgetting')
- motor inadequacies ('I'm all fingers and thumbs with the sewing needle, Mum'), or
- lack of motivation ('I don't see why I should!').

With this type of learning (and another which we will come to), we are less concerned with the *consequences* of behaviour, but more interested in the *antecedents* of behaviour (i.e. what goes before, or leads up to, the particular action). For example, a child might learn vicariously to fear a teacher because s/he has observed him treating another child harshly. All of this is not to deny the importance of consequences in observational learning. A child's imitations – actual performance – of various socially approved behaviours are given even greater impetus by praise and encouragement; in other words, they are reinforced by 'social' (or 'symbolic') rewards. S/he will also be more likely to imitate if s/he sees that the model's actions have rewarding or prestigious consequences. Think of the many television characters, watched avidly by children, who achieve outcomes favourable to themselves by violent means.

The symbolic rewards described above regulate behaviour. The child is likely to be willing to obey distasteful social rules because s/he wishes to have his or her parents' approval or avoid their disapproval. Their words of approbation increase his or her self-esteem. And, in this way, s/he develops patterns of behaviour that conform to the social norm. Not all human behaviours require external reinforcements; children often learn to solve problems simply for the pleasure of solving them. Successful imitation may contain its own rewards. Many of our activities and strivings are, in this sense, self-reinforcing.

4. Cognitive learning

The critical role of cognitive processes in childhood learning (e.g. Bruner 1975) led to a reappraisal by many psychologists of the significance of 'private events', and the cognitive mediation of problem behaviour. Thus, we arrive at propositions that thoughts, feelings and behaviour are causally related, and that phenomena such as schemata, attributions, opinions and self-statements require investigation in order to understand children's psychological difficulties (Kendall and Gosch, 1994). This form of learning will reappear in almost all the following chapters.

5. Social learning

Here the emphasis is on the crucial fact that rewards and punishments, and other events, are mediated by human agents and within attachment and social systems, and are not simply the impersonal consequences of behaviour. Children do not simply respond to stimuli; they interpret them. They are relating to, interacting with, and learning from people who have meaning and value for them. They feel antipathetic to some, attached by respect and/or affection to others, and thus may perceive an encouraging word from the latter as rewarding (i.e. positively reinforcing), but from the former as valueless, perhaps even aversive. As Bandura (1977) claims, stimuli influence the likelihood of particular behaviours through their predictive function. Contingent experiences create expectations rather than stimulus-response connections. The failure to comprehend such meanings – as seen, for example, in the child with a semantic-pragmatic disorder or Asperger's disorder – has a devastating effect.

The Adaptive Role of Fear

'Do fears have an adaptive function, and do they facilitate development?' This question put by Ollendick and King (1998) may seem paradoxical. But the answer is 'yes'. Fear is a natural response to events that are threatening to a child's personal security; in fact it is a vital adaptive, indeed survival, reaction which every mother makes use of in training her child to avoid dangers. It can also be adaptive in preparing them to cope with emergency situations. In such crises, the child experiences a variety of physical sensations such as a pounding heart, shivering and trembling, 'butterflies' in the stomach, dry mouth and perspiring hands. These reactions are due to physiological mechanisms built into the body. The physical sensations are by-products of the changes in body chemistry which take place as adrenaline is released into the blood-stream (see chapter 3 on the autonomic nervous system). Consider a cat asleep in the garden. A dog appears. In a moment the cat is alert and ready either to fight or to escape up the nearest tree. This sudden alerting is known as a 'fight–flight' reaction. As soon as the cat sees, hears or smells the dog, a message goes to thalamic centres in its brain, which send out an alert within a split second. Messages also pass to the adrenal glands, where there is an outpouring of adrenaline that keeps the system toned up until the crisis has passed. This defence mechanism is essential to the cat's survival. Without its prompt intervention the cat might well be killed. This same mechanism saved our primitive ancestors from extinction. Cavemen had to be constantly on the alert to protect themselves from animal predators or tribesmen from another territory. Modern men/women retain a modified form of the 'fight–flight' reaction as a built-in device. It comes under the control of the autonomic nervous system.

Today we have less opportunity to fight back, or flee from real dangers, than did our preliterate ancestors. In modern times our fears are more likely to be anxieties about our ability to succeed in a competitive society, about our competence, prestige and status in a complicated social structure, and about our loneliness and lack of significance in the huge impersonal machine of society. Even children are not immune from such worries, exposed as they are to adults' uncertainties while remaining full of their own self-doubts. When the rather disturbing physical sensations already described occur in the absence of objective fear-provoking situations, they are called anxiety attacks. More and more frequently, such attacks are a reaction to the symbols of potential danger. Exams provide a good example. Failure to pass is not a threat to a child's *life*, but it *is* a threat to her or his self-esteem, and it certainly has dangerous implications for their future. Although some people can shrug off such stresses imposed by modern society, the high incidence of neurotic breakdown, in both children and adults, shows that many cannot do so. The consequence of living in a civilized society – where expressions of fear, aggression and resentment must be constantly suppressed – is the development of neurotic attitudes and psychosomatic conditions in vulnerable individuals.

Childish fears

Fear can be produced in infants by making a loud noise behind them or by going through the motions of dropping them. Until s/he is about 6 or 7 months of age, a baby will probably show no concern about being with strangers, but from then on it is quite common for this to change. Babies gradually learn to discriminate between familiar people, like mother, and the other – unknown – people in the world. In many infants, the first fear of separation from mother is quickly followed by a fear of people who are strange or new to them. This fear may generalize, becoming a widespread fear of the unfamiliar and unknown. Later, the situations that pre-school children fear are still mainly those linked to their sense of security and their apprehensions over strangeness and suddenness. Things beyond control – like darkness, large barking dogs, noises, storms, the ocean, the doctor or strange people – are typically feared by youngsters. As children get older, their fears change from the tangible to the intangible. There is an increase in the number of fears of the occult, the dark, being alone, accidents and injuries, bad people, the loss or death of relatives, medical treatment, high places, ridicule and personal failure, and dying or ill health. These fears are generally 'outgrown' in the natural way that the youngster outgrows toys and childish enthusiasms. A summary list provided by Ollendick and King (1991) is given below.

- Infancy
  - Loss of support
  - Loud noises
  - Strangers
  - Things which 'loom up'
- 1- to 2-year-olds
  - Separation from parents
  - Strangers
- 3- to 4-year-olds
  - Darkness
  - Being left alone
  - Insects and small animals
- 5- and 6-year-olds
  - Wild animals
  - Ghosts
  - Monsters
- 7- and 8-year-olds
  - Aspects of school
  - Supernatural events
  - Physical danger
- 9- to 11-year-olds
  - Social fears
  - Fears about wars
  - Health and bodily injury
  - School performance

Generalized Anxiety

Fear and anxiety are not always adaptive, and when extreme (i.e. dysfunctional) they are referred to as generalized anxiety disorder (GAD). It often begins during childhood or adolescence and involves excessive worry and anxiety about such matters as school performance, social relationships, the health of significant others, and events in the world around (see Mattis and Ollendick, 2002). For instance, older children with GAD may worry a good deal of the time about their health, their mother's health, their school work and whether they have made themselves unpopular with their classmates by being courteous to the teachers. Such concerns are likely to be accompanied by additional symptoms, including restlessness, being easily fatigued, difficulty concentrating, irritability, muscle tension, and sleep disturbance. While almost all children and adolescents experience some degree of worry, the worries of a youngster with GAD are disproportionate to reality.

Parental fears

The need to achieve is one of the earliest and most stable human motivational attributes. Sadly, our achievement-oriented society often breeds a fear of failure in children and adolescents, at times amounting to a neurotic disorder. A counterpart of the fear of failure in their carers is a widespread anxiety about their aspiration to be a 'good parent'. Mothers, as the targets of endless media articles and programmes on 'ideal motherhood' are the particular victims of what, essentially, is an undermining message (see p. 57). It is a subversive chimera as no one can define a culture-free unitary gold standard of parenthood, or operationalize 'correct' childcare practices. Not surprisingly, the failure of vulnerable (i.e. non-sceptical) mothers to be wholly effective – 'revealed' particularly, when one has a problematic child – results in anxiety, guilt, and feelings of inadequacy. Fortunately, there is some reassurance in the following words of Bruno Bettelheim:

> In order to raise a child well one ought not try to be a perfect parent as much as one should not expect one's child to be, or become, a perfect individual. Perfection is not within the grasp of ordinary human beings. But it is quite possible to be a good enough parent.
>
> A Good Enough Parent (Knopf-Random House, 1987)

Note: The problem of extreme anxiety that takes the form of panic attacks is discussed in chapter 14.

chapter five

Early Childhood: The Pre-School Stage Socialization and Cognitive Development

The condition of man . . . is a condition of war of everyone against everyone.

Thomas Hobbes (1588–1678): *Leviathan*, Pt. i, Ch. 4

Everything is good when it leaves the Creator's hands;
Everything degenerates in the hands of man.

Jean-Jacques Rousseau (1712–1778): *Emile* I, I

Socialization and Self-Control

Children have to be inducted into the codes of their society by a long and complex process of learning, or socialization. The initially asocial infant is required to develop over the long term, through interaction with caregiving adults, into a mature adult who accepts the norms of his or her society, and who will act upon them without continual supervision. S/he, in turn, will transmit these norms to his or her own children. In addition s/he should be able to understand the function of rules so that s/he is able to contribute to their modification and development.

The human species is unique in having as its main mechanism of social regulation a system of conceptually formulated rules, roles, values and conventions. The child's understanding of these social mores develops and increases in sophistication hand in hand with his or her growing conceptual (cognitive) maturity. The Swiss psychologist Jean Piaget's seminal contribution to our knowledge of the processes involved is discussed below. The norms of conduct, of course, vary widely from culture to culture. Cultural studies of parents' attitudes to parenting, child-rearing practices, and level of involvement in parenting, in Caucasian American, Hispanic American, African

American, Asian American mothers and fathers in two-parent families reveal some variations, but also far more cultural similarities than differences when socioeconomic status is controlled. The finding of similarities is perhaps not surprising given the common American citizenship. Nevertherless, ethnic groups tend to emphasize self-control and doing well in school. They place greater demands and expectations on their children because of the difficulties their children face, as they perceive it, in their journey through life.

The relationship between parental child-rearing strategies and the economic mode of subsistence – gathering-hunting-fishing as opposed to pastoralism-agriculture – have been studied. In the case of the latter (societies preoccupied with food accumulation) children are socialized to be conscientious, compliant, responsible, conservative, to adhere to the rules, and to respect authority. These are attributes likely to ensure the survival of the group. Parents foster obedience by strict discipline and careful monitoring. Children are trained to carry out agricultural tasks and care for the well-being of animals. (Berry et al., 1992.)

By way of contrast, children in communities that rely on daily hunting and food gathering as means of subsistence (a relatively low concern with food accumulation) are socialized to be individualistic, self-reliant, independent, venturesome, imaginative, assertive. The emphasis is on becoming self-sufficient adults. The maintenance systems, social stratification, and economic mode of subsistence are strongly associated with the actions the parents inculcate in their offspring. These are strategies that are functional (i.e. have survival value) for the adult generation-to-come.

Learning and Identification: Social and Moral Awareness

According to contemporary theories a child, through learning and identification, acquires both the content of his or her parents' social expectations, and a willingness to act in accordance with moral codes and rules. Immanuel Kant, in his *Critique of Practical Reason* observed that:

> *Two things fill the mind with ever-increasing wonder and awe,*
> *The more often and the more intensely the mind of thought is drawn to them:*
> *The starry heavens above me and the moral law within me.*

The wonder and awe continue in the minds of scientists to this day, generating a huge research literature. They identify as many as four facets that constitute moral awareness and behaviour:

1. Resistance to temptation: the 'braking' or inhibitory mechanism against misdemeanours that work even when the child is not being observed.

2. Guilt or the acute emotional discomfort that follows transgression and may lead to confession, reparation, or self-blame.
3. Altruism, representing various pro-social acts of kindness, helpfulness, generosity, sympathy, empathy and service to others.
4. Moral belief and insight, covering all aspects of what people think and say about morality, including their willingness to blame others who do wrong.

Each of these components is complex and related one to the other in a complex manner. The evidence concerning resistance to temptation in private suggests a personality trait of some generality. But it is also clear that situational factors exert a powerful influence. According to Wright (1971), the evidence suggests that moral self-restraint is one aspect of a broader control factor, a generalized capacity to check or suppress one's impulses in situations that do not necessarily raise moral issues.

Cognitive processes contribute significantly to these moral and more general control mechanisms. As children grow older they are better able to conceptualize right and wrong; they gradually learn sets of rules taught them by parents and teachers. These developments are facilitated by an interaction with authority figures who behave rationally, and who explain the reasons for their requirements, and by the individual's own experience in taking the role of authority.

Piaget (1932) demonstrated how the logic of children's moral reasoning changes radically from the age of 4 until adolescence. During the early stages of moral development the rules are felt to be absolute; morality is a unilateral system based essentially upon authority and, as such, external to the child. From the age of about 7 years onwards, children increasingly experience relationships that involve mutual respect – relationships between individuals of equal status; thus they meet other children who do not always share their views. By the age of 10 years the system of morality has undergone considerable change so that children now perceive rules to be society-made. Morality is very much a matter of negotiation and compromise; the rules can be changed if agreement can be obtained. With adolescence the young person enters the final phase of moral development when morality is seen as a matter of individual principles.

Piaget believed that the mature understanding of rules goes with an ability to keep them. On this point Kohlberg (1976) is particularly critical of both learning and psychoanalytic approaches to moral development. In his view, behavioural psychology and psychoanalysis have always upheld what he sees as a Philistine view, that fine moral words are one thing and moral deeds another. Kohlberg suggests that morally mature reasoning is quite a different matter, and does not really depend on 'fine words'. The person who understands justice is more likely to practise it. His view of the stages of moral development is outlined in table 5.

Table 5 Kohlberg's stages of moral development

Stage	Level
	1: Pre-conventional reasoning
1	Moral reasoning determined by avoiding punishment and obedience to perceived authority figures
2	Moral reasoning is hedonistic, with consideration only for person's own needs based on the balance of rewards and punishment
	2: Conventional reasoning
3	Individual becomes aware of the needs of other, with relationships becoming the most important factor in moral reasoning
4	Moral reasoning becomes concerned with maintaining society's rules and laws for the sake of upholding society itself
	3: Post-conventional reasoning
5	Individual perceives that society's laws are a contract between themselves and society; however, under certain circumstances laws can be broken
6	Moral reasoning determined by self-chosen ethical principles, and these may over-rule society's laws when they conflict

Social Cognition

This is a term used to describe a field of research and theory related to the area of moral development, one that focuses on the child's understanding of social relationships. Some of the elements of this social cognition are:

- Empathy and role taking: This is the ability to see things from the other person's point of view, i.e. to empathize with them, to feel for them.
- Self-control: Low self-control is characterized by impulsive behaviour, the apparent absence of thought between impulse and action. It is manifested by a failure to stop and think, a failure to learn effective ways of thinking about social situations, and a failure to generate alternative courses of action.
- Social problem solving: Social problem solving refers to the process, in a given social situation, of generating feasible courses of action, considering the various outcomes that might follow, and planning how to achieve the preferred outcome.

Robert Selman, author of *The Growth of Interpersonal Understanding* (1980), is one of the most influential thinkers in this field. He devised a series of stories that describe relationships and dilemmas within relationships. Children hear (or read) these stories and are then asked to say what the characters in the story should, or would do. Based on an analysis of their answers Selman

Table 6 Selman's five levels of social understanding

Approximate age	Level of social understanding	Characteristics of child's social understanding
3–6	0	The child is capable of taking only an egocentric perspective. He or she may realize that other people experience things differently in a physical sense, but cannot yet appreciate that other people feel or think in a different manner from him or herself
5–9	1	The child is now capable of taking a subjective differentiated perspective. He or she appreciates that other people feel and think differently and is aware that people may act differently from how they feel but does not yet realize that other people also perceive the same things about him or her
7–12	2	The child is now capable of adopting a self-reflective and reciprocal perspective. He or she appreciates that there is two-way traffic in social relationships/interactions – that each member of a pair knows the other may think differently ('I know that you know that I know'). Relationships are perceived as being truly reciprocal
10 15	3	The child is capable of adopting a third-person and mutual perspective. At this stage (early formal operations) he or she is able to stand apart from a relationship (i.e. outside it), and view it as if he or she were a third person. Relationships involve mutual coordinations, mutual satisfactions
12–adult	4	The child is now capable of adopting an in-depth and societal-symbolic perspective. The young person understands that other people's actions are influenced by their upbringing, by their personalities, and by social forces. He or she is able to take these factors into account

Adapted from Selman's theorizing (1980)

proposed five stages or levels in children's and adolescents' ability to adopt a social point of view or perspective-taking (see table 6).

Social Compliance

Stayton and her co-workers (1971) make the point that no distinction is made, usually, between the process of learning the rules of society and the

first (and most important) step in the socialization of the child. This occurs
when children develop a *willingness* to do as they are told. What they learn
will depend on the nature of their parents' demands, but the development of
an initial disposition toward compliance may be critical for the effectiveness
of all further attempts at training them. If children lack this tendency they
will remain, in many ways, strangers to their society, unidentified with it,
regarding its rules and values from an external point of view.

Stayton et al. (ibid.) question another assumption. The basic question in
the theory of socialization is put as follows: 'what must be done to children
in order that they will act in accordance with the rules of their society?' The
implication here is that the 80 or 90 per cent of the child population who are
normally socialized have become so only as a result of specific adult interventions designed to foster learning or identification. Atypical or unsocialized
children are seen as instances in which the socialization process has failed.
These theorists reverse the earlier question to: 'what must be done to children
in order to estrange them from their society?' As they point out, when the
question is posed in this way, it turns attention from the problem of socializing the majority, to ways of preventing or correcting the failures of
socialization in a deviant minority.

The authors touch on another assumption that is often taken for granted.
In most treatises on socialization, it is implied that there is a fundamental
antagonism between a child and her or his society, between natural behavioural tendencies and cultural constraints. As they put it, some writers regard
society as inimical to the wholesale development of the person's true nature.
Others consider society as necessarily inhibiting the anarchic impulses of the
individual for the good of the whole. Alternatively, Stayton et al. (ibid.) also
believe (and we have seen some of the experimental evidence in support of
this view) that human beings have evolved as a social species. Infants are
genetically biased toward certain social activities. The family is a microcosm
of society for which infants are pre-adapted; and children are fundamentally
social from the beginning. In other words, a disposition for obedience and
compliance, in fact for socialization in general, is the product of proper social
development rather than the result of a rigorous and specialized training
regimen.

These optimistic and pessimistic polarities find philosophers like Jean-
Jacques Rousseau and Thomas Hobbes at opposite ends of an ideological spectrum regarding the nature of human nature. Parents often adopt similarly
opposing attributions (theories or beliefs) about the nature of children's
behaviour, and the extent to which they should be proactive or reactive in
their parenting role. Some feel that they should take a direct, even intrusive,
part in educating and training their children, in other words strict discip-
linarians, always on the lookout for that naughty little 'demon' to emerge.
Others believe that children are basically good: active learners, who develop
through their own experiences and the niches (such as access to enriching

opportunities) provided for them by their parents and teachers. The child is likened to a plant that should be allowed to flourish without interference, broadly self-directed, apart from the adult provision of emotional and intellectual 'nutrients'.

Stayton et al. (ibid.) add a rider to their general proposition about socially biased children. Clearly, as a child matures, increasing parental intervention becomes necessary. A child will not conform 'naturally' to all the rules of his or her parents or society, no matter how benevolent the home environment may be. Many a parent with a disobedient child (not to mention teachers) may be surprised to hear the more optimistic (some would say romantic) 'nature knows best' metaphor embraced by Rousseau and his present-day acolytes. Perhaps a 'golden mean' exists somewhere between the two philosophical extremes, an understanding by lay-persons – the so-called 'authoritative mothers' – that there are both light *and* dark shades in the make-up of children, the former to be encouraged, the latter discouraged (see Baumrind, 1971).

It is the child's initial willingness to comply that is critical, and this seems to be a natural emergent, but one that will be 'fuelled' powerfully by the affection and respect that accompanies a secure attachment to caregivers. Attachment theorists have extended the 'reach' or influence of early attachment events into adulthood. There is evidence that the attachment patterns of infants and their early relationships with their mothers influence later cognitive and social development (Bowlby, 1969; 1988). (See chapter 11 for a discussion of failures of attachment and faulty socialization.)

The Development of Aggressive Behaviour

In the Freudian canon aggression is an instinct. Repression, in Sigmund Freud's view is the only answer to the development and control of the hostile tendencies of human beings. Albert Einstein conducted an interesting correspondence with Freud on the theme of the inevitability of war. He believed that aggression is learned, and that it should be possible for a society based on pacific values to raise children who find violence antipathetic. War for them would be an alien concept. Freud, after all a man who was of the opinion that civilization is built upon repression, could not agree.

It would not be difficult to construe aggression as inborn instinctive behaviour. Signs of rage are thought to appear in young infants. Facial expressions associated with anger in adults have been seen in infants as young as 4 months old. Although even younger infants do look displeased if thwarted, their expressions cannot be reliably classified as angry by observers. By 7 months of age children are using anger to communicate their feelings and they will turn their face towards their mother even if she is not the cause of their anger.

Young children tend to hit out when frustrated. Typical displays of undirected anger in young children include jumping up and down, breath holding, screaming, and so on. The younger the child, the stronger are its demands for the immediate gratification of all its wants. As the child gets older, random, undirected or unfocused displays of emotional excitement become more rare, and aggression that is retaliatory more frequent. It may consist of throwing objects, grabbing, pinching, biting, striking, calling names, arguing and insisting. A child will perhaps bite when frustrated, an older child may hit or throw something at the frustrating person. It is not easy for young children to learn to 'wait patiently', to 'ask nicely', and to be generous, considerate and self-sacrificing.

Understanding the distinction between hostile and instrumental aggression is important because, as Guerin and Hennessy (2002) point out, it is the key to understanding one of the early changes in the types of aggressive behaviour that children display.

- Instrumental (proactive) aggression is behaviour that is intended to obtain something e.g. pushing a child off a tricycle so that you can have a go yourself.
- Hostile (reactive) aggression aims specifically to inflict harm or hurt on another person.
- The types of aggression that are typically aimed at causing psychological rather than physical harm are referred to as relational aggression and can include exclusion and gossip.

There is now a considerable body of research (reviewed by Guerin and Hennessy) that provides an insight into the way in which aggressive behaviours change as children get older, and the personal, family and neighbourhood influences that are associated with differing levels of aggression. From birth onwards, there are individual differences in assertiveness and passivity that tend to persist in many as they grow older. From early on, children have a repertoire of some 14 'coercive behaviours', including temper tantrums, crying, whining, yelling and commanding, which they use (wittingly or unwittingly) to influence, often quite legitimately, their parents (Patterson, 1982). At times influence develops into outright manipulation and confrontation.

Coercive actions decline steadily in frequency from a high point around 2 down to more moderate levels at the age of school entrance. The older 'aggressive' boy or girl displays coercive behaviours at a level commensurate with a 2- to 3-year-old child and, in this sense, is an exemplar of arrested socialization. What usually happens is that with increasing age, certain coercive activities (e.g. whining, crying, tantrums) are no longer acceptable to parents; these behaviours then become the target for careful monitoring and sanctions, which in turn are accompanied by reductions in their frequency and intensity. By the age of 4, there are substantial improvements in children's ability to hold in check their negative commands, destructiveness and attempts to coerce by aggressive means. By 5, most children use less negativism, non-compliance, and negative physical actions than younger siblings.

Guerin and Hennessy (ibid.) ask whether there are gender differences in the expression of aggression. Are boys more aggressive than girls? Their answer is that it depends on what one means by aggression. If aggression is defined as physical or verbal attack on another person, then research studies suggest that boys are more aggressive than girls. However, if relational aggression is included in the definition there may be fewer sex differences in aggressive behaviour when sibling groups are studied. Dunn's (1984, 2000) investigations showed that boys and girls showed fairly high levels of physical aggression with their siblings. The gender differences first emerge in the pre-school years. During infancy few researchers report any gender differences in aggression, but this changes during the pre-school years. In particular, in naturalistic settings (e.g. in children's homes and preschools) boys have been observed to engage in more verbal and physical conflict and to be more forceful in their use of aggression. Guerin and Hennessy (2002) state that there are a number of possible reasons for these differences:

* Boys are more impulsive than girls, and this may lead them into many more conflicts over the possession of objects.
* Gender differences in aggression may be influenced by girls' greater abilities to use verbal negotiating skills to prevent conflict escalating into aggression.
* The differences may in part be influenced by biological differences, added to by differing social expectations for the display of aggression.
* There are gender differences in the ways in which boys are treated by their parents, particularly fathers. Fathers typically engage in more boisterous and physically energetic play with their sons than with their daughters.

Anxious and insecure attachment patterns have been found to predict problems in the child's later development, and 'pattern D' (disorganized and disorientated) infants appear to be especially at risk for developing aggressive and antisocial behavioural problems. The more serious (atypical) patterns of aggressive activity are discussed in chapter 13.

Sex-Role (Gender) Identity

The term 'sex-role' refers to those psychological characteristics that are *typical* of one sex in contrast to the other – a matter of debate in contemporary society. From birth to 5 years of age children are socialized into their appropriate sex-role (as society defines it). However, the process begins with the chromosomes. Gender is imposed on each individual from the moment when fertilization takes place, when a particular combination of maternal and paternal chromosomes determines the gender of the embryo (see p. 22). It takes several weeks of embryonic life before the first slight signs of sexual differentiation are manifested. The embryo develops without showing any sexual characteristics until the primordia of the sex glands (the gonads) show themselves as masculine or feminine. In human embryos, the rudimentary testes and ovaries can be distinguished by microscopic examination at the sixth week of life.

Clearly, from a psychological perspective, the newborn human is not sexually differentiated. General patterns of sexual behaviour – such as identification with a particular gender, choices of heterosexual, homosexual or bisexual partners, sexual arousal and stimulation, and styles of sexual gratification, are extremely complex in nature. Among atypical conditions is sexual inversion (transsexualism) which refers to the identification with and adoption of the psychological identity of the opposite sex. (See Money, 1993; Rutter, 1971; and chapter 7 for a further examination of this topic.)

Sex-typing

Sex-typing is the process by which the child learns the concept of gender – the behaviour and attitudes thought culturally appropriate to his or her sex. This involves the following:

• Distinguishing between the sexes
• Categorizing themselves as male or female
• Realizing that gender is stable (i.e. not subject to changes from day to day)
• Appreciating that there are critical differences, such as in the genitalia
• Realizing that there are differences, such as the clothes boys and girls wear, which have no effect on gender
• Developing gender 'scripts' which are representations of the things that boys and girls do
• Going on to develop gender 'schemas' – the cognitive structures that are used to organize the categories 'male' and 'female'.

(See Anhall and Morris, 1998; Carr, 1999; Levy and Fivush, 1993.)

Gender identity and sex-role are acquired in childhood in roughly the following chronology:

• Second year of life: child begins to distinguish between 'masculine' and 'feminine'.
• By third year of life: showing preference for one sex-role or the other.
• By 4 years of age: divides the world into male and female people, and is preoccupied with boy/girl distinctions.

- By the age of 7: is passionately committed to shaping his or her behaviour to what is 'appropriate' to his or her biological sex; shows anxiety or anger if accused of behaving like the opposite sex.

Once the standards of sex-role behaviour are learned, they are not easily altered. Rigid and stereotypical sex-roles are being challenged in many Western societies to an extent not acceptable (generally speaking) in Eastern societies.

Genetic, anatomical, hormonal, environmental, cultural and social factors all play a part in determining the huge variety of expressions of human sexuality. The precise importance of these factors, relative to each other, is still arguable. Undoubtedly, as numerous research studies indicate, sex-role behaviour is strongly influenced by parents' rearing of their children (providing differential models, expectations and reinforcers) and by children's identification with, and imitation of, parents (Herbert, 1998a).

Socializing Tasks

The toddler stage of pre-school development challenges children with a host of tasks: physical, social and psychological. They need to achieve a sense of adequacy and learn skills such as locomotion, speech, and how to eat 'properly'. There are many 'don'ts' (too many in some families) to conform to. Children have to learn to check their impulses, irrational, sexual, aggressive and acquisitive. They are forbidden sexual play, and not allowed to hit and hurt other children, or to 'steal'. They are forbidden to lie and cheat. These issues raise the question of the child's dawning comprehension of what is socially appropriate and what is not, and the requirement to exert self-control. In particular at this stage of development there is the need to establish physical control over bladder and bowels.

Toilet training

'Potty training' is the phrase commonly used to describe the steps parents take in helping children to develop bowel and bladder control (a physical achievement) and teaching them where to put faeces and urine (a social skill). Dollard and Miller (1950) point out that within a relatively short space of time the toddler must learn, at the risk of losing his or her mother's esteem, to attach anxiety to all the cues produced by excretory materials, to their sight, smell and touch. They must learn, in addition, to deposit faeces and urine only in a prescribed and secret place, and to clean their body. And later still, they must learn to suppress unnecessary verbal reference to these matters.

Control of the bowels is attained before bladder control. The developmental sequence is generally as follows:

1. Bowel control at night
2. Bowel control during the day
3. Bladder control during the day
4. Bladder control at night.

The sequence may vary for children. Some achieve bowel and bladder control 'simultaneously'. Girls tend to be quicker than boys in becoming continent (i.e. developing control). A child might be considered toilet trained when s/he is able to use the toilet (or potty) reasonably independently, perhaps with assistance over bottom wiping and clothing. Many parents make the issue of toilet training a rod for their own backs. They try too hard, too soon or too late; warfare with the toddler breaks out – perhaps needlessly. Knowledge of the norms (what to expect in typical development), especially the wide range of individual differences, should help parents to feel a bit less hurried and more relaxed about this teaching task.

There is much variation in the age at which children achieve control in different cultures and within our own culture, depending on the expectations of their parents. A study by Kirk Weir (1982) of 706 3-year-olds in an outer London borough, showed the following:

- 23 per cent of boys and 13 per cent of girls were wet by day (wetting more than once a week); 55 per cent of boys and 40 per cent of girls were wet by night, and
- 21 per cent of boys were 'soilers' (i.e. had soiled at least once during the previous month); in the case of girls it was 11 per cent.

Most children have achieved bowel control by both day and night at between 42 and 48 months of age, thus 4 years is a realistic minimum age for judging there to be a problem in bowel control, called encopresis (see chapter 11). The incidence of day and night wetting declines with age. At the age of 5 to 7 years 2 to 4 per cent of children wet (at least once a week) during the day, and approximately 8 per cent are wet at least monthly. There is no one age at which children cease to wet the bed.

There is a gradual decrease in the number of children who wet the bed: from every child at birth, to 1 or 2 in every 100 children at age 15 (see table 7).

Cultural values have an influence on when parents would want their child to stop bed-wetting. In some cultures bed-wetting is not seen as a problem at all, and in others night-time dryness is seen as an important developmental task to achieve as soon as possible. Every newborn comes into the world with an inability to control wetting, either during the day or at night. The young infant's development is such that when his/her bladder

Table 7 Frequency of bed-wetting

Age in years	Approximate number of children in every 100 who wet the bed
2	75
3	40
4	30
5	20
6–9	12
10–12	5
15	1–2

is full of urine an automatic or reflex action occurs and the bladder empties regardless of the time of day or where the child is. As children get older they eventually gain control of their wetting so that they can 'hang on' when they have a full bladder, and delay wetting until they can get to the toilet. For most children this control that they learn during the day transfers to night-time; they learn to hold on for the whole night or to wake up when their bladder is full and take themselves to the toilet.

Five years is a realistic minimum age for judging there to be a problem in bladder control (called diurnal or nocturnal enuresis) – (see chapter 11). The ability to stay dry at night usually occurs after learning to stay dry during the day. Nearly ninety per cent have that skill at 3 years of age. Some children do not begin to develop night-time control until after their third birthday, so there is no need to worry at an earlier stage if a child is somewhat slow to achieve success.

Active training is most effective when the child is 'ready' (generally between 18 and 24 months, probably nearer the latter). There is no one right way of training. There are quite likely to be setbacks. Learning many skills is like learning to ride a bicycle: there may be wobbles, falls and other setbacks before becoming confident and perfect in riding performance.

Toileting skills

James Anthony (1957) describes the complexities of the learning process for the child, reminding us that from the child's eye view, the toilet ritual, as practised by adults, must sometimes appear as an exacting and complex ordeal far removed from the simple evacuations into the nursery pot. It is his or her business, with maternal prompting, to become aware of defecation cues in time, to stop their play in response to them, to inhibit immediate excretion, to search for and find an appropriate place for the purpose, to ensure adequate privacy for themselves, to unfasten their clothes, to establish themselves securely on the toilet seat, and to recognize an end-point to the proceedings. Next they must cleanse themselves satisfactorily, flush the toilet, refasten their clothes, unbolt the door and emerge successfully to resume their disrupted play at the point where they left off. No wonder, for some young children, it hardly seems worth while to go to all that trouble.

Skills required include:

- Having words (e.g. wee/poo) for the urine and faeces, and for the places they are deposited in (e.g. potty, toilet)
- Sitting on the toilet
- Going to the toilet (e.g. indicating need to caregiver, going unaided)
- Managing clothing/wiping at toilet
- Having control (continence)
- Bladder control.

When it comes to bladder training, at 18 months of age most children are physically mature enough to hold their urine for between 1 and 2 hours without much leakage. Their coordination – being able to sit comfortably on the potty or toilet, for example – would be another sign of readiness, and also their ability to understand simple instructions. There are large individual differences in this readiness. Children are expected to achieve satisfactory bladder control during the day by the time they start school. Parents and teachers may tolerate occasional lapses in the infant school, but thereafter an incontinent child is likely to come under increasing social pressure and possibly teasing.

A very high level of skill is needed before the bladder can be properly controlled during sleep. Some children find this a difficult skill to learn, just as some children find it difficult to learn to swim or to ride a bicycle. It is perhaps not surprising that some children do not learn bladder control as infants, or easily lose their ability (especially when under stress) to control the bladder at night. We should perhaps be surprised that so many do manage to learn such a complicated skill, and not surprised that children with disabilities may be delayed. It is likely that unpleasant experiences involving stress and coercion make the learning of bladder control (as with other skills) more difficult.

Bowel control

The control of elimination via the bowels and rectum means the inhibiting of processes which are, at first, completely involuntary. The baby's muscles must mature until they are strong enough and coordinated enough to hold back the waste products that are trying to emerge from his or her body. Of all the muscles in the trunk region, those that control the organs of elimination, are the slowest to come under voluntary control.

The total time required to complete bowel training has been found to be less when it is initiated relatively late. Sears et al. (1957) were able to show that when mothers began bowel training before the child was 5 months old, nearly 10 months (on average) was required for success. But when training was begun later (at 20 months or older) only about 5 months were required. Children whose toilet training was begun between 5 and 14 months, or after 19 months, manifested fewest emotional reactions during training.

Meal-time training

Meal-time problems are a common cause of worry for parents. Typical difficulties are: 'bad table manners', refusing to eat or eating painfully slowly, getting up from the table, finicky eating habits, faddiness, tantruming and crying. The setting for a family should (or could) provide an important opportunity for children to enjoy family life, and learn interactive skills; instead, it seems only too often (especially with pre-school children) to become the occasion for open warfare.

In a London study of 3-year-olds, 16 per cent were judged to have poor appetites, while 12 per cent were considered to be faddy. There were no sex differences in the rate of difficulties, but the problems were found to persist for 1 year in about two-thirds of these children and to continue for over 5 years in about one-third. In a study of 5-year-olds, over one-third of the children were described as having mild or moderate appetite or eating problems. Two-thirds of these were considered to be faddy eaters, while the remainder did not eat enough (cited in Herbert, 1998a).

Personality theorists (notably the Freudians) have always emphasized the importance of early satisfying feeding experiences in the development of personality traits (e.g. oral optimism v. pessimism) and parent–child relationships. During the early weeks after birth, many of an infant's waking hours involve feeding. The feeding situation is an important component of the bonding process between parent and child (see Herbert, Sluckin and Sluckin, 1982). While it is not contentious to suggest that the development of positive feeding patterns is significant to the child's well-being, the fuss made by early theorists about the long-term effects on personality development are nugatory. Of course, this is not to deny that it is important to make a child's feeds as relaxed and pleasant occasions as possible.

Cognitive Development

Of the many ways in which children change and mature on their way to adolescence, perhaps the most fascinating, and most significant, are those to do with cognitive development. Its relevance to socialization and education gives it a particular importance theoretically and practically.

Jean Piaget (1896–1980)

The seminal work in this field is that of Jean Piaget. He developed an open-ended, conversational technique, similar to a clinical interview, for eliciting children's thinking processes. He argued that in order to understand them we have to examine the qualitative development of their ability to solve problems. Piaget likened children to little scientists. He used observations and small-scale experiments, in addition to the conversational dialogues, to enter the children's minds. His approach is basically a biological one (see Piaget, 1950). He proposed that intelligence is an aspect of the person's adaptation to his or her environment. Adaptation is about a person's intellectual striving to establish a state of equilibrium between him/herself and their surroundings. In Piaget's view, the term 'intelligence' has a very specific meaning, namely, the coordination of operations.

An operation is the mental action a person performs in adapting to his or her environment. In Piaget's more technical language '. . . operations are actions which are internalizable, reversible, and coordinated into systems characterized by laws which apply to the system as a whole'. All these systems are governed by the overriding principle of equilibration. This involves putting things into relation with one another so as to achieve a system that is stable, consistent or non-contradictory. As children mature they acquire organized patterns of thought or action that are used to cope with, or explain, some aspect of experience. Piaget uses the term 'organization' to refer to the infant's inborn capacity to coordinate existing patterns of thought and elaborate them into ever more complex systems. Such a system is called a schema.

Adaptations of any kind consist of an interweaving of two processes that Piaget calls 'assimilation' and 'accommodation'.

Assimilation refers to the way children reshape their experience to fit their own level of functioning. They adapt the environment to themselves so that assimilation represents their use of their environment as they conceive it. Experiences will be absorbed to the extent that they can assimilate, preserve and consolidate them in terms of their own subjective experience. When youngsters grasp a stick, they are assimilating the stick to the grasping action (or schema); they are turning the stick into 'something to be grasped'.

Accommodation, by contrast, refers to the way children's experiences reshape their way of behaving. It is really the converse of assimilation, and involves the impact on the child of the actual milieu itself. To accommodate is to perceive and incorporate the experience provided by the environment as it actually is. At the same time that the youngster is assimilating his or her stick, s/he has to accommodate to it, in the sense that the grasping schema has to adapt to the weight, size, length and texture of the stick.

It was Piaget's belief that we continually rely on the complementary processes of assimilation and accommodation to adapt to our environment. Children's intellectual development is reflected by the complexity of their schematic structure. This is influenced by the variety of environmental objects which are available for them to assimilate and which simultaneously produce accommodation. If you watch children at play, using mud and blocks of wood, you will notice that they create them to their imagined theme in a manner that has assimilation operating at a maximum, while accommodation is at a minimum. On the other hand, accommodation to what an adult says or does is functioning at a maximum, while assimilation is at a minimum.

Piaget partitions intellectual development into stages, or periods of growth, on the route to what he refers to as adult thought. These are arbitrary divisions, because development is a continuous process, but they provide a convenient way of viewing the nature of changes in intelligence and thinking as these take place. The growth of intellect is measured by the increasing use of accommodation: the ability to alter old strategies or make new ones to solve unfamiliar problems. Flexibility of thinking is the key to this concept of intelligence.

In a child's intellectual development from his or her birth until maturity, four main periods are distinguished. These periods, although they can only be related to approximate age ranges, come in a fixed order – what Piaget called an invariant developmental sequence. They appear earlier or later, depending on the individual child. It is better to think of them in conjunction with the child's mental age, rather than his or her chronological age, since some intellectually impaired children never reach the higher levels of intellectual development. Children cannot skip stages because each successive stage builds on the previous stage and represents a more complex level of thought.

1. THE SENSORIMOTOR STAGE

The first stage, which Piaget calls the period of sensorimotor intelligence, lasts until a child is somewhere between 18 months and 2 years old. During this period, the foundation for thought is laid down. The infant uses sensory and motor capabilities to explore, and s/he learns to identify the main features of the world about them. At first, infants have no knowledge that a world 'out there' exists; they are only aware of their own feelings. Piaget, in his 1954 study, *The Construction of Reality in the Child*, called this stage of affairs, in which the baby's world is centred upon him/herself without being aware of themselves at the centre of something else, *egocentrism*. Infants are unaware that objects cohere and persist, and that the world works by external laws rather than by their actions.

Pinker (1997) likens infants to the man in the limerick 'skit' on the idealist philosophy of Berkeley:

> *There once was a man who said 'God*
> *Must think it exceedingly odd*
> *If he finds that this tree*
> *Continues to be*
> *When there's no one about in the Quad'.*

During this period, babies seem to become intrigued (and delighted) with the mastery of such 'simple' responses as picking up things, blowing, falling backwards on a cushion, and making certain sounds. Their intelligence is displayed in their actions. A major development is the acquisition of a primitive sense of 'self'; another is the development of object permanence – the understanding that objects continue to exist when they are out of sight. Children now begin to internalize behavioural schema so as to produce images or mental schema.

Piaget's observations of infants during the sensorimotor stage have been confirmed, by and large, by subsequent researchers. However they suggest that he probably underestimated children's mental capacity to organize the sensory and motor information they absorb (e.g. Baillargeon and De Vos, 1991).

2. THE PRE-OPERATIONAL STAGE

The second stage called the pre-operational stage lasts from around 2 to 7 years of age. Piaget (1950) describes the intellectual development of the toddler as occupying this stage. It divides into two periods:

1. The pre-conceptual stage lasts until children are about 4 years old. They learn the basic use of language for simple communication. Children are continually investigating; they discover new symbols such as how a stick can represent a sword. They become imaginative in their play activities. As yet their thought is not organized into concepts and rules. Several systematic errors in basic logic appear in children's thinking. One of these is the error of realism that refers to their conviction that everything they see is viewed in the same way by other individuals.

2. Intuitive thinking comes next and is a phase during which children wrestle with problems regarding the interpretation of their environment. They are now using language in a more complex and subtle manner. Piaget argues that thought shapes language far more than lan-

guage shapes thought at this stage. Deaf children are able to reason and solve problems despite limitations in their language. Children are intuitive about relationships because they cannot give reasons. They can say 'Daddy is Mummy's husband', but they cannot say why this is so.

Although the pre-operational child can represent things and events to him or herself, s/he cannot differentiate between the general and the particular, so their reasoning leads them into some fascinating fallacies. Children are still without true concepts. There are as yet many limitations to their development of logical thinking, consistent explanations and coherent arguments.

Piaget was correct in pointing out difficulties that pre-operational children have with conservation and other reasoning and problem-solving tasks. They often judge that a piece of clay is 'more' if it is rolled from a spherical shape into a long cylindrical shape. Later researchers have discovered that given appropriate contextual cues and wording, young children are more competent at these earlier than was thought possible by Piaget (e.g. Donaldson, 1978).

3. THE CONCRETE OPERATIONAL STAGE

Piaget's third stage covers roughly the period from 7 to 11 or 12, and is one of concrete operational thinking. In the second stage, children began to think in language, but now they manage to see events from different perspectives. They have acquired concepts involving complex relationships. Very important is the fact that they now have a mental representation of a series of actions. The youngster now has the mental capacity to order experience, and relate it to an organized whole, but at first only in relation to objects that form a familiar part of his or her environment. Nevertheless, thinking has become much more familiar because of its wider focus on different aspects of a task at the same time. Many of Piaget's ideas of developments at this stage have been confirmed by subsequent experimentation.

4. THE FORMAL PROPOSITIONAL STAGE

The fundamental difference between the period of concrete operational thinking and Piaget's fourth stage of formal propositional thinking has to do with the real and the possible. It is during adolescence (roughly the years from 11 or 12 to 15) that children begin to free their thinking from its roots in their own particular experiences. Logical thinking is no longer restricted to the concrete or the observable. Adolescents' cognitive operations are reorganized in a way to permit them to operate on operations, or to put it another way, to think about thinking and thinkers. They become capable of general propositional thinking. Thought is now systematic. (We return to this in chapter 7.)

Piaget's theory has had an enormous impact on the knowledge base of developmental psychology (Beilin, 1992). But it hasn't escaped criticism. Later research indicates that the achievement of formal operational thinking is more gradual and haphazard than Piaget assumed (e.g. King, 1985; Martorano, 1977). The notion of universal and invariant stages has been challenged (Bjorklund, 1995) at both the level of theory and research. Piaget thought of cognitive development as a spontaneous process that did not necessarily depend on direct instruction from adults. His theory depicting children as learning primarily from interactions with, and explorations of, the environment, have had (critics like Pinker maintain) an invidious influence on some aspects of educational practice, notably where a more didactic approach is appropriate. (See Case and Okamoto, 1996, for an elaboration of Piagetian theory.)

Lev Vygotsky (1896–1934)

The Soviet psychologist Lev Vygotsky's writings have had a significant influence since their relatively recent translation into English (1962). Vygotsky was deeply affected by Marxist ideas and thought of cognitive development as a socially mediated process achieved through interactions with, and instructions from, knowledgeable members of the community. He believed that the dialectic, the discussion and reasoning that occur in cooperative social dialogues between children and their socializing agents, were crucial to children's understanding of culturally significant activities. Piaget largely excluded the role of significant cultural and social influences on human development, in his theorizing.

Cultural variations

An interesting example of the risk of such an omission is provided by a demonstration of how context gave Zimbabwean (Harare) children of 9 a more advanced understanding of economic principles than their British equivalents. Using a mock shop and a shopping game, it was shown how the Harare children, who were involved in their parents' small businesses, possessed the motivation to understand concepts of profit and loss. The British children, unlike their counterparts, had not mastered key trading principles and strategies such as buying for less than the price that one sells at, or the setting aside of profit for the purchase of new goods to sell.

Although the development of similar thinking patterns to those described by Piaget are to be found in other cultures such as the USA, Africa, UK and

China (e.g. Goodnow, 1969), there are those who argue that some of the tasks are culture-bound. They are thought of as reflecting cognitive styles demanded by Western industrialized societies. The methodology lacks clarity in the language used or the context provided (Donaldson, 1978). Researchers have demonstrated that when the task and its context are made clear to children, they may be able to exhibit logical thought well before the limits suggested by Piaget.

To be fair, he did recognize that there may be unevenness in development in his stage theory. A child can achieve conservation of liquids but may fail at a class inclusion task. Conservation of number precedes others, particularly that of weight. Piaget termed this uneven development horizontal *decalage*. When counting procedures are modified, 3-year-olds demonstrate an understanding of number conservation concepts (Gelman, 1972). Children as young as $2\frac{1}{2}$ can understand some basic principles of counting (Gelman, 1979).

Vocabulary

The ability of the toddler to communicate is now developing at a fast and accelerating rate. The average child at the age of $2\frac{1}{2}$ comprehends some 1000 words and has a vocabulary of around 600 words; by the age of 5 or 6 it has increased to about 15,000 words (Pinker, 1994). By the age of 3 children have the wherewithal to form sentences and carry on a conversation (Bloom, 1991), a development that appears to require a vocabulary of 100 to 200 words. By 24 months the longest sentences include four and five words; by 30 months sentence length has almost doubled. This is critical in facilitating the social training (socialization) mediated by parents and other caregivers.

Play

Play is the natural medium of childhood and another significant facet of social development. But is it spontaneous or an end in itself? Does it have a purpose? Philosophers and psychologists have puzzled over these and many other questions over many years. For them, play is serious business. The first person to advocate the study of children's play in order to understand and educate them, was Rousseau in the eighteenth century. For Herbert Spencer (1878) play was important for its role in allowing children to expend their 'surplus energy'. Karly Groos (1901) was of the opinion that play offered children the opportunity to rehearse survival skills that would be required in later life. Many theories have been advanced since then to explain the meaning and utility of play in childhood. Anna Freud (1946) believed that through the interpretation of play and its symbolism (as with dreams) the therapist could enter the enter the child's inner life and unravel the child's conflicts. Virginia Axline (1947a) provides a fascinating account of play therapy at work in her analysis of a child named Dibs.

All of this emphasis on the social significance of play is rather solemn; after all, play is meant to be fun. Nevertheless, while children are enjoying their games, they do learn about rules and the norms of their culture. The naturalistic nature of children's play provides an unmatched arena for observing them being themselves, and for assessing functional abilities in all developmental domains. Structured experimental play sessions have produced many insights into children's views of the world, their preoccupations, and attitudes and relationships (e.g. Bandura, 1969). The so-called 'projective techniques' used to study personality depend on unstructured play, story-telling, picture-completions, drawing and painting (Anastasi, 1987).

Given that play changes as the child matures an understanding of the typical developmental patterns will benefit a clinician's assessment of the implications of a child's atypical problems. Parten (1932), observing young children's play in nursery school, concluded that social development proceeds in three stages:

1. Solitary play (involving non-sociable play behaviour)
2. Parallel play (limited side-by-side social participation)
3. Cooperative social play.

This seems to be an oversimplification. Children do not simply evolve from one stage to the next. Rather, the distribution of time they spend within each mode of play changes as they grow older.

Piaget proposed that children's play progresses through three stages as they get older:

1. Practice play (the first 2 years of life): This involves the simple repetition of different actions for what Piaget calls 'functional pleasure'. A child who engages in functional play with repetitive immature motor actions as his or her preferred play mode may be exhibiting a delay in cognitive social development.
2. Symbolic play: The use of different symbols is the major achievement of the pre-school stage of development. Symbolic play occurs when the child transforms the physical environment into make-believe, pretend play, beginning at around 18 months and reaching a peak at 4 to 5 years. It takes him or her into the world of fantasy.
3. The increasing organization of make-believe play culminates in what Piaget called 'games with rules' at the age of around 6 or 7 years. They

may be made-up games with spontaneously created rules. They may be games like football and cricket with rules that are formal and public.

Undoubtedly free play promotes creative thinking ability and problem-solving skills. And, as the American philosopher and poet Ralph Waldo Emerson wrote in his *Journals* (1834), 'it is a happy talent to know how to play'.

Theory of Mind

Children begin to attribute mental states to themselves (and others) and use language in a variety of ways to indicate these states of mind (Wellman, 1990). Leslie (1987) proposes that it is only from the second year of life that the normal child unequivocally displays this ability. The first clear manifestation is the emergence of pretence. (Autistic children have serious difficulties with pretence, a matter discussed in chapter 15.) In the following 2 or 3 years a representational second-order *theory of mind* develops so that a child comes to understand that mental states are interpretations of the world that may be true or false and which influence individuals in choosing appropriate or inappropriate actions. Second-order representations are involved in many accomplishments such as thinking and reasoning about the content of one's own and other people's minds (referred to as 'mentalizing'). The systematic application of mentalizing arises from the individual's theory of mind, a calamitous lack, as we shall see, in autistic children.

Research on theory of mind developed from efforts to determine whether chimpanzees are aware that individuals experience cognitive and emotional states (Premack and Woodruff (1978). The contentious conclusion that chimpanzees do have a theory of mind meant an implicitly invidious comparison with deaf children, who were said to be delayed in developing a theory of mind. Marschark (1993) has challenged this claim (convincingly if not absolutely) by examining stories told by deaf and contrast hearing children, rather than by the most often used 'false belief task' (see appendix I for a reference to a variety of FBT assessment methods).

Children typically develop a theory of mind with profound effects on social life and on communication in general. Such a theory allows children to interpret overt behaviour by reference to invisible mental states. In this way they can distinguish 'really meaning it' from 'just pretending'. If there should be a fault in metarepresentational ability (the ability to form second-order representations), this would be devastating for the development of a theory of mind. Without a theory of mind such everyday social nuances as pretend, deception and bluff would be incomprehensible. The idea that there is a way of knowing what 'makes people tick' would be

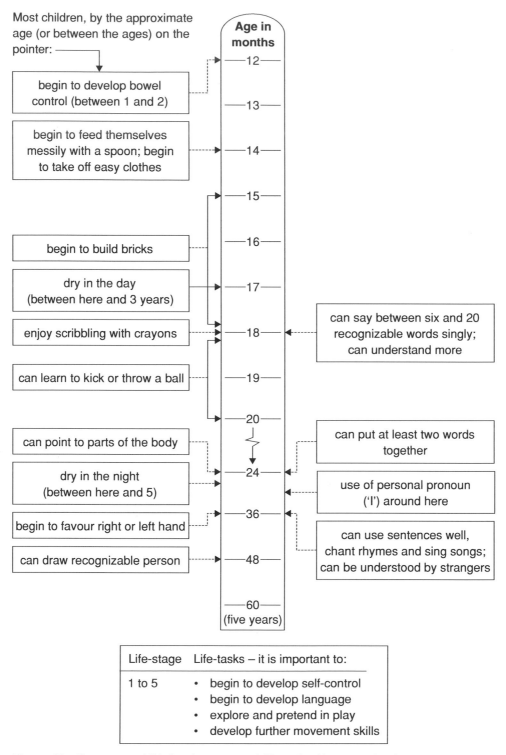

Most children, by the approximate age (or between the ages) on the pointer:

Age in months

begin to develop bowel control (between 1 and 2)

—12—

—13—

begin to feed themselves messily with a spoon; begin to take off easy clothes

—14—

—15—

begin to build bricks

—16—

dry in the day (between here and 3 years)

—17—

enjoy scribbling with crayons

—18—

can say between six and 20 recognizable words singly; can understand more

can learn to kick or throw a ball

—19—

—20—

can point to parts of the body

can put at least two words together

dry in the night (between here and 5)

—24—

use of personal pronoun ('I') around here

begin to favour right or left hand

—36—

can draw recognizable person

—48—

can use sentences well, chant rhymes and sing songs; can be understood by strangers

—60— (five years)

Life-stage	Life-tasks – it is important to:
1 to 5	• begin to develop self-control • begin to develop language • explore and pretend in play • develop further movement skills

Figure 18 Summary: child development and life-tasks (the pre-school years)

totally alien. This subject is pursued further when we discuss autism in chapter 15.

The pre-school years have been notable for the changes and skills demanded of the child. A sample of these tasks is described in figure 18.

Note: The atypical aspects of this stage of development are discussed in chapter 11.

chapter six

Middle and Late Childhood
The School-Going Child

We are moulded and remoulded by those who have loved us; and
though the love may pass, we are nevertheless their work, for good
or ill.

Francois Mauriac

Developing a New Individuality

The years of middle childhood are notable as a period in which youngsters'
interactions with the people in their home and school environments help
them to shape their personality, their individuality. The seriousness with
which life is approached through work, and a preoccupation with what can
be achieved, assist them to develop a sense of industry. In Erikson's (1965)
framework of psychosocial development, the theme of this period of life is in
a sense of duty and accomplishment – laying aside fantasy and play and
undertaking real tasks, developing academic and social competencies. There
is a human need called 'effectance motivation', a powerful desire to learn
and exercise skills, to carry out constructive tasks, and to do them well.
When successful, such circumstances – alongside the genetic factors that are
thought to account for about half of the variation in *happiness* from person to
person – contribute to children's enjoyment of life.

Erikson maintains that children like to be mildly but firmly coerced at this
stage into the adventure of discovering that they can learn to accomplish
what they would never have thought of themselves. Such things owe their
attractiveness to the very fact that they are not the product of fantasy but
the product of reality, practicability, and logic. They provide a token of sense
of participation in the real world of adults. Children are therefore probably
as amenable as they are ever likely to be, to learning, and open to the
direction and inspiration of others. What gets in the way of such readiness or
subsequent achievements are emotional problems, excessive competition,
personal limitations, or other conditions that lead to experiences of failure.

These may result in crises leading to feelings of inferiority and poor work habits. If the child fails to develop skills and social competencies she or he is likely to suffer a sense of inadequacy or incompetence.

Elkind (1967) described the pragmatic-optimistic nature of school-aged children. The pragmatism shows itself in their concern with how things work, and how to produce things of meaning and value that will receive the approval of others. Success in small endeavours feeds a sense of optimism about mastering new skills and acquiring new abilities. A source of this optimism for children according to Elkind, is their belief that there are unlimited years in which to attain their goals, and to master the skills necessary to become an adult. The pragmatism that accompanies this optimism about themselves results in an attitude that persistent effort at a task eventually ends in its accomplishment. Achievement motivation is one of the earliest and most stable attributes displayed by children, especially if 'fuelled' by parental encouragement and/or pressure (McClelland, 1961).

The ever-increasing importance of social and extrafamilial influences in the child's life has been discernible in the earlier developmental phases described in previous chapters. In order to achieve trust, autonomy and initiative it was necessary for the child to mix with an increasing number of people. Now, by going to school, his or her social universe is significantly extended. Where previously the parents and family were the main agents of socialization, in middle childhood, teachers, friends and peers now become important additional social influences. However, in many ways, children of this age turn their backs on adults and become immersed in the community of children. There are fairly crucial implications in the balance of power between parents and 'outsiders'. If the balance is tilted too much in favour of peer group influence or too much to parental influence, the effects tend to be undesirable (Herbert, 1987b). The inability or failure to make friends can have serious consequences for the child, a matter dealt with below.

There is a marked contrast between the playful existence of the pre-school child with a nurturant mother near at hand, and the life of the school-going youngster. Even in today's more informal play and nursery schools, children are faced with exacting disciplines and intellectual demands which can constitute quite an ordeal. The stresses of the new situation are often too much for the overly dependent child. During these long hours in the classroom there is no appeal to a protective mother. The child is forced to rely on his or her own resources although they may (if the teacher lets them) relate to 'her' in a clinging manner, as a surrogate mother.

Most parents have had to cope, and successfully by and large, with the occasional reluctance of their children to go to school. But there is a group of children whose determination goes beyond mere reluctance to set off for school. They dig their heels in, and no one can budge them. We are no longer dealing with 'typical' reluctance to go to school, but the untypical problem of a school refusal, a subject for chapter 12.

It is no exaggeration to say that the key to children's happiness at school, and therefore to the effectiveness with which they learn, is the teacher. The 12-year-olds who were questioned in Moore's study in 1966, regarded the schools they had attended primarily in terms of how the teachers had treated them. The qualities they appreciated in a teacher were helpfulness, clear explanations, firmness in keeping order, fairness, humour, kindliness and good manners towards the class. They resented anything they saw as unfair: shouting, ranting and grumbling in the class, confusing instructions, boring teaching, physical punishment and, most of all, humiliation of individual children. Teachers' attitudes in any school are bound to vary, and different teachers suit different children. Inevitably, there is an element of chance in all this. In general, from about the age of 7 on, it is probably a good learning situation for a child to have to adapt to teachers of varying personalities.

In many studies, a teacher's behaviour has been shown to be an enormously powerful influence – affecting the social and emotional climate of the classroom, and the status relationships among the children (see Goldstein, 1995). It also affects the individual child's behaviours, moral attitudes and intellectual performance. The primary-school teacher influences not only the child on whom she is focusing her attention, but the onlookers as well. If the teacher delegates some of her authority and power, and if her acceptance of the pupils in the classroom is widespread and not confined to a few 'pets', she is able to increase the social and intellectual interactions between her pupils. In this way she is able to reduce conflict and anxiety in the children. Such democratic behaviour is claimed to stimulate independent working habits, independent thought, and a sense of moral responsibility.

Rules and Values

Schools are in a powerful position to exert influence on their students; children spend almost as much of their waking life at school as at home. They enter an environment providing work and play for nearly a dozen years. The school introduces boys and girls to social and working relationships and to various forms of authority that they would not experience in the family. The areas of academic success, social behaviour, moral values and occupational choice represent major spheres of influence by teachers as well as parents in the socialization of young people. Rutter and a team of researchers, in their 1979 study of London secondary schools, found that children and adolescents are more likely to show socially acceptable behaviour and good scholastic attainment if they attend certain schools (regardless of their catchment area) rather than others (Rutter, Maughan, et al., 1979).

The strong 'message' to emerge was that school values and norms appear to be more effective if it is clear to all that they have widespread support. Discipline is easier to maintain if the pupils appreciate that it relates to generally accepted approaches and does not simply represent the whims of the individual teacher. The particular rules which are set and the specific disciplinary techniques which are used are probably much less important than the establishment of some principles and guidelines which are clearly recognizable, and accepted by the school as a whole.

Expectations of Parents

A study by Okagaki and Sternberg (1993) explored the difference between parental and school expectations with regard to appropriate child behaviour. Immigrant parents from Cambodia, Mexico, the Philippines, Vietnam, and native-born Anglo-Americans and Mexican Americans with children in kindergarten through first grade were asked a series of questions. They covered their child-rearing beliefs, their expectations for their children's school behaviour, their beliefs about what teachers should teach children, and their perceptions of the characteristics of an intelligent child. The results revealed that immigrant parents believed that it was more important for a child to conform to external standards than to develop autonomous behaviour. However, American-born parents perceived it was more important for a child to develop autonomy than to conform to external standards. Furthermore, parents from all immigrant groups perceived that non-cognitive characteristics, such as motivation and practical school skills, were either more important or as important as cognitive characteristics, such as problem-solving skills and verbal ability.

Commitment to education

There is evidence (e.g. Stigler, Lee and Stevenson, 1987; Chen and Stevenson, 1995; Stevenson, Chen and Lee, 1993) that Asian students spend more time being educated than American students – 95 per cent v. 80 per cent of their time 'on-task' such as listening to the teacher and completing assignments. They are encouraged, supervised and coerced to a high degree by parents who are strongly committed to the educational process. They express higher expectations for their children than American parents, and communicate frequently with the school about their offspring's progress. The consequence of such a commitment to education appears to be the outperforming of American school children by scholars in China, Taiwan and Japan, in mathematics, reading and other subjects (e.g. Geary et al., 1996; Stevenson, Chen and Lee, 1993).

Social Skills and Friendships

Apart from the obvious skills such as learning to read and write, crossing the road safely, counting the correct change, and developing good judgement, there are social skills which, because they are not obvious or readily taught, come hard to some youngsters. These are the skills that we use when we meet strangers, make small talk, encourage acquaintanceship, attract friends and fit in with groups of people.

Youngsters who cannot get on with other children, who are lacking in social skills, who are clumsy or shy, often lead miserable and lonely lives. They may lack the vital skills of social sensitivity, 'small talk', and of forming accurate impressions of other people – the foundations upon which personal liking, leading to the attraction of acquaintances, and thereby friendship, is built. Children who are the most popular or influential members of groups, and the most effective leaders, tend to have these attributes in abundance. Of course there are children who possess the requisite social skills but have little opportunity to practise them and thus gain confidence.

The process by which people are initially attracted to each other and finally become friends, can be represented symbolically by a 'funnel' with a series of filters in it. Each person has such a figurative 'funnel', with filters designed to fit his/her particular criteria for a friend. At the opening of the funnel is the first criterion, proximity, which determines the eligibles. Before any kind of attraction can be established there must be opportunity for the children to come into contact. Ordinarily, friendships evolve out of some direct face-to-face contact. Children who live close to one another are more likely to become friends than those who live some distance apart, and children who interact frequently are more likely to become friends than those who interact rarely. Youngsters who live in isolated areas, or whose parents artificially isolate them from other children, may have difficulty in making friends. The pool of eligibles is too limited.

Homogamy ('like attracts like')

Further filters will work to narrow the field gradually. In general, the filters select 'similar individual characteristics', 'common interests or values', and 'similar personality'. Someone who successfully passes through these filters becomes a friend. The second filter works on the basis that like attracts like. There is little or no evidence that opposites attract in children's friendships. Pairs of friends, in fact, tend to resemble each other in several respects: social maturity, age, weight, height and general intelligence. Friendly, energetic, capable, responsive and daring youngsters are attracted to each other, possibly because they understand one another and can fulfil their mutual needs.

Friendship choices are influenced to a significant extent by similarities in social background, religious affiliations and ethnic-group membership. The most significant influence on the formation of friendships is the belief that another is similar to oneself; this is more important than whether or not he or she is actually similar. Children also tend to choose as friends those with characteristics considered desirable in terms of the values of their group. Children at this stage tend to choose friends from those who live in the same neighbourhood, or who are in the same class at school, and who are about the same age. Even at this tender age children tend to choose friends who have the same status as themselves. In choosing friends, primary school children (after the age of 8 or so) prefer members of their own sex. Clearly, the second 'filter' suggests that birds of feather do flock together.

Some children are attracted to others whose needs complement their own, although this is rare. For example, a dominant child may become friendly with someone who is predominantly submissive, but the principle that 'opposites attract' is the exception, not the rule. Research workers have demonstrated that persons tend to choose others whom they perceive as choosing *them*. In other words, people like others who they believe view them in a favourable light.

Popularity and unpopularity

Friendship patterns change with age. Psychologists who have conducted investigations of school and playground friendships find that friendly contacts between children increase between the ages of 2 and 5. During these years, children form their first friendships, generally, but not exclusively, with members of their own sex. Popular children can be distinguished as early as the nursery school phase. They are frequently sought out as playmates, while others are frequently ignored. Some are systematically shunned by their peers (see chapter 12). However, evidence shows that, in general, the interaction of pre-school or nursery school children is characteristically more friendly and cooperative than hostile and competitive and, indeed, even the most aggressive youngsters at this stage make more friendly than aggressive overtures to other children. Friendships at this age are relatively casual, transient and unstable, and they probably have few important or enduring effects on a child's personality.

After 5, the development is towards closer attachment to a few special children though, at this stage, peers in general become very important. When asked to name their best friends, youngsters often choose children with highly esteemed personality traits. The older ones in this age range emphasize friendliness, cheerfulness, tidiness and cleanliness.

In middle childhood friendships are fairly unstable; interests change easily at this period, and 'old' friends may be unable to satisfy new needs. The capacity for building lasting friendships gradually increases during childhood and adolescence. As the child grows older, interests become focused, and friendships gradually increase in quality, depth and reciprocity, and are therefore much more likely to be enduring. Below the age of 11 or 12, girls are more socially active than boys, and tend to establish more intimate and confidential relationships with each other. The capacity of the older child to form friendships, and to maintain them on the basis of meeting others' needs as well as his or her own, is thought to be a strong indication of developing social maturity.

Psychologists, have used a technique called sociometry to explore the choices children make of a 'best friend', and the nature of the attraction of particular children. Pupils in a class may be asked to choose a partner to share a desk, to help with a project, or to ask to a party. In a typical class, about one child in five turns out to be an isolate. None of his classmates chooses him. Such children usually have personality problems, both as a cause and as a consequence of rejection. Unpopularity is a feature associated with bullying. At the other extreme, most groups have a few popular members, chosen by many of their classmates.

It is important to distinguish popularity – general attractiveness to others – from the ability to form specific friendships. The psychological factors associated with one are not necessarily associated with the other. Popular children may have many admirers but few friends. Being singled out for admiration by many may even tend to isolate a person from close personal relationships. This is especially so if the qualities or accomplishments that invite popularity are envied by others who lack such gifts. It is also possible that the psychological components that initially attract one person to another are not those that lead to lasting friendships and sustained loyalties.

Exchange Theory

Immature, self-centred children are not always able to manage the give-and-take of friendship. What is called 'exchange theory' gives us pointers to why this should be so; it provides one method of evaluating friendships. In this theoretical model, social interactions and relationships are compared to economic bargains or the exchange of gifts; they are seen as a ratio of rewards and costs. All activities carried out by one individual, to the benefit of another, are termed 'rewards', while detrimental activities – hostility, anxiety and embarrassment – are counted as 'costs'. If a child forgoes a reward (e.g. loses the approval of his family) because he engages in some form of social interaction (e.g. associating with a delinquent), this, too, is termed a cost. The ratio of rewards to costs is called the 'outcome'. If the outcome is positive, it may be said to yield a 'profit', if negative, it is termed a 'loss'. So, before we can be said to be attracted to a potential friend, the 'reward-cost outcome' must be above the 'comparison level', a standard against which satisfaction is judged. Selfish or aggressive people, by their actions, tilt the balance towards the loss or debit side.

Siblings: The Longest Lasting Relationships

Around 80 per cent of people in the UK and the USA have grown up with brothers and sisters, and as Judy Dunn (2000) observes, our relationships with our siblings are quite likely to be the longest lasting (longer than our parents or partners) we will ever have. Development is influenced by the intensity and intimacy of sharing a home, parents, and each other's company (often benign, sometimes hostile) for years on end. In the latter case, the outcome may be the fostering of aggression, feelings of inadequacy and low self-esteem. In the former, affectionate, supportive and companionable interactions are a bonus to the young person's development. Relationships, which are frequently a mixture of both, and which often change as the siblings mature, contribute to their social understandings and skills.

Patterson (1982) has shown that siblings reinforce each other's aggressive behaviour by retaliating, teasing and escalating conflict. There are links between sibling influence and deviant behaviour in adolescents (see chapter 13). As mentioned earlier, the arrival of a sibling is consistently found to be linked to increased problems for first-born children: sleeping problems, feeding and toilet problems in young children, withdrawal, dependency and anxiety have all been reported (Dunn, 1993). Obviously, adjustment problems are not simply attributable to misconceived parental actions, but also the effect of poor sibling relationships (see Dunn, 2000, for a detailed review of this area).

Note: There is more detail about children who lack social skills in chapter 12.

chapter seven

Adolescence: Leaving Childhood Behind

Lousy stinking school on Thursday. I tried my old uniform on, but I have outgrown it so badly that my father is being forced to buy me a new one tomorrow. He is going up the wall but I can't help it if my body is in a growth period can I? I am only five centimetres shorter than Pandora now. My thing remains static at twelve centimetres.
Sue Townsend: *The Secret Diary of Adrian Mole Aged 13¾*

The Changes of Puberty

Adrian Mole, tormented teenage 'offspring' of author Sue Townsend's imagination, manifests in this fragment from his diary several common adolescent preoccupations: bodily changes, genitalia, school, relationships with parents and, not least, himself and the opposite sex. To use an old cliché, Adrian is in a stage of 'transition', between childhood and adulthood. If he is confused, so are the adults when it comes to describing the boundaries defining adolescence. It is revealed by metaphors such as the 'in-between stage', and the 'no-man's land between childhood and adolescence'. It has also been referred to as a 'tunnel' into which young people disappear, displaying certain kinds of character. They are then 'lost to sight' for a few years. According to this metaphor you never know what is going to emerge at the other end – a daunting prospect for parents and teachers (if true) when they've put so much time, effort and affection, into preparing the children in their care for adulthood.

That there is necessarily a stage of transition from 'irresponsibility' to 'responsibility' has been widely, but not universally accepted. Age does not have the same significance in all eras or cultures. Some cultures, notably preliterate ones, had 'rites of passage' that took children directly from their childhood to adult status. Others, as in the West, extend the dependency of childhood (because of the cost of housing, unemployment or higher education) into an adolescence lasting into the mid-twenties. The St Lawrence Eskimos simply distinguish boys from men and girls from women, following the tradition of many preliterate societies that identify puberty as the point of transition from childhood to adulthood. Some theorists reject altogether the notion of adolescence as a distinct stage of development. They repudiate the idea that at puberty every child somehow takes on a qualitatively different persona, or engages in radically different developmental tasks, more or less overnight. Rather the child grows by imperceptible degrees into a teenager, and the adolescent turns by degrees into an adult. Others disagree.

The fact is that many parents await their child's approaching adulthood with a sense of gloomy foreboding. They anticipate the adolescent years as something to be confronted rather than shared. It is often the case that they are apprehensive that they may 'lose' the closeness, the affection, and the degree of parental authority they feel to be important in the relationship with their son or daughter. Although in Western societies this may be a common parental expectation (apprehension) that their children's adolescence will be marked by challenges to their authority, in societies where filial piety and respect between members of a family are encouraged, indeed insisted on, conflict between parents and the 'young adults' is not anticipated. Confrontations may occur, however, where there is a cultural mismatch between the values of (say) older generation immigrants to a Western society, and attitudes their offspring are absorbing from peers at school and elsewhere.

Of course, adolescence can be traumatic for some individuals, but it is by no means necessarily so. Nor is it some 'alien land' through which all children have to travel. The popular (and professional) notion that adolescence *is* different from the whole of development which precedes it, and the whole of development which follows it, is of relatively recent origin. Among the early proponents of this view was G. Stanley Hall in his 1904 treatise on the subject, *Adolescence: Its psychology and its relationship to physiology, anthropology, sociology, sex, crime, religion and education*. His belief, that adolescence is necessarily a stage of development associated with emotional turmoil and psychic disturbance, was to become so deeply rooted, reinforced by a succession of psychoanalytically orientated writers, that it persists to this day. This 'storm and stress' conceptualization (built on eagerly by journalists in sensational features on feral teenage hooligans and vandals) has filtered down to the public as a vaguely 'demonological' theory of adolescence. Certainly the psychiatric profession, with its biased sample of clinic-attending youngsters, has tended to take a jaundiced view of adolescence. Hutter in the 1930s described adolescence in Alice in Wonderland terms as a period of development in which normally, abnormalities so often happen that 'it is abnormal that everything passes normally'. Anna Freud, writing in the 1950s on 'Adolescence' in the journal *Psychoanalytic Study of the Child*, said it was 'abnormal' if a child kept a steady equilibrium during the adolescent period. The adolescent manifestations, in her view, come close to symptoms of the neurotic, psychotic or dissocial type, merging into almost all the mental illnesses.

In the 1960s the child psychiatrist Gillespie wrote that the contrasts and contradictions so characteristic of adolescence produce an impression of instability that leads sometimes to a mistaken suspicion of a schizophrenic illness.

Clinicians mainly see disturbed or deviant young people. When the evidence is based on unbiased investigations of 'run-of-the-mill' adolescents rather than impressionistic data, it is clear that adolescence, for all its difficulties, can be negotiated successfully by children who enjoy intuitive, sensible parents and economic security (see Aggleton, Hurry and Warwick, 1999; Coleman and Hendry, 1999; Herbert, 1987c; Rutter, 1979). What is required is an acceptance of the essential continuity of important aspects of personality from childhood, through adolescence, and on to adulthood. The 'changeling' phenomenon, in the sense of some radical change, is somewhat unusual. Nevertheless, dramatic physical and psychological changes are features of adolescence, and an understanding of these processes can be of benefit to harassed young people and their parents.

The End of Childhood

Puberty often brings about a degree of self-centredness in the erstwhile child. The body the child has taken for granted becomes the focus of attention; so much is happening. The very ground on which the young person has been standing so securely up to now begins to shift. If there is any one event that makes adolescence stand out from the rest of childhood, it is the radical nature of the growth that occurs at the time. These physical, physiological and mental changes transform children into young adults.

Cognitive changes

By the end of middle childhood, youngsters become capable of *propositional thinking*. They can propose hypotheses and deduce consequences. Their language is now fast and versatile. They may be critical of, and even despise, what they now perceive as their hopelessly out-of-date parents. As Mark Twain (1835–1910) so aptly put it: 'When I was a boy of fourteen my father was so stupid I could hardly stand to have him around. At twenty-one I was astonished at how much he had learned in the past seven years'. We now begin to see the fundamental difference between *concrete operational thinking* of the previous phase of cognitive development, and the new stage which Piaget (1950) called *formal propositional thinking*. The difference is essentially to do with the real and the possible. It is during adolescence, roughly the years from 11 or 12 to around 16, that children begin to free their thinking from its roots in their own particular experience.

Gender differences

There are some interesting differences in the nature of intellectual functioning in boys and girls, although it is difficult to separate out heredity and environment as causes of these differences. Intellectually, they get off to a good start – being slightly ahead of boys on average, on intelligence tests during the first 4 years of life. They are more articulate. They literally have the first word (on average) and, one might note, because of the longevity of females, the last one too. They learn to read more easily. The intellectual differential soon vanishes at school, although girls still excel on verbal fluency tests – using more words, telling longer stories and in fact giving support to the stereotype that females talk more than males. It is not until high school that boys draw ahead of girls on mathematical skills. Boys do better than girls on tests of spatial ability and to some extent on abstract, analytical types of reasoning. It is necessary to be cautious about these generalizations. Much of the 'received wisdom' about differences in academic ability and performance between males and females, is now being challenged as stereotypes that result, in part, from limited career opportunities and restricted expectations.

Physical changes: the growth spurt

Adolescence begins in biology (at puberty) and ends in culture (i.e. when young people take on an independent existence). It is, for these reasons, a moveable feast and one stretching over 6 or 7 years. Given this, it makes better sense to think in terms of early, middle and late adolescence, rather than a monolithic undifferentiated stage of development. Growth in virtually all parts of the body is sharply accelerated. It tends to be most rapid at the periphery and to move in toward the trunk, so the young adolescent appears to be gangly, 'all hands and feet'. Of course, size eventually gets back into proportion. For both sexes there is an increase in size of shoulders and hips, arms and legs, height and total body weight. Boys undergo a significant increase in their muscle tissue and strength, whereas girls develop more fatty tissue, producing their softer and more rounded contours. All of these events are referred to as the adolescent 'growth spurt' (see figure 19).

Because the peak in growth rate occurs at different times for different parts of the body, the basic balance of the body is temporarily disturbed – producing, for some, a disconcerting sense of disequilibrium. The many physical upheavals encountered by youngsters seem to require a focusing in on themselves while they adapt to change, and come to terms with their new (or modified) body and self image. Self-absorption at such a time would seem eminently reasonable. Nevertheless, parents sometimes become over-concerned when their children become, as they see it, egocentric and self-centred.

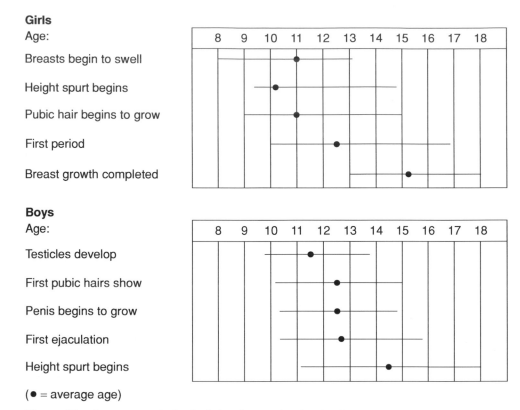

(● = average age)

Figure 19 Age range of physical developments at puberty

Girls are on a quicker physical developmental timetable than boys. At puberty they are developmentally 2 years ahead of boys. The physical changes of puberty continue for about 2 years and have a significant impact on the erstwhile child's body image and, building on that foundation, his or her self-image. The end of childhood for the girl is sign-posted by an increase in the growth rates of breasts, ovaries and uterus (womb). One may find an early-developed girl at the age of 12 who is already physically a woman, with fully developed sexual characteristics and destined to grow very little more in height. At about the same age, and therefore in the same classroom and social group, may be a later-developing girl who is just about to begin her growth spurt at the age of 16. One is a mature-looking and possibly quite sophisticated young adult; the other is (or looks like) a pre-pubescent child. One can see how illogical it is to generalize too much about the so-called female 'teenager'. The same conspicuous differences might also be apparent in boys of 14 or 15.

Around 15 per cent of adolescents reach maturity early, an event that affects males and females in different ways. A girl may be concerned about becoming impossibly tall – outstripping her peers even further at adolescence

– because she is already tall before the event. However, girls who are already tall as pre-adolescents, tend to reach the adolescent growth spurt earlier than other girls. Once she and her maturing peers have passed the period of rapid adolescent growth, their height relationships are more likely to return to those of pre-adolescence. Thus her worst fears of being a 'giant' among midgets are unlikely to materialize. If a boy is short he may view this picture in reverse, fearing that he will be a midget among giants. Short boys may appear to be losing ground as a result of delays in the adolescent growth spurt, only to return later to an approximation of their initial height relationships with their fellows.

Physical signs of sexual maturity

Menstruation is generally a signal that a girl is producing ova and is capable of becoming a mother; a girl's first period is therefore a notable landmark in her life. For some girls the menarche is an unwelcome sign that they will have to assume responsibilities and burdens, of which males have little inkling. For others this assumption of womanhood is a proud, exciting and welcome event; however they appear to be in the minority. Surveys suggest that a very small proportion of girls (about 10 per cent) when asked about their reactions to the onset of their menses demonstrate such enthusiasm. Most report that they are indifferent. A significant number experience worry or anxiety and a few are terrified. Today, children are told a great deal more about their approaching puberty than used to be the case only a few decades ago. In spite of this, many young adolescent girls await or experience the first signs of maturity with anxiety. A female child might connect the menstrual blood with the dismay associated with a bleeding wound.

These physical and physiological changes that take place (on average) at 12 in girls are due to the action of hormones. The average age of the menarche for Edwardian girls was fifteen. Only a minority began their periods while at school. By the 1960s it had reduced to 13 years of age. Today the menarche may be:

- Early (fast track): 15 per cent are earlier than 13 years of age (some as early as 10 years)
- On time, at around 13 years: about 70 per cent of girls
- Late: 15 per cent are later than 16 or 17.

It is thought that the age of menarche has gradually become lower since Victorian times because of better nutrition. Certainly girls who are deficient in iron, through dietary deficiencies or other reasons, are likely to have a delayed menarche.

By the age of 16, the average boy is fully developed sexually and is capable of becoming a father. One of the main indicators is ejaculation or emission. The word 'testes' comes from the Latin for 'witness'. The presence of testicles was a witness to a man's virility and his potential as a father. There is an increase in the size of testes, scrotum and penis, the child becoming a man in physical characteristics. In typical boys there is roughly a 5-year variation in the age at which puberty is reached.

Some boys and girls react adversely to the fact that nocturnal emissions (wet dreams) and menstruation happen, respectively, in a manner that is beyond their control. They may regard these phenomena as shameful in some way, and therefore keep them a secret out of embarrassment. Many of the fears are quite irrational but have their roots in childhood fantasies. A male child might treat nocturnal emissions with the same disgust as a wet bed.

Hormonal changes

Puberty is not just a matter of changes in the size and shape of the body. Physiological developments in glandular secretion, particularly those affecting sexual function, occur. Until arriving at puberty, males and females have similar quantities of both sex hormones in the bloodstream, with only a slightly greater proportion of the sex-relevant hormone. Thus boys have nearly as much oestrogen (the female sex hormone) as androgen. At puberty, however, there is a sharp increase in the secretion of the sex-related hormone. The pituitary gland at the base of the brain starts to produce two hormones, the gonadotrophic hormones, which it releases into the bloodstream. These complex chemical substances are actually the same in both sexes; in boys they are produced together continuously, whereas in girls they are produced one after the other in accordance with the monthly menstrual cycle.

The two hormones are the follicle-stimulating hormone (FSH) and the luteinizing hormone (LH). In boys, the FSH 'instructs' the testes to start making sperm cells, and the LH (also called the interstitial-cell-stimulating hormone) causes the testes to start making testosterone, the male sex hormone. Both the pituitary hormones cause the testes to grow, but it is testosterone that produces the other changes of puberty. These include the growth of the penis, and the deepening of the voice owing to the enlargement of the larynx. Boys' voices break, at times shifting alarmingly from low basso to high contralto. Boys also develop hair on the face, body and limbs. The same hormone causes loss of hair on the scalp in some men later. Acne spots on the face and back are also the result of a sudden excess of testosterone at puberty.

In girls, the FSH stimulates the ovaries to release ova (egg cells) and to produce the female sex hormone oestrogen. The LH causes changes in the ovaries and the secretion of the other female sex hormone, progesterone.

Hormones from the ovaries produce physical changes, including the development of the breasts and uterus, the growth of pubic hair and the more rounded female shape.

Adolescent Sexuality

How the changes and variations in sexual drive that accompany hormonal development are translated into overt sexual behaviour, depend on personal values, peer pressures and cultural variations in sexual mores. Attitudes that range from permissive to restrictive, are conveyed to the adolescent in sex education at school, and by parental efforts (often thwarted), at control. In the West, adolescents' attitudes toward their sexuality have become increasingly liberal or (as they might see it) 'liberated' over the last century.

The National Survey Of Sexuality and Lifestyles, a Medical Research Council project, presents several important findings about how adolescents in the UK express their sexuality (Wellings et al., 1994):

- A majority of boys and girls masturbate.
- One in five young people under the age of 16 are sexually active: 26 per cent of girls and 30 per cent of boys report having sex by the age of 16. These activities are generally within brief romantic relationships; they include kissing, fondling, intercourse, mutual masturbation and oral sex.
- First-time sexual intercourse takes place at least 3 years earlier on average, than was the case two or three decades ago.
- Working-class and lower educational level youngsters begin sexual intercourse 2 years earlier than middle-class youths and those with educational aspirations.
- Those with strong religious affiliations and those of Indian origin delay their first experiences of sexual intercourse until later in life.
- The first sexual experience for boys tends to be primarily motivated by curiosity; for girls, being in love.
- 33 per cent of males express regret having had sex early; 66 per cent of females do so.
- Up to 50 per cent of sexually active adolescents use no contraception.
- 50 per cent of girls could talk to their parents about sex compared with 33 per cent of boys.

Teenage parenthood

Teenage parenthood is thought by some to be a central link in the 'cycle of disadvantage': thus children of teenage mothers are a group of particular interest to the study of intergenerational transmission of poverty, mental health and other social problems. The empirical evidence drawn from a vast literature on adolescent parents (mainly mothers) presents an almost comprehensively negative picture of the unpreparedness of teenagers for the burdens and responsibilities of parenthood (see chapter 13).

Homosexual, lesbian and bisexual development

Methodologically sound studies of gay, lesbian and bisexual (GLB) adolescents are in short supply (see Anhall and Morris, 1998; Rutter, 1971), hence the paucity of reliable generalizations about this aspect of adolescent development. Clearly, homosexual and lesbian experimentation are commonplace in adolescence; longer term attraction to the same sex or both sexes is reported in under 10 per cent of the population. Being called 'names' such as 'queer' and 'dyke' plus a host of others can, and is meant to, hurt. How others see us and think of us (implicit in those names) is of vital importance to the way we perceive ourselves – our self-image. This has particular bearing on how adolescents deal with their dawning realization of the permanence of homosexual feelings and identifications. The experience of 'coming out' is unique to GLB adolescents – a fraught action for many, and possibly the source of the proposal (as yet unproven) that they are at risk of developing psychopathology. Various adjustment problems have been reported in the literature, including attempted suicide, substance use and abuse, conduct problems, and academic difficulties.

In gay and lesbian adolescents sexual and self-identity undergo the following transitions in development (see Carr, 2002; Laird and Green, 1996; Money, 1993):

- Defining oneself as homosexual (gay) or lesbian following experiencing a sense of being different or alienated from heterosexual peers of the same gender as oneself.
- A later reinforcement of this growing awareness by attraction to and/or intimacy with same-sex peers, followed by the dilemma of whether to deny or accede to homoerotic feelings.
- These feelings and subsequent choices are likely to be influenced by homophobic or tolerant attitudes within the family, society and the peer group.
- In the case of the former there may be a denial or suppression of a gay/lesbian identity leading to depression, drug abuse, absconding and even suicide in extreme cases.
- In the latter reaction, one of understanding and refraining from expressions of contempt and rejection, the path of accepting a gay identity becomes viable and fulfilling.

Fortunately, there is today a generally much more enlightened attitude to gay and lesbian people, an acceptance of sexual preferences being a matter of differences rather than deviations.

Attitudes to premarital sex

Although adolescents have become more accepting in their attitudes to premarital sex, this does not imply that there is a massive rise in casual sexual relationships. Young people, and particularly girls, continue to emphasize the importance of love and stable emotional attachment in premarital sex, although intended marriage or an engagement is not so often seen as a prerequisite of such relationships. Girls display more conservative attitudes to sexual issues than boys. They are more likely than boys to have been in a 'steady relationship' when they first experienced sexual intercourse. The emphasis tends to be on a stable relationship with one sexual partner at a time, so-called serial monogamy. Most youngsters wish to get married and have children. Certainly a committed relationship is generally thought to be essential for the rearing of children, and, although a majority would wish such a longstanding commitment to take the form of marriage, a substantial minority reject such a view. A majority of adolescents say they expect sexual fidelity after marriage.

Identity and Self-image

The establishment of a clear sense of identity is one of the major tasks of adolescence (Erikson, 1968). Allport (1937) describes two aspects of the self-image: the way the individual sees her or his present abilities, status and roles; and what they would like to become, their aspirations for themselves. When there is a large discrepancy between the teenager's self-image ('myself as I am') and his or her idealized self ('myself as I would like to be') there is also likely to be anxiety and over-sensitiveness, in close attendance. At the foundation of adolescent self-awareness – the self-image – is a representation of their body: what it is like, and how it looks to others, a self-perception strongly influenced by cultural norms. The importance of body image to our culture as a whole is obvious in terms of the widespread expenditure of time and effort that is given to the body's appearance, by means of fashionable clothes, skin preparations, cosmetics, tattoos, facial jewellery, even plastic surgery. For many young women intense dieting and exercising, and some-times purging, are the extremes required by fashion (see chapter 15 on anorexia nervosa). In some cultures, the need to alter the body's appearance is expressed in bodily mutilations or facial scars (e.g. the Zulu nation of old). Members of a culture may radically revise their idealized body image with

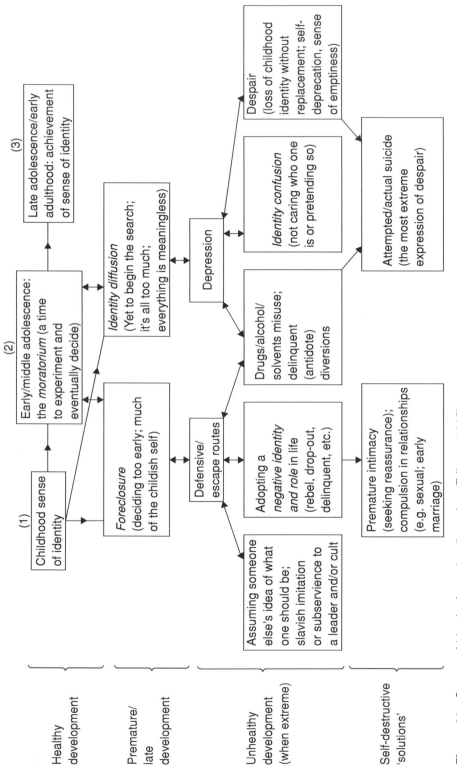

Figure 20 Stages of identity formation (based on Erikson, 1965)

the passage of time, or under the influence of a global culture like the American one.

Children absorb the attitudes of others towards their body and they may possess a body image that is reassuring, even pleasing (Carr, 2002). They may, however, come to view their body and its parts as off-putting and shameful. It is important for youngsters' self-esteem that they should perceive how other persons see them, and that they should be able to compare their self-image with the expectations they believe others have concerning what they should be like. The individual's perception of her or his appearance to a particular group of other persons, or some other significant individual, is referred to as their 'subjective public identity'. Teenagers may have as many such identities as there are groups of significant other persons who they believe perceive them in a distinctive way. In collectivist cultures the emphasis is usually very different from individualist (e.g. Western) cultures where, as we have seen, the self is conceived as autonomous and largely independent of others. The self tends to be defined in terms of group identity and interdependence with one's fellow members of the community. Group goals are likely to have primacy over personal goals (see Triandis, 1995).

Marcia (1980) proposes, in a model similar to Erikson's (see below), four ways in which adolescents arrive at a sense of who and what they are:

1. Foreclosure: Parents or authoritative figures in the community inculcate ideas (vocational, political, ethnocentric and religious) which the adolescent submissively accepts. The values endorsed tend to be authoritarian.
2. Identity diffusion: The young person, devoted to fun and excitement and 'living for the day', makes no firm commitment to personal, social, political and vocational plans or beliefs.
3. Moratorium: A number of roles are 'tried out' before arriving at a settled identity. Along the way (sometimes a period of considerable duration) delinquent or unconventional (opting out) identities may be assumed before a stable sense of self is arrived at.
4. Achieving a clear identity: This entails the achievement (not premature or too long delayed) of a strong commitment to a consistent value system and a 'healthy' adjustment to the world of significant relationships, work and leisure.

Erikson (1968) sets out the stages of identity, and their implications, as shown in figure 20.

The development of identity doesn't always proceed smoothly, but what evidence we do have calls into question Erikson's belief that adolescents usually suffer a *crisis* over their identity. Most teenagers actually have a positive but not unrealistically inflated self-image and this view of themselves tends to be fairly stable over the years (Herbert, 1987c). It is important to remember that children do not face all of the 'hurdles' of adolescent development at one time. Different challenges (e.g. sexuality, new relationships, changes in body and self-image identity and independence issues) are spread out over several years. Children have strengths, and they generally bring forward into maturity their positive attributes. They don't suddenly lose these characteristics which most parents have so assiduously nurtured.

Having said all that, it is clear to anyone working in the social, health or educational services that there are some very real problems in adolescence. Fortunately, the serious, as opposed to day-to-day difficulties, affect a relatively small minority (see chapters 13 and 14).

The Ending of Puberty

If the physiological changes of puberty are most commonly taken as the onset of adolescence, it is sociological phenomena, such as status, duties, privileges, the end of education, the right to marry and enjoy economic independence, which are most frequently cited as the termination of adolescence. These matters depend on the traditions, laws, and requirements of society, many of which appear contradictory and hypocritical to the adolescent. Orme (2000, p. 3) observes that '. . . our law . . . doles out adulthood in spoonfulls one at a time. During the last hundred years, the ages of fourteen, fifteen, sixteen, seventeen, eighteen, and twenty-one have all been fixed as thresholds when a child may stay alone at home, leave school, do full-time work, marry, drive a vehicle, join the armed forces, suffer capital punishment, or vote in elections. Nor have the thresholds stayed constant; some have been raised and others lowered.'

As we have seen, the dramatic heightening of sexual awareness and increased sexual arousal brought about by hormonal changes brought in their wake psychological implications for teenagers who have to manage powerful heterosexual or homosexual feelings and desires. Parents have to deal with their offspring's increased (and, in part, hormone-driven) assertiveness (see Carr, 2002). The tendency to stigmatize adolescence as the 'terrible teens' has meant that countless parents have brought to life a self-fulfilling prophecy that condemns them to endure, rather than enjoy, their child's entry into young adulthood. We began the chapter with imaginary Adrian Mole's anxieties, and now bring it to a close with a real-life quotation from one of my teenage patients, one that nicely illustrates her insecurity – a mixture of pessimism and optimism. When asked, in an assessment exercise, to write about herself 'as she is', she wrote:

'Lately I've been in a daze, and I can't think straight. Maybe because some of my brain cells are dying and I'm just about sixteen. My whole world is changing. Before I used to have a regular routine and all I was concerned with was school. But now I'm thinking of my future.'

part iv

Atypical Development
The Hazardous Route

Now, here you see. It takes all the running you can do,
To keep in the same place.
If you want to get somewhere else,
You must run at least twice as fast as that!
Lewis Carroll: Through the Looking Glass

Issues of Assessment, Definition and Measurement

The complex developmental and health problems of children represent an enormous challenge for the clinical assessment of the individual differences required for the provision of personalized services and supports. To achieve this, the chapters in this section of the book on atypical development proceed in parallel with earlier ones that dealt with the typical (i.e. normal) aspects of development from conception to adolescence. It is impossible to proceed to a discussion of atypical development without commenting briefly on issues of terminology and diagnostic classification. Conceptual inconsistencies in this area have constituted a long-standing problem for carers, clinicians, and researchers.

In the chapters to come I describe developmental and clinical disabilities in traditional terms (they are widely used in practice and in the literature) but I also include, where appropriate, a dimensional developmental perspective on atypical problems. My underlying premise, as was strongly emphasized in the introduction to the book, is that children with disabilities and chronic conditions progress through common developmental stages and are characterized by individual differences.

Simeonsson and Rosenthal, in their invaluable text *Psychological and Developmental Assessment* (2001), are of the opinion that 'instead of a diagnostic and categorical conceptualization of disability, a developmental approach focuses on the commonalities and variations of development across major domains. These domains are reflective of the child's interactions with the physical and social environments and can be assessed by measures of cognition, communication, personal and social development, and behavior.' (p. 22). The authors (ibid.) state that theory and research confirm these assumptions and require a dimensional perspective in addition to (some would say instead of) a categorical view of disability. Clearly, such an approach requires a multimeasurement assessment strategy.

In their opinion there are three concepts that contribute to a dimensional desideratum. These are outlined below.

1. THE CONTINUUM OF REPRODUCTIVE CASUALTY

In this concept, developmental disabilities are not construed as a unique diagnostic entity but as variations of a common process, with a focus on similarities rather than differences in children who are developmentally disabled or chronically ill (see Pasamanick and Knobloch, 1961).

2. THE CONTINUUM OF CARETAKING CASUALTY

Here the emphasis is on the caretaker's role as a powerful influence on developmental outcomes – positively modifying or delaying/distorting them. The outcomes are not discrete entities but are manifested across a continuum. They are the expression of similar developmental processes covering both the prenatal and postnatal periods (see Sameroff and Chandler, 1975).

3. THE CONTINUUM OF CENTRAL NERVOUS SYSTEM (CNS) DYSFUNCTION

Clinicians use this concept to emphasize the associated deficits that arise from a common underlying dysfunction of the CNS. Both the spectrum of difficulties (expressed disabilities) and the underlying dysfunction are taken into account (e.g. Herbert, 1964).

The movement towards a dimensional analysis of developmental disability is actually a *return*, as is plain when one looks at the publication dates of the studies on impairment continua. Theorists have a tendency, when time has passed by, to reinvent the wheel.

The Journey Begins Again: Prenatal Influences

We began the book with the basic units of inheritance present at conception (the chromosomes and genes) that provide the blueprint for the child-to-be's future development. As a brief reprise: all of the human bodily cells (with the exception of the sperm and ovum) contain a nucleus within which are 23 pairs of chromosomes. Half of each pair originated from the mother, the other half passed on by the father. Pairs 1 to 22 of the chromosomes, referred to as autosomes, are collectively responsible for the individual's biological and physical inheritance.

The sperm and ovum are different, each containing only half the number of chromosomes present in the body cells, in other words 23. These are the sex chromosomes. It is at fertilization that they complement each other so as to form 23 *pairs*. If the 23rd pair contains two X chromosomes it indicates a female; the possession of an X and Y chromosome indicates a male.

Each chromosome consists of thousands of genes; the genes contain DNA (deoxyribose nucleic acid). The coded information therein – our inheritance – is the source of what we are and what, in large part, we become. The term 'inheritance' refers to characteristics the infant is born with, the genetic heritage from one or both of the parents. There are other attributes the infant is born with which are not necessarily inherited, but have occurred during intrauterine development. These are referred to as 'congenital' factors.

The child's journey began in chapter 1 with conception, and it is here that we resume the story. Now it is the hazardous (atypical) events, involving inherited abnormalities that we begin with.

Genetic Influences: Inherited Abnormalities

At the very start, at conception, problems may be encountered because of aberrations in what is inherited – usually a defect of the genes or of the chromosomes as a whole. Gene disorders are of a sub-microscopic kind, involving substitutions of a single base-pair, or alterations of DNA sequence over a very short length of chromosome. Any of the 46 chromosomes in the human complement can undergo abnormal changes. Chromosome disorders are microscopically visible alterations to the chromosome set, either of number (loss or addition of a whole chromosome), or of structure (translocation, deletion or duplication of part of one or more chromosomes). A very large number of genes is involved in even the smallest detectable abnormalities of this sort.

Karyotyping is the procedure whereby chromosomes are counted and laid out, with the band patterns on each quite visible. As all body cells carry the same 23 pairs of chromosomes, this procedure can be conducted on any cell in the body. Human chromosomes are classified by size and the position of the centromere, the point at which the arms of dividing chromosomes, the chromatids, join. They are allocated to five groups (referred to by the letters A to E), to numbers 1 to 22 (the autosomes), and to Xs and Ys, according to whether they are female or male sex chromosomes. In each chromosome the short arm is labelled p and the long arm q. The location of chromosome abnormalities (deletions, breakpoints, etc.) can thus be described in terms of the number of the chromosome involved, the arm on which it is situated (p or q), and the band in which it is positioned. The use of + or – signs indicates additional or absent chromosomal material. An example of how a karyotype

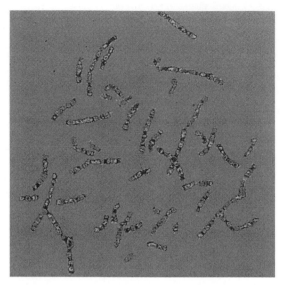

Figure 21   Digitized light micrograph of the 46 chromosomes from a normal human (constituting the full 'karyotype', i.e. the total number of chromosomes found in nearly every cell of the human body): each cell contains 22 matched pairs of chromosomes (one member of each pair is from the mother and one from the father) plus one sex-determining pair (the only pair that differs between the male and female karyotype: XX, female; XY, male)
(Custom Medical Stock Photograph/Science Photo Library)

of a male with a shortened long arm of chromosome 18 can be indicated, is thus: 46, XY 18q–.

Chromosomal Abnormalities

Loss of abnormal concepti

The percentage of infants born with serious genetic defects is small, major chromosomal abnormalities affecting 0.5 to 0.75 per cent of unselected new-borns. It is estimated that between 40 and 60 per cent of miscarriages occur because the mother's body rejects and expels a fetus with chromosomal abnormalities. Were this not to occur (and the uncomfortable aphorism 'nature knows best' come to mind), the result would be a stillbirth or a profoundly handicapped live-born child. Damage or defect in the ovum or sperm can be manifested before, during, or after conception. And every stage of a pregnancy may be involved in the loss (i.e. rejection) of a defective conceptus.

Only about 10 per cent of spontaneous abortions are detectable because most are re-absorbed (resorbed) into the mother's body. It is estimated that some 16 per cent of defective eggs in contact with sperms fail to fertilize. A further 15 per cent that have been fertilized are rejected at the cleavage stage prior to implantation. 27 per cent are lost by the second week, coinciding with the first missed period (menses), and an additional 8 per cent by the second missed. Evidence suggests that around half to 60 per cent of the spontaneous abortions in the first 3 months of pregnancy have aberrant chromosomes – prevalence rates so similar to others found in various parts of the world, that they would seem to represent a basic biological error rate (Rosenblith, 1992).

There are many types of chromosomal abnormality, some of them detectable by tissue tests. Some of the main chromosome aberrations are:

- Trisomy, which involves one extra chromosome per cell (i.e. 47). Outcome: Down's Syndrome with trisomy of chromosome 21. Among other outcomes are Patau's and Edward's syndromes, which are rare and extremely abnormal.
- Monosomy, which involves one too few chromosomes (i.e. 45). Outcome: Turner's syndrome; Klinefelter's syndrome.
- Triploidy, which involves a complete extra set of chromosomes (i.e. 69). Outcome: lethal.
- Tetraploidy, which involves twice the normal number of chromosomes (i.e. 92). Outcome: lethal.
- Deletions: Terminal deletion 5p. Outcome: cri du chat syndrome.
- Inversions: Percentric inversion 9. Outcome: normal phenotype.
- Duplications: Isochromosome X. Outcome: infertility in females.
- Fragile sites: Fragile X. Outcome: intellectual impairment.

The syndromes mentioned above are described briefly as follows:

1. Down's syndrome (DS) (Trisomy 21) is one of the most common congenital chromosomal abnormalities, affecting one in 700 newborns. It is also the most widely known of the chromosomal anomalies perhaps because of their high survival rate, the sheer amount of research carried out on the condition; and also (although many would question this) their charm, affection and humour. Down's syndrome was at first referred to as *mongolism*, named after the man who described it in 1866. Most chromosomal aberrations arise as a result of a non-disjunctive disturbance in meiotic divisions, i.e. a failure to disjoin. It can occur in male and female alike. Chromosomal trisomy in Down's syndrome is a result of non-disjunction. Lejeune, Gautier and Turpin were the first to point this out, in 1959. The most frequent aberration occurs on the 21st chromosome, which carries an extra chromosome (trisomy 21). The

Figure 22   A 3-year-old girl with Down's syndrome (Hattie Young/Science Photo Library)

children are characterized by small features and head size, a tongue that tends to protrude, slanted eyes that have folds of skin at their inner corners, low muscle tone, fine hair and skin, and not uncommonly, congenital heart defects. The degree of handicap varies. The majority suffer from intellectual impairment, although there are relatively small numbers who obtain scores on IQ tests within the low average range.

In the first few months of life the child with Down's syndrome displays atypical motor behaviour: muscular hypotonia (floppiness), and an atypical timetable of emergence and dissolution of reflexes. At most stages these children function less well on tests of motor function than their typical peers. There appears to be no satisfactory explanation of their motor problems (see Henderson, 1985). We return to the child with Down's syndrome in a later discussion of learning disability.

2. Turner's syndrome involves an absent chromosome, a single X chromosome in the female (X0 instead of XX). It is characterized by underdeveloped reproductive organs and breasts, short height and sterility. Hormonal treatment at puberty normalizes sexual appearance, but does not produce fertility.

3. Klineflelter's syndrome involves an extra X chromosome in the male (XXY) and the condition is characterized by infertility, small testes, long limbs, and feminine appearance. There may be mild intellectual impairment. Male hormone treatment normalizes masculine body appearance.

4. Cri du chat syndrome involves the deletion of the one arm of the chromo-
    some pair 5, and is characterized by a shrill cry ('cry of the cat') in the
    newly born. There is an abnormal heart condition, and retarded physical
    and intellectual development.

There are some 220 developmental defects and syndromes involving 14
systems, ranging from the skeletal, cranio-facial, and neurological, to structures and functions affecting growth, and size or shape of limbs and skull
(see Buys, 1990). Infants with physical defects are likely to have genetic
problems that are detectable at birth; they constitute about 6 per cent of all
infants born alive. Twenty per cent of these suffer from effects of known
genetic transmission (e.g. club foot, cleft lips and palate, neural tube defects);
a further 3 to 5 per cent have anomalies due to chromosomal abnormalities.

Hazards

Phenotype abnormality is to be expected only when the total material on the
chromosome set is 'unbalanced' that is, there is monosomy or trisomy for part
or whole of one or more chromosomes, rather than the normal disomy within
the set. Accidents to chromosomes usually take place during the formation of
the individual egg (ovum) and sperm cells, on a one-off basis. However parents
may, in fairly rare cases, carry a so-called balanced chromosome abnormality,
which leads to the repeated production of chromosomally abnormal eggs or
sperms. As a result of cell division, there is either a failure of the chromosomes
to separate properly (affecting the number of chromosomes), or the problem
occurs during recombination (unequal lengths of chromosome pairs crossing
over) which may produce deletions, rearrangements and inversions. Faulty
cell division leads to malformations in 3 to 8 per cent of all fertilized eggs.
Less than 1 per cent of all newborns have a chromosomal abnormality.

Genetic Accidents

Any deviation from the norm in genetic information is called a mutation.
The DNA structure of the gene may be wrongly copied, so that the message
of that part of the genetic code is lost or changes. Such changes occur in
exceptional circumstances such as exposure to excessive radiation. They can
occur spontaneously, but this is rare, about once in some 50,000 generations
for any particular gene.

A mutant gene can be passed on from one generation to the next in
exactly the same way as a normal gene. This is because errors affect the egg
and sperm cells so that they become a permanent characteristic. This is the
basis of evolutionary change, for better or worse. It is generally for the

worse; on the whole the effects of mutations are deleterious. The resultant pathological condition is often self-limiting owing to its severity, and the inability of the affected individual to reproduce.

It is possible for an environmental intervention to mitigate an inherited defect. An example is provided by one of the gene's basic functions, the determination of the architecture of protein molecules. Genes control protein and enzyme synthesis. One gene is responsible for the synthesis of one enzyme. Phenylketonuria is an example of a form of intellectual disability that is controlled by a single abnormal gene. In this condition an enzyme necessary for normal development is not produced. This enzyme is required to convert phenylalanine into tyrosine, and its absence means that phenylalanine accumulates in body tissues. This results in the interference with cerebral development and functioning. The unconverted phenylalanine is secreted in the urine as phenylpyruvic acid and the condition can be identified by a simple chemical test, now carried out as a matter of routine in the first weeks of life. If identified, the infant is put on a diet that is free of phenylalanine, an intervention that prevents intellectual impairment.

Patterns of Genetic Transmission

A single defective gene that results in a genetic disorder can be either dominant or recessive, a mutation, or attached to the X chromosome. Abnormal chromosomes that result in genetic disorders are usually new mutations, but may be inherited.

Autosomal dominant disorders

Although a family history in these disorders is common, individuals may carry a new mutation. Failure to pass on dominant genes to offspring means that fatal diseases that they produce remain rare. They usually involve structural and physical abnormalities. The most common genetic disease *familial hypercholesterolaemia* (FH) is detectable by a blood test at birth. It presents a manageable risk to health despite the extremely high blood cholesterol levels that predispose the sufferer to heart attacks. Huntington's Chorea, a condition that usually appears in middle age, is characterized by jerky movements and progressive mental deterioration.

Autosomal recessive disorders

These usually involve an enzyme deficiency that leads to some pathological biochemical event (e.g. an accumulation of toxins in the nervous system). A normal dominant gene usually masks a defective recessive gene. In the case of both parents carrying a defective recessive gene, each of their offspring has a one in four chance of inheriting both recessive genes (and therefore one of several disorders) or neither, and a two in four chance of being a carrier. Examples of recessive disorders are as follows:

- Cystic fibrosis (CF) is the most common autosomal single recessive gene disorder of the secretory epithelia that affects their ability to transport salt and water. This anomaly leads to heavy, dehydrated mucus in the airways. It is a condition that mainly affects the lungs and the digestive system. The breathing exercises, incessant and robust physical attention the parents have to pay to the child (pounding the chest walls), along with other treatments, have increased the quality of life and life span of these children. Over 60 per cent survive into adulthood.
- Tay-Sachs disease is a fatal condition inherited as an autosomal recessive condition involving degeneration of the brain. The gene responsible for breaking down a toxic product into a non-toxic one in the neurons is absent. As a result there is an inability to produce a crucial enzyme, hoxosamidase A. The effects begin at around 3 to 6 months after birth. When lipids accumulate in the nervous system they cause brain damage and eventual death. Few children live beyond 3 years, and no effective treatment is available. Less severe cases may survive longer.
- Phenylketonuria (PKU) was described above.
- Thalassaemia produces anaemia and chronic ill health. Not all cases are severe, and some victims of the disease may survive for many years.
- Sickle-cell anaemia is indicated by the sickle shape of the red blood cells. They lack the full capacity to carry oxygen. It results in poor physical growth and secondary infections such as pneumonia.

Some of the conditions described above have prevalence rates that vary in different cultural or ethnic groups. Tay-Sachs disease is linked to a chance mutation in Jewish families about 200 years ago. The aberrant gene has been passed on across several generations. There is a predisposition in people of African and Caribbean origin to develop sickle-cell anaemia. Births to these ethnic minority parents exceed 15 per cent of all deliveries.

X-linked disorders

Abnormalities of the sex chromosomes take several forms. The various conditions stem from defective genes on the X chromosome of the 23 pairs. The defect would be masked if a normal X chromosome is present and in such a case, does not show itself. Since females have two X chromosomes, the defective X acts like a recessive gene in the female, but like a dominant one in the male. Therefore there is a much higher probability that the disorder

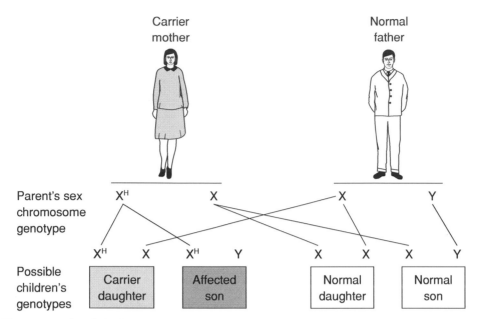

Figure 23   Sex-linked transmission of a recessive condition (haemophilia): a carrier mother can pass on the haemophilia to half (on average) her sons because there is no countervailing gene on the Y chromosome; a daughter of the carrier mother will not inherit the haemophilia itself unless her father has the disease

will be passed from mother to son. In males, with their Y chromosome instead of a second X chromosome, the disease will express itself. Examples of conditions affected by defective genes are:

- Haemophilia, an absence of the blood clotting factor VIII is one such disorder, and causes profuse bleeding from any external or internal injury. It may be dominant across the generations before it makes its appearance to the surprise of the family. A diagnosis can be made from a sample of fetal blood at 18 to 20 weeks of pregnancy.
- Duchenne muscular dystrophy is the most common form of X-linked disorder, and can be detected before birth. It affects one boy in 5000. The sufferers lose the ability to walk and are usually confined to a wheelchair for their relatively short lives.
- The fragile-X syndrome is perhaps the most common inherited intellectual disability. Large ears, a prominent jaw and large testes are among physical features associated with the disorder. Psychological features include behavioural problems, autistic characteristics and hyperactivity.
- Turner's syndrome is the one visible case of a monosomic person – one with a totally missing chromosome. The karyotype is 45, X0 (where the zero stands for the missing chromosome). An estimated 95 per cent of these conditions are aborted spontaneously. They appear to be normal

females at birth. Their sexual characteristics are immature, and they never commence menstruation. They are shorter than average; most have normal intelligence.

Prenatal, Antenatal and Neonatal Screening

Blood tests may be advised in order to detect problems such as iron-deficiency, Rh factor, immunity toxoplasmosis, gestational diabetes, sickle-cell disease, thalassaemia major and minor, and HIV. Tests such as chorionic villus sampling or amniocentesis may be suggested if the mother and her baby are at increased risk of complications. Genetic counselling is important if there are family or ethnic predispositions to inherited disabilities or diseases such as haemophilia, sickle-cell anaemia, cystic fibrosis, Tay Sachs disease, or Thalassaemia. Older would-be mothers and women with a history of stillbirths may also wish to be reassured by a genetic counsellor.

A neonatal screening test is not the same thing as a diagnostic test. It has to be relatively easy to administer to large numbers of apparently healthy babies, and be able to detect in that population, with minimal false positives and negatives, most cases of the disorder being screened. Neonatal screening for phenylketonuria (PKU) involves the analysis of drops of blood from a heel-prick sample. The test was introduced nationally in the UK, in the 1960s. Screening for congenital hypothyroidism (once called cretinism), introduced in the early 1980s, is also available. Without preventive interventions both disorders usually lead to permanent profound learning disabilities.

Behavioural Genetics

The notion that genetic influences are significant determinants of behaviour would have invited controversy in the not very distant past. However, a great deal of research in the last 25 years or so, has led to a better appreciation of the genetic contribution to many individual differences, including:

- personality
- intelligence (50 per cent of the variance)
- behaviour problems, and
- self-esteem (even something as apparently 'psychological' as this attribute is heritable: 32 per cent in women, 29 per cent in men).

Behaviour geneticists sometimes refer simplistically to the 'genes for this or that behaviour or psychopathological condition'. Rutter et al. (1999a, p. 18) caution that 'it is necessary to reject some of the over-enthusiastic claims that genetic influences are overwhelmingly influential on psychopathology and on psychological functioning generally, or that quantitative behavioural genetics constitutes a theory. It is nothing of the kind. Rather, it constitutes a method for partitioning population variance (for some trait) into the various types of genetic and environmental effect.' Rutter and his colleagues (ibid.) also emphasize how important it is to avoid terminology that implies a much more deterministic role for genes than is warranted by the evidence. Their responsibility for the susceptibility to the development of a particular psychological disorder is only a partial one. Even the finding that there is a genetic effect is, in itself, opaque with regard to the actual causal processes that are involved in aetiology. Richard Dawkins, in his book *The Selfish Gene*, reminds us, at a broader level, that no matter how much knowledge and wisdom is acquired during life, not one jot will be passed on to the children by genetic means. Each new generation starts from scratch.

Neuropsychological Causation

There are several psychological disorders that have a neurological substrate. They include schizophrenia, conduct disorders, affective disorders, and anxiety problems (Baron et al., 1995; Cody and Hynde, 1999). Others include developmental problems such as autism, dyslexia, dyspraxia and cerebral palsy. Neuropsychological assessments that are required for these problems might include:

• Differentiation of functional conditions from organic disorders
• Differential diagnosis of subtypes of neurodevelopmental disorders such as dyslexia
• Assessment of areas of strengths and weaknesses (deficits) in children with organic disorders
• Report of current neurophysiological status
• Report on the rate of improvement or deterioration
• Assessments of current and pre-morbid level of cognitive development
• Development of plans for rehabilitation and remediation.

The interaction of heredity, neurobiology, and environment is a continuing theme in the chapters to come.

chapter eight

The Perilous First Journey
The Inhospitable Environment

Discontent stirs up such affections in the body
As are inimical both to body and mind and must needs . . .
Spoil the child in the womb; such are anger, passion, hatred,
Fear of things to come, fear of things past, sorrow, sighing and
grief of mind.

Nicholas Culpeper (1616–1652)

Maternal Stress and Inherited Abnormalities

Is it possible that a mother's emotions can influence a child before it is born? In the folklore of all societies there exists the persistent belief that the emotional experiences, attitudes and behaviour of the pregnant mother can affect the child she carries by disrupting the pregnancy and thus, its future. Psychologists, as far back as the 1940s, began to investigate the influence of psychological stress on the physiological and behavioural responses of human offspring while in the womb, and following birth (e.g. Sontag, 1941, 1944). In subsequent years, researchers have found significant correlations between:

- Women who had been unhappy about their pregnancy and babies who were described as upset (e.g. Ferreira, 1960)
- Mothers who were stressed to a high degree during pregnancy and infants who tended to be very active, irritable, and irregular in their feeding, sleeping and bowel movements (Stott, 1966)
- Severe and prolonged emotional stress and premature delivery, low birth weight, stunted prenatal growth, and birth complications. Mothers who are victims of domestic violence are four times as likely to have low birthweight babies than mothers who are not subjected to such chronic stress (Browne and Herbert, 1997).

The other side of the coin is the suggestion that optimistic contented mothers pass on these 'positives' to their babies in the form of longer gestational time and physical well-being. The prevention of premature and low birthweight births (see chapter 9) is considered to be the most important desideratum in enhancing neonatal health. Stressful periods of short duration such as an argument, a frightening experience, or a minor fall, have few if any harmful consequences for the mother or her unborn child (Brockington, 1996).

Transmission of emotional stress

The emotional bond between mother and unborn infant is the medium whereby maternal activity, fatigue, emotionality and personality are postulated to influence the activity level, irritability and autonomic functioning of the fetus. For example, when a mother becomes emotionally aroused her glands secrete powerful activating hormones such as adrenaline that crosses the placental barrier, entering the fetal bloodstream, and accelerating the fetus' motor activity. Stress hormones divert blood flow to the large muscles and impede the flow or oxygen and nutrients to the fetus, possibly contributing to the stunting of its growth. Stress may undermine the mother's immune system, making her and her fetus vulnerable to infectious diseases (Cohen and Williams, 1991). The common accompaniment to prolonged distress is a poor appetite, and a need to smoke, drink alcohol and use drugs. All of these activities have an influence on growth retardation and low birthweight. Many mothers, however, seem capable of resisting such adverse effects despite their unhappy circumstances because of their ability to mobilize skills for managing stress.

Much of the evidence on the precise effects of maternal stress on her unborn child is extremely difficult to evaluate It tends to be based more on correlations found in retrospective evidence than evidence arising from the direct experimental manipulation of variables. It is notoriously risky to infer cause–effect relationships from *post facto* measures of association. The reason for the bias towards correlational studies is the ethical consideration that precludes direct experimentation. Observations of the effects of prenatal influences on the child's postnatal development may be contaminated by the influences of the mother's management of her baby after birth, and by genetic factors which cannot be controlled. Despite these difficulties and caveats it seems likely that babies of women who are tense, anxious or stressed during pregnancy are adversely affected. Precisely what the causal mechanisms are, is difficult to extricate because the dependent measures vary from investigation to investigation.

Biological Adversity

The journey embarked upon by the zygote can go badly wrong from the outset, at or around the point of fertilization. An ectopic pregnancy is one that develops outside the uterus. An egg from the ovary is fertilized and becomes implanted (usually) in the Fallopian tube. As the fertilized egg enlarges, the Fallopian tube stretches and ruptures, causing potentially life-threatening internal bleeding. In the early stage there is:

- A missed menstrual period or a heavy, painful period
- An unexplained vaginal spotting or bleeding
- Lower abdominal pain and cramps
- Pain in the shoulder.

In the late stages there is:

- Sudden, sharp, severe abdominal pain caused by the rupture of the Fallopian tube
- Dizziness, fainting and shock (paleness, drop in blood pressure and cold sweats).

Only about half of all fertilized ova implant firmly and move on to the next stage of development. A high proportion of the failures is either genetically abnormal and thus fail to develop, or they implant themselves in a location incapable of sustaining them, resulting in miscarriage (Moore and Persaud, 1993). It is estimated that three zygotes out of four fail to survive the prenatal stage of development.

Even when the blastocyst (fertilized egg) is safely implanted in the uterine wall there are many hazards to face. The point was made in a previous chapter that the uterine environment is almost always a benign and hospitable place in which to develop. In relatively unusual circumstances there are physical and psychological influences that, by disturbing the host mother, can disrupt the tenant, notably during the period of the embryo. These stressors include maternal disease, malnutrition, fatigue, tissue damage, intense emotion and extreme environmental conditions. Active substances are transmitted to the embryo by transplacental transfer and these may be capable of affecting its neural, endocrinal, or other structures.

Teratogens

The term teratogen is applied to any disease, chemical, drug, or other environmental agent capable of harming a developing embryo by causing severely retarded growth, physical deformities, deafness, blindness, brain damage, and also death. It comes from the ancient Greek word meaning 'creating a monster', a fact that makes it a particularly unfortunate term. The list of possible sources of adversity for the unborn child is a dauntingly long one. Teratogenic influences include:

- Maternal illnesses: rubella (German measles), chicken pox, diabetes, toxoplasmosis
- Sexually transmitted diseases: syphilis, AIDS, genital herpes, cytomegalovirus (CMV)
- Drugs: thalidomide, alcohol, marijuana, tobacco, cocaine, amphetamines, barbiturates
- Environmental hazards: radiation, chemicals, various pollutants, domestic, gardening and industrial products
- Diet: malnutrition, poor diet
- Maternal age
- Paternal exposure to environmental toxins
- Miscellaneous: vaccinations, passive smoking, raw meat, cat litter trays, commonplace painkillers (e.g. aspirin and paracetamol).

Not all embryos or fetuses are equally (or always) affected by a teratogen. The short- and long-term effects depend on the prenatal and postnatal environments respectively, as well as the baby's and mother's genetic makeup. The same defect can be caused by different teratogens; any one may produce a variety of defects. The longer the exposure, or the greater the 'dose' (potency) the higher the probability of a seriously damaging consequence.

The following teratogens are amongst the most widely publicized and harmful of the noxious agents.

- AIDS is one of the main causes of death in American children from birth to 4 years of age. In Africa it is decimating a generation of children. The transmission rate from affected mother to infant is between 20 and 25 per cent. There is evidence that mothers who are treated with AZT experience a significantly lower transmission rate (see chapter 16).
- Rubella (German measles) is most dangerous when contracted by the mother in the first few weeks of pregnancy. Hearing impairment, cataracts and heart defects are the most common abnormalities suffered by the child. If contracted in the last 6 months of pregnancy, the probability of the fetus suffering an adverse effect reduces to around 10 per cent (Moore and Persaud, 1993).
- Radiation: The effect of radiation depends on the amount and the time of exposure during pregnancy. Exposure of less than 5 rads, typically prescribed for diagnostic X-rays, has not been observed to cause malformations or growth retardation. Nevertheless, alternative procedures such as ultrasound are advised by some practitioners (see Bathshaw and Perret, 1992).
- Thalidomide: The highly visible effects of this drug (arrested growth of arms and legs) tell us that the pregnant mothers of some of our fellow citizens were prescribed teratogenic medication. They took it most probably between days 21 and 35 of the pregnancy.

- Alcohol ingestion has a potentially serious consequence referred to as *fetal alcohol syndrome* (FAS), the leading cause of learning disability (mental retardation) in the USA. The children have small heads and facial deformities, mild to severe cognitive impairment and attention-related problems.
- Cocaine appears to produce no recognizable deformities, but is associated with prematurity, low birthweight, and withdrawal symptoms in the baby.
- Smoking tobacco and marijuana share a similar effect with cocaine, of constricting the blood flow to the placenta from which the fetus derives its nutrients. This results in low birthweight. Higher rates of behaviour problems and learning difficulties are reported in children whose mothers smoke heavily during pregnancy.
- Malnourishment (e.g. excessive dieting) in pregnant women: Babies born to poorly nourished mothers tend to be small and thin; they undergo changes to their metabolism and to their hormonal and circulatory systems that predispose them to disease. These children are reported to be more likely than average to suffer heart disease, hypertension, diabetes and strokes (report by David Barker to the European Society of Human Reproduction and Embryology annual conference in Lausanne, 2001). Barker states that it is the mother's whole-life experience that counts, not just what she eats while she is pregnant. Lifestyle becomes particularly important if a child was born small. Becoming obese at any point is much more dangerous for people who were small as infants.

For prospective parents who come to the gloomy conclusion that their only 'safe bet' is to hide in some isolated place for the duration of the pregnancy, there are reassuring guides written by Miriam Stoppard (*Conception, Pregnancy and Birth*) and Virginia Apgar and Jean Beck (*Is My Baby All Right?*). They provide checklists of things to do or not to do, actions that can significantly reduce the likelihood of having an impaired baby. Considering that most infants, by far, enter the world in good health, it is surely better to emphasize the positive opportunity during pregnancy to do everything possible, at all times, to facilitate their growth and development in the womb.

It is therefore important to be aware of the timing of intrauterine events. Those physical agents that are capable of altering the design of morphology of the organism have their most deleterious effect during the germinal period (first 2 weeks), and the embryonic phase (2 to 8 weeks) when the organ systems are first emerging (see chapter 1). Pregnancy sickness ('morning sickness') seems to coincide with the period of maximum vulnerability to teratogens, peaking at around 6 to 8 weeks. It is a cross-cultural phenomenon. One speculation is that this very uncomfortable state that besets so many pregnant women is, in evolutionary terms, an adaptive mechanism to protect the embryo against various teratogenic agents (e.g. toxic chemicals in certain foods that might not do the mother any harm, but which could damage the embryo).

From about the beginning of the third month of life to birth (the fetal stage) various illnesses and toxins can produce permanent damage. However, once an organ or body part is fully formed (the notable exceptions being the eyes, genitals and nervous system) they are less susceptible to damage. In the first 5 per cent of babies who are not perfectly normal at birth, there are many whose defects and difficulties may prove to be mild, transient or reversible.

> **Note:** In chapter 9 we turn to the atypical experience of the infant-to-be as s/he approaches the time to be born – the hazardous perinatal stage of his or her journey.

chapter nine

The Hazardous Perinatal Period
The Atypical Route

Difficult birth, difficult child

Ancient Chinese saying

By the time the baby is born, s/he is an extraordinary survivor. Only 31 per cent of all conceptions complete the prenatal journey to become living neo-nates. However, the vast majority of babies who do survive, are in a healthy state. Of those that do not complete the journey, 58 per cent are developing organisms that do not survive the germinal period. About 20 per cent of babies-to-be fail at the embryonic stage, and roughly 5 per cent of fetuses are aborted spontaneously or are stillborn (see Moore and Persaud, 1998).

The Apgar Test

In the first minutes of life, a baby takes his or her first 'fitness' test, the *Apgar test*, named after Virginia Apgar (1953) who developed it. It is designed to evaluate the health and status of the baby. A doctor or nurse checks the infant's physical condition by looking at five standard characteristics which are rated from 0 to 2, recorded on a chart, and totalled – giving a range of from 0 to 10. The Apgar score includes the following checks:

Pulse/heart rate – strength and regularity

100 beats per minute	Score 2
Below 100	Score 1
No pulse	Score 0

Breathing – maturity and health of the lungs

Regular breathing	Score 2
Slow, irregular breathing	Score 1
None	Score 0

Movements – muscle tone
Active movement	Score 2
Some movement/limited flexion	Score 1
Limp/flabby	Score 0

Skin colour – effective oxygenation of the blood
Pink skin all over	Score 2
Bluish extremities (arms/legs)	Score 1
Totally blue skin	Score 0

Reflexes – response to stimuli
Crying	Score 2
Whimpering/grimace	Score 1
Silence/no response	Score 0

(In black and Asian children, the colour of the membranes of the mouth, of the whites of the eyes, of the lips, palms, hands, and of the soles of the feet, are examined.)

It is quite common for neonates to have scores lower than 10 in the first round, since babies usually have blue fingers and toes on arrival. At the 5-minute evaluation, the majority of babies score 9 and 10. Seven or better indicates that the infant is not at risk. A score of 4 to 6 indicates that the infant requires assistance in establishing normal breathing patterns. Scores lower than 4 indicate that the baby is in a critical condition and often requires an active intervention (probably intensive care) in order to survive. A low Apgar score tends to signal that the baby is quite likely to have a developmental disability. Around 12 per cent of babies with Apgar ratings lower than 4 at 5 minutes may develop disabling conditions such as cerebral palsy, intellectual impairment and seizures. Fortunately, low-rated infants are by no means always denied normal development.

The Apgar test may not detect more subtle complications. A second test designed by Berry Brazelton (1984), called the *Neonatal Behavioural Assessment Scale*, can be administered a few days after birth, to assess the strength of 20 inborn reflexes, in addition to changes in the infant's state, and reactions to comforting and other social stimuli. A low NBAS score provides a warning that problems may emerge.

Outstanding acoustic characteristics of the newborn cry seem to be related to the integrity of the nervous system. Many pre-term babies, and infants with disabilities (e.g. Down's syndrome, meningitis, encephalitis) where there are neurological complications, have atypical patterns of crying involving penetrating, grating sounds. Among a group of high-risk infants, those with more shrill and high-pitched cries had significantly lower IQ scores at 5 years of age.

Survival Repertoire

One of the significant indications of the preparedness of infants for some of the rigours of their journey through life, is their possession of a repertoire of instinctive survival reflexes that help them to adapt to their new surroundings and to satisfy basic needs. Reflexes are the names given to the newborn's ability to respond motorically to sensory stimulation of particular kinds, in predetermined (i.e. canalized) ways. There are several adaptive reflexes, some having more obvious survival value than others. They include:

- Rooting, a head-turn in response to the stimulation of the corner of the mouth, preparatory to sucking.
- The sucking reflex is elicited by having a nipple in the baby's mouth. Deprivation of oxygen during birth may prevent the appearance of both of these vital reflexes.
- Reflexes such as swallowing, blinking, sneezing, and coughing are all adaptive and are retained for life.

The primitive reflexes, so-called, include the following:

- The Moro reflex refers to the way the infant arches his back in response to a loud noise, also extending his or her legs and throwing their arms outwards. The reflex will have disappeared by the time the baby is 6 months of age.
- The Babinski reflex is a response to stroking the sole of the foot from the toes toward the heel; the big toe extends and the smaller toes spread out. The reflex disappears by the first year's end. It may not be present in newborns with lower spinal cord damage.
- Palmar grasp. This refers to the grasp precipitated by pressing the baby's palm with a finger. It disappears by 3 to 4 months as the baby moves on to voluntary grasping.
- Walking. When held under the arms with feet touching the surface the infant lifts one foot after the other in a walk-like position. This reflex tends to disappear by 2 months of age.

Primitive reflexes, like the swimming reflex and the grasping reflex, may have useful functions (Thelen, 1984). They are controlled by the lower subcortical areas of the brain and are lost once the higher centres of the cerebral cortex begin to guide voluntary behaviours. If they, or other reflexes, are not present at birth, or if they last too long in infancy, there would be reason to be concerned about a possible neurological difficulty. Particularly important are the actions that function primarily in social situations, notably the attractiveness of auditory and visual stimuli provided by caregivers and other adults to babies soon after their arrival in the world.

- They turn their heads towards patterned sounds rather than monotonic stimuli, particularly if these sounds are within the frequency range of human speech.
- They are attracted to the human face in motion, the advantage being that it is at just at the right height to fixate with ease.
- There is interest shown in stimuli that move around, in general.

There are other proactive activities designed to give babies an early orientation to the social world. Newborn infants smile and cry for a variety of reasons, at first without social meaning. But this soon changes. As we shall see in later chapters these physically and socially adaptive capacities (most dramatically in conditions such as profound learning disability and autism) may be impaired or absent.

Birth Complications

We have seen, in chapters 1 and 2, how the first 9 months of life present the embryo and later the fetus, with a succession of hurdles to overcome. Birth complications are part of a continuum that begins before the first contractions, and continue in the subsequent months and years. They are much more likely in the following circumstances:

- Low fetal weight
- Pre-term birth
- Genetic abnormality
- Exposure to teratogens
- The mother is unusually small
- The mother has medical problems.

The final hurdle – the process of being born – is in many ways the most dramatic. Certainly a child who has developed normally during the nine prenatal months can be seriously harmed by some accident during the process of birth. Looking at the size of a neonate's head, and considering the dimensions of the birth canal, one might be excused for thinking that the otherwise extraordinarily well-adapted human body is poorly designed for the rigours of delivery. Injuries can be caused by an exceptionally long labour, abnormal positioning of the baby, direct trauma to the brain, as a result of damaging haemorrhages, or mother–child Rh factor incompatibility.

Rh factor incompatibility

A dangerous situation can result from the condition known as Rh incompatibility (erythroblastosis). It involves an incompatibility between the infant's blood type and that of its mother, resulting in destruction of the infant's red blood cells (haemolytic anaemia) after birth, by antibodies from its mother's blood. The signs in a newborn are:

- Paleness
- Jaundice (yellow skin and eyes) that begins within 24 hours after delivery
- Unexplained bruising or blood spots under the skin
- Tissue swelling (oedema)
- Breathing difficulties
- Fits
- Lack of normal movement
- Poor reflex responses.

Problems arise if the mother is Rh– and the baby is Rh+. Because Rh+ is dominant, an infant with an Rh+ father could inherit an Rh+ gene from him, even though the mother is Rh–. During delivery a small amount of the infant's blood is absorbed by the mother through the placenta, stimulating her body to go into defensive mode. Her body considers the baby's Rh+ factor to be an alien substance and her immune system tries to eliminate it by producing antibodies. These antibodies cross the placenta and attack the infant's blood, producing in it, a chemical substance called bilirubin. Babies with high levels appear jaundiced, i.e. quite yellow. If untreated brain damage may ensue. The antibodies are produced after delivery, so the first infant is not affected. With succeeding pregnancies, the risk of damage to the fetus increases; the antibodies in the mother's blood destroy fetal blood cells.

   To prevent this risk to the child, medical supervision early in the pregnancy is essential, to determine the risk of Rh incompatibility. Special anti-Rh gamma globulin is given to the mother at 28 weeks gestation and within 72 hours after delivery, or following a miscarriage, ectopic pregnancy or abortion. This prevents the formation of antibodies that might affect future infants. At the time of writing this section, a fetus whose life was in danger because of serious Rh complications, was saved by a blood transfusion conducted *in utero*.

Prematurity

Crises within the perinatal time frame are frequently the result of prematurity. Babies weigh different amounts at birth, some being very small; and not all gestate for the full term of 38 weeks. Prematurity and other complications of pregnancy and birth are associated with an elevated risk of fetal and neonatal death, usually due to the damage sustained by the central nervous system. In the past babies studied for their premature status (e.g. Drillien, 1964) were categorized together if they weighed less than 2500 g (5.5 lb). Definitions, today, are rather more refined than that.

- Small for date or low birthweight (LBW): Infants who are small for gestational age are seriously under-weight. Even when born close to their normal due date, these infants are below the tenth percentile of full-term babies weight at birth. This means they weigh less than 2000 g. The optimum weight range for infants – the weight that is thought to involve the lowest risk of later disability or death – is between 3000 and 5000 g (6.6 to 11 lb). All babies below 2500 g (around 5.5 lb) are described using the generic term *low birthweight*. Those below 1500 g (about 3.3 lb) are usually referred to as *very low birthweight*, while those below 1000 g are called *extremely low birthweight*. Advances in neonatal medicine over the last decade and a half ensure that many more very low birthweight (3.3 lb < 1500 g) infants survive than did previously, with some evidence that morbidity rates are also improving. Nevertheless, babies who are of low weight for their gestational age (more than two standard deviations below the mean) are at higher risk of serious complications than their normal counterparts. They are more likely to die during the first year, or suffer more abnormalities of the nervous system. Pressure during birth may cause the fracture of bones in their delicate skulls. Should this happen in the vicinity of nerve centres, there may be temporary or permanent injury to some of them, or to the sense organs, particularly the ears and eyes.
- Birth before term: Infants born at least 1 month before their estimated date of birth are defined as *pre-term infants*. The limit for viability of pre-term babies is at about 23 to 24 weeks of gestation or about 500–600 g. Survival at 25 weeks and beyond is fairly routine, but still fraught with risk, requiring intensive care. The 'grey area' is between 22 and 24 weeks of gestation. The chances of survival are much less and the likelihood of disability much greater. This gives rise to many ethical issues that are extremely difficult to unravel. Why some babies arrive early is not fully understood. In about 30 per cent of pregnancies pre-term birth occurs because there is some infective process. There are organisms in the vagina that become pathogenic, and make their way up into the uterus causing problems in the fetal membranes. Contractions occur to remove the fetus from possibly terminal danger – a protective outcome for baby and possibly the mother as well. In a further 20 per cent of pregnancies the health of the fetus or the mother makes it imperative that the baby be born premature. In the remaining 50 per cent it is not known why there is an early entry into life.

A primary task facing the newborn is state regulation. A baby born very immature is in many ways a different organism than a full-term baby, and the problems they experience affect almost every organ they possess. Given the improved survival rate of very low birthweight infants, has the prevalence of handicapped infants increased? It is argued that over the years the rate of handicap in immature babies has reduced, because neonatologists have learned new skills and developed very sophisticated technology. It certainly takes what looks like 'space age' technology plus specialist neonatal nursing and medical expertise in intensive care units, to monitor and replace the life-supports the uterus would have provided. Premature babies are often delivered by caesarian section because there is less of a risk to an infant that is already under varying degrees of stress.

Causes of prematurity

The reported 'causes' of prematurity (usually expressed as factors that are *associated* with prematurity) are many and varied. (The meaning and significance of correlations constitute a potential 'minefield' (see Herbert, 1990).) The putative determinants include primiparity, maternal age, malnutrition, multiple births, pyelonephritis, vaginal bleeding, prolonged rupture of membranes, habitual abortion, previous history of infertility, acute infections, and toxaemia during pregnancy. Twenty per cent of all premature infants are born to adolescent girls (Goldberg and Craig, 1983). There is a predisposition to perinatal complications in women from deprived low socioeconomic circumstances in which there has been inadequate prenatal care and stress-related difficulties such as alcohol and drug abuse. Mothers who smoke and drink heavily, use drugs, or are malnourished are likely to deliver undersized babies. Excessive alcohol consumption and substances such as cocaine constrict the blood vessels and starve the placenta, resulting in prematurity, placental separation, and fetal distress during delivery (Kopp and Kaler, 1989; Lin, 1993).

Various illnesses and conditions may predispose women to premature delivery and birth complications:

- Hypertension: Pregnant women sometimes suffer from high blood pressure in the second half of pregnancy. If combined with oedema (accumulation of fluid in tissues) and/or protein in the urine it may result in toxaemia of pregnancy or pre-eclampsia. The condition will persist until after delivery, and carries a significant risk of prematurity and intrauterine growth retardation.
- Diabetes: In this condition the fetal pancreas produces excess insulin which results in abnormally low levels of blood sugar levels (hypoglycaemia). If not treated it results in brain damage in the infant.

- Herpes: This active viral infection can be transmitted from the mother to the relatively immune-deficient infant during delivery. It causes death in 60 per cent of infected infants and significant neurological damage in half of the survivors.

Among other adverse conditions that put a pregnancy at risk are the following:

1. Placenta praevia: Normally the placenta attaches itself high on the uterine wall, away from the cervix. The placenta covers the cervix partially or completely. Any change in the cervix, such as the softening and dilating that occurs close to delivery, can cause the placenta to separate from the uterus and bleed. This may be life threatening to the unborn child. Placenta praevia occurs to some degree in one out of 250 pregnancies. Illness or accidents that disrupt the functioning of the placenta can retard fetal growth and lead to a baby who is pre-term or small for date. Small-for-date infants are often malformed, undernourished, or genetically abnormal.

   The problem shows itself as sudden painless bleeding during the second or third trimester of pregnancy, especially the last 13 weeks. The risk for the mother of suffering from placenta praevia increases if she has:
   - fibroid tumours of the uterus,
   - diabetes mellitus,
   - had previous uterine surgery,
   - had multiple previous pregnancies and deliveries; and if
   - the foetus is in an abnormal position, or
   - the mother is over 35 years of age.

2. Premature rupture of the amniotic sac: This condition may precipitate premature labour or lead to infection or fetal deformities.

3. Structural abnormalities: The mother's pelvis may put her at risk if it is too small to allow the passage of the baby's head (cephalopelvic disproportion) or it may dilate too early (incompetent cervix), which can result in premature delivery or miscarriage.

4. Uterine contractions: If the uterus contracts too forcefully, it can interfere with fetal circulation, causing oxygen deprivation or bleeding in the brain. The fetus is designed to withstand the stress of labour, which usually involves a reduction in the amount of blood reaching the brain (ischaemia) and the amount of oxygen in the blood (hypoxaemia) during passage through the birth canal, but if these reductions are too great a normal fetus is more likely to die than survive.

Birth by caesarian section is a common procedure in placenta praevia. The delivery of the baby is through a cut into the abdominal wall, thus transforming a birth-event into a major operation from which the mother needs time to recover. In the past mothers were always given a general anaesthetic for a caesarian as a matter of routine, which meant that the mothers were unconscious right through the birth of the baby and for some time afterwards. However, nowadays some mothers who need to have a caesarian section choose to have their babies delivered with the help of an epidural injection. This is an injection into the space between the vertebrae at the base of the spine that numbs all (or most) sensation from the waist downwards. Thus the mother is fully conscious when her baby is removed from the womb. This has some advantages and also allows the father to share with the mother the moment of birth. Birth by caesarian section can retain some of the features of a normal confinement. Such babies, after all, are fairly unstressed.

Consequences of prematurity

To be born prematurely is an immediate developmental setback, not untypically compounded by multiple medical complications requiring invasive and sometimes prolonged treatment. The strongest perinatal indicator of difficulties to come is the number of days the infant spends in the intensive care unit. Fortunately, the presence of short-term effects does not necessarily mean that there will be long-term consequences of an adverse kind. Outcomes are especially positive when parents are sensitive to the factors that promote and stimulate healthy development (Caughy, 1996).

Nevertheless, prematurity at birth is correlated with various later complications. For example, children in less stable, deprived homes, experience more emotional problems and manifest long-term intellectual and academic deficits (see Baker and Mednick, 1984; Kopp and Kaler, 1989). Other outcomes include:

- Intellectual difficulties: The general finding for very low birthweight children in terms of intellectual development, is that they are one-half to one standard deviation (7 to 15 IQ points) below their peers.
- Stature: The small-for-date babies are more likely than pre-term infants to remain small in stature throughout childhood, to experience learning difficulties and manifest behaviour problems at school, and to perform poorly on IQ tests (Goldenberg, 1995; Lin, 1993).

The premature infant is vulnerable with regard to several physical complications, including:

- Intracerebral haemorrhages: bursting of blood cells particularly in the ventricles with implications for leg movements and the risk thus of spastic diplegia (Graziani, Pasto and Stanley, 1986).

- Retrolental fibroplasia (retinopathy of prematurity): the detachment of the retina that can lead to blindness, a condition associated with high concentrations of oxygen given to babies with respiratory distress syndrome (RDS) (Bathshaw and Perret, 1992).
- RDS develops within a few days of birth and is suffered by 60 per cent of infants born at or before 32 weeks, when they are unable to produce surfactant to keep the alveoli open. Most survive with treatment.
- Sudden infant death syndrome (SIDS), commonly referred to as 'cot death', is defined as the sudden death of an infant or young child that is unexpected by its history and in which a thorough post-mortem fails to demonstrate an adequate cause of death. There have been mentions of sudden and unexpected deaths in the *Old Testament*, in Roman records, and in the twelfth- and thirteenth-century legal and medical literature. SIDS is poorly understood, although several environmental associations (e.g. overnight temperature, sleeping position, climate) and biological correlations (e.g. centrally determined sleep apnoea) have been reported. The necessary and sufficient causes of SIDS remain to be discovered, despite the best efforts of investigations dating from the 1950s. SIDS has serious and prolonged psychological effects on parents and siblings.
- Behavioural difficulties: A long history of research indicates problems such as excessive distractibility, hyperactivity, hyper-irritability, impaired intellectual capacity, hypersensitivity to sound, personality disturbance and reading difficulties (e.g. Shirley, 1938). Pre-term children, as rated by teachers, display more behaviour problems than controls (normal birth-weight children) and are less well adjusted to the school environment. This applies to all social classes and appears to result from a general failure in self-regulated functions (see Kopp and Kaler, 1989; Korkman, Liikanen and Fellman, 1996).

Follow-up evidence

Drillien (1964) studied (longitudinally) the sequelae of premature births in over 1000 mothers. Using the *Bristol Social Adjustment Guide*, she tested the school-going children at ages 6 and 7. She found that the proportion of youngsters considered maladjusted or unsettled increased as birthweight decreased. Obstetric difficulties – severe complications of pregnancy and/or birth – were associated with an increased risk of disturbed behaviour in the offspring. An intensive investigation of 112 babies whose birthweight was 3 pounds or less revealed defects of vision in 37 per cent of those who were of school-going age. Eight per cent had some degree of congenital defect. Other defects included cerebral diplegia (18 per cent), epilepsy (7 per cent) and speech defects (8 per cent). At 5 years or more, one-third of this subgroup were below the fifth percentile for mature controls in weight; nearly one-half were behind in height and over one-quarter in both weight and height. Over one-third were likely to be 'ineducable' (a politically incorrect term these days) in ordinary schools for reasons of physical or intellectual impairment or both. Only 30 per cent of the school-age children could be described as manifesting no disturbance of behaviour.

Drillien (ibid.) found that the most common behaviour problems associated with very severe prematurity (birthweight of 3 pounds or less) were hyperactivity and restlessness. These problems, and distractibility, are probably the only types of childhood behaviour disorder that can be associated (with any degree of confidence as to causality) with perinatal factors. However, it would not be surprising if other conduct disorders of a reactive nature (e.g. delinquency) followed on the educational and social failures frequently experienced by hyperactive, restless and distractible children (see chapter 12).

The findings of this study are somewhat compromised by the undifferentiated definition Drillien applied to premature infants. Classifications are now more precise; and differentials in outcomes resulting from refinements in specifying the type and nature of the prematurity, and the quality of the long-term care provided, are much more taken into account.

Birth Trauma

Much has been made in the past of the translation of the neonate from the 'tranquillity' of the womb to the busy world outside this sheltered environment. The notion of a psychological 'birth trauma' (Greenacre, 1945) has not proved susceptible to proof or disproof, although this has not deterred many people from employing a form of therapy based upon liberation from the prolonged and allegedly traumatizing influence of the birth process. The emotional trauma is seen as the prototype for later anxiety attacks.

Leaving aside the psychological ramifications of being born, there is little doubt that the birth process is the most hazardous single event in a person's life. An average period of labour lasts for about 12 to 14 hours for first-time mothers and about 7 hours for subsequent babies. Labour lasting well over 12 hours the first time or 9 hours in subsequent labours may require, following an examination, an intervention. Breech delivery refers to the position in which babies are born feet or buttocks first. The umbilical cord can easily become tangled or squeezed in this situation, interrupting the baby's supply of oxygen. Breech babies are often delivered by caesarian section to protect them against anoxia (Lin, 1993).

Anoxia

The development and normal functioning of the brain depends upon large supplies of oxygen conveyed to it by the blood. A reduction in this blood supply results in a shortage of the oxygen necessary for the maintenance of brain metabolism. Perinatal anoxia (a lack or deficiency of oxygen) affects nearly 1 per cent of babies. Permanent brain damage can result if breathing is delayed for more than 3 to 4 minutes, a greater tolerance of oxygen starvation than is possible for older children and adults.

Anoxia can be caused by many factors. Brief, intermittent periods of severe anoxia may be associated (as we have seen) with the rhythmic uterine contractions of labour. It may be mild but prolonged in the case of partial, premature separation of the placenta. It can also be relatively brief in duration but exceptionally severe in the case of complete placental separation, massive loss of blood by the mother, or other complications of labour and delivery. In many cases the infant's supply of oxygen is interrupted because the umbilical cord has become tangled or squeezed during childbirth, as can easily occur when infants are lying in the breech position. Anoxia can also occur if sedatives given to the mother cross the placental barrier and interfere with the baby's breathing.

Consequence of oxygen deprivation

The hippocampus (important in establishing a continuous record of memories) is one of the most sensitive areas of the brain. It is frequently damaged by anoxia. If damage to the brain is widespread and affects the integrity of the temporal lobes, intellectual impairment is highly probable. There is evidence that babies born precipitately after a short, sharp labour, or born after their mothers have endured difficult pregnancies (such as full or partial placenta praevia) tend to be irritable, hyperactive and difficult as babies and as older children. Precipitate labour (i.e. of less than 2 hours' duration) has potentially detrimental effects on later intellectual development because it introduces the infant to oxygen too suddenly with the result that she may suffer from anoxia.

Early studies, notably in the 1960s, were full of pessimistic findings of correlations between asphyxia at birth and the incidence of neurological abnormalities between one and five years from birth. Among these were correlations between anoxia and perceptual and psychomotor deficits, over-excitability, low developmental quotient scores in the first 2 years of life, and quite specific temperamental attributes in later life. The affected children were unusually sensitive, over-reactive to stimuli, with a tendency to become upset when customary routines are upset (Ucko, 1965). Pasamanick and Knobloch (1961) referred to the relationship between complications of pregnancy and birth, and behaviour disorders in children, as a 'continuum of reproductive casualty'. Understanding the causal processes that underlie such short- and long-term longitudinal correlations is a central and continuing task for researchers in the field of developmental psychopathology (see discussion on pp. 177 and 178).

There is little doubt that in extreme cases human babies do suffer gross and sometimes fatal brain damage from birth asphyxia and resultant oxygen deprivation. But the extent to which this lack of oxygen contributes, over the long term, to the much more common minor degrees of neurological impairment, intellectual impairment, or behaviour problems, remains to be established. As always, one has to be cautious about interpreting correlations, as they do not necessarily indicate a causal relationship, although they may be suggestive of cause and effect. Children who experience mild anoxia are often irritable at birth and tend to score below average on tests of motor and mental development throughout their first 3 years of life (Sameroff and Chandler, 1975). However, the differences between typical (normal) children and atypical (i.e. mildly anoxic) children become smaller and smaller and are usually not detectable by 7 years of age. There is certainly no compelling evidence to date that mild anoxia has any lasting effects on children's motor skills or intellectual development (Vaughan, Kopp, and Krakow, 1984).

Goodman (1994, p. 173) challenges the perinatal danger theories. He states that 'generations of medical students have been taught that cerebral palsy, mental retardation and epilepsy are commonly due to perinatal complications. This view is almost certainly false. Obstetric and neonatal complications are common but are generally innocuous'. Thus in one study, over half the normal controls had experienced one such complication. He adds that even severe perinatal complications are usually harmless. Goodman provides evidence for his claim in his detailed review.

He goes on to observe that 'since the fetus is an active participant in the delivery process, and not simply a passive passenger who is expelled when his or her time is up, it is not surprising that an abnormal fetus is particularly liable to an abnormal birth'. It is possible that perinatal complications compound whatever damage has already occurred prenatally, just as labour may compound the existing damage in spina bifida. When it comes to the aetiological link between birth complications and brain damage, he cautions that 'neurological theories about aetiology are as error-prone as psychiatric theories'. In his opinion, if birth complications are not common causes of overt brain disorders such as cerebral palsy, it is even less likely that they commonly result in minimal brain damage manifesting itself solely in behavioural or learning difficulties.

Parental Attachment to Atypical Infants

Adverse events during the perinatal period seem capable of affecting the mother's feelings for her baby. The sudden change in hormone levels referred to in chapter 2 (i.e. a dramatic reduction in progesterone and oestrogen) following childbirth is thought to be a principal cause of the so-called 'baby blues' (not statistically atypical) and the more serious malaise diagnosed as 'postnatal depression'. Doubtless, the thought or dawning realization of the unconditional responsibility for a totally dependent normal, or atypical disabled child, has its impact on a woman, particularly (but by no means exclusively) a first-time or single mother and, notably, an exhausted one.

Infants are very susceptible to 'unnatural disruptions' (e.g. a depressed mother's blank face or mistimings of her responses) in the interactional sequences between themselves and their mothers (Murray and Trevarthen, 1985).

Williams and Carmichael (1985) studied a group of Australian women who were depressed after they had their first baby. They reported significantly more problems than the contrast group of non-depressed mothers. These difficulties included:

- A failure to establish a relationship with the infant on the postnatal ward
- Difficulties in developing a routine pattern of management of the baby
- At home the baby cried a great deal, fed poorly, slept irregularly and was resistant to soothing
- The infant's behaviour made the mother angry and frustrated
- Some mothers experienced depression weeks after delivery, with similar interaction problems.

Robson and Kumar (1980) noted that maternal affection was more likely to be lacking after delivery if the mother had had a forewater amniotomy and had, in addition, either experienced a painful and unpleasant labour, or been given more than 126 mg of pethidine. Such indications of indifference are not usually long lasting.

The question has been raised as to whether maternal attachment may be affected by the particular circumstances of the postnatal care of prematurely born babies. Low birthweight and pre-term infants are typically placed in a special care nursery. This procedure increases the chances that the mother and infant do not have as much opportunity to interact intimately in the early days following birth, as those born at term.

To begin with, premature birth can be a somewhat traumatic experience for the mother. The low weight of the baby can itself be worrying. A mother who smoked during pregnancy may be concerned, with some justification, lest she herself is to blame for the baby's low birthweight. Thus, at the time, her anxiety may be due as much to these and related factors, as to the enforced separation from her baby. Whatever feelings she harbours towards her baby are clearly the result of a complex set of events and experiences, and certainly are not solely the result of the absence of skin-to-skin contact, about which (as we have seen) there has been so much fuss. If all goes well with the infant in the special care unit, and the parents can clearly observe this in the course of frequent visits, then their anxiety is likely to be allayed. There is no evidence that in such circumstances parental love and attachment will in any way be diminished.

A research group (Leifer and colleagues) compared the actions of mothers of full-term babies, and two groups of mothers of premature babies. There were those who were only allowed visual contact with the baby after her placement in the intensive care unit, as was then customary, and an experimental group who were allowed to participate in care-taking as far as was practicable. Mothers of the full-term babies did maintain more ventral contact between themselves and their babies, and did smile more at the infants than mothers of the premature ones. However, 1 month after the baby's discharge from hospital, no differences were found between mothers of full-term and premature babies in many other attachment activities (holding, affectionate touching, looking at, talking to, laughing or singing to the baby) or the time devoted to interaction with the baby, outside care-giving. The two groups of mothers of premature infants showed no differences at all in maternal actions, although mothers in the group who had experienced the longest separation were still somewhat less confident about their care-taking skills. Nothing significant emerged from this investigation that demonstrated unequivocally any lasting disruption of normal maternal behaviour in the 'separation' group (Leifer, 1972).

To be discharged from hospital and to return home without her baby is a situation fraught with difficulty for any mother. It is a situation that is contrary to the expectations of her friends and neighbours. A good deal of explaining has to be done, which may or may not be somewhat distressful or tiresome. In the end, sooner or later, the baby is returned to the mother: and there is no evidence that the mother's feelings towards her infant are in any way permanently distorted. Of course, parental access to their babies in special care units is to be greatly encouraged for a variety of good reasons: but practical common sense, rather than concern over the existence of a critical bonding period, should decide upon visiting arrangements.

Those are the conclusions that can be reasonably drawn from the present state of knowledge. However, that is not to say that our knowledge in this field is adequate or satisfactory. As one group of authors say, the present 'scientific' evidence on the adverse effects of parent–child separation in the immediate neonatal period is partial and incomplete. There is, however, a good deal of evidence that babies can weather prolonged early parental separation and thrive in every way thereafter. There are also numerous indications that mothers can, in favourable circumstances, function perfectly well after being reunited with their premature babies, care for them competently, and become attached to them as strongly as do mothers of full-term babies.

As is usual in so many areas of research into early child development, the studies have concentrated mainly on maternal attitudes. Depending on the nature and severity of the disability, a firm diagnosis may be possible at any time, ranging from birth onwards. The clearest diagnosable type of handicap at birth is a congenital abnormality of structure. According to the Department of Health statistics, there are up to 40 such babies born each day in Britain, and the survival rate is increasing all the time. If the mother is initially unaware of the infant's disability, then clearly the development of maternal attachment remains unaffected until the time she learns about it. And even then, whatever the child's age, her feelings about the child may remain substantially unaltered one way or another. If the mother learns about her baby's handicap at birth, she is, of course, likely to be markedly affected by the news. The question is whether her love for the baby then develops normally or not; and if the latter we may ask whether her bond of affection is weaker, stronger or different in quality from what it might otherwise have been.

How then do mothers and the rest of the family react to the birth of atypical infants? One systematic small-scale study was carried out in the hope of finding an answer (Johns, 1971). Not at all surprisingly, the initial emotional reaction of the mothers was found to be anxiety, shock or dismay in facing an unexpected crisis. This overshadowed the satisfaction normally accompanying childbirth. After a time interval, some mothers tended to play down the problem, and early mothering care seemed essentially unaffected. Studies like this are very useful in suggesting how doctors, nurses, counsellors and social workers can best manage a situation that is sometimes fraught.

It is very difficult to predict what the impact of the birth of a handicapped infant is on the development of the mother-to-infant bond. When asked, most mothers express the view that it is best for them to be told as soon as the doctor suspects a physical or a mental disability in the infant (McMichael, 1971). They wish to be given truthful and clear information. However, some mothers adopt what looks like a defensive stance and deny the diagnosis. They certainly often continue to hope that the doctor will be proved wrong. Such denial is not uncommon immediately following diagnosis and goes on for some days or weeks, or even longer, before it finally abates. The doctor has to decide how soon he or she is in a position to tell the parents of their infant's disability; also how much to tell them. For one thing, young mothers are sometimes so overwhelmed by the initial news that they cannot take in much more than the barest outlines of the situation. Finally, the problem faced by the doctor is not only when and what to tell the mother but also what not to tell her. It is often a question of not giving the parents information that could be misinterpreted, sparing them any unnecessary worry, and, for some, grief.

I am conscious of not having stated in an unequivocal manner whether there is anything different and special about maternal attachment to physically disabled infants. There are reports of resentful and rejecting mothers. Equally, many mothers are exceptionally loving and devoted to their handicapped children, and commonly say that the child has enriched their family life. One has only to work in a paediatric development centre to witness the unconditional care and love bestowed on many children with major disabilities.

Stillbirth and Infant Death

It is only too apparent that several conditions described in this chapter can lead to death, an issue we address further in chapter 16. Although, at no time, are mothers prepared, mentally and emotionally, for the death of their baby at birth (think of that initial, inevitable question: 'Is it all right?'), losing the infant nevertheless comes as a devastating blow. This reflects the considerable emotional investment that has already been made in the baby-to-be. Bonding has a fairly specific connotation as we have seen, and it is very much a two-way process between mother and child. So it is debatable whether we can refer to the emotional investment as bonding – that attachment which is discriminating and specific and which ties her to her offspring in space and over time. In a way this is splitting semantic hairs. In the words of the poet, Henry Wadsworth Longfellow (1807–1882):

> *It is difficult to know at what moment love begins;*
> *it is less difficult to know it has begun.*

A mother's feeling of loss is likely to be all the stronger if she has (earlier) felt her baby living and moving. Even in the recent past, mothers were often prevented from seeing their dead babies in the mistaken belief that 'what you have not seen you won't miss'. Currently it is a common practice to allow parents to see and, if they so wish, touch the dead infant. Underlying this change in hospital routine may be a view that unless a bond has formed through skin-to-skin contact with the baby, mourning cannot occur. This is an implied rather than explicit tenet, and more likely to be voiced at case conferences and ward rounds than debated in the literature.

Whatever the truth of the matter, there are sound psychological reasons for managing the death of an infant, and the family's, and particularly the mother's grief, with sensitivity and flexibility. Standish (1982) interviewed 32 women who had had a stillbirth or neonatal death, 6 and again

14 months after the death of their babies. Although 6 months after the event, life had apparently returned to normal for most of them, and even more so 14 months on, she found the mothers still very preoccupied with the events that had led to their loss. The dead baby was far from forgotten.

Of particular concern in this matter of the mother's (and, indeed, the family's) attachment to the stillborn infant, is the effect on the offspring who follow an emotionally unresolved bereavement. A study by Hughes, Turton et al. (2001) of 53 infants born next after a stillborn baby and 53 control infants of primigravid mothers, confirmed previous clinical observations that next-borns are at risk of psychological and behaviour problems in later childhood. The authors of the research conclude that the strong association between disorganization of infant attachment and maternal state of mind with respect to loss suggest that the mother's state of mind may be causal, and raises interesting theoretical questions about the mechanism of inter-generational transmission, and practical ones about the necessity for raised consciousness in professionals who work with bereaved mothers.

In situations of fetal death or stillbirth, socially or culturally prescribed customs are, too often, lacking. Some couples will want to see the infant, perhaps hold it, and may desire photographs. There may be a funeral and burial involving close family and friends where the ritual of saying goodbye brings comfort at this time of loss. For some couples, this difficult time of loss and grief is mitigated through the support they receive through this open process of recognizing the death of their infant. For others the fetus may be disposed of at the hospital, and the couple may grieve in the absence of any healing ritual. In either situation, the loss is very painful. For the young couple inability to cope with the loss may require professional help. There is increasing recognition of the need for mothers to recognize the dead infant as a person and to grieve the loss (Clunies-Ross and Lansdowne, 1988). Recognizing the baby as a person and making the death public tend to aid the healing process for the mother and father (see chapter 16).

chapter ten

Early Childhood
Atypical Physical,
Sensory and Motor Development

Cassius: *But soft, I pray you. What, did Caesar swoon?*
Casca: *He fell down in the market place, and foam'd at mouth,*
           and was speechless.
Brutus: *'Tis very like. He hath the falling sickness.*
                                    William Shakespeare: *Julius Caesar*

Physical Disorders and Disabilities

Neurological damage has been implicated in the aetiology of behaviour problems, specific learning difficulties, infantile autism and cerebral palsy, to mention only a few of the areas I shall be considering. Of major concern, among the atypical disorders linked to cerebral dysfunction, is epilepsy.

Epilepsy (seizure disorders)

Epileptic seizures ('fits' in common parlance) occur because some abnormal locus of the brain's electrical activity escalates and spreads into an area of cortex. Behavioural reactions are involved to the extent that the areas corresponding to motor and sensory functions represented on the brain are involved.

We saw above, a literary account of an epileptic seizure suffered by the eponymous hero of Shakespeare's play. Medical practice had to await Hippocrates' treatise on epilepsy (400 BC) to appreciate that the brain was the seat of the disease. The ancient Greeks believed it to be a sacred disease brought about by an invasion of the body by a god. His hypothesis was forgotten for some 25 centuries. It awaited the development of the discipline neurology to rescue it from the alienists who by then were seen as the main custodians of 'mad' epileptics (see Reynolds, 1988). In 1873 Huglings Jackson redefined epilepsy in neurophysiological rather than clinical terms, as occasional, sudden, excessive, rapid and local discharges of grey matter.

Only in the last four decades has the diagnosis 'epilepsy', per se, been removed from national and international classifications of psychiatric illness. Epileptic seizures were classified by the 1981 Commission on Classification and Terminology of the International League Against Epilepsy, using more appropriate terms to describe the underlying pathology. The sub-types of epileptic seizures are as follows.

GENERALIZED SEIZURES

In these, both hemispheres of the brain are involved simultaneously; they account for nearly half of all cases of epilepsy. Tonic-clonic seizures, absence seizures, myoclonic seizures and atonic seizures are all forms of generalized epileptic seizures.

- Tonic-clonic seizures (grand mal seizures) involve the entire body. The tonic (rigidity) phase is followed by a clonic (oscillating, jerking) phase. From a stiff posture to cessation of convulsions may take two to four minutes. The person may experience an aura (a warning sign, like seeing coloured flashing lights) briefly prior to an attack, with no memory of the attack itself and a state of deep restful sleep afterwards. A child who remains in a state of convulsion for more than 15 minutes is said to be in *status epilepticus*, and will require an emergency intervention.
- Absence seizures (petit mal seizures) last only seconds, and may be quite difficult to see in the child, as the body posture and muscle tone remain the same. The eyes appear somewhat glazed and the child is literally absent in mind from the situation s/he is in. Nor can this 'unawareness' be brought to an end by prompting. Such interruptions in consciousness occur dozens of times a day in some children. They are not aware of the episodes.
- Myoclonic seizures are characterized by powerful abrupt contractions of muscles, which may involve the entire body or a part of it. Atonic seizures involve just as sudden a loss of muscle tone, such that the child may need to wear a helmet to avoid head injury in case of an inevitable fall.

PARTIAL SEIZURES

These are more common than generalized seizures. The brain abnormality is usually restricted to one hemisphere, and most of the children affected have some prenatal brain insult. Partial seizures can be categorized as simple or complex:

- Simple partial seizures are those in which the child retains consciousness. The symptoms include twitching, or oscillation of the hand, arm or leg. If the abnormal discharge of electrical activity occurs in sensory areas of the cortex, visual, auditory or olfactory sensations may also be present.
- Complex partial seizures (temporal, or psychomotor seizures) are those in which the child is unaware of the seizure activity, which may last up to several minutes. Some characteristic symptoms are staring, blinking, lip-smacking, finger-tapping, grimacing and other rapid automatic actions.

An extensive research literature on epilepsy and cognitive impairment (e.g. Besag, 1988) suggests that:

- The cognitive characteristics of epilepsy are very varied and multifactorially determined.
- Epileptic children are significantly at risk of having learning disabilities.
- Nevertheless, most children with epilepsy are of normal intelligence and the intellectual ability does not deteriorate.
- A small subgroup does deteriorate intellectually.
- In these children, although there is conflicting evidence, it appears that what contributes to the intellectual deterioration may be:
  - early age of onset
  - frequent seizures
  - prolonged seizures
  - association with pre-existing brain damage
  - mixed seizure types occurring together
  - status epilepticus.

Cerebral palsy (CP)

Cerebral palsy provides a good example of the symptom diversity shown by children covered by a single diagnosis associated with lesions to the central nervous system. Several different motor disorders are referred to under that generic term. These disorders are the result of lesions that can occur at a number of levels within the system of motor control. For example lesions in the cortex or in its projections into the corticospinal tracts produce spasticity – abnormal muscle contractions and inability to perform voluntary movements freely and smoothly. CP begins in infancy and continues throughout life. The number and severity of the symptoms vary widely among children with CP:

- Early sucking difficulty with the breast or bottle
- Lack of normal muscle tone (early)

- Slow development (walking, talking)
- Unusual body postures
- Stiffness and muscle spasms (later)
- Purposeless body movements
- Poor coordination or balance
- Crossed eyes
- Deafness
- Convulsions
- Various degrees of intellectual impairment.

The source of defects associated with cerebral palsy include:

- Birth injury, including prolonged oxygen deprivation
- Use of drugs during pregnancy that damage the fetus
- Infections, such as German measles, in the mother during pregnancy
- Rh incompatibility or bile blockage in the newborn
- Meningitis or encephalitis during infancy or childhood.

We return to the subject of cerebral palsy below.

Neurofibromatosis (Nf)

Two different genes are affected: Nf 1 is caused by a change in a gene on chromosome 17. This abnormal gene is a dominant one. When the parent suffers from Nf each child has a 50 per cent chance of inheriting this abnormal gene. Nf 2 is caused by a change in a gene on chromosome 22. Because Nf 1 and Nf 2 are due to changes in different genes, they do not occur in the same family. They cause growths or tumours to form on nerves and may occur anywhere in the body.

Nf is one of the most common genetic disorders and its most common form is Nf 1. It is sometimes referred to as peripheral neurofibromatosis or von Recklinghausen's disease. This is the type we shall deal with here. One in every 2500 babies born has Nf. But even though Nf is relatively common, not many people have heard about it. It occurs in every racial and ethnic group and affects both sexes equally. Some signs of Nf 1 are usually visible within the first year of life. Other signs of Nf 1 may develop as people get older. For example, Lisch nodules of the iris are unusual in young children but commonly develop in teenagers and adults. Neurofibromas frequently appear or grow during the hormonal changes that occur in teenage years and during pregnancy.

While Nf 1 can affect almost any organ in the body, many people have only a few difficulties. Children can live a normal and productive life. Some will only have café-au-lait spots and neurofibroma, but others may have more difficult problems. At the present time it is impossible to predict what kinds of problem an individual will have; no two people are affected in exactly the same way, even within the same family.

Children with Nf 1 usually have normal intelligence, but as many as 40–60 per cent have short attention span, hyperactivity, or some difficulty coping in school. Nf 1 frequently causes learning difficulties in children. It may affect physical appearance. In addition, tumours may form along nerves anywhere in the body.

Problems with visual perception are common and may make spelling and arithmetic more difficult. Headaches and difficulties with hearing are also common with Nf 1 and may affect schoolwork. The condition frequently affects growth. People with Nf 1 may be shorter, or have slightly larger heads, than the average person. Nf 1 may also affect the growth of bones. A few people will have actual shrinkage of bones.

Among other serious consequences of neurological damage are the following:

- Athetosis involves damage to basal ganglia and other extrapyramidal structures, resulting in uncontrollable writhing head, arm, and hand movements – particularly volitional activity.
- Ataxia is associated with damage to the cerebellum, resulting in difficulties with balance, or inability to perform fine movements such as reaching out for, or holding an object.
- Spina bifida is associated with that birth defect where the spinal cord has failed to close properly; in the most severe cases, spinal nerves will be outside the spinal column in a sac, usually in lower spinal levels. Youngsters with the disorder may exhibit flaccid paralysis and no sensation from the body, from the level of the lesion, down. Muscles that do not receive any innervation gradually waste away or atrophy.
- Hydrocephalus may be associated with spina bifida, which disrupts the circulation of the cerebrospinal fluid; it may also be caused by congenital abnormalities, or meningitis, an infection of the protective membranes of the central nervous system. Children with this type of neurological condition, with or without myelomeningocele, can present a variety of symptoms depending on the site, onset, duration, and shunting. Problems include difficulty sustaining attention and disinhibited behaviour (Baron et al., 1995).
- Expressive aphasia involves damage to Broca's area in the frontal lobe, resulting in difficulty in planning and executing sequential speech movements. In severe cases there may be an inability to talk.
- Receptive aphasia involves damage to Wernicke's area in the temporal lobe, resulting in difficulty comprehending verbal language and responding appropriately.
- Cortical blindness is associated with damage to the occipital lobes, resulting in an inability to see or to interpret visual images, despite normal vision and intact visual nerves.

- Auditory processing disorder involves parietal/temporal dysfunction, resulting in difficulty comprehending oral language; it may be reflected by measures such as problems in following directions or learning new vocabulary items.
- Visual processing disorder involves a parietal/occipital dysfunction. A result may be a difficulty deriving meaning from visual stimuli, making visual interpretations, or reproducing visual forms.

The neuropsychological impact of bacterial meningitis and haemophilus influenza (especially in children who contract the diseases before 1 year of age) includes later cognitive, linguistic and reading difficulties.

Congenital Physical Anomalies

Among these are:

- Waardenburg syndrome: children have an unusual facial appearance, with a white forelock of hair and irises of different colours. Also present are congenital deafness and consequent developmental disabilities.
- Treacher-Collins syndrome: children have low-set ears with malformations, widely spaced eyes, flattened cheekbones, absence of lower eyelashes and cleft palate. Intelligence is normal but there may be language delay due to frequently occurring conductive hearing loss. During infancy there may be feeding problems, apnoea and nasal obstruction.
- Osteogenesis imperfecta (brittle bone disease): children are very susceptible to bone fractures and deformities due to an underlying abnormality of collagen formation. They also have bluish eyeballs, translucent skin, and possible hearing impairments.
- Williams syndrome (Elfin Facies syndrome): children have full lips and cheeks, short stature, hoarse voices, and star-like patterns to the iris. There may be mild to moderate mental handicap, hyperactivity and heart and kidney complications.
- Marfan syndrome: children tend to be tall, thin in stature, with spidery limbs, chest deformities and hypermobile joints. Intelligence is normal, but attention deficit hyperactivity disorder and learning difficulties are commonplace.

Minor physical anomalies

Bell and Waldrop (1982) recorded a relationship between behavioural problems in general, temperament and minor physical anomalies. The latter are slight irregularities or deviations in the child's physical make-up. They include small or large head circumference, slightly malformed ears, high steepled palate, no ear lobes, curved fifth finger, wide gap between first and second toes – all cumulative indications of deviant embryological development.

Abnormalities of Haemoglobin

Haemoglobin is the chemical in red blood cells that carries oxygen. Sickle-cell disorders are present where the red blood cells become sickle-shaped due to lack of oxygen, dehydration or infection. The frequency is between one in 60 and one in 280 in infants born to parents originating from Africa and the Caribbean, and rather less in infants born to parents from the Mediterranean, Middle East, India and Pakistan, and only occasionally in North Europeans. Sickled cells clump together in the blood vessels leading to severely painful crises. Affected children are more likely to get severe infections, which can be fatal. Diagnosis by screening allows the baby to start on regular antibiotics and be immunized, reducing this risk. Screening for sickle-cell disorders may also identify other abnormalities of haemoglobin such as thalassaemia major (see p. 187).

Impairments of Vision

An understanding of the development of blind children should reveal how significant sight is in the development of children who can see. However, there is no single accepted definition of blindness or visual impairment. It is therefore not surprising that the actual incidence or prevalence of the condition are difficult to estimate. In fact, most so-called 'blind' children can see something, although their vision may be severely restricted or limited to a minute area of their visual field. This preponderance of partial-sightedness has led to a preference for the terms visual handicap or visual impairment. What the visually impaired, partially sighted child can see will depend on whether her or his vision is peripheral (which means s/he cannot see straight ahead or read the printed page), or central only (allowing him or her to read print but restricting ease of getting around). There is a wide range of visual impairments from blurred vision and short sightedness to total blindness. In the USA visual impairment or blindness is defined if the child has a visual acuity for distant vision of 20/200 or less in the better eye, with best correction; or a visual field of 20 degrees or less.

Two children with the same limited visual acuity may see things very differently if one (say) learns to use his or her residual vision efficiently, a sign perhaps of a higher intellectual level. Studies of the development of blind children indicate that vision undoubtedly makes a significant contribution to the manner in which sighted children develop (see Lewis, 1987).

They can achieve levels of development in certain skills comparable to those of sighted children, however other aspects of their development may not reach the same levels. In general the course of language development is similar to the pattern found in sighted children, but deficits or delays in adaptive behaviour and social skills are common.

Vision enables children to make sense of their environment rapidly and efficiently, and sighted children integrate their various experiences at an earlier age than visually impaired children, giving them a great advantage. Blind children reach for objects later than sighted children, and they are later in getting moving. At no time in development are cognition and motor development more intertwined than in infancy, both being significantly influenced by vision or its absence. Visually impaired youngsters cannot bring together all their separate experiences, tactile, auditory, kinaesthetic and others, in the same way as sighted children. Blind infants reach all their motor milestones later than their sighted contemporaries. They generally skip crawling. Walking tends to be delayed. Because maintenance of muscle tone is in part mediated by vision, in its absence fine motor skills are held up.

Their understanding of themselves as separate beings, but sharing certain attributes that distinguish them from objects, comes more slowly than is the case with those who can see. The point in time at which they realize they are different from sighted children seems to be at about 5 or 6 years (Burlingham, 1979). Fortunately vision is not entirely essential to making sense of the environment (e.g. an understanding of the concept of permanence of objects and people) otherwise the world they live in would be a closed book to them. Nevertheless, because the child's sensory deficits prohibit her or him from reaching for objects, this has the effect of delaying object concept from 1 to 3 years.

Although blind children tend to be delayed in certain aspects of their intellectual development, the delays for most are not large. They appear able to develop similar concepts to sighted children although how they 'get there' may differ. Certainly, by preschool years when logical thought begins to supersede visual perception as the major learning modality, blind children demonstrate equivalence to their sighted peers (Reynell, 1978).

Some parents find it difficult to talk to their blind infant; the absence of eye contact and a somewhat expressionless face can make communication and sometimes relationships awkward. Many of these impediments vanish when the child begins to speak. Speech connects the blind child to his or her world in many physical and social ways. A vital ingredient in the acquisition of language is the parents' awareness of the child's reliance on experience via modalities other than vision, and their sensitivity to making their own language relevant to the world of the blind learner. Lewis (1987) states that researchers emphasize the role of the blind child's environment, and believe it to be far more important than the nature of the blindness itself.

Aetiology

The causes of visual difficulties may be the result of:

- Prenatal (e.g. inherited) conditions
- Injuries or poisoning
- Exposure to drugs or medical interventions (excess oxygen), and infectious diseases
- Congenital factors (e.g. cataracts, glaucoma, optic nerve atrophy, retinopathy of prematurity).

Impairments of Hearing

Sound is of critical importance in the development of children who can hear. So what of those who cannot do so? Deafness, like blindness, is rarely total. There is usually some residual hearing. It is not a homogeneous condition; it can vary in several ways, for instance in frequency (measured in hertz, Hz) or intensity (units of sound measured in decibels, dB). The frequencies that are important for speech development fall between 250 and 4000 Hz. A person with a loss of intensity up to 55 dB would hear sounds but have difficulty without a hearing aid of interpreting them. These children are described as partially hearing. Children experience increasingly severe difficulties in hearing with losses of over 55 dB. Deaf children with a loss of over 90 dB may just be able to hear a very loud noise close up. The frequency range for the normal ear is from around 20 to 20,000 Hz. The pattern of loss of hearing will determine, depending on whether vowels or consonants can be discriminated, the problem of interpreting speech. The frequency components of consonants and vowels are to be found, generally speaking, above and below the threshold of 1000 Hz. About 50 per cent of cases of deafness are genetic, the other half of unknown origin.

Many children with hearing impairments, despite improvements in diagnostic methods, are 2 or 3 years old before their hearing loss is detected. Research indicates that young deaf children seem to know almost as much about objects and people as hearing children (Lewis, 1987). Their understanding, however, may be qualitatively different. Sound would not appear to be essential, despite being important, for these and other developments. Deaf infants are able to manipulate symbols as demonstrated by their early use of signs and pretend play. Sound is not necessary for cognitive development in the early stages of life although the influence of the child's environment increases as time goes by. Alternatives to the spoken word become necessary. A deaf baby usually begins to babble like a baby with hearing but it ceases at about 9 months of age (Meadow, 1980). Only a particularly bright deaf child will have as many as 200 words at 4 or 5 years of age compared with the hearing child's vocabulary of 2000 or so words. The deaf child has problems with writing and reading as well as having problems producing and comprehending spoken language. Much depends on the nature and extent of the child's hearing loss.

The developmental of language, cognition and thought is intimately related to the primary method of communication. Families are faced with many choices with regard to the methods of communication and education, ranging from oral/aural approaches to varieties of contact sign language communication systems.

Emotional expression and theory of mind

The expression and understanding of emotions are of particular importance in everyday communication. Most hearing children, by the age of 3, understand that other people's *actions* are governed by their beliefs and desires; by 5 they comprehend that *emotions* also depend on these subjective states of mind. They also demonstrate the capacity to attribute to others, beliefs that differ from their own. Deaf children frequently have difficulty understanding other people's emotions. Can an impaired theory of mind account for this, as has been suggested? Pretend play is less imaginative in these children than hearing children; there are also difficulties in relating to people socially and in communicating – features of autistic children who suffer from so-called 'mind-blindness' (see chapter 15).

The suggestion of an impaired theory of mind seems unlikely in the light of a study by Rieffe and Terwogt (2000). The experiment focused on the spontaneous use of mental states in explaining other people's emotions by 6- and 10-year-old deaf children. They were compared with their hearing peers. Within both age groups, deaf children referred to others' beliefs as often as their hearing peers and their references to people's desires even exceeded those of hearing children. The reason for this preponderance may be that deaf children, in their daily lives, are compelled to express their own desires and needs emphatically and unambiguously.

The valid assessments of visual and hearing, as well as other sensory and motor impairments, so vital for educational and developmental policies and decisions for children, are fully described by Simeonsson and Rosenthal (2001).

Motor Impairments

A child with a motor impairment is likely to be restricted in how s/he is able to interact with the environment. Clearly the nature and seriousness of the limitation will vary with the extent of the impairment. As examples of motor disabilities I have chosen to concentrate on cerebral palsy, muscular dystrophies, and dyspraxia.

Cerebral palsy (CP)

Cerebral palsy is another complex condition, so multifaceted that it makes it difficult to define. As we saw earlier, it is a disorder of movement and posture resulting from a permanent, non-progressive defect or lesion of the immature brain. There may be additional difficulties involving vision, hearing, speech and intellectual ability. Many children with CP may also suffer from fits. Given different combinations of disabilities the differences between children with CP tend to outweigh the similarities.

• Spasticity: most children with CP seem stiff and rigid, a result of damage to the motor cortex.
• Athetoid: these children suffer from an excess of uncontrollable movements due to damage to the frontal ganglia. These interfere with normal body movements.
• Ataxia: this condition involves poor coordination of movement and disturbed balance and is due to damage to the cerebellum.

CP is estimated to occur in from 15 to 25 babies per 10,000 infants born alive. Some early signs of CP include the following:

• Weak cries or a weak sucking reflex, showing little interest in their surroundings
• Adopting a floppy rag-doll position typical of the hypotonic infant, or an arched position with too much muscle tone
• Asymmetrical reflexes between two sides of the body or persistence of primitive reflexes (see chapter 9) are evident
• Persistent clenched fists, or too early hand preference
• A discrepancy between the rates of cognitive and motor development.

Children with mild neuromotor impairments meet expected milestones linguistically and cognitively, but this is not the case with motor skills.

The types of cerebral palsy where the limbs are involved are as follows:

• Hemiplegia, which refers to paralysis on either the right or the left side of the body, involving the upper and lower extremities on the affected side.
• Diplegia refers to the legs being more affected than the arms. The symptoms are evident in both lower extremities. The cortical damage involves bilateral lesions from the midline out, as the feet and the legs are represented on the medial portion of the primary motor area of the frontal cortex.

- Quadriplegia refers to involvement of all four limbs, and is related to extensive cortical damage. The trunk muscles and those for the oral musculature may be involved. The result is communication difficulties and feeding problems. Severity of brain damage may result in various medical complications, mental retardation, associated sensory impairments such as hearing and vision loss, and seizures.

CP is always a congenital problem, and one that can develop after birth, the result of:

- meningitis (around 10 per cent of children with CP)
- encephalitis, and
- a variety of trauma to the brain (e.g. fractures) or inside the brain (e.g. tumours).

The main determinants occur during the prenatal or perinatal stages of development; they include Rhesus incompatibility (now treatable with a blood transfusion to the baby, and of late, the fetus itself), maternal rubella and anoxia.

Muscular dystrophies

The clinical symptoms of muscle weaknesses are differentiated by age of onset, muscle groups, progressiveness of muscle deterioration, and genetic factors. Duchenne or pseudohypertrophic muscular dystrophy (DMD) is the most common form. It tends to be terminal in adolescence or young adulthood. A psychoeducational assessment is vital as there are reports of decreased intellectual function, notably reading difficulties.

Dyspraxia

The fairly frequent problem of clumsiness was discussed in the 'typical development' half of the book (chapter 4). The more serious form of clumsiness, called developmental dyspraxia, gets its name from the conjunction of two Greek words: 'dys' meaning bad, and 'praxis' meaning ability to perform sequences of co-ordinated movements so as to achieve an objective. There have been at least 11 different labels applied to the disorder, indeed some clinicians have questioned (as they have the term 'dyslexia') its usefulness as a diagnostic term.

The area of the brain required for complex combinations of movement, is typically fully developed by 5 to 7 years of age. In the dyspraxic condition we have a disorder of the higher cortical process involved in the planning and execution of learned, volitional, purposeful movements occurring in the presence of *normal* reflexes, power, tone, and sensation. Children with dyspraxia make more movement and action errors than other children of the same age. Their finger movements are affected so that doing up buttons and laces are tasks of great difficulty, as are drawing and writing neatly. Problems with gross bodily movements are evident in the child's awkwardness in throwing or catching a ball, also trying to hop and skip. Poor skills in perceiving shapes and copying designs may result in the child being slow to learn to read.

Because there are no obvious or dramatic neurological signs and symptoms of such brain malfunction, the underlying condition often goes undetected. As a result, clumsy children tend to receive less sympathy and understanding than other handicapped children. The problem (which occurs in 1 to 2 per cent of children in the general population, and is far more common in boys than girls) tends first to be noticed and worried about by parents, but taken seriously in the school situation. Teachers become concerned at the child's awkwardness of movement, the clumsiness at gym and sports, and the difficulties with the fine muscular control demanded by writing.

Dyspraxic children may suffer a great deal as a result of rebukes from parents and teachers for their 'ham-fisted' and ungainly behaviour, and as a consequence of teasing and mocking from their playmates. They do not get picked for team activities and can nurture a sense of being inferior – an outsider. Because children who are severely uncoordinated are unable to do many things that most children take for granted, and more and more unwilling to expose their 'incompetence', it is often assumed that they are oppositional and 'spoiled'. They are often accused of laziness or misbehaviour, and even suspected of being mentally 'dull'. It is hardly surprising that they become, with the passing of time, diffident about attempting manual and sporting skills. Punishment and scorn are so frequently their lot, their physical difficulty is quite likely to become an emotional problem. The child feels s/he has been unfairly treated, loses trust and confidence in those in authority, not to mention in themselves.

It is usually the role of the educational psychologist (sometimes the clinical child psychologist) to review assessment evidence, and to prepare a plan to meet the needs (physical, psychological and educational) of the child.

Impairments of Speech and Language

Stuttering

This problem is also referred to as 'stammering' and is a disorder of speech rhythms. The flow of speech is disrupted by blocks and tensions that produce hesitations, repetitions, or prolongations of sounds. The continuity of diction is broken by clonic and tonic spasms of the muscles that participate in the mechanism of speech. It is well known that emotional factors can affect speech mechanisms; normal speakers occasionally stutter with strong emotion and people who stutter may experience a particularly severe blockage in speech in times of distress. In fact, at the best of times, there is a considerable degree of overlap to be observed in the speech features of persons classified as stutterers and those classified as non-stutterers. Andrews and Harris (1964) have identified three categories of stutter:

1. Developmental stuttering, being of early onset (2 to 3 years) but lasting only a few months
2. Benign stuttering, characterized by late onset (mean age $7\frac{1}{2}$ years) but tending to spontaneous remission after about 2 to 3 years
3. Persistent stuttering, with an onset between $3\frac{1}{2}$ and 8 years.

A majority of cases have their onset between the ages of 3 and 5 years. After the age of 9 the onset of stuttering is unlikely. Andrews and Harris (ibid.) in a survey of over a thousand school children found an incidence of 3 per cent; this figure rose to 4.5 per cent if cases of transient stammering lasting up to 6 months were included.

There are those who are critical of definitions of stuttering that emphasize the lack of fluency in speech because they see stammering as a disorder of communication not of speech. They define persistent stuttering as a problem manifest in progressive dissolution of communication. The disorder is thought to be expressive of a disharmony in the interrelation between psychic processes and the linguistic encoding process, irrespective of possible neuropathological conditions.

Specific language delay (SLD)

SLD is a term applied to:

*   Expressive delays in which the child's ability to use expressive spoken language is significantly below the appropriate level for his or her mental age but in which language comprehension is within normal limits. These are the most common forms of SLD.
*   Mixed receptive–expressive delays, which are the most handicapping. The child's understanding of language is below the appropriate level for his or her mental age. Expressive language is markedly impaired in nearly all cases and abnormalities in word-sound production are common.

SLD is distinguished from secondary language delay associated with autism, hearing loss or intellectual disability (Rapin, 1996). Children with receptive delays only are very rare.

Expressive language disorder is indicated by:

- The absence of single words (or word approximations) by 2 years
- The failure to generate simple two-word phrases by 3 years.

Restricted vocabulary, overuse of a small set of general words, word substitutions, short utterances, syntactical errors, misuse/failure to use articles, pronouns, prepositions, etc., and omissions of word endings are some of the later indications of an expressive disorder (WHO, ICD-10).

Mixed receptive–expressive language disorder is indicated by:

- Failure to respond to familiar names by the first birthday
- Inability to name a few objects by 18 months of age
- Failure to follow simple, routine instructions by the age of 2 years
- Later difficulties include inability to understand grammatical structure (negatives, questions or comparatives)
- Lack of understanding of more subtle aspects of language (e.g. tone of voice).

Language delays are more common in boys than girls. The language delay, and its not uncommon associated delay in speeded fine-motor skills (but not general clumsiness), may both reflect an underlying neurological immaturity. They find their manifestation in slow information processing and limited information-processing capacity (Bishop, 1992). Genetic factors play a significant role in specific receptive–expressive language disorders. Psychosocial factors are not significant causal influences, but may play a part in maintaining language difficulties.

Much of the information that enables individuals to understand and express themselves in speech appears to be stored in the left parietal cortex in right-handed people. The use and understanding of language may be impaired in several ways. Penfield and Roberts (1959) are of the opinion that there are no really pure forms of language defect. However they present evidence that relatively small lesions may in some cases produce impairments where one aspect of language is much more disturbed than others. The commonly quoted examples of this are expressive impairments of speech associated with lesions in the region of the rolandic fissure, and dyslexia, usually accompanied by dysgraphia associated with parieto-occipital lesions.

Language disorders in autism

Language disorders are a major feature of autism (see chapter 15). The development of language is an important prognostic factor and it has been demonstrated that adult outcome is related significantly to whether or not the child developed useful speech by 5 to 6 years (e.g. Lotter, 1978). The parents of a child suffering from an autistic disorder may be initially puzzled, and gradually more and more concerned, about what seem to them to be untypical behaviours in their baby. The areas of disturbance that increasingly worry them are:

1. Sensorimotor
2. Speech and language
3. Relationships to people, objects and events.

For the moment we shall restrict ourselves to the last two.

SPEECH AND LANGUAGE

Birth to 6 months: the baby

*   does not vocalize
*   cries in a way not related to its needs.

6 to 12 months: the baby

*   does not imitate sounds, gestures, or expressions
*   may stop babbling.

12 to 24 months: the baby

*   makes no speech or only occasional words
*   stops talking
*   does not develop gestures
*   repeats sounds in a non-communicative manner.

RELATING BEHAVIOURS

Birth to 6 months: the baby

*   makes no anticipatory social responses
*   has absent or delayed smiling response
*   makes no or poor eye-contact
*   fails to respond to mother's attention
*   fails to respond to toys.

6 to 12 months: the baby

*   fails to show affection
*   has difficulty engaging in baby games

- shows no interest in toys
- does not wave bye-bye
- pushes objects away.

12 to 24 months: the baby

- displays no distress on separation
- shows unusual use of toys (e.g. lines up objects).

Executive Functions of the Brain

Theorists stress the importance of a healthy physical constitution as a pre-requisite for sound social and educational training (socialization). This applies particularly to the physical integrity of the brain and its executive functions. The term 'executive functions' is an umbrella construct for a group of interrelated functions that are responsible for purposeful, goal-directed, problem-solving activities: initiating, inhibiting, planning, organizing, shifting, self-monitoring, controlling emotions, and having access to a 'working memory' (holding information in mind) (Gioia, Isquith, and Guy, 2001). The term *metacognition* is used by educationists and clinicians to describe this role of oversight, regulation, and organization of a multitude of vital cognitive functions.

The developmental course of the executive functions (from infancy through the pre-school and school-going years) parallels the protracted course of neurological development, particularly with regard to the pre-frontal regions of the brain, a system highly and reciprocally interlinked through bi-directional connections with:

- the limbic (motivational) system
- the reticular activating (arousal) system
- the posterior association cortex (perceptual/cognitive processes and knowledge base), and
- the motor (actions) regions of the frontal lobes.

The course of development of the executive functions of the brain varies across individuals in terms of timing and content.

This complex control system must always be on the alert, attending selectively to what is crucial in the individual's ever-changing surroundings, processing information and regulating countless adjustments required in his interaction with the environment. Functioning like a computer of a homeostat, the brain maintains the life-preserving physiological equilibrium in the body. It stores and integrates vast amounts of information, and exercises choice over how and when to react to particular situations. Each and every second of waking life, more than a hundred million electrical impulses flow into the brain. Even during sleep, more than fifty million neuronal 'messages' are being relayed, every second, to and from the brain and different parts of the body. All this requires a staggering level of dependability and delicacy of analysis, in times of calm and crisis, health and disease, and around the clock, for years on end.

Neurological Damage

The brain fortunately, under normal circumstances, is a remarkably sturdy and reliable instrument (Herbert and Kemp, 1969). It is relatively rare for the brain to be seriously impaired. It can be compared with an incredibly intricate machine. Like a machine, it can go wrong; but unlike most machines, its standards of reliability are remarkably high. A formidable problem of automation is the fact that no man-made device is yet able to maintain itself so as to provide precise and dependable standards of performance over really prolonged periods of time. There are several properties of the brain that promote this reliability and efficiency. Specialization and flexibility are combined in the organization of the nerve cells in such a way that speed and accuracy are assured, and an additional bonus of compensatory capacity (plasticity) which allows it to circumvent emergencies, sometimes including even disease or damage to brain tissue. The superfluous number of functional units in its construction provides a latent reserve so that certain brain centres can undergo a dynamic readjustment of their function and take over from other damaged parts. (See Battro, 2001, for the story of Nico who was given a right hemispherectomy at the age of 3.) This plasticity is more available to children, whose brain development is still in a state of flux, than it is to adults, whose brains have matured. Nevertheless, there are limitations to what 'neuroeducation' can achieve.

The integrity of the brain and nervous system is a crucial determinant of a child's success in adapting to his or her internal and external environment. Even an instrument as robust and well protected as the brain can be impaired. Impairments to this integrity may be detected early on in the infant's life by an examination of its reflexes (see p. 197). The brain is the site for by far the majority of the developmental disorders of childhood. There is no singular core dysfunction of the executive functions. Deficits and/or dysfunctions are present in several specific disorders, including ADHD, leukaemia, Tourette's disorder, acquired brain injuries, and psychiatric disorders (e.g. pervasive developmental disorders).

Rutter, Tizard and Whitmore (1970) estimate, on the basis of their epidemiological studies of children on the Isle of Wight, that 5 per cent of the population of children is brain damaged in some way. The reasons why a malfunctioning brain can be so devastating become clear when you think of the adaptive functions it mediates: learning, thinking, language, perception, emotion, fine and gross motor skills, to mention but a few. A list of the dysfunctions commonly associated with brain damage illustrates the potentially serious implications for the child's adaptation at home or at school (Herbert, 1964):

- Motor incoordination, overactivity (hyperactivity)
- Perceptual anomalies
- Learning and memory deficits
- Distractibility (difficulties of attention)
- Language and other communication difficulties
- Problems of concept formation
- Intellectual disabilities.

The brain's functions may be adversely affected by injuries (such as a blow, a fall or some penetrating wound), oxygen deprivation (e.g. asphyxia at birth), infections, tumours, degenerative diseases, mechanical trauma (brought about by difficulties during birth), toxic influences on the embryo *in utero*, and genetic aberrations. The effects of brain malfunctioning do not always show themselves in the obviously handicapping problems like cerebral palsy, blindness or deafness. Apart from the influence of brain injury itself on emotional and physical tone and control, any one of these functional difficulties listed earlier may lead to behavioural problems in the child.

The original injury may be so 'minimal' that there are not always clear-cut neurological signs to assist in a neurological diagnosis. And yet the insidious and cumulative effects of the cerebral dysfunction itself, plus the fact that it so often goes undetected, make the child vulnerable to stress. Minimal brain damage (or minimal cerebral dysfunction), as it is called, can have effects on the motor and sensory abilities of children, and on the functions with which they interpret the messages from their environment, and coordinate their reactions to such information.

It is less common today to refer to brain-damaged or neurologically impaired children as if they comprise a homogeneous group (terms like 'minimal brain damage'), which they are certainly not. Who would be satisfied with a doctor's diagnosis that one was 'body-damaged'? The popular stereotype of the brain-damaged child was a cluster of symptoms made up of overactivity, motor incoordination, impulsiveness, distractibility and perceptual disturbance. In fact the symptoms resulting from different types of brain injury are, not surprisingly, very diverse (Herbert, 1964); and the stereotype – the unitary syndrome – applies to only a very small proportion of the cases of brain injury in the general population.

Goodman (1994) has described the organic (neurological) and psychosocial pathways that lead from brain to behavioural abnormalities, via outcomes that are:

- Direct and physical
- Direct and psychoeducational
- Direct and neurobiological.

Such adverse effects (mixed psychopathology, reactive psychiatric disorders) in turn, and in circular fashion, exacerbate the personal problems of the victim and his or her family.

Tics and Tourette's Syndrome (TS)

TS is a rare (four to five per 10,000) neurodevelopmental disorder defined by the presence of chronic, multiple motor and vocal tics of childhood onset (DSM-IV: APA, 1994). Typically tics develop at 6 to 7 years of age, show a fluctuating course, and decrease in severity during adulthood. Although they are common in childhood and frequently short-lived ('transient tic disorder') they may be part of a progressive and debilitating syndrome called Tourette's syndrome/disorder (named after Gilles de la Tourette) – a syndrome that lies at the extreme end of the tic continuum. Tics are sudden, repetitive, stereotyped movements, or vocal sounds that are brief and rapid and may involve multiple muscle groups. They occur at random intervals, but can be exacerbated by stress, fatigue or underlying medical illness. Eye tics such as eye rolling and blinking are the most common first symptoms. Facial tics such as grimacing and nose twitching, and vocal tics such as sniffing, grunting, coughing and throat clearing, are the next most common.

The average age of onset (from world studies) is 7 years. The precise aetiology of TS is unknown. It was once thought to be of psychodynamic origin, but is now considered to be a neuropsychiatric brain disorder influenced by genetic, environmental (e.g. perinatal), hormonal and other extra-genetic influences (see Cody and Hynde, 1999). Twin studies certainly indicate a strong genetic component. Chronic tics together with Tourette's disorder were the first child psychiatric disorder to figure in molecular genetic studies (see discussion in Rutter et al., 1999a,b).

Coprolalia is the best known of the vocal tics and consists of the involuntary interruption of the flow of the person's speech with various unprovoked obscenities. Only a relatively small proportion of children suffering from Tourette's disorder display no worsening of the tics.

The phenotype TS is claimed to include various other conditions. It may be associated with:

- Obsessive–compulsive disorders (OCD)
- Learning disorders
- ADHD
- Autism

- Eating disorders
- Substance abuse.

Psychosocial consequences of TS include:

- Poor school achievement
- Social difficulties
- Self-consciousness
- Embarrassment
- Irritability
- Depression.

Although autism (another neurodevelopmental disorder) and TS are distinct disorders, they share certain behavioural features: echolalia, obsessive–compulsive behaviours, and abnormal motor behaviour.

Head Injuries

Many children suffer a bang to the head at some time, but only a few of such bumps cause major problems. However, in a few cases, the neurological sequelae are serious and far-reaching. A review by Middleton (2001) has listed the following factors as aids to evaluating the significance of a head injury:

1. Injury variables
   - cause
   - severity
   - type of injury
2. Child variables
   - pre-morbid functioning
   - age
   - developmental level
3. Cognitive and emotional problems that arise
4. Parental beliefs and knowledge about the injury
5. Overall effect of the injury on the family as a whole.

As many as 2.5 per cent may have sustained a head injury leading to attendance at an accident and emergency department during childhood. The causes of injury differ according to age:

- Infants under 2 years: non-accidental injury
- Young children: falls

- Middle and older children: injuries due to pedestrian or bicycle accidents, or in sports
- At all ages: as passengers in cars involved in accidents.

As in cases where children with severe head injuries sometimes do exceptionally well, there are also some with mild injuries who do not. A number of children are a self-selecting group in terms of vulnerability to head injury, often incurred crossing roads. Risk factors include:

- Pre-morbid behaviour difficulties
- Poor attention
- Impulsivity
- Overactivity.

Children's brains are still immature and in a phase of rapid development. There is a belief that plasticity may enable them to develop normally if there are focal lesions (see Battro, 2001). Most children with an injury sufficient to cause localized injury (unless it is a penetrating wound) may well have experienced diffuse axonal injury (e.g. shearing and acceleration/deceleration damage). This may prevent other areas of the brain from taking over new functions (Middleton, 2001).

Those areas of the brain developing most rapidly are most vulnerable. Thus younger children are more at risk of developing global rather than focal problems. Damage to the brain in infancy can affect subsequent brain growth. Suffering damage to some areas in early childhood may not give rise to major problems until early or late adolescence, when these areas (such as the frontal lobes) become fully functional.

Progress at school is commonly affected following moderate or severe head injuries. A painstaking multilevel assessment is critical as there are many possible explanations. They include:

- Mild hemiparesis
- Poor motor coordination
- Tremor
- Sensory impairments (vision and hearing)
- Epilepsy
- Diabetes insipidus
- Weight gain
- Fatigue proneness
- Early onset of puberty
- Loss of self-confidence/self-esteem
- Slower rate of leaning
- Loss of skills
- Poor attention/distractibility

- Memory difficulties
- Problems with visuomotor (e.g. perceptual) skills.

The frontal lobes are particularly vulnerable in traumatic brain injury with consequential disruption of its executive functions. For example:

- Monitoring/organizing/integrating functions
- Holding a goal in mind
- Basic attention and orientation
- Working memory
- Metarepresentation skills such as somatic representational skills and semantic representational skills.

chapter eleven

The Pre-School Child
Atypical Behaviour

The children now love luxury. They have bad manners, contempt for authority, they show disrespect to their elders and love to chat in places of exercise.
They no longer get up when their elders enter the room.
They contradict parents, chatter before company, gobble up dainties at the table, cross their legs and are tyrants over their teachers.

Socrates (469–399 BC)

This critique by Socrates of the shortcomings of children and, by implication, their parents and teachers, resonates with contemporary criticisms of the lack of discipline. Here is another commentary:

'Our earth is now degenerate, children no longer obey their parents.'

An Egyptian priest inscribed this six thousand years ago. It would seem that the issue of parental control has been a preoccupation from time immemorial. It certainly is a particular concern today when it comes to dealing with the pre-school child's development.

The Authoritative Parent

Healthy personality development and satisfactory social relationships can be described in terms of a balance between children's need to make demands on others, and their ability to recognize the demands which others make on them, a proposition put forward by Bowlby and Danziger, and discussed in part I. The balance is perhaps best illustrated in the philosophy of what is called an 'authoritative parent' (Baumrind, 1971). In the case of the mother (for example) she appreciates both independent self-will and disciplined conformity. Therefore, she exerts firm control at those points where she and her child diverge in viewpoint. But she does not hem the child in with restrictions. She recognizes her own special rights as an adult, but also the child's individual interests and special ways. The authoritative parent affirms the child's present qualities, but also sets standards for future conduct. She gives reasons (and other inductive methods) as well as using power to achieve her objectives. Her decisions are not based solely on the consensus of the group or the individual child's desires, but she also does not regard herself as infallible or divinely inspired. This authoritative parent seems too good to be true – a paragon of textbook virtues – nevertheless, it does represent an approach to child-rearing which many American, and other Western parents, wish to emulate or approximate.

Consequences of authoritative child care

Diana Baumrind (ibid.) has produced evidence for the assertion that the firm control of authoritative parents facilitates the development of competence and self-reliance in young children by encouraging responsible, purposeful and independent behaviour. Such an outcome is possible only if the control is not restrictive of their opportunities to experiment and be spontaneous. The key seems to be to strive for a workable balance of power. If children are never given any control in family relationships, power struggles tend to occur and they will strive to get control in inappropriate ways.

Socialization

Children's demands, commands, and occasional defiance arise, in large part, as a typical side effect of the requirements of socialization. The infant is intolerant of the thwarting of his or her desires. The younger children are, the stronger are their demands for the immediate gratification of their wants, and they tend to get angry when frustrated. In fact, infants do express rage. Other displays of undirected frustration and anger in young children include jumping up and down, breath-holding, and screaming.

Parents generally wish their children to be contented, so it is not surprising if signs of frustration, distress, sadness and misery are difficult for them to bear. The cry of the human infant is pitched at a level, and varied in such a way, as to be nigh impossible to ignore or get used to. This effect applies especially if it is the parent's offspring who is crying. Adults will go to great lengths to quieten the child – 'comforting' it by nursing it, or getting out of bed repeatedly to its calls, and so on – but as others might view it, 'capitulating' to it. Parents' 'philosophical' attitudes towards childhood (differences that are highly visible in the way children are treated in other nations and cultures) result in very different attributions (see chapter 5).

Parental behaviour is liable to be moulded (i.e. shaped) by the infant's powerful and persistent demands. Two- and three-year-olds seem to know just when throwing a tantrum will leave parents uncertain, undermining their sense of authority. Say 'no' at the checkout counter of the supermarket and parents have to cope with the embarrassing drama of screams, kicks and sit-ins from a canny 3-year-old, while a shop full of people look on, summing up the hapless parent's performance. Up to a point, disobedience is undoubtedly adaptive (functional) and its absence, as a manifestation of mindless servility, would be a matter of concern. Parents' commands may be unreasonable. How else (other than by exerting self-willed defiance at times) does a child establish and develop her or his own individuality?

The child's increasing cognitive maturity, for example, her or his cognitive differentiation of self from others, allows the toddler to recognize causal relationships in a more realistic manner. Among the realities perceived is her/his relative impotence in the power structure of the home. Ausubel and Sullivan (1970) postulate this to contribute to the devaluation of the child's ego. But it also transforms what Lawrence Kohlberg refers to as the child's assimilation of the interesting, into a desire for power and control over things and people (Kohlberg, 1963). This motivation, and the child's maturing differentiation of her/himself from others are thought to be essential for the perception and subsequent imitation of the behaviour of models. When the adult does something fascinating, the child wishes to see if s/he can also do it. According to Ausubel and Sullivan (ibid.) the next best thing to being omnipotent is to be a satellite of people who are.

There is a 'trade-off'. The child has to accept *volitional dependency*, becoming subservient to the will of his parents. This demand for the subordination of the child's will is counterbalanced by more *executive independence* (i.e. being allowed, indeed required to do more for her/himself). We now get a situation in which the child who has previously accepted help without any fuss, empowered by increasing self-awareness insists (sometimes inconveniently from the parents' point of view) that s/he display their competence by managing on their own. This can lead to the so-called negativistic crisis where the child not only defies the parent, but also does the opposite of what was wanted.

As the child gets older, random, undirected or unfocused displays of emotional excitement become more rare, and aggression that is retaliatory more frequent. It is not easy for young children to learn to 'share their toys', 'wait patiently', 'ask nicely', and be generous, considerate and self-sacrificing. Typically, coercive actions decline steadily in frequency from a high point around two years of age, down to more moderate levels at school-going age. With increasing age, certain of the child's coercive actions (e.g. whining, crying, tantrums) are no longer acceptable to parents. These behaviours become the target for careful monitoring and sanctions, which in turn are accompanied by reductions in their frequency and intensity.

By the age of 4 there are substantial improvements in children's ability to hold in check their negative commands, destructiveness and attempts to coerce by aggressive means. By 5, most children use less negativism, non-compliance, and negative physical actions than younger siblings. There is a reduction in temper tantrums. At 9, more than 50 per cent of boys, but only 30 per cent of girls, are having quite frequent explosions of temper. Some of the differences in aggressiveness between boys and girls may be due to the fact that parents in Western culture tend to disapprove more of aggression in girls than in boys.

Assertive/Commanding Behaviour in Young Children

Parents are sometimes taken by surprise by the fractious temperament of their newborn babies and by their resistance to changes of routine and even the simplest training requirements. This is what one mother told me about her infant:

> 'From the first day that I saw my adopted son Paul I realized that he was more lively than his sister Janis and wouldn't be content to be in a room by himself. He would scream; and I went through endless months wondering if I was feeding him correctly, whether he had a pain or was unhappy. Meanwhile, other problems were emerging. He would never sleep during the day like other babies, and eventually wouldn't sleep at night either; and when I went to cuddle him he would scream, bite or kick and this showed itself particularly at bath time and changing time.'

From the time they are born children have the behavioural repertoire to 'shape' their parental actions in directions that are not always welcome to their caregivers. In the technical language of psychologists, they possess a formidable range of 'negative reinforcers' to direct at their parents and others. They are capable of delivering, in addition to their delightful smiles and sounds, a repertoire of some 14 coercive behaviours: psychologically 'aversive' stimuli, including crying, whining, yelling, temper tantrums, and commanding, emitted if they don't get their own way (Patterson, 1982). From early on they are used (wittingly or unwittingly) to influence their parents. At times influence is transformed into outright confrontation and control.

Adverse Temperamental Attributes

Adverse temperamental attributes like the ones described above, can seriously worsen relations between parents and children, especially if there is a marked 'mismatch' between the parent's and child's personality. It is possible to demonstrate different styles of temperament in babies soon after birth. Quite apart from the emotional distress experienced by the parents, they have to cope with a child whose disorganized condition makes his or her signals more difficult to interpret and whose unusual demands cause confusion and inappropriate reactions in the parents. Pathological crying, disturbed sucking patterns, unusual waking-sleeping rhythms, and distractibility are but some of the infant characteristics with which some parents are confronted.

Children's inborn, idiosyncratic characteristics, and their large differences in sensitivity to their environment, make implausible Watson's notion of a purely environmental 'programming' of the child. Any nurse who has duties in a nursery of newly born babies, or any mother who has had several children and can thus compare her babies, knows that they differ markedly in temperament from the very beginning. Such is the potency of these characteristics that they often 'shape' parents' child-management in a direction they had no wish to go.

Thomas, Chess and Birch (1968) carried out research with New York families that was to prove highly influential. They demonstrated just how important these constitutional aspects of personality – the temperamental qualities of the child – are, in the unfolding of normal behaviour and atypical behaviour problems. An intensive study of 136 children measured temperament in terms of nine descriptive categories:

- activity level
- rhythmicity
- approach and withdrawal
- adaptability
- intensity of reaction
- threshold of responsiveness
- quality of mood
- distractibility/attention span, and
- persistence.

They classified babies according to clusters of temperamental characteristics; these groupings were referred to as 'difficult', 'easy' or 'slow to warm up' babies. The authors found that 65 per cent of their original babies could be assigned to one of the general 'types' of temperament. Some 40 per cent of the children fell into the so-called 'easy' category, a group highly rewarding to rear, while 10 per cent were 'difficult', or to use an unkind but heartfelt description used by many of the research participants, 'mother-killers'. Another 15 per cent of the babies were 'slow to warm up'. These infants combine negative responses of mild intensity to new stimuli with slow adaptability after repeated contact. Infants with such characteristics differ from the difficult child in that they withdraw from new situations quietly rather than loudly. They do not usually exhibit the intense reactions, predominantly negative mood and biological irregularity of difficult children. The remaining 35 per cent or so of children showed a mixture of characteristics not fitting into any of the typologies.

The 'Difficult' Child

The study identified a cluster of temperamental traits that typify the difficult children. The first is the predominance of intense reactions. These children shriek more frequently than they whine, give belly laughs more often than smile. They will express their disappointment not with a whimper, but a bang. Frustration characteristically produces a violent tantrum. Pleasure is also expressed loudly, often with jumping, clapping and running about.

Frequently, difficult children exhibit withdrawal behaviour when exposed to new features of the environment. In general, difficult infants manifest a predominantly negative mood. This means that they cry more than they laugh, and fuss more easily than they express pleasure. Negative moods are usually evident at times when the child is experiencing new situations and new demands, especially if they react to them by withdrawing.

Slow adaptability to change (much more marked than the 'slow to warm up' children) manifests itself in different ways at different age periods. In infancy, the babies typically withdraw from new experiences. Eventually they adapt, but only after frequent and repeated exposure to a given situation. For example, the difficult infant may kick and scream during his or her first bath, and for a long period of time they may continue to behave in this way each time they are placed in the water. However, if children are bathed daily for several weeks, there will be a gradual but noticeable lessening of their negative activity, and eventually they will show either a quiet acceptance of the bath or a vigorous positive reaction to it with laughing, splashing, and playing. But, they may now frequently protest and cry when taken out of the water. Difficult children typically follow this pattern of very slow adaptability in most new situations, and reveal a need for many familiarizing exposures to them before they can make a positive adjustment. If given an opportunity to experience the new situation without being pressured for an immediate positive response, such children adjust eventually.

These children tend to be irregular in biological functioning which shows itself in a variety of ways, being particularly evident in the early months and years of life. They sleep irregularly and, in many cases, seem to need less sleep in a 24 hour period than the average infant of the same age. The child may awaken two or three times a night at unpredictable intervals, while at other times he or she may sleep for as long as 5 or 6 hours at a stretch. Such babies do not quickly develop lengthened periods of sleep. It is not at all unusual to find that, during their first 2 or more years, the parents were frequently awakened by his or her crying and could not get them to sleep through the night, no matter what training procedures they used.

Patterns of elimination are typically irregular. There is considerable variability in the timing, frequency, and size of bowel movements. Often, the only thing that is predictable is irregularity itself. As a result, toilet training procedures do not always work.

The authors comment that to the observer the problems may seem to reflect poor care. However, what looks like 'bad' mothering is often the mother's confused reaction to a difficult child, rather than a primary cause of the child's problems. Many conscientious mothers are made to feel guilty and anxious when a child is so tempestuous and defiant. When the problems persist, her feelings sometimes explode in anger at the 'unlovable' child, putting her in the 'wrong', and making her feel guilty. In such cases the problem is not the simply the parent's, but the parent's and the child's, and results from a downward spiralling pattern of interaction between the two.

There is evidence (Thomas and Chess, 1986) that even as early as the second year of life, and before the manifestation of symptoms, children who were later to develop behaviour problems requiring psychiatric attention showed particularly difficult temperamental attributes (70 per cent of the so-called 'difficult' category). Although difficult children, who are so very 'thin skinned', are likely to become shy and timid and to develop other emotional problems, they do not always do so. Children are not immune to their parents. Thirty per cent of those studied in this instance adjusted slowly, especially those with resourceful, robust parents. Only 18 per cent of the easy children developed such problems.

Temperament should not be reified in the sense of being conceptualized as a fixed unmodifiable 'entity'. Environmental factors shape the manner in which temperament is displayed as the child gets older and, indeed, changes in temperament over time have been shown to be correlated with parental characteristics (Cameron, 1978). Having said this, there does seem to be a genetic component. Identical twins are more like each other in several of the various attributes than are the two children in a non-identical pair (Torgerson and Kringlen, 1978).

Oppositional Defiant Disorder (ODD)

Clearly, most children who manifest challenging behaviours, so commonplace during toddlerhood, do not go on to develop more severe conduct problems. Nevertheless, 'mental alarm bells' should begin to ring if a quality of extremeness (in terms of frequency and/or intensity) or persistence (duration) of the non-compliant/aggressive behaviour, is observed. With regard to the persistence criterion, a child's behaviour might be assessed as 'aggressive' if, at an older age, he or she displays coercive activities commensurate with those of a 2- to 3-year-old child. It is, in this sense, an exemplar of arrested socialization. Concern would also increase if there were many other coexisting problems. There seems to be a typical developmental progression from early in life (between the ages of 3 and 8) when some children begin to display extreme oppositional and confrontational behaviour, followed often by a gradual progress into increasingly severe patterns of antisocial and perhaps, even, delinquent activity.

In the case of children with ODD, their parents may come to realize that they have become 'obedient parents' and that a tyrannical child seems to be 'running' the household. Some children enter a stage of sheer 'bloody mindedness' referred to, when it is extreme, as oppositional defiant disorder. An example is given below.

> Scott has displayed aggressive, defiant behaviour of an extreme nature since he was a toddler. Although initially his parents were told by professionals he would 'outgrow' these problems, they found he became increasingly aggressive and defiant. He was kicked out of four nursery groups before he started school. The parents report that they have tried every discipline strategy they could think of such as time-out, yelling, hitting and taking away privileges, and grounding him. They feel that none of these approaches has worked with him. The parents report feeling isolated and stigmatized by other parents with more 'normal' children and feel that his teachers blame them for his misbehaviours.
>
> An evaluation of his behaviour at school reveals inattentiveness and distractibility in the classroom, aggression towards his peers – particularly during breaks – and frequent reports of teacher calls to his mother to take him home from school because of unacceptable and uncontrollable behaviour. His intellectual performance is within the normal range yet his academic performance is grossly underachieving. His school absences and physical fights have resulted in frequent contact with his parents and threats of expulsion.

Developmental progress of ODD

THE CHILD (SEE ALSO CHAPTER 13)

The logic of attempting to intervene early in the pre-school years with positive disciplinary rules and with clear limits is compelling. Parents like Scott's feel they have lost control of their children. Some children are difficult to rear from birth, particularly for socially isolated or unwell parents who have several children, poor housing and inadequate means. Their behaviour makes parenting seem very unrewarding. Parents tend to describe their children (especially those with attention deficit hyperactivity disorder (ADHD), which is co-morbid with ODD) as overactive, easily 'wound up', excitable, loud, wild and out-of-control. Moreover, their offspring have trouble listening and concentrating even for brief periods of time. Their activity level is so frenetic at times as to make their safety and their survival a matter of continuous and exhausting surveillance. Parents express concern about their child's seeming inability to learn from experience. They observe their child suffering the negative consequences of a particular action, yet repeating the same self-defeating behaviours within a short time.

Children's invariable refusal to comply with parental requests compounds the misery. They seem to control not only the parents but also the entire family, by virtue of the power they command through their indomitable willpower. Parents tend to lose their self-confidence, and may feel compelled to seek professional help. (See Webster-Stratton and Herbert, 1994.)

PARENTS: FAULTY SOCIALIZATION

There is another group of parents whose contribution to the development of their children's ODD is, in a sense, more direct and active. Numerous studies carried out in different parts of the world, over many years, have made clear the causal role of ineffectual or dysfunctional parents and families (see chapter 13; Herbert, 1987b). The developmental literature provides clear guidelines for the conditions conducive to the acquisition of internalized rule (norm) formation. These include firm moral demands made by parents upon their offspring, the consistent use of sanctions, techniques of punishment that are psychological rather than physical (i.e. methods that threaten withdrawal of approval), and an intensive use of reasoning and explanations (i.e. inductive disciplinary methods). A variety of economic, social and family conditions preclude the operation of these factors in the lives of some children (see chapter 1).

Developmental (Physical) Task Problems

Feeding difficulties

The severity of eating difficulties described by parents can range from simple feeding problems to failure to thrive due to emotional abuse or insufficient nutrition. Parents can become very worried about slight losses of appetite in their child while others will not notice that their child is malnourished.

FINICKY EATING

Parents differ in the amounts of food they expect children to eat, or need nutritionally. Growth charts are more reliable than arbitrarily labelling the child as a 'poor' or 'finicky' eater. Almost every child becomes fussy about food at some time; toddlers often show changing likes and dislikes for particular foods. At some ages, this is simply a matter of disliking certain tastes or textures or being more interested in experimenting, playing and talking than eating. However, some children learn to be difficult after observing other family members who are finicky.

DISRUPTIVE BEHAVIOUR

There are several disruptive mealtime behaviours, including stealing food from others, eating spilled food, aggressiveness to others at the table, destructive acts such as throwing food, drink, plates and cutlery, screaming and tantruming.

PSYCHOLOGICAL PROBLEMS

Anxiety, depression or reactions to adverse (perhaps abusive) relationships within the family may cause the child to stop eating. The child may fail to thrive.

NON-ORGANIC FAILURE-TO-THRIVE

This is a term used to describe infants and children whose growth and development are significantly below age-related norms and in whom no physical causes can be detected. These children frequently appear to be withdrawn, depressed, lethargic, anxious, whiny and tearful. These problems are frequently the outward and physical signs of emotional abuse and/or neglect (Iwaniec, Herbert and Sluckin, 1988). In severe cases of failure to thrive admission to hospital provides an environment where close observation of feeding patterns and mother–child interactions can occur.

Enuresis

When children wet the bed, it seems that their brain is not properly aware of the amount of urine in the bladder, allowing it to empty automatically while they are sleeping. Whether a child has been wet all his/her life, or has more recently lost control of his/her bladder, s/he needs special help in the difficult task of learning bladder control. This applies to children over the age of 5, an age at which a majority might be expected to be continent at night.

Enuresis is not only a source of embarrassment to the sufferer, often invoking ridicule or punishment, but it can place an intolerable burden upon family relationships – especially in those large families living in overcrowded conditions, where several children may wet the bed. For the majority of enuretics, to be a bed-wetter carries adverse emotional consequences, and

these children tend to exhibit some degree of reactive emotional disturbance. Even when this is not apparently the case, enuresis imposes a limit
on the child's choice of activities; few enuretics can happily go camping or
stay with friends. In own-homes and residential establishments, the daily
wash of bed linen is unpleasant and onerous. All too often both natural
parents and house-parents are forced into a fatalistic acceptance of enuresis
as an inevitable correlate of child upbringing.

Nocturnal bed-wetting (at least once a week) occurs in approximately
13 per cent or 14 per cent of 5-year-old boys and girls respectively (Rutter,
Tizard and Whitmore, 1970) (some estimates make the rate higher). The
prevalence rate is 1 per cent to 2 per cent for youngsters over 15 and adults.
Enuresis is a very common occurrence amongst children in residential establishments, and many cases continue (if untreated) into late adolescence or
even adulthood. Daytime wetting (diurnal enuresis) is present in approximately one in ten nocturnal enuretics.

PRIMARY ENURESIS

This problem represents a behavioural deficit. The child has never gained
control of nocturnal wetting.

SECONDARY ENURESIS

Here the child reverts to bed-wetting after a period of being dry. The child's
control may, anyway, have been tenuous at best. A period of stress may
produce the regression.

A further distinction can also be made between children who are 'regularly'
and those who are 'intermittently' enuretic.

CAUSATION

The origins of nocturnal enuresis would seem to be multifactorial. Enuresis
may have its origins in faulty learning. Because the peak age-range for the
emergence of continence is between $1^{1}/_{2}$ and $4^{1}/_{2}$ years of age, it could be
said that there is a 'sensitive' period for the emergence of night-time dryness. Harsh 'pressurizing' of the child or (conversely) complacent neglect of
training may lead to a failure of this development. Emotional problems are
then superimposed when the child is made to feel acute shame at his or her
'babyish' ways. Only too often – a point made already – they have to endure
punishment, scorn and ridicule at home and school. Among other contributory causal influences suggested are urological and medical factors, deep
sleep, small functional bladder capacity, genetics, maturation and developmental disorders, also a variety of psychological factors.

1. PHYSICAL CAUSES

It is wise to have the child examined by a doctor in case there is an infection or some other physical cause. As many as 10 per cent of all cases of enuresis are the result of medical (physical) conditions, most commonly urinary tract infections. Approximately one in 20 female and one in 50 male children with enuresis have such an infection. Other uncommon physical causes are chronic renal or kidney disease, diabetes, tumours and seizures. Such potentially important causes should make an expert physical examination a matter of routine.

2. EMOTIONAL INFLUENCES (ANXIETY)

Children who wet the bed tend to be nervous children. What is not certain is the precise nature of the relationship between feeling anxious and wetting the bed. A popular view is that the child wets the bed because s/he is anxious. In other words, the anxiety causes the bed-wetting. This idea is supported by the fact that several studies have shown that after the success-ful treatment of bed-wetting there is usually a decrease in anxiety and an improvement in the way the child feels about her/himself. This explanation seems plausible when we think about the problems of being labelled as a 'bed-wetter'. The child is often ridiculed by her/his brothers and sisters and may even be ridiculed by parents. It is even very difficult to hide from neighbours, given the frequent appearance of sheets and blankets on the clothes line. It would not be surprising if child who is enuretic became very anxious about his or her 'problem'.

Encopresis (soiling)

Because research suggests that soiling (and children who soil) cannot mean-ingfully be compartmentalized, into disorders with physical, as opposed to psychological, aetiologies, or into any other recognizable groupings, a broad and simple definition of encopresis will have to do:

> A soiling child refers to any child over the age of 4 and under the age of 16 who regularly soils his/her underwear and/or bed.

WHAT HAPPENS IN SOILING?

Normally, when stool enters the rectum, causing it to stretch, sensory nerves are stimulated. These nerves send a message to the brain telling us we are full and need to evacuate. However, when the child withholds stool (for whatever reason), her rectum enlarges slowly over weeks and months. Eventually it becomes so large that it can no longer be suddenly stretched by the passage of stool into the rectum. At this point the child no longer knows if his or her rectum is full or not. Because the appropriate messages are not getting through, a large, hard impaction of stool forms in the rectum. The constipation becomes so severe that it leads to a partial blockage of the bowel.

Some of the motions liquefy and leak around the impacted area, soiling the child's underwear. Children with encopresis due to rectal impaction cannot prevent themselves from soiling. They are unaware of their blockage and unable to prevent the leakage. The soiling occurs because the child has lost the normal anal reflex through excessive constipation and subsequent dilation of the bowel. This problem is referred to as retention and overflow. Sometimes (after about 1 to 3 weeks, when the rectum is so loaded that messages get through) a stool (a large hard lump of faecal matter) is let out when the child's muscle relaxes. The child usually doesn't realize that it is happening until it is too late. Some children, fearing ridicule or punishment, hide the evidence – the soiled clothing.

Encopresis has the following characteristics (see Clayden and Agnarsson, 1991):

- It is not an uncommon problem. Three in every 100 children entering primary school at five years will still be soiling. Between 7 and 8 years, about two out of 100 children are soiling. At 12 years, about one in every 100 boys (and some girls) are still soiling.
- Because of the shame felt about this problem, and the attempt by many families to keep the soiling a secret, the figures quoted above may be underestimates.
- Constipation, or hard bowel movements, cause pain, irritability and a decreased appetite.
- A child's emotional state (due to stress/trauma) can affect the functioning of the bowel. Thus, soiling may result from distressing individual and/or family life-events.
- Many parents are likely to think (shamefully) that their child has a unique problem because most parents have never heard of another with a soiling problem.
- Some children have never established bowel control (primary encopresis). When bowel control has been established for at least 6 months before the soiling begins, it is referred to as *secondary encopresis*.
- Soiling is not a unitary symptom, but a many-sided syndrome. For example, it can lead to fear, embarrassment and a lowering of self-esteem in the child, which leads on to yet other social ramifications.
- He or she is quite likely to be taunted, teased, even bullied at school because of the problem. (Children have been suspended from school because staff find soiling so difficult to manage.)

- For the family, there are feelings of bewilderment, frustration, failure, revulsion and anger. Soiling tends to engender negative responses from parents. It is one of the most common precipitants of physical abuse incidents. Soiling is sometimes associated with behaviour problems such as non-compliance and defiance.
- More boys soil than girls.
- Children of all levels of ability soil.
- Children from all walks of life soil.
- There is a highly significant association between enuresis and encopresis.
- There is a relationship between soiling and low birthweight.

Children have to be taught to become clean, that is to say they have to be toilet-trained. It doesn't just happen! This point is of vital importance for work with children who soil. Principles of learning and training (or re-training) strategies are of great significance. In most cultures bowel training is the responsibility of the mother, and most children have successfully learned bowel control between the ages of 2 and 4, irrespective of the training methods used, if not too early when they were applied. The learning task is quite a daunting one. Complex social learning (i.e. psychological) processes, as we saw in chapter 5, are involved in the control and social response to an essentially physical activity (defecation). Undue pressure is the last thing in the world to facilitate learning. If this learning occurs under stress it may break down under stress.

CAUSATION

There is no uniform causation for all cases of soiling; it comes about in different ways and for quite different reasons. Rigorous assessment is therefore crucial. The search for antecedent influences which may be linked with the problem produces a list of factors ranging from the intellectual (e.g. learning disability); the physical (e.g. constipation); the psychological (e.g. fear of the toilet) or social (neglectful or coercive training in toilet habits).

1. PHYSICAL CAUSES: CONSTIPATION

The vast majority of cases of soiling are a result of chronic constipation and stool withholding. Children of any age who have hard movements (pain may also be caused by an anal fissure) may respond by stool withholding. When they feel the urge to have a bowel movement, they are afraid of pain and respond by holding the stool in. The role of the colon and rectum is to absorb water from the stool, so the longer the child withholds (voluntarily or involuntarily), the harder and more painful his/her bowel movements become. A 'vicious cycle' is created of stool withholding, causing more painful bowel movements, causing more stool withholding, and so on.

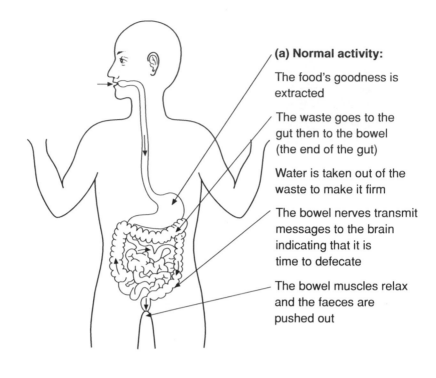

(a) Normal activity:

The food's goodness is extracted

The waste goes to the gut then to the bowel (the end of the gut)

Water is taken out of the waste to make it firm

The bowel nerves transmit messages to the brain indicating that it is time to defecate

The bowel muscles relax and the faeces are pushed out

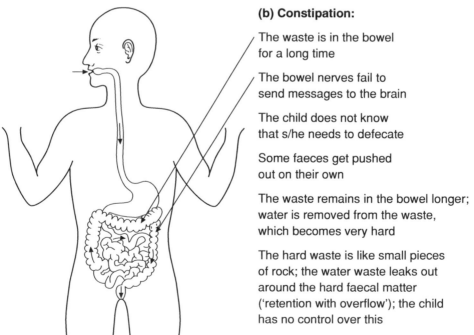

(b) Constipation:

The waste is in the bowel for a long time

The bowel nerves fail to send messages to the brain

The child does not know that s/he needs to defecate

Some faeces get pushed out on their own

The waste remains in the bowel longer; water is removed from the waste, which becomes very hard

The hard waste is like small pieces of rock; the water waste leaks out around the hard faecal matter ('retention with overflow'); the child has no control over this

Figure 24   (a) The process of bowel activity; (b) Constipation: retention with overflow

When the bowel is frequently overloaded, the rectal muscles become *overactive* while concurrently the anal muscles relax reflexly in response to the rectal activity (Clayden, 1988). Thus, as the muscles go on churning to eliminate the blockage, the child has no voluntary control over what happens below, and s/he soils. No wonder a child said to me: 'It's not me who soils, it's my bottom'. His bottom seemed to him to have an independent existence!

2. OTHER PHYSICAL CONDITIONS

These include undiagnosed Hirschsprung's disease, intestinal obstructions, congenital abnormalities, gastrointestinal disease, brain injury and developmental delay (see Clayden and Agnarsson, 1991).

3. PSYCHOLOGICAL DETERMINANTS

The word 'determinants', rather than 'causes', is deliberately chosen, as the psychological factors associated with soiling may be secondary to the soiling – an 'emotional overlay' which contributes to the onset, the maintenance or exacerbation of the symptoms. Cause is too precise a word.

Among the psychological determinants (see Bellman, 1966) are:

• coercive training/punitive remedies on the part of parents
• the role of anxious/overprotective mothers and/or overly strict fathers
• a tendency of children with encopresis to be nervous
• a tendency also to refuse food, and
• a tendency to suffer from learned helplessness.

4. ENVIRONMENTAL FACTORS

Among the predisposing environmental influences are:

• stressful environments (Butler and Golding, 1986)
• poor toilets at home or at school
• separation (and other traumatic) experiences, and
• dietary factors: eating a diet deficient in fibre (and drinking excessive milk) can cause constipation in older children.

chapter twelve

The School-Going Child
Atypical Behaviour

The children who need love the most will always ask for it in the
most unloving way.
Quotation by Russell. A. Barkley (1996) of a retired
teacher's comment to the mother of a hyperactive child

Educational Failure

For academically successful teenagers, attendance at school should be a bridge
between the world of childhood and the world of adulthood. Youngsters
who do well at school tend to enjoy good health, have average or above-
average intelligence and well-developed social skills. They are likely to have
a good opinion of themselves, and the ability to gauge accurately their effect
on others. For children unwilling or unable to learn, school is the place
where confrontation against society is likely to take root. A sense of failure
often manifests itself in a facade of rebellious disruption behind which the
student hides. Failure in a world orientated toward success has significant
consequences for the well being of children and adolescents, not only at
school but also in other facets of their lives. In discussing these children it is
helpful to consider the emotional and behavioural difficulties associated with
underachievement at school within the following categories:

- internalizing disorders
- externalizing disorders
- developmental disorders.

There is an empirically established distinction between the externalizing
problems (aggression, lying, stealing and disobedience) that disrupt the well
being of others, and the internalizing disorders such as anxiety, phobic fear,
shyness, depression, and timidity that lead to distress mainly to the child

him/herself. A major source of distress originates in emotional difficulties such as separation anxiety and friendlessness at school and elsewhere.

Insecurity Based Problems

Erickson, Sroufe and Egeland (1985) have established a clear link between early insecure attachments and later development of behaviour problems, bringing attachment research into the domain of the clinic. It is hypothesized that many conduct problems are strategies for gaining the attention or proximity of caregivers who are unresponsive to the child's pro-social communications (Greenberg and Speltz, 1988). Individual children develop an attachment 'strategy', a behavioural strategy they mobilize when under threat. This strategy (as we saw in part II), and the longer term implications of attachment, have been investigated in laboratory situations. Infants (usually under 18 months), and their parents, enter a strange room in which there are toys. The infant is observed (i) while with a parent, (ii) with a stranger who enters the room, (iii) when the parent leaves the room, and then (iv) when the parent eventually returns. Some are *secure* in this. Other infants show extreme distress when their mothers return after the brief separation, and cling to them but are inconsolable. These babies are said to demonstrate *anxious* or *insecure attachment*. Others ignore mother on her return and react to her no differently than to the stranger. They are described as displaying *avoidant attachment behaviour*. There are other subgroups, particularly ones in which infants display both heightened avoidance of the mother when reunited with her, as well as heightened resistance to comforting. Crittenden (1988) has shown that these infants can be judged erroneously as 'secure'. What is of particular interest about them is that they are disproportionately likely to have been abused and/or neglected. It is important to remember that the patterns of behaviour described above do not necessarily persist, and they are not necessarily indicators of a serious rift in the relationship between parent and child. However, they are worth following up in an assessment. This is a theme I shall return to in chapters 14 and 16.

A fascinating link across the generations is evident in the finding that children's responses in the *strange situation* at 12 months can be predicted on the basis of parental *adult attachment interview* measures obtained during pregnancy (Fonagy, Steele and Steele, 1991). Mothers of children classified as secure tended to show coherent and collaborative discourse about their own childhood relationships with their parents, valuing attachment, and providing an 'objective' and internally consistent account. It is suggested that secure mothers are able to see, in mentalizing terms, such separation experiences from the child's perspective, responding to them empathetically and supportively. Mothers of children classified as avoidant tended to demonstrate a 'dismissing' account of attachment-related experiences. Those rated as ambivalent or resistant, tended to be 'preoccupied' with past attachment experiences, and appeared to be angry, passive, or fearful. Finally, mothers of children categorized as disorganized, tended to display striking lapses in monitoring of reasoning and discourse while discussing loss or abuse.

Maccoby (1980) is of the opinion that the parents' contribution to attachment can be assessed and identified within four dimensions of caregiving style:

1. Sensitivity/insensitivity. The sensitive parent meshes his/her responses to the infant's signals and communications to form a cyclic turn-taking pattern of interaction, whereas the insensitive parent intervenes arbitrarily, and these intrusions reflect his/her own wishes and mood.
2. Acceptance/rejection. The accepting parent acknowledges in general his or her responsibility for childcare, demonstrating few signs of irritation with the child. The rejecting parent, on the other hand, has feelings of anger and resentment that eclipse his/her affection for the child, often finding the child irritating and resorting to punitive control.
3. Cooperation/interference. The cooperative parent respects the child's autonomy and rarely exerts direct control. The interfering parent imposes his/her wishes on the child with little concern for the child's current mood or activity.
4. Accessibility/ignoring. The accessible parent is familiar with her or his child's communications and notices them at some distance, hence s/he is easily distracted by the child. The ignoring parent is preoccupied with her or his own activities and thoughts. S/he often fails to notice the child's communications unless they are obvious through intensification. S/he may even forget about the child outside the scheduled times for caregiving.

These dimensions are inter-related and together they determine how warm the parent is to the child and what the possibility of rejection is likely to be.

Children who show secure attachment to their mothers are likely to be more sociable than children who do not. Waters, Wippman and Sroufe (1979) assessed children's attachment behaviour at 15 months, and observed their social behaviour at nursery school at the age of three and one half years. The securely attached children were clearly more sociable than those who were not securely attached. For example, they were more popular with other children, more sensitive to their feelings and more likely to initiate play activities (see also Main and Weston, 1981; Shaffer, 1999).

Reactive Attachment Disorder (RAD)

Many theorists believe (somewhat controversially) that it is possible to define a specific disorder arising from extreme disturbance of the development of child-to-parent attachment. The person with such a syndrome is described as follows:

- Superficially engaging, charming (phoniness)
- Lack of eye contact
- Indiscriminately affectionate with strangers
- Lacking ability to give and receive affection (not cuddly)
- Extreme control problems: often manifest in covert or sneaky ways
- Destructive to self and others
- Cruelty to animals
- Chronic, crazy lying
- No impulse controls
- Learning lags and disorders
- Lacking cause and effect thinking
- Lack of conscience
- Abnormal eating patterns
- Poor peer relationships
- Preoccupied with fire, blood, gore
- Persistent nonsense questions and incessant chatter
- Inappropriately demanding and clingy
- Abnormal speech patterns
- Passive-aggression, provoking anger in others
- Unusually angry parents.

Few children with RAD will exhibit all of these symptoms.

Peer Group Problems

Many children for a variety of reasons that remain somewhat obscure, lack some of the crucial social skills required to cope with life at school and elsewhere, in a satisfactory manner. Social skills and friendships were discussed earlier in the book, and the point was made that deficiencies in peer relationships are implicated in a wide range of problems:

- Problems in peer relationships (lack of friendships, rejection)
- Inability to be appropriately assertive
- Victimization (e.g. by bullies)
- Social withdrawal
- Aggression.

Children suffering developmental delays are commonly unable to express themselves socially so as to be accepted by peers.

Rejection

The role of peer rejection in the development of psychopathology has been the subject of more research than any other area concerned with peer relationships (see Deater-Deckard, 2001). There are links with externalizing disorders (e.g. aggression and hyperactivity) and internalizing problems (e.g. anxiety and depression). The child's status (popular v. unpopular) may be established as early as toddler-hood, and is moderately stable over the longer term. Children find it difficult to gain acceptance by their peers if they are aggressive or hyperactive, and the resulting social isolation tends to reinforce and exacerbate their disruptive behaviour. Children who are the target of persistent bullying and who lack visibility or support within the peer group, are liable to develop internalizing problems such as poor self-esteem, loneliness, anxiety and depression.

Social Skills Problems

There are several explanatory models for these problems. Among them are:

• The situational model: The assumption here is that some children fail fully to develop proficiency (or lose it) due to the lack of opportunity to practise or use skills.
• The interference model: The skills are there but are not being expressed because emotional and/or cognitive factors interfere with their performance (e.g. anxiety, criticism, and low self-esteem).
• The social learning model: The assumption underlying the skill-deficit model is that the child's incompetence is the result of faulty socialization or ineffectual learning, the result often of the absence of caring foundational relationships with significant adults and children.

The learning and reinforcement of antisocial behaviour (particularly the coercive modelling of misuse of substances) provides a good example of a maladaptive peer socialization process. The antisocial youngsters teach each other delinquent attitudes and activities by means of conversational and behavioural rewards (mutual approval, esteem, etc.). Delinquency is discussed in chapter 13.

Social phobia

Social phobias represent the extreme end of the continuum of social difficulties like shyness. The youngster experiences considerable anxiety and avoidance of parties, physical education, going out with members of the opposite sex, performing in school plays or debates – indeed a wide range of social activities. Communication itself may become impossible, as with the following childhood problem.

Selective Mutism

The child who *elects* to remain silent in the presence of others, or (more accurately) *selects* to whom he or she will talk, is a phenomenon which was described a long way back in literature in Jane Austen's *Sense and Sensibility* (published in 1811), but relatively recently in clinical publications. The earlier diagnostic term 'elective mutism' has been superseded by the term 'selective mutism' (SM). SM children are reported to have age-appropriate speech development, but appear 'stuck' at the stage children often pass through at about 2 to 3 years, which is characterized by excessive shyness. Selective silence tends to occur most frequently in school, presenting a formidable problem in the classroom (Baldwin, 1985). In 4 to 5 year olds, shortly after initial school entry, the prevalence of non-speaking in school is about 7 per thousand among a sample of Birmingham (UK) children. However, a sharp decline in the number of non-speakers occurs over the next 20 months. The disorder represents less than 1 per cent of child guidance and social work referrals in the USA. A Swedish population-based study of older children (7- to 15 year-olds) by Kopp and Gillberg (1992) found a rate of 18 in 18,000 children.

Selective mutism, although a well-established diagnostic entity in DSM-IV, has received little empirical investigation. Several studies (e.g. Sluckin, Foreman and Herbert, 1990) have attempted to isolate individual and demographic factors associated with, and possibly predisposing children to, selective mutism. SM children, it appears, have been exposed to greater family discord and a greater number of environmental stressors than controls. Moreover, they frequently come from families with a history of some form of psychopathology.

Reed (1963) was possibly the first author to propose that SM might be a learned pattern of behaviour. Thus a child's differential pattern of communication might be subjected to a functional analysis with respect to the frequency of talking (speech) in certain situations and/or to certain individuals. Adults (teachers in particular), in response to a selectively mute child's silence, often adopt a pattern of verbal interaction which reinforces the child's non-verbal behaviour.

School Refusal

Until the 1930s, the different forms of persistent absence from school were all referred to as *truancy*. In the 1930s a form of truancy characterized by neurotic features (worry about the safety of the mother, fear of the teacher, nervousness on returning home from school) was identified. In the early 1940s a type of emotional disorder in children, associated with intense anxiety leading to prolonged absence from school, was described as *school phobia* (see review by Heyne and Rollings (with King and Tonge), 2002). The following vignette illustrates several features of this anxiety disorder:

> Ben, aged 9, an only child, refused to go to school, and would speak to no one but his parents. These problems (together with bouts of bed-wetting) had begun after episodes of bullying at school, coinciding with the serious illness of his grandmother, who lived in the same house. Always a solitary and timid boy at school, Ben became noticeably more shy and preoccupied. At home, where he had previously been a pre-cocious, domineering child – 'a loveable little tyrant', in his mother's words – he was pale and weepy, and morbidly concerned about his mother's health. In the mornings he would complain of various ailments, and express a dread of going to school. His mother was at her wits' end and couldn't cope with his fears and physical symptoms, which seemed to get worse with each succeeding day. No entreaties, blandishments or threats would persuade him to return to school.

Lionel Hersov's seminal research led to the adoption of the diagnostic term *school refusal* (Hersov, 1960). He showed that non-attendance difficulties may have nothing to do with specific situations arising from circumstances in the school setting (see also King, Hamilton and Ollendick, 1998: King, Ollendick and Tonge, 1995). It may arise from a variety of anxieties: separation from parents; a worry about illness in the family; concerns about domestic violence at home. Some of the difficulties described above may, if extreme and/or persistent, go beyond reluctance to leave home in the morning, to an outright refusal to go to school.

In the case of Ben, his distress appeared to be related to fears connected with school and home situations. A fairly common aspect of school refusal is *somatization* – the somatic manifestation of psychological difficulties. Such a tendency to experience and communicate somatic symptoms and distress cannot be accounted for by pathological findings. Ben's mother, as so often occurs in families with a non-attending child, attributed his problems to physical illness, and this belief led her to take the boy on several fruitless visits to the doctor in search of a medical 'cure'. The symptoms (which obviously must be checked out) are usually the physical accompaniments of intense anxiety. We are dealing with a predominantly psychological disorder, but not one to be identified with that other form of school non-attendance called *truancy*.

Heyne and Rollings (with King and Tonge) (2002) suggest that school refusal differs from truancy in a number of important ways:

- Children who *truant* usually conceal their failure to attend school from the family. The parents of children who refuse to go to school (school-refusers) are aware of the problem. The child usually remains at home, despite exhortations, bribes or threats from alternatively worried or angry parents.
- Children who *refuse* to go to school may be away from school for weeks or months at a time, sometimes intermittently, sometimes persistently.
- The school refuser is usually a good student with vocational goals while the truant dislikes school and is usually an indifferent or poor student.
- Truancy is more often associated with the diagnosis conduct disorder rather than with the type of emotional disorder associated with anxiety symptoms. Children who truant tend to get involved in antisocial behaviour, often leading to delinquent activities. Truancy has been referred to as 'the kindergarten of crime'.
- Children who refuse to go to school seldom display antisocial behaviour, but do exhibit fearful, avoidance behaviour such as clinging to parents, refusing to get dressed in school uniform, refusing to get in or out of the car during travel to school, and refusal to go through the school gates.

School refusal is reported to affect about 1 per cent of the school-aged population. It occurs across the age range, with some suggestion of a higher prevalence in pre-adolescence and adolescence. The disorder is equally common in boys and girls. There is a normal distribution of intelligence and no clear evidence that learning disabilities are disproportionately represented in the general school refusal population. Socioeconomic level and family composition do not appear to be influences on school refusal.

King, Ollendick and Tonge (1995) conclude their review of the school refusal literature by acknowledging that its aetiology is still not fully understood. Causation varies from child to child. A broad range of precipitating factors associated with the home, the school, and the individual, contribute to the development of school refusal. They include:

- Fear of some aspect of the school environment such as doing tests, social rejection or isolation, having to use the school toilets, the child's perception of his/her ability to cope with school (ibid.). For example, students unsure of their ability to establish close friendships or achieve academic tasks may be predisposed to avoid school.
- The transition from primary school to secondary school.
- Illness in a family member.
- Family stresses such as moving home or parental separation.

Maintenance factors

The particular reinforcing influence militating against the child's return to school is the relief ('drive reduction') at escaping from the fear-eliciting stimulus of school. There are also so-called 'secondary gains' associated with having access to the television, computer games, toys, pets and many other benefits of life at home (including, sometimes, a nurturant and thus 'colluding' parent). An understanding of the factors contributing to an individual child's school refusal is best gained by a thorough assessment conducted with the parents, the child and teachers, using a multimethod problem-solving approach (e.g. Ollendick and King, 1991).

Attention Deficit and Hyperactivity at School

'Fidgety Phil'

He won't sit still
He wriggles
And giggles
The naughty restless child
Growing still more rude and wild
Heinrich Hoffman (1808–1894)

The hyperactive child is the cause of significant and frequent complaints at school. As many as 3 to 6 per cent of school-age children are estimated to have attention deficit hyperactivity disorder (ADHD). Clearly, the hyperactive child is no new phenomenon; nor are the conduct problems that young Phil (above) was said to display. Sir Alexander Crighton in 1798 described one type of attentional problem in young people in a way that meets the criteria listed for *inattention* under ADHD in DSM-IV. In a series of lectures in 1902, to the Royal College of Physicians, an English paediatrician Frederic Still described 20 children in his practice who showed little 'inhibitory volition', a lack of sustained attention and who were, among other things, aggressive, defiant and resistant to discipline. One century on, Russell A. Barkley (1990) described ADHD as the most recent diagnostic label for children presenting with significant problems with attention, impulse control, and overactivity. Children with ADHD, he added, are a heterogeneous population who display considerable variation in the degree of their symptoms, the pervasiveness across situations of these problems, and the extent to which other disorders occur in association with it.

Hyperactive children are like the proverbial elephant: difficult to define, but, by golly, we know one when we see one – or teach one. Their nomadic wilful style in the classroom is their hallmark. Behaviour can be so disruptive and frenetic that they may be referred to a GP and thence to a psychologist, psychiatrist, or paediatrician, by teachers (and parents) who feel demoralized by their inability to manage their disruptive behaviour in the classroom (and at home), or to teach pupils with such short attention spans.

The attentional component

William James (1890) describes attention as the taking possession by the mind, in clear and vivid form, of one out of what seem several simultaneous possible objects or trains of thought. He says that 'focalization and concentration of consciousness' are its essence. It implies withdrawal from some things in order to deal effectively with others. The ability to apply persistent concentration over a period of time depends upon intact cortical and subcortical brain function. In the 1970s, the focusing on attentional deficits of hyperactive children went into the ascendance, as researchers and clinicians became disenchanted with the earlier emphasis on overactivity as the *sine qua non* of the disorder. The disorder was even renamed attention deficit disorder (ADD) in the 1980 DSM-III giving predominance (for several years) to attentional problems over symptoms of extreme activity levels. After all, some children have attention problems but are not hyperactive; some, indeed are slow and lethargic, and less impulsive or aggressive than ADHD children.

It is all very well to talk about attention deficits but what constitutes a deficit, a deviation from the norm that is disabling? Many factors will affect how well a child attends: the type of activity, what has preceded the activity throughout the child's day, and the child's level of interest in the task. Children often daydream or become preoccupied with intrusive worries when emotionally disturbed by distressing life events – an 'off-task' activity that annoys teachers.

Call (1985) estimates that a developmentally appropriate length of attention for a sustained attention activity, such as viewing television, is as follows:

2 years old: 7 minutes
3 years old: 9 minutes
4 years old: 13 minutes
5 years old: 15 minutes
6 to 7 years old: 60 minutes

These times are presented as guidelines only; children vary greatly in their attention spans. However, children with attention disorders will find it challenging to maintain attention on a structured task for these lengths of time.

Cooke and Williams (1987) outlined six levels of normal development of attention control, based on Jean Reynell's research. These levels may be used to assess the child's development of attention skills.

Level 1 (birth to 1 year)

Level 1 is characterized by extreme distractibility, in which the child's attention shifts from one object, person, or event to another. Any new event (such as someone walking by) will immediately distract the child.

Level 2 (1 to 2 years)

Children in level 2 can concentrate on a concrete task of their own choosing but will not tolerate any verbal or visual intervention from an adult. These children may appear obstinate or wilful but, in fact, their attention is single-channelled, and they must ignore all extraneous stimuli in order to concentrate upon the task at hand.

Level 3 (2 to 3 years)

Children's attention is still single-channelled in level 3. They cannot attend to competing auditory and visual stimuli from different sources. For example, they cannot listen to an adult's directions while playing but, with the adult's help, they can shift their full attention to the speaker and then back to the game.

Level 4 (3 to 4 years)

The child in level 4 must still alternate full attention (visual and auditory) between the speaker and the task, but now does this spontaneously without needing an adult to focus that attention.

Level 5 (4 to 5 years)

By level 5, attention is two-channelled; that is, the child understands verbal instructions related to the task without interrupting the activity to look at the speaker. The child's concentration span may still be short, but group instruction is possible.

Level 6 (5 to 6 years)

In the final stage, auditory, visual, and manipulatory channels are fully integrated, and the child's attention is well-established and sustained.

For school-based observations Claire Jones (1994) provides observational questions/criteria for the teacher as follows:

• Does the child impulsively answer questions (or select answers in forced choice formats) without appearing to think about alternatives?

- Does the child fidget even when appearing interested in the task?
- Does the child's conversation appear random or sound like a 'free flight of ideas'?
- Does the child look away from the task in response to noises or visual distractions? Does the child comment on external noises or objects in the room that are unrelated to the task at hand?
- Does the child frequently ask questions such as 'When will this be over?', 'What's next?' or 'What other things can we do?'?
- Does the child yawn after activities requiring sustained attention?
- Does the child doodle in class or draw on hands, clothing, and other things?
- Does the child stare off into space or appear to be 'glass-eyed'?
- Does the child lose papers, assignments, books, and the like?
- Are the student's desk and backpack messy and disorganized?
- Is the child able to stay alert during tasks requiring sustained attention?
- Does the student appear to lack persistence?

Barkley (1990) provides a review of this disorder. A more technical discussion of the mental health aspects of ADHD follows in chapter 13.

Severe (Profound) Learning Disabilities

In chapter 15 we shall be examining the severe learning difficulties (referred to in the diagnostic manuals as 'mental retardation'). As we shall see the functional impairment in these conditions tends to be defined in psychometric terms, a practice we shall look at critically.

Specific Learning Disabilities

Children who suffer from specific learning problems such as severe difficulties with reading, spelling, writing and arithmetic reflect educational rather than medical criteria. There are three basic distinctions in the diagnosis of low scholastic achievement.

1. Type of skill involved – reading, spelling, maths
2. Failure to achieve educational skills v. later loss of these skills
3. General v. specific learning disabilities.

The child with these problems exhibits a disorder in one or more of the basic psychological processes involved in understanding or using spoken or written language: knowing, learning, listening, thinking. As talking, reading, writing, spelling and doing arithmetic are affected adversely, such disorders can have a devastating effect on school attainments. Reading problems tend to be persistent (Maughan, 1995).

They are commonly associated with psychiatric disorders so it is not surprising that they figure in DSM-IV (APA, 1994). Rates of behavioural problems in the classroom and more pervasive psychiatric problems (e.g. emotional and conduct disorders) are elevated in reading disabled children. There is an impressive amount of evidence pointing to a link between school failure and juvenile offending.

Specific learning disabilities are often divided as follows:

- General reading backwardness. Poor reading performance forms part of a wide pattern of intellectual difficulties.
- Specific reading retardation. The reading deficit is discrepant from the child's general abilities (i.e. expectations based on age, grade and IQ).

Whether these two categories constitute distinctively different groups remains a contentious issue (Maughan and Yule, 1994). They are not the result of low IQ, but rather a particular way in which the brain and nervous system *process information* extracted from the perceptual input from the environment. The development of reading and reading disabilities is the most intensively researched domain, notably within cognitive psychology. It is the best understood of the disabilities. Clearly a complex range of cognitive skills is involved in the task of reading. Learning to speak English as an alphabetic language, can be extremely complicated (see Nation, 2001). Letters and groups of letters map on to pronunciation in a systematic way. However, the relationship between orthography (print) and phonology (sound) is only quasi-regular, for example there are words that have similar pronunciation but look as different as *beat*, *ski*, *street* and *thief*, or words like *steak* and *teak* that look similar, but sound very different. Comprehension must follow, and the minority of children who are poor at decoding tend to have weak comprehension. For some children, notably those with dyslexia, the two sets of skills develop out of step. In their case decoding is slow, effortful, 'painful', and error prone. Yet their actual comprehension of what they have read can be excellent (Snowling, 2000). This compares with the 10 per cent of children in middle childhood who are poor comprehenders despite having well-developed decoding skills.

In addition, Maughan and Yule (1994) observe, the reader must make fine visual discriminations including closure (as between o and c), line to curve transformations (as between u and v), and rotational transformations (e.g. b and d, or m and w). The ability to make these transformations follows a regular developmental course. In written English, left-to-right sequencing, both of letters within words and words within sentences, is also crucial for accurate reading: 'god' is not the same as 'dog', nor 'dog bit man' the same as 'man bit dog'.

The information-processing model (IPM)

The information-processing approach to reading difficulties assesses the dys-function in the components required for solving problems. According to Andre and Phye (1986) the cognitive IP system has the following components:

- Input: vision and audition for the reception of information.
- Short-term memory: storing and transforming the information.
- Long-term memory (storage).
- Executive function: controls the flow of information and decides on, selects and performs operations on the information.
- Output buffer: filters information so that resources of attention are directed to new and important information.

The 'to-and-fro' movement (reciprocal *feedback* and *feedforward*) of information within the components listed above, constitutes the processing. A controlled processing mode is uppermost when a child is learning a new skill; later automatic processing takes over, reflecting his or her proficiency. Learning in the school setting requires a balance between the two modes for optimal functioning. Bottom-up processing (as in inductive thinking) and top-down processing (as in deductive thinking) is another IP strategy for solving problems (see Gerber, 1993).

The child with short attention span is at a great disadvantage, as is the child with sensory impairments. The IPM is particularly concerned with attentional, memory and perceptual processes and the interrelationships between them. Learning disability may be indicative of an imbalance in the use of these strategies to extract meaning from the outside world.

Dyslexia

This is a subset of the specific reading difficulties we have been considering, and it is a contentious one. It is a common developmental disorder, affecting 3–10 per cent of children, and is frequently referred to in educational circles. Many talented people have overcome what can be an extremely disabling problem. Artists like Rodin, Leonardo da Vinci and Turner are cited as ex-amples of a link between dyslexia and exceptional visuo-spatial skills. Many other talents in fields ranging from architecture, engineering and science to music and athletics – people such as Albert Einstein, Thomas Edison, Alexander Graham Bell, Walt Disney, Hans Christian Anderson, Yeats, Gen-eral George Patton, and Winston Churchill – have been mentioned among the outstanding sufferers from dyslexia.

Developmental dyslexia is differentiated from acquired dyslexia, the latter being a loss of existing language skills as a result of brain damage (e.g.

physical injury). Central to the concept of developmental dyslexia is the notion of unexpected reading problems, in the sense that some children experience difficulties with the acquisition of reading and writing that cannot be attributed to poor hearing or vision, low intelligence or inadequate educational opportunities. They arise from anomalies of development that affect both written and spoken language (Miles, 1990).

A wide variety of symptoms is displayed in the dyslexic syndrome, and for that reason experts in different fields provide a variety of definitions. The most frequently recognized characteristics include:

- Severe reading, spelling and writing delays
- Reversals of symbols
- Time and space confusion
- Disorganization
- Difficulty with comprehension.

In theory, there are two kinds of dyslexic children: those who cannot read because they have difficulty in making sense of what they see, and those who cannot read because they find it hard to make sense of what they hear.

Sensory perceptions affected in dyslexia include:

1. Vision
In the individual with dyslexia:

- Shapes and sequences of letters or numbers appear changed or reversed
- Spelling is incorrect or inconsistent
- Words or lines are skipped when reading or writing
- Letters and numbers appear to move, disappear, grow or shrink
- Punctuation marks or capital letters are omitted, ignored or not seen
- Words and letters are omitted, altered or substituted while reading or writing.

2. Hearing
For the dyslexic child:

- Some speech sounds are difficult to make
- Digraphs such as 'ch' and 'th' are mispronounced
- 'False' sounds are perceived
- S/he appears not to listen or hear what is said
- Sounds are perceived as quieter, louder, farther away, or nearer than actuality.

It is difficult to detect children who cannot fully make sense of what they hear. Basically, this involves an inability to distinguish between similar sounds, like the middle sounds of the words 'fan' and 'fun'. Reading is a problem to a child with this kind of difficulty because, although s/he sees two different words on the page, the teacher's voice is saying the same sound for both of them.

Balance/movement
The child may also display:

- dizziness or nausea while reading
- poor sense of direction
- an inability to sit still
- difficulty with handwriting, and
- problems with balance and coordination.

Two types of dyslexic individual have been described in the literature:

1. Some are totally unable to learn to read. They are still struggling with putting sounds and letters together to decode words when they reach adulthood. They cannot recall symbols or combinations of symbols. Words they know do not look familiar on the page. Their level of ability to recognize words is around that of a 9-year-old child, despite the years of remedial reading help they may have received.
2. Others can read words quite well, sounding coherent when reading aloud. But they find that they cannot always understand what they are reading. They have to repeat a sentence several times to make some sense of it. There is a severe difficulty in writing. The symbols of language are a source of great frustration.

A distinction is made between developmental phonological dyslexia and developmental surface dyslexia. The former is a condition in which reading is based on whole-word information rather than on translating letters into sounds. The latter is a condition in which reading is based on translating letters into words rather than on whole-word information. These are not necessarily 'pure' categories. The majority of children who are dyslexic have features of both forms of dyslexia (Ellis, 1993).

The theory that most credibly accommodates most cases of developmental dyslexia, is the phonological deficit hypothesis. Shaywitz (1996) explains that when a child is dyslexic a deficit within the language system impairs his or her ability to segment the written word with its underlying phonological compound. There is evidence that the difficulties of dyslexic individuals are less severe with regular languages like Spanish and Italian than with irregular languages such as English or Danish (Miles, 1990).

It would appear that the causes of developmental dyslexia tend more to the biological than the environmental. It is suggested, on the basis of MRI (magnetic resonance imaging) and other studies that there is a neurological basis for dyslexia. No single neuroanatomical marker represents dyslexia, but rather a combination of structural variations awaits discovery. The condition often runs in families and a genetic factor has been identified. It does not mean that all cases of dyslexia are inherited. Shaywitz (1996) using functional MRI on large numbers of dyslexic and non-dyslexic children and adults found significant neural differences in the inferior frontal gyri that are in the frontal lobe areas mainly associated with language.

Summary

The question of whether dyslexia 'exists' as a specific condition is still debated. Children who fail to learn to read are notable for the variety as well as the complexity of their difficulties. There is certainly no one particular teaching method that will remedy such reading or other educational problems. There are on the contrary many approaches to the teaching of reading, some of which are more useful for particular children than others. It is unhelpful to try to separate into different camps the dyslexics and the non-dyslexics. Remedial education is more likely to succeed by sorting out each 'struggling' reader's particular problems according to his or her strengths and weaknesses.

Maughan and Yule (1994) are among the sceptical theorists. They maintain that most efforts to separate out a dyslexic core from within a broader group of children with specific reading retardation have largely failed. They add that it is now widely accepted that dyslexia is not a scientifically or clinically useful definition, partly because there is no consensus on how to operationalize it, but largely because it is a negative rather than a positive definition. Many educationists would disagree.

part v

Atypical Development
Mental Health and
Mental Illness

The greatest thing in the world is to know how to be self-sufficient
Michel de Montaigne (1533–1592)

Positive Mental Health

Clinicians tend to become vague when they are asked to define 'positive mental health' as opposed to mere 'normality' (see Jahoda, 1958). It seems easier to describe the nature of dysfunctional mental life (i.e. psychopathology). Sigmund Freud described normality as the facility to work and love (in its broadest sense) effectively. For children, the former – the ability to work constructively – applies mainly to their attainment at school, something that tends to be adversely affected by psychological disturbance. The latter criterion refers to the individual's ability to forge lasting and friendly relationships with others, notably warm and affectionate relationships (where appropriate) with partners, offspring, siblings, parents, classmates, and other peers. In adults healthy adjustment to life is usually taken to mean self-awareness, maturity of judgement, stable emotional development, and self-actualization (i.e. recognizing and realizing one's potential). Mental health for children might include the individual's ability to tackle life's tasks with reasonable efficiency – adapting to his or her own growth and developments, and the complex demands, social, emotional, and intellectual, made upon them. Needless to say, there are cultural variations in defining positive human attributes, as anthropologists like Margaret Mead have illustrated. Certainly, collectivist cultures are likely to be disapproving of the individualism implied in the introductory Montaigne quotation from his *Essays* (1, xxxix). There have been acrimonious debates over the years about the nature of mental illness and mental health. The anti-psychiatry movement of the 1960s, led by clinicians like Szasz (1960) and Laing and Esterson (1964) rejected the labelling (i.e. classification) of conditions such as depression, schizophrenia and the neuroses as 'mental illnesses'.

Mental Illness

The popular view of mental illness is that there is a breaking point – a fairly precise point – at which some overwhelming emotion, profound physical illness, or excessive fatigue leads to a 'nervous breakdown'. It is loss of self-control that is one of the main distinguishing marks in what the public regards as 'insanity' or 'madness'. People can usually tolerate peculiar behaviour, eccentric ideas and strange manners and speech, as long as the individual does not do anything that threatens their own, or other people's safety. It is very much the same for the individual. It is often at the point when they have to admit that they have lost their self-control ('I am no longer in charge of my own mind'; 'I cannot control myself') that people doubt their own mental health. People are also likely to label behaviour as 'not normal' if it is generally unpredictable and/or incomprehensible (i.e. without apparent meaning).

It is, of course, much more complicated than that. How does one recognize that a change (which might be labelled 'mad', 'insane', or, to use the correct psychiatric term, psychotic) has actually taken place? Certainly we are not dealing with clear-cut opposites when we refer to issues of mental health v. mental ill health, nor are the syndromes or constellations of symptoms clear-cut. It is one of the most vexed problems when 'diagnosing' the presence or absence of a reified *mental illness*, that the 'symptoms' often represent an exaggeration of attributes occurring in 'normal' people. When does a sense of injustice, resentment, or suspicion, amount to a delusion of persecution – an indication of paranoia? When is shyness and solitariness abnormal; when is a concern with tidiness obsessional; or brittle eccentricity a sign of Asperger syndrome? These are not easy questions to answer.

Definition and classification

Clinicians define the psychoses as mental functions so profoundly disturbed in the acute phase, that sufferers are incapacitated from participating in everyday activities. They usually show, *inter alia*, signs of thought disorder, which gives the odd or irrational nuance to their talk and actions. Essentially, there is an alteration of that central aspect of his or her personality: the self. It is not the 'split personality' beloved by Hollywood – the Jekyll and Hyde syndrome – but rather a desynchronizing fragmentation of various aspects of self that usually work harmoniously together. It should not be forgotten that there are many mentally ill patients who do not show such extreme symptoms. The neuroses are, in comparison with the psychoses, relatively mild mental disorders, characterized by symptoms such as free-floating anxiety, phobias, depression, hysteria, obsessions and compulsions. The emphasis must be on the word 'relatively', as these conditions are capable of causing great personal suffering.

Psychiatric classifications are described in great detail in the ICD-10 and DSM-IV diagnostic manuals, published by the World Health Organization and the American Psychiatric Association respectively. The disruptive behaviour disorders are classified in these taxonomic systems under the general rubric 'psychiatric disorders'. However, antisocial disruptive behaviours such as oppositional defiant and conduct disorders are not mental illnesses, but rather developmental aberrations involving personality and social deviation (see chapter 13). The term *antisocial behaviour* refers to a heterogeneous developmental dimension with the common theme of an extreme failure of the individual to conform his actions to expectations of some authority (e.g. parent or teacher) or to societal norms. The behaviours can range from chronic conflicts with authority (e.g. non-compliance, defiance, argumentativeness, to violations of social norms (e.g. truancy, running away from home) to serious violations of the rights of others (e.g. aggression, vandalism, fire setting, stealing). The antisocial disorders described above are described in chapter 13, as is 'delinqency' – an administrative term encompassing a variety of illegal activities.

On the basis of traditional categories, published by the Department of Health in 1995, the prevalence of psychological disorders for adolescents is as given in table 8.

Psychiatrists differentially diagnose 'mental illness' by the presence of clusters of symptoms (syndromes) illustrated, for our purposes, in the American Psychiatric Association's 1987 *Diagnostic Statistical Manual* (DSM-IIIR). A developmental theme was introduced for the first time in this third edition of the manual. It thus provided more than a diagnosis (see Carr, 1999). As a

Table 8 Prevalence of adolescent mental health problems

Disorder	Prevalence (%)
Schizophrenia	1.0
Major depression	2–8
Attempted suicide	2–4
Suicide	7.6 per 100,000 (15–19 yrs)
Obsessive–compulsive disorder	1.9
Anorexia nervosa	0.5–1.0
Bulimia nervosa	1.0

Table 9 DSM-IIIR multiaxial classification system (only major entries and axes I and II are included)

Axis I	Axis II
Clinical syndromes	• Developmental disorders • Personality disorders • Disorders usually first evident in infancy, childhood, or adolescence
	Cluster A
Organic mental disorders	• Paranoid
Psychoactive substance use disorders	• Schizoid
Schizophrenia	• Schizotypal
	• Delusional (paranoid) disorders
	Cluster B
Mood disorders	• Antisocial
Anxiety disorders	• Borderline
Somatoform disorders	• Histrionic
Dissociative disorders	• Narcissistic
Sexual disorders	• Sleep disorders
	Cluster C
	• Avoidant
	• Dependent
	• Obsessive–compulsive
	• Passive aggressive
	• Personality

'multiaxial classification system' it added a set of independent dimensions (axes) which are coded or rated along with the psychiatric diagnosis. Axes I and II (outlined in table 9) are used to describe the patient's current condition, i.e. clinical and developmental (or personality) conditions. Axis III lists all the patient's physical disorders (e.g. bronchial asthma, epilepsy, hypothyroidism). Axis IV contains a 'severity of psychological stressors' scale, involving a rating. Axis V is an estimate of the patient's level of function at the time of the assessment and his or her highest level of function during the past year.

Psychiatric classifications persist despite their weaknesses, presumably because the advantages outweigh the disadvantages, and because no better descriptive system has been developed. They facilitate comparisons across research reports and clinical articles. There is today an increasing consensus about the key features of schizophrenia. The consensus about psychiatric categories made by clinicians has been improved, by standardizing the questions asked in diagnostic interviews. The *International Pilot Study of Schizophrenia*, published by the World Health Organization in 1988, which investigated the diagnosis of schizophrenia in nine countries, found that similar, fairly tight, criteria, using standard decision-rules for assigning diagnoses to constellations of symptoms, were adopted in seven. Broader criteria were used in the USA and USSR.

It is still necessary to bear in mind that the diagnostic systems are not infallible and the 'labels' they attach to individuals should not be accepted uncritically or without giving careful thought to their implications for the young person. Detailed assessments of the functional strengths and weaknesses of the *individual* provide the professional with more information vital to a clinical formulation and treatment plan, than membership of a particular category, no matter how helpful that may be. The two approaches go best together, as tends to be the practice these days.

Professional boundaries with regard to the assessment and treatment of psychological ('clinical') problems have become somewhat blurred and permeable. This has arisen in part because of the increasing tendency of practitioners to offer help and to conduct therapy on an interdisciplinary basis, or to work collaboratively within multidisciplinary teams. Who does what is not always a clear-cut matter of the psychiatrist doing X, the clinical psychologist doing Y and the social worker doing Z and so on. What, in the end, is crucial in deciding to assess and/or intervene in a clinical problem at some level, is that there is the necessary expertise, the support and approval of the agency and a clear line of consultation and supervision with the professional ultimately responsible for the case or patient.

Society's concern about children with mental health problems is justified given their high cost in personal suffering and economic implications. In the case of the antisocial problems these include the cost of incarceration of juvenile offenders, the costs associated with vandalism of public property, and the costs to the victims of such children and adolescents, and not least the perpetrators of such misery – the young people themselves. Another disorder that has antisocial elements is hyperactivity, which, as we saw in chapter 12 affects teachers and parents who find hyperactive children so difficult to train and control. Concern about other disorders such as child and adolescent psychoses, or the pervasive developmental disorders, are particularly worrying because of the shortage of treatment personnel and facilities, and the failure (with some exceptions) to discover effective remedial and preventative interventions (see Carr, 2002; Herbert, 2002; Rutter and Taylor, 2002).

Note: Disorders ranging from 'neurotic' and psychotic conditions to pervasive developmental disorders, are described in chapters 13, 14 and 15.

chapter thirteen

Adolescence: Unsocial and Antisocial Behaviour

The Child is father of the Man

William Wordsworth (1770–1850)

Prejudice

Compliance to social attitudes is not always desirable. Racial and religious prejudices are not innate. It could be argued that a prime example of 'unsocial' socialization and the consequent distortion of social interactions (described earlier) is the development (and encouragement) of bigotry and prejudice. Children and adolescents who become deeply prejudiced often do so by default, because parents didn't bother to check on what their children were learning – or because of careless or malicious example that their children are likely to emulate. The individual tragedy is that prejudiced people (and extreme past and present examples might be children brought up in apartheid South Africa, the Balkans, Northern Island, and Rwanda) lose trust in people and in themselves.

The development of prejudice (Allport, 1954)

As children, we may learn to hate and despise other colours and creeds, but there is nothing inevitable about this process. In the initial development of prejudice there is a growing awareness by the child of himself and others in terms of racial identity. It has been found that children under 4 are aware of differences between people, but that they do not show signs of prejudiced behaviour. When they are between 3 and 4, they learn race-related words, concepts and attitudes. By the time they are 5, they have a fairly clear sense of ethnic identity. It is only after this age that fully fledged racial attitudes, possibly followed by prejudiced actions, are established.

Even then, attitudes are not rigid. Although a child may start school with the words and even the sentiments of prejudice, these will not harden into an attitude of bigotry until he is in junior, or even senior school. It all depends on the environment in which these ideas take root. Then, the emotional accompaniment of prejudice may vary from cold indifference to patronizing tolerance, from derisive rejection to violent hostility. But whatever form it takes, it stunts the sufferer's personality and closes many doors to him.

Few parents consciously teach their children to be prejudiced, but children imitate their parents' attitudes. They absorb their parents' prejudices by noticing restrictions placed on their playmates, and listening to remarks that denigrate, say, Protestants, Irish, Germans, West Indians or Japanese, not to mention politicians, students, and children with particular accents. And, as children grow older and spend more time with their friends, they also pick up attitudes and prejudices from them.

Racism and childhood identity

Milner (1997) has attempted to counter-balance the traditional 'passive' view of prejudice (racism in particular) of the kind described above. He states that it is simply necessary to acknowledge that children are not bemused bystanders to the process, looking on while adults instil in them their own views, much as they have to queue for vaccinations outside the school medical room. Rather they act in order to make their world manageable. The proper place, according to Social Identity Theory, he suggests, is one that reflects well on the individual and the group in comparison to other groups. A view of the world or attitudinal climate that *already* 'inferiorizes' certain groups and provides a ready-made scheme of things that automatically 'superiorizes' the child, may well seem to answer this need for majority-group children. On top of this, of course, comes the tangible encouragement to adopt the views of parents and peers in the socialization process, reinforcing the child's own motivation. Miller asserts that it is certainly not that racism in the childhood years is a trivial matter. It is that the 'seeking', absorbing and reproducing of racist ideas may have rather more to do with the developing identity needs of the child than the objects of those attitudes. They function to bring positive increments of self-definition during a period in which the child has little else from which to fashion a positive identity; and that they may rapidly be replaced by other sources of status and self-esteem when they become available. Race attitudes do not have such a central role in the child's identity that, except in a minority of individuals, they endure into adulthood. They peak in hostility at around 6 to 7 years of age (Pushkin and Veness, 1973).

The authoritarian personality

There is also evidence supporting the view that prejudice represents an aspect of a general character type. Put another way, the child's personality type is the main determinant of whether he will be excessively prejudiced. Prejudiced children tend to be rigid, illiberal, intolerant and punitive in their general attitudes. Like adults who have 'authoritarian personalities', these children usually manifest marked feelings of inadequacy, inferiority and insecurity, combined with a tendency to show blind deference to authority. They feel unloved and unwanted, and frequently come from unhappy or broken homes. Parents transmit to their children the personality type that predisposes a child to assume bigoted attitudes.

A large-scale study carried out in the United States, revealed that individuals most susceptible to the influence of fascist movements seemed to have a distinct personality syndrome. It was comprised of submissiveness to authority, cruelty to those in lower positions, rigid thinking, intolerance of ambiguity, and an unusual repression of their own impulses (Adorno et al., 1950). Many such people had grown up in homes where self-expression was limited and rigidly controlled, especially by the father. As a result, they tended to identify with the father in order to avoid his hostility, and to bottle up their own hostility, which was later expressed towards other disliked authority figures or minority groups.

The persons who contain within themselves a large store of resentment and aggression may be disposed to displace these on to others. Fearing retaliation, they try to displace their aggression on to the weaker members of society, and on to minority groups. Some psychologists believe that the greater the degree of frustration undergone by individuals the greater is their aggression.

Prejudice may be (as it is with adults) a 'psychological crutch' used by immature and emotionally damaged children, or it may come about because of a desire to conform to group expectations. There is variation in the degrees of prejudice shown, and this often depends on the sort of environment in which a child lives. For example, countries practising discrimination produce prejudiced children.

To some extent, prejudice arises through ignorance. It may sometimes amount to a deliberate restriction of one's own exploration and understanding of others; more often, it represents a fear of what one does not know or understand. If people behave differently from ourselves, we question their failure to conform. If this is highlighted by differences such as those of skin colour, language or customs, intolerance may be increased. But if we can learn more about other people through social contact, their differences may seem less threatening.

There is a self-defeating quality in society's attitude towards prejudice, and to the discrimination that follows in its wake. The victims of persistent prejudice either withdraw or become aggressive and resentful. This increases the antipathy felt toward them.

Risky Sexual Activity

Parents are not necessarily old-fashioned, hypocritical or puritanical if they have reservations about their teenagers being sexually active. Many are afraid that youngsters might be hurt or exploited if they embark on a sexual relationship too soon, before they are more experienced and emotionally mature. What puts particular pressure on parents is their perception of some of the awful risks their children may confront at this age: unwanted pregnancies, the exploitation of naivete, sexually transmitted disease, not least AIDS. Between a third and a half of sexually active adolescents do not use contraceptives during first sexual intercourse (Gerrard, 2000). One in five sexually active American teenagers contracts a sexually transmitted disease (STD) such as syphilis, gonorrhea, chlamydia, genital herpes or AIDS (see Carr, 2002, on sexually risky behaviour during adolescence).

The incidence of teenage pregnancies in the United States is higher than in Canada and most European nations. Britain has the highest teenage pregnancy rate in Europe, and one of the highest of any industrialized country. A significant proportion of young women conceive more than once in their teens; one in eight who had their first baby in their teens went on to have a second child before they reached the age of 20. One in six teenagers who had an abortion in 1997 had already had an abortion or a live birth. Eight thousand of the 90,000 adolescents who become pregnant every year are under 16; 2200 are 14 or younger. There is evidence of an association between very early sexual activity and social disadvantage, as well as antisocial behaviour (Bingham and Crockett, 1996; Tubman, Windle and Windle, 1996).

Teenage parenting

The risks here are related to the social, emotional, educational and physical disadvantages so evident in the pregnant adolescent's background (e.g. Blake and Lile, 1995; East 1992), and those of the father of her child-to-be. Among the correlates of early pregnancy are:

- A tendency to drop out of school
- Conduct problems
- Disciplinary difficulties
- Social competence skill and problem-solving deficits

- Poor resources in the home backgrounds
- Disturbing childhood experiences
- Diminished social and psychological coping
- Vulnerability to physical and emotional abuse
- Substance use
- A raised risk of birth complications
- An adverse influence on siblings.

In relation to the care of their infants, teenage mothers tend to display high levels of parenting stress. They appear less sensitive to their children's needs and display less responsive interactions than adult mothers. They have poor play skills. Adolescent mothers express less satisfaction with parenting than older mothers, and are at risk of abusing their children.

Sadly, many of the numerous programmes designed to prevent teenage initial (or repeat) pregnancies have had disappointing outcomes. Grandparents (often intensive, ongoing and 'hands-on'), and other agencies, can and do play an important role in supporting and mentoring teenage mothers, notably by helping them to stay on at school. This appears to be one of the major influences mitigating the adverse effects on the young mothers' opportunities for living a fulfilled life in the future (see a description of programmes in Blake and Lile, 1995; Zippay, 1995).

Teenage fathers

In addressing adolescent pregnancy, researchers have paid relatively scant attention to the male partners. Teenage fathers have been reported (e.g. Blake and Lile, 1995), relative to age-matched non-parenting male peers, to have less support from friends and the community, lower general life-satisfaction, and lower self-esteem. As a group, they tend to develop psycho-somatic problems and emotional difficulties, depression, guilt, educational or work difficulties, and anxiety. Relative to adolescent mothers they have lower general life-satisfaction, and attitudes that stress the increased responsibility of parenthood. Abandonment of the paternal role is fairly commonplace. Adolescent mothers report increased maturity and being kept out of trouble, as a result of parenthood.

The litany of negatives above undoubtedly gives a jaundiced view of adolescent sexuality. Of course there are countless examples of teenage love/ sexual relationships which provide growth-enhancing, memorable, and happy life-experiences that enhance the teenager's progress toward maturity. Nevertheless, many adolescents (according to surveys) believe that they have sexual problems of one kind or another, and comment on the intense anxiety they suffer. Harmonious sexual relationships (specifically) are relatively infrequent, feelings of insecurity fairly common (Gerrard, 2000).

Drug Use and Abuse (Farrell and Taylor, 1994)

The terms 'drug abuse' and 'drug misuse' refer to the observation that a particular form of drug taking is a harmful (abuse) and/or socially unaccept-able way of using that substance (misuse). 'Users' are likely to develop 'tolerance' for a drug, which means that their body has adapted to the repeated presence of the drug so that higher doses are required to maintain the same effect. The body may react with withdrawal effects to the sudden absence of a drug to which it has adapted; they involve severe physical discomfort. When this occurs and leads to a compulsion to continue taking the drug so as to avoid these symptoms, we speak of 'physical dependence'. The more important and widespread problem of 'psychological dependence' refers to an irresistible psychological compulsion to repeat the stimulation, pleasure or comfort provided by the drug's effects.

Use of alcohol, tobacco and marijuana is high among youth. I have chosen to use the word 'unsocial' rather than 'antisocial' to describe these problems. The *recreational* use of drugs of all kinds, and the existence of an extensive adolescent drug culture is so pervasive that the term 'antisocial' is generally inappropriate. Smoking, drinking, and illicit drug use have all increased among American and British youth. Surveys in the UK indicate that by the age of 19 some 90 per cent have drunk alcohol, 60 per cent have tried smoking, 50 per cent have used cannabis, and 20 per cent have tried drugs such as stimulants, solvents, hallucinogens or opiates (see Carr, 1999). In the US about 93 per cent of youth graduating from high school report having tried alcohol with about 41 per cent reporting that they experienced binge drinking. As many as 42 per cent of high school seniors report having used illicit drugs during the 1996 academic year with marijuana being the drug most commonly used (Winters, 1998).

This is not to deny that there are antisocial, often criminal aspects, con-nected with the dealing in drugs, and the means by which many addicts obtain the money to satisfy their habit. The description 'unsocial' is not (except perhaps in the eyes of parents) an entirely satisfactory generic term, given the vulnerability of children to exploitation and degradation. There is concern that children at pre-teen ages are having greater access to drugs such as cocaine and heroin (Thurman, 1997).

Many proponents of recreational drug-taking argue that the regular use of drugs like marijuana is little different in its health and social (if not legal) implications than the use of other drugs such as alcohol and nicotine. Even if true, such a comparison scarcely constitutes reassuring information. Avail-able evidence suggests that the habitual use of drugs by adolescents is unso-cial in the sense that it *can* have adverse long-term effects on them and eventually their offspring. For example, increased substance abuse has links with delinquency, crime, arrests, and a range of conduct problems (Winters,

1998). There is a particularly strong tendency for antisocial behaviour and psychiatric disorder in childhood to precede drug and alcohol problems in a complex interplay between the two. They predispose each to the other, and to some degree reflect the same underlying liability. It is estimated that between 5 and 10 per cent of teenagers under 19 years of age have drug problems serious enough to require a professional intervention.

Due to the availability and increased use and abuse of drugs and alcohol, the discrepancy between the estimated need for substance abuse treatment in the UK and US and its availability is deeply worrying. Increased usage of substances, pressure for legalization of marijuana, and continuing lack of information about indicators of causation and treatment success give rise to continuing concern.

The key factor in drug taking is opportunity – the availability of drugs and people to tempt and 'prompt'. Users have generally been exposed to drugs by their peers or by people (not infrequently family members) whose values incline toward non-conformity or even deviance. Rebelliousness, low self-esteem, a poor sense of psychological well-being, depression, and low academic aspirations are among the characteristics commonly found in adolescent drug users. The boredom and hopelessness of unemployment also play their part. Substance abuse presents a similar picture. High-risk drug taking is defined as uncontrolled use, whether or not it is already demonstrably harmful. A person is also taking an unacceptable risk if he or she is a regular user, that is, taking drugs at predictable intervals.

It isn't easy to be on the lookout for signs that may lead one to suspect drug use, because some of the signs are not uncommon in adolescence generally. There is often a gradual change in the adolescent's habits and a general lethargy. Other signs include aggression, loss of interest in schoolwork, sports, hobbies, and friends; furtive behaviour and frequent lying; bouts of drowsiness and sleeplessness; unexplained disappearances of money and belongings from the home. Heroin addicts usually stop bothering about their appearance, their speech may become halting, and they tend to drop old friends and take up with new ones. Users of heroin may receive unexplained messages or telephone calls, followed by an immediate and unexplained departure. Spots of blood may be noticed on their clothes, and needle marks on the back of the hand and the inside of the elbow. There may also be thickened brownish cords under the skin where veins solidified as a result of the injections.

Antisocial Behaviour: Conduct Disorders

Profile of children with antisocial disorders

The conduct disorders (CDs) refer to a heterogeneous category of antisocial disruptive behaviour disorders with the common theme of an extreme failure of the individual to conform his or her actions to expectations of caregivers (parents), teachers, or to societal norms. The behaviours can range from endless conflicts with authority (e.g. non-compliance, defiance and argumentativeness) and violations of social norms (e.g. truancy, running away from home), to serious violations of the rights of others (e.g. aggression, vandalism, fire setting, stealing, even murder).

Frick et al. (1993) conducted a quantitative meta-analysis of 60 factor analyses of conduct problem behaviours with a combined sample of 28,401 children and adolescents. The analysis generated two bipolar dimensions:

1. Overt behaviours involving direct confrontation with others, and covert behaviours not involving direct confrontations.
2. A destructive–non-destructive dimension of behaviour. The intersection of these two bipolar dimensions resulted in a division of conduct problem behaviour into four quadrants:
    (i)   the oppositional behaviours tend, as we saw in chapter 11, to emerge first (median age of onset 6 years), followed by
    (ii)   the aggressive behaviours (median age of onset 6.75 years),
    (iii)   the covert property destructive behaviour (median age of onset 7.25 years), and
    (iv)   the status violations (median age of onset 9 years).

Society's concern about children who indulge in these kinds of activities is justified given their high costs. These include the pain and suffering of their victims, and not least the harm done to themselves – the perpetrators of such misery. Their antisocial behaviour is, in the end, self-destructive. These 'aggressive', antisocial children are at increased risk of developing a veritable litany of problems later in life such as truancy, alcoholism, drug abuse, juvenile delinquency, adult crime and interpersonal problems (see Farrington, 1995). It also involves incalculable financial burdens on the community: the cost of incarceration of juvenile offenders and the costs associated with vandalism of public property.

Whatever the origins of the conduct disorders (and they are many sided), the child's difficulties create a 'ripple effect' affecting the family in ever-widening circles (see Webster-Stratton and Herbert, 1994). They have their impact on:

•   The parents: repeated episodes of verbal and physical aggression towards other children lead to their rejection and ridicule by others – adults and children. This is a key element in the tension between parents of children with conduct disorders and parents of non-challenging children, contributing to their feelings of humiliation, rejection and isolation.
•   The marital relationship, particularly arguments over the management of the child.
•   Other siblings, involving acts of violence.

- The extended family (notably grandparents) through their collective concern over the child's actual or incipient delinquencies.
- The family's relationships with the community, particularly the school and the police.

The origins of CD

Social learning theorists suggest that children and adolescents with such potentially serious antisocial problems are deviant because, *inter alia*, their early social learning/conditioning is ineffective. Youngsters with oppositional, conduct and (later) delinquent disorders demonstrate a fundamental inability or unwillingness to adhere to the rules and codes of conduct prescribed by society at its various levels. Such failures may be related to:

- the *lapse* of poorly established learned controls
- the *failure* to learn these controls in the first place, or to the fact that
- the behavioural standards a child has absorbed *do not coincide with the norms* of that section of society which enacts and enforces the rules.

Children who begin to show conduct problems before adolescence are usually referred to as 'childhood onset conduct disorders' (see chapter 11). However, there is a substantial number of young people who begin showing antisocial behaviour as they approach adolescence, without any history of oppositional activity during childhood (Loeber, 1991; Loeber et al., 1992). They are referred to as 'adolescence-limited conduct problems'. These youngsters are less likely to persist with their antisocial actions into adulthood. Boys displaying childhood-onset conduct problems are more aggressive and have more neuro-psychological deficits than boys with the adolescent limited pattern. It would seem from these longitudinal findings that onset in childhood is the more serious pattern of dysfunction, whereas the adolescent limited pattern may be better considered an *exaggeration* of normal developmental processes.

Most children who display the more extreme types of conduct problem do not change the activities in their antisocial repertoire, but simply add to them. That is to say most children with the more severe activities at the top of a figurative pyramid (with a large base and a smaller peak) *continue* to show conduct problems from the lower levels as well (Frick, 1998).

Stability of antisocial behaviour

There seem to be children with conduct disorders who show more stable patterns of antisocial behaviour than others. One influence, as we have seen, is the age of onset. Other indicators of stability include:

- The number of co-existing conduct problems
- Multiple types of conduct problems (Loeber, 1991)
- Attention deficit hyperactivity disorder (Farrington, 1991)
- Lower intellectual levels (Farrington, 1991)
- Having a parent with an antisocial disorder (Loeber and Hay, 1997).

Causation

The conduct disorders represent one of the most intensively studied of all forms of childhood psychopathology, yet there is still a debate over how accumulated findings should be interpreted. Why do defiant, antisocial trajectories develop? Why do they broaden and deepen with development in some children, yet taper off in others? And why are they so difficult to deflect once stabilized?

Faulty social training

A vast amount of cross-cultural research, over many years, has demonstrated that disharmonious home backgrounds, the breakdown of discipline, parental loss, and broken homes, are among many variables that are linked aetiologically to conduct disorders (Herbert, 1987b; Rutter, Tizard and Whitmore, 1970; Webster-Stratton and Herbert, 1994). Parent skills training is one of the priority interventions with families and children where CD problems cause such misery in the home, at school and elsewhere (see Herbert, 2002; Herbert and Wookey, 1998; Kazdin, 1997; Webster-Stratton and Herbert, 1994).

Attention Deficit Hyperactivity Disorder (ADHD)

ADHD and conduct disorder are co-morbid, so this is an appropriate place to continue the description in chapter 12 of this complex disorder in its context as a psychiatric disorder. ADHD represents one of the most common reasons why children are referred to mental health practitioners, and it is one of the most prevalent childhood mental health disorders. Only 10–20 per cent of ADHD children reach adulthood free of any psychiatric diagnosis, functioning well and without significant symptoms of their ADHD. The findings of the Cambridge Study in Delinquent Development, a prospective longitudinal survey of over 400 London males from age 8 to age 32 (Farrington, 1991), indicated that hyperactivity and impulsivity are among the most important personality or individual factors that predict later delinquency. A combined measure of hyperactivity-impulsivity attention deficit at ages 8 to 10 demonstrated that it significantly predicted juvenile convictions independently of conduct problems at age 8 to 10. A major problem of interpretation of these findings centres on the marked overlap between hyperactivity and conduct disorder (Taylor, 1994). It is difficult to know how far the results might have reflected the continuity between childhood antisocial behaviour and adult antisocial behaviour. Richman, Stevenson and Graham (1975) found that restlessness at age 3 predicted conduct disorder at age 8. Other attributes of ADHD such as sensation seeking, daring and risk taking and poor concentration are also related to delinquency.

Diagnosis

The diagnosis is affected by a variety of cultural views. It has been said that attempting to define ADHD is like entering a semantic jungle. There has been a proliferation of terms put forward to describe the hyperactive child, among them labels that imply causation (e.g. post-encephalitic behaviour, minimal brain damage, brain damage syndrome, and organic drivenness). Then there are those without a clearly hypothesized aetiological basis (e.g. minimal brain dysfunction and cerebral dysfunction); and descriptive labels which avoid implications about pathology (e.g. hyperkinetic impulsive disorder and hyperactive child syndrome).

ADHD is a neurodevelopmental disorder with core symptoms of inattention (see chapter 12), impulsiveness and hyperactivity. The latest version of the *Diagnostic and Statistical Manual* (DSM-IV: APA, 1994) codes and classifies three subgroups of conditions under the umbrella term attention deficit hyperactivity disorder:

1. Attention deficit hyperactivity disorder, predominantly *inattentive type*: The patient has recently met the criteria for inattention but not for hyperactivity-impulsivity. (This is the so-called attention deficit disorder of the earlier version of DSM.)
2. Attention deficit hyperactivity disorder, predominantly *hyperactive-impulsive type*. The patient has recently met the criteria for hyperactivity-impulsivity but not for inattention.
3. Attention deficit hyperactivity disorder, *combined type*. The patient has recently met the criteria for both inattention *and* hyperactivity-impulsivity.

Most ADHD children have symptoms of the 'combined type'.

Observation, usually by the clinician, aided by information from parents and the classroom teacher, is the initial tool in effectively documenting the child's level of activity, attention and distractibility. Observations should occur in a variety of settings, including the following:

- During solitary, parallel, and group play
- At home with parents, siblings, and other significant people
- At school (classroom/playground)
- In new environments such as the clinic playroom, the psychologists' consulting room, or the supermarket.

The goals of the observation are:

- To describe the child's general behaviour and how it relates to the criteria set out in the DSM-IV or ICD-10 (see below).
- To observe skills in a variety of areas to determine whether developmental delays are present.
- To note any atypical behaviours that warrant more formal testing; for example, weak visual-motor skills noted in copying a design, motor incoordination (clumsiness), or cognitive difficulties.

Attention span

At least six of the following *often* apply:

- Fails to pay close attention to details or makes careless errors in schoolwork, work, or other activities.
- Has trouble keeping attention on tasks or play.
- Doesn't appear to listen when being told something.
- Neither follows through on instructions nor completes chores, schoolwork or jobs (*not* because of oppositional behaviour or a failure to understand).
- Has trouble organizing activities and tasks.
- Dislikes or avoids tasks that involve sustained mental effort (homework, schoolwork).
- Loses materials needed for activities (assignments, books, pencils, tools, toys).
- Is easily distracted by external stimuli.
- Is forgetful.

Hyperactivity-impulsivity

At least six of the following *often* apply:

Hyperactivity
- Squirms in seat or fidgets.
- Inappropriately leaves seat.

- Inappropriately runs or climbs (in adolescents or adults, this may be only a subjective feeling of restlessness).
- Has trouble quietly playing or engaging in leisure activity; appears driven, always 'on the go'.
- Talks excessively.

Impulsivity
- Answers questions before they have been completely asked.
- Has trouble awaiting turn.
- Interrupts or intrudes on others.

Barkley, in his 1996 book *Taking Charge of ADHD*, cautions us never to view these criteria as infallible; they are simply guidelines or suggestions for identifying the possible presence of ADHD. He is of the opinion that the criteria have the following problems:

- DSM-IV criteria make no adjustments for age. Since children are less likely to show the listed behaviours as they mature, using one cutoff score for all ages means too many young children and too few older children will be diagnosed as ADHD.
- The guidelines make no adjustment for gender, despite the fact that we know young girls show the listed behaviours less than young boys. So little girls will have to have more severe behaviour problems compared to other girls to be diagnosed as ADHD than little boys compared to other boys.
- DSM-IV requires that the behaviour problems show up in two of the three settings of home, school, and work. In practice this means that parents and teachers must agree that the child has ADHD before the child can be given that diagnosis – and experience shows that parent–teacher disagreement is quite common.
- The DSM criteria do not tell us just how deviant from normal a behaviour must be to be inappropriate.

Whatever the confusions and contradictions of making a DSM or ICD diagnosis many, if not most, practitioners would say that there is sufficient agreement at a descriptive level, and in implications for treatment (see below), to justify the term ADHD. It has resource implications in the sense of developing appropriate services for these children and obtaining a Disability Living Allowance for their parents.

Co-morbidity and differential diagnosis

In children, a number of conditions may complicate the differential diagnosis of ADHD. The complications are as follows:

- Children with learning disabilities learn slowly and may be overly active and impulsive, but ADHD patients, once their attention is captured, are usually able to learn normally.
- Unlike children with an autistic disorder, ADHD patients communicate normally.
- Depressed patients may be agitated or have a poor attention span, but the duration is not usually lifelong.
- Many patients with Tourette's disorder are also hyperactive, but those who only have ADHD will not show motor and vocal tics.
- Other behaviour disorders (oppositional, conduct) may involve behaviours that annoy adults or peers, but they appear purposeful and are not accompanied by the feelings of remorse typical of ADHD behaviour. However, many children with ADHD also have conduct disorder or oppositional defiant disorder as well as Tourette's disorder.
- Children reared in a chaotic social environment may also have difficulty with hyperactivity and inattention.

It should be remembered that in a clinician's consulting room, some children with ADHD are able to sit still and focus attention well. Thus, the diagnosis is best made on the basis of historical information, and a rating of a wider range of situational observations (Herbert, 1987b). Whatever the difficulties, technical or ethical, of applying a diagnostic label, many parents find that it relieves them of much guilt and self-blame.

The course of ADHD

The onset of ADHD is placed no later than 7 years of age for more than half of those diagnosed as such, the disorder often being recognized later in life for girls than boys. The high degree of activity when present in early childhood tends to peak at around 5 or 6 and then undergoes a slow downward trend by adolescence. Some children outgrow the ADHD problem altogether; others certainly improve but remain somewhat impaired. Estimates suggest that 70–80 per cent are likely to continue to display symptoms in the adolescent years; furthermore, such symptoms (over-activity and behaviour problems) may persist for 50–65 per cent of children into adulthood.

Causation

Although research on the causes of ADHD remains inconclusive, there is compelling evidence linking the disorder to genetic, prenatal, environmental or physical factors.

HERITABILITY OF ADHD

Studies employing family methods demonstrate that ADHD is highly heritable. First-degree relatives of children diagnosed with ADHD are at markedly elevated risk for the disorder. Twin studies have indicated a genetic component in ADHD. Full-siblings of hyperactive children are more likely than half-siblings to be hyperactive themselves (Barkley, 1990). Heritability estimates employing a behavioural genetic methodology indicate that approximately 65 per cent of individual differences in attention, 70 per cent of individual differences in parent-rated impulsivity activity and 83 per cent of observed variation in composite ratings of ADHD symptoms are attributable to genetic variation (see reviews by Denney, 2001; Rutter et al., 1999a,b).

NEUROLOGICAL FEATURES AND BRAIN CHEMISTRY

ADHD sufferers have been found to have the following neurological features:

• Small sized corpus callosum (i.e. likely dysfuntion of neurodevelopment in ADHD)
• Differences in the size of the caudate nucleus (i.e. affecting the ability to regulate inhibition of motor responses.

It is thought that the neurological evidence (see review by Cody and Hynde, 1999) supports the heterogeneity of ADHD. Some of the brain areas implicated in the core attentional component of the disorder include:

• The superior temporal cortex
• The inferior parietal cortex
• The corpus striatum structures
• The rostral midbrain structures
• The hippocampus
• The pre-frontal cortex.

Evidence from several investigations supports the proposition that genetic biological factors (of the type described above) are related to abnormalities in neurological function, in particular to disturbance of brain neurochemistry (e.g. Cody and Hynde, 1999; Shaywitz, 1987). A number of studies, investigating with techniques such as PET scan (positron emission tomography) and magnetic resonance imaging (MRI), have explored the neurological substrates of ADHD during the last decade and a half. In the PET scan procedure, radioactive substances that emit positrons are used to label glucose, which is then introduced into the body by injection so that it may be traced in the brain. Using the PET scan, the glucose can be tracked as it is absorbed by the brain and used as fuel. The most active parts of the brain use the largest amounts of glucose.

The rate at which the brain uses glucose – its main energy source – is lower in participants with hyperactivity of childhood onset as compared with normal participants. Zametkin and his fellow researchers have determined that the frontal lobes of the brain are involved in regulating attention, emotional responses, and activity level (Zametkin and Rapoport, 1986). In addition, the frontal lobes play a role in planning, an area in which children with attention disorders typically have great difficulty. Children or young adults who have had some type of damage in the frontal lobe area seem to have great difficulty controlling impulsive actions. Although they are able to function in a perfectly normal intelligence range, their ability to plan and to abide by rules seems to be impaired.

MOLECULAR GENETIC FINDINGS

There is evidence for the hypothesis that the disorder results from the brain's inability to regulate itself appropriately via the neurotransmitters dopamine and norepinephrine. These are not the only neurotransmitters involved. There appears to be a chemical imbalance or shortage of certain neurotransmitters in the brain. Several studies in recent years have linked two genes associated with dopamine function to hyperactivity: the D4 dopamine receptor (DRD4) and the dopamine transporter gene (DAT1).

DIETARY FACTORS

Although there is some evidence that diet may be a factor in ADHD for some people, recent UK research shows that only a small proportion of children respond to dietary help. Studies by the US government have never confirmed the theory of a dietary basis to ADHD.

Overview

Barkley's (1996) conclusions, following a comprehensive review of the literature on the aetiology of ADHD, are that studies endorse a biological predisposition, as is the case in severe learning disability. In both heterogeneous conditions a variety of causal influences (e.g. pregnancy and birth complications, acquired brain damage, toxins, infections, and heredity) can play their part, through some fault in a final common pathway in the nervous system.

In the case of ADHD, it would seem that hereditary factors play the largest role in the occurrence of these symptoms in children. It may be that what is transmitted genetically is a tendency towards dopamine depletion in, or at least under activity of, the pre-frontal–striatal–limbic regions and their rich interconnections. Neurological studies are converging on the conclusion that a dysfunction in the orbital–limbic pathways of the frontal area (and particularly the striatum) is the probable impairment that gives rise to the primary features of ADHD, notably its *behavioural disinhibition* and diminished sensitivity to behavioural consequences or incentive learning.

It is the behavioural and learning implications that require – whatever the medical intervention – a psychological input (see Herbert, 1987a; Webster-Stratton and Herbert, 1994). ADHD can be exacerbated by pregnancy complications, exposure to toxins, or neurological disease, but also by social factors (such as environmental and family adversity, dysfunctional child-rearing and management, or educational environment).

Bullying

Involvement in bullying has long-term negative effects for both victims and bullies (see Guerin and Hennessy, 2002). The most common forms of bullying are verbal and physical abuse, such as name calling, physical attacks etc. Other behaviours include psychological aggression such as excluding a child from a group, intimidation and threats; they cause hurt and distress.

Most children will experience or witness bullying at some point in their school career.

Guerin and Hennessy report that:

- Approximately one-third of children in primary school report that they have been bullied in a given term, while around 10–15 per cent had bullied others.
- Of those involved in bullying, the majority report infrequent involvement, with very few reporting being involved 'once a week' or more often.
- There is less involvement in bullying in secondary school. There appears to be a decreasing trend in reported involvement in bullying as children get older.

Delinquency

The term 'juvenile delinquent' is an administrative term, not a clinical diagnosis. It is perhaps the most noteworthy of atypical manifestations in adolescence, reaching a peak at 15 years for boys and 14 years for girls. Although conduct problems in young children can create misery for everyone concerned, the disturbance is often contained within the home or classroom, although sometimes at great cost. As children grow, persistent defiance of authority, combined with a refusal or inability to show self-restraint, become more serious in their implications. They extend more and more beyond the confines of the child's life at home and school. The reverberations of such children's misdemeanours may eventually lead not only to the diagnosis 'conduct disorder', but also earn them, if they infringe the law, are apprehended and found guilty, the designation 'juvenile delinquent'.

Insecure attachment

There is evidence suggesting that much adult psychopathology, including the development of delinquent behaviour, is due to the failure of young children to attain secure attachments to a primary caregiver (see Rutter, 1970a, 1972, 1995). It has been theorized that attachment to significant others is conducive, especially for males, to the development of conventional attitudes, forming a bond between the juvenile and society, thus preempting delinquent attitudes and activities. In cases of extreme parental neglect, the child may be deprived of any opportunity to form a selective attachment. Such deprived children may suffer from reactive attachment disorder. They fail to respond to the normal social stimuli, tend to withhold close bodily contact, and have difficulties forming relationships later in life. Insecurely attached children (relative to secure children) tend to be:

- Less cognitively competent
- Less able to show social proficiency
- Less able to get along well with their peers
- More likely to develop emotional or behaviour problems.

Retrospective and prospective studies suggest that most antisocial adults have childhood histories of antisocial behaviour (see Farrington, 1991). Estimates from prospective studies suggest that around 40 per cent of children with conduct disorders will exhibit antisocial personality disorder as adults. Over half the children with conduct disorders will not go on to antisocial activities as adults. Maltreatment, and witnessing parental aggression during early childhood, are predictive of children developing conduct problems (Browne and Herbert, 1997; Moffitt and Caspi, 1998). The presence of delinquency/ criminality in a parent is a further determinant. It is associated with a three- to fourfold increase in the rates of similar problems in the offspring (Farrington, 2002).

It is clear from self-reports of delinquent-type activity that large numbers of young people engage in delinquent acts (e.g. petty thefts, vandalism) for several years before they receive a police caution or are found guilty (Herbert, 1987b). Such activities tend to decline after the late teenage years when a majority begin to 'merge' with the broadly law-abiding members of the community. However, there is a small but hard core of adolescents who habitually break the law. Among these recidivists is a group that is amongst the most dangerous and/or intractable offenders who pass through the revolving doors of the justice and penal systems, and the health and social services.

Personality Disorder

There are children and teenagers conspicuous for their fundamental inability or unwillingness to adhere to the rules and codes of conduct prescribed by society at its various levels: family, school and, indeed, the community at large. A psychiatric classification of psychopathic (or sociopathic) personality disorder denotes a pattern of antisocial activities, a syndrome that sets psychopaths apart from other people. It is a term so pessimistic about prognosis, and so therapeutically nihilistic, that there is a reluctance to apply it to children and adolescents. In any event, it is a contentious diagnosis, unreliable and value-laden. The belief that psychopaths differ quantitatively and qualitatively in general from ordinary citizens remains, nevertheless, an article of faith for many clinicians and researchers.

The classical delineation of psychopathy, clearly over-inclusive and highly subjective, is that proposed by Cleckley, in his seminal work *The Mask of Sanity* (1976). He included the following attributes:

- Superficial charm
- Above average intelligence
- Absence of delusions
- Absence of anxiety
- Considerable poise, calm and verbal facility
- Unreliability
- No sense of responsibility
- Untruthfulness, insincerity
- Lack of remorse or sense of shame
- Antisocial behaviour, often unmotivated, poorly planned, impulsive
- Poor judgement; inability to learn from experience
- Total self-centredness, pathological egocentricity
- Incapable of love and deep (as opposed to superficial) attachments
- Poverty of deep emotions
- Lack of insight
- Lack of ability to see self as others do
- Ingratitude for any special consideration shown to him/her
- Objectionable behaviour
- Poorly integrated sex life
- Failure to have any orderly lifestyle or life-plan.

This litany of negatives, especially when associated with horrific and apparently mindless acts of violence, tends to be polarized in debates about crime and punishment. Are such perpetrators 'mad' or 'bad'? Are they treatable? Should they be locked away for life? Is capital punishment the appropriate response to some of their more appalling, incomprehensible deeds?

This is our cue to look briefly at the issue of the delinquent youngster's moral development and reasoning. The terms conduct disorder and delinquency seem to suggest moral judgements. And the suggestion is that offenders use less mature moral reasoning than non-delinquent youngsters.

Moral Development

Moral reasoning

Kohlberg (1963, 1976) argues (as we have seen in the first half of the book) that moral development progresses through a number of levels, with different stages at each level. At the lower stages moral reasoning is characterized by its concrete nature and egocentricity. At the higher stages moral reasoning is guided by abstract notions such as 'justice' and 'rights' and is much more social in orientation. Following this model, offending is said to be associated with a delay in moral reasoning development, so that given the opportunity for crime the delinquent does not have the ability to control and resist temptation. A body of research studies has examined this proposition, and reviews are available (Herbert, 1987b). The broad consensus is that these experimental studies are equivocal: some suggest that delinquents use less mature reasoning than non-offenders, others fail to show any difference between offenders and non-offenders. Two procedural explanations have been offered to account for the varied empirical findings:

- The first is that moral reasoning is correlated with other cognitive developmental processes which, in an experimental study, should be controlled in order to determine true between-group differences in moral development.
- The second is the heterogeneity of the offender population, which means that there are *within-group* differences that should be taken into account when searching for differences *between* offenders and non-offenders.

It appears therefore that the link between moral development and delinquency is unlikely to be either simple or direct. While there are indications that youth offenders use less mature moral reasoning than non-offenders, this difference is probably mediated by the level and functioning of other sociocognitive abilities:

- by sex
- age
- type of offence
- experimental procedures such as type of moral problem, and
- the selected measure of moral development – with the contrast between moral *content* and the *process* of moral reasoning being of particular importance.

Gene–environment interactions (GrE) in antisocial activities

The interplay between nature and nurture is perhaps most dramatically illustrated in the field of antisocial behaviour. For example, adverse environments tend to have only a weak effect in increasing the susceptibility to antisocial activity when there is no genetic risk (as indexed by the presence or absence of antisocial behaviour in the birth parents). But the effect is very marked when adverse parenting is associated with genetic risk. It has been reported that in the absence of either genetic or environmental risk, the rate of adult criminality was only 3 per cent. With environmental but no genetic risk the rate rose to 6 per cent. With genetic but no environmental risk it rose further to 12 per cent. When both genetic and environmental liability were present the rate reached 40 per cent. Other adoptee studies have produced comparable results (see Rutter et al., 1999a,b).

chapter fourteen

Psychological and Psychiatric Disorders

As the twig is bent the tree's inclined

Alexander Pope (1688–1744)

Mental Health Problems

We are not only dealing with physical health and developmental problems such as those described earlier in the book, but also mental health problems that arise in the context of atypical development. Research studies provide a knowledge base of the major social and biological factors that put children at high risk of developing mental health problems.

On a 'family adversity index', which combines six variables associated with childhood psychiatric/psychological problems, the risk rises with each increase in the adversity score on the following items (see Rutter and Quinton, 1977):

- Father an unskilled worker
- Overcrowding: at least four children or more than one person per room
- Persisting marital discord or one-parent family situation
- Maternal depression or neurosis
- Delinquency in the father
- Institutional care of the child exceeding 1 week in duration.

Other high-risk factors, which are estimated to increase the likelihood of developmental problems fourfold if two are present and tenfold if four are displayed, include:

- Single or teenage parenthood
- History of:
  - parental drug taking
  - parental failure to provide cognitive stimulation in the home

- parental abuse
- excessive parental criticism/inconsistent discipline
- parental psychiatric history
- parental disengagement from their children's school experience
- domestic poverty.

Biological factors might affect children with;

• Learning disability
• Delayed language and reading
• ADHD.

(See Blanz et al., 1991; Farrington, 2002; Webster-Stratton, 1991.)

The complexity of the factors contributing to dysfunctional behaviour is illustrated by the multifactorial chart shown in figure 25.

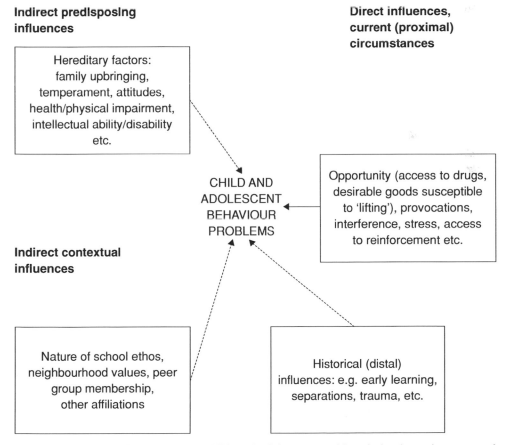

Indirect predisposing influences

Hereditary factors:
family upbringing,
temperament, attitudes,
health/physical impairment,
intellectual ability/disability
etc.

Direct influences, current (proximal) circumstances

CHILD AND
ADOLESCENT
BEHAVIOUR
PROBLEMS

Opportunity (access to drugs,
desirable goods susceptible
to 'lifting'), provocations,
interference, stress, access
to reinforcement etc.

Indirect contextual influences

Nature of school ethos,
neighbourhood values, peer
group membership,
other affiliations

Historical (distal)
influences: e.g. early learning,
separations, trauma, etc.

Figure 25 Levels of influence on child and adolescent problem behaviour: the range of causal and contributory factors is large and bewildering

In the 1960s, Michael Rutter and his colleagues conducted a study in the Isle of Wight that was to become a classic among investigations of the incidence of mental and other health problems in children (Rutter, Tizard and Whitmore, 1970). They discovered that mental health problems were relatively common (one child in ten), and that there was considerable overlap, children with one kind of disorder tending to have others in addition. Emotional difficulties (e.g. anxiety, depression, fears) and disruptive problems (oppositional defiant behaviours, conduct problems, hyperactivity) formed the bulk of the problems.

In a broadly comparable study directed by Robert Goodman (the 1999 *Office for National Statistics Survey of the Mental Health of Children and Adolescents in Great Britain*) the findings were similar. A small number had rarer conditions such as autism or psychosis. Associations were explored between physical and mental health problems and a variety of social and family influences. There were strong effects of social disadvantage on the rates of problems. Children who were living in relative poverty had a rate of problems that was three times greater than the rate of children whose family was well off. The rates were higher than the overall rate (10 per cent) in children from single parent families (nearly 20 per cent) and reconstituted families (around 15 per cent).

Both deprivation and the stress of adapting to new family relationships appear to have a key role in determining these associations. Where there has been an increase over the 50 years between the two studies in children's mental health problems (as indicated by rates of suicide, drugs, serious depression), physical health has improved.

Specific child and adolescent disorders

Table 10 provides a list of specific child and adolescent mental health disorders and their prevalence, drawn from a 1995 UK Department of Health report.

Estimated prevalence rates of mental health problems in children from other cultures, are listed below:

Table 10 Prevalence of mental health disorders

Disorders	Prevalence (as a %)
Emotional disorders	4.5–9.9 (of 10-year-olds)
Conduct disorders	6.2–10.8 (age 10)
Hyperactivity	1.7 (primary school age)
Encopresis	2.3 (boys); 0.7 (girls) (7–8 years)
Depression	0.5–2.5

Indian children	8.2–9.4 per cent
Chinese children	8.3 per cent
Sudanese children	29.0 per cent
Malaysian children	6.1 per cent
Puerto Rican	18.0 per cent

The major mental health problems are described in the following sections.

Anxiety States

There is no doubt about the power of fear to alter and disrupt thought and behaviour. Anxiety (which has been called fear spread thin) can erode our capacity to enjoy life. It is a condition that varies along a continuum from a reaction of arousal, which at relatively low levels may enhance performance to one of panic that is immobilizing. The condition arises in large part from a subjective appraisal by the person that there is a threat to his or her physical or psychological well-being.

Four separate systems make up the anxiety response.

1. Physiological: the person's response via the autonomic nervous system – adrenaline is secreted, heart rate increases, sugars flow to the muscles.
2. Behavioural: the person's observable behaviours.
3. Affective: the person's experience and feelings.
4. Cognitive: the person's *self-statement* (what a person thinks/says about and to him- or herself) ('I can't cope with this').

The systems are not neatly synchronized one with another, i.e. changes in one system are not immediately reflected by changes in the others.

Anxiety disorders are among the most prevalent forms of psychopathology during childhood and adolescence. The 'internalizing disorders' are manifested by about 2.5 per cent of pre-adolescent children. Their prevalence increases somewhat by adolescence, and we find that boys and girls are about equally prone to them. We know as a result of longitudinal studies that, for the most part, young people who suffer from emotional disorders become reasonably well-adjusted adults. In a sense these difficulties are the emotional equivalent of 'growing pains'. They come and go; nevertheless they sometimes persist, and can reach levels of intensity that cause all-round suffering.

When is an 'emotional problem' really a problem?

This question highlights the importance of a developmental context for explaining a child's fearfulness, as ongoing stress in life is not uncommon.

Fear, anxiety and, indeed, panic may be appropriate or normal (i.e. usual) responses to particular situations. Fear is adaptive when appropriate and within limits and an absence of fear has serious implications for a person's normal development. The defining criteria of psychopathy include the absence of appropriate anxiety/fear reactions to wrong doing. Post-traumatic stress disorder involves a typical (normal) and intense fear reaction to an abnormal situation (disaster).

Fear is not necessarily a maladaptive reaction. Indeed, it is functional in the sense of having positive survival and reward value: 'driving' the individual to maximum efficiency for 'fight or flight' in the event of extreme threat or toning him or her up for peak performance in activities such as examinations, acting, and athletics. In crises or demanding situations, the child experiences a variety of physical sensations such as a pounding heart, shivering and trembling, 'butterflies' in the stomach, dry mouth and perspiring hands. These physiological mechanisms are built into the body, and processed by the 'autonomic nervous system'. The physical sensations are by-products of the changes in body chemistry that take place as adrenaline is released into the blood stream. This outpouring of adrenaline keeps the system toned up for maximum efficiency of the body, until the crisis has passed. For many aspects of human performance, an 'inverted U-curve' relationship is postulated between efficiency of performance and level of anxiety. Parents also make use of the child's fear in teaching the child to avoid danger; anxiety (about the loss of love or approval) is vital for ensuring compliance and the internalization of rules and values in the task of socialization.

What, then, is abnormal fear or dysfunctional anxiety? Context is one criterion. Is the fear proportionate to the objective threat inherent in a particular situation? The physiological accompaniments of the 'fight or flight' response to threat, if they are chronic and unresolved by action (given the constraints of life at home and at school and the fact that many of the threats are symbolic rather than real), may contribute to the aetiology of psychophysiological disorders.

Context for childhood fear is a wider criterion than that for adults. Children's fears (as we saw in part III) show a clear pattern as they grow up – each stage would seem to have its own set of 'adjustment' crises or anxieties. Particular fears are so common at different ages that a child referred for being fearful may be experiencing the kind that are age-appropriate rather than developmentally 'abnormal'. The parameters that separate behaviours defined as phobic from the anxieties, avoidance, fears, indecisiveness, and obsessions shown by all children at one time or another are their *frequency* and *intensity*, also their *duration* and *pervasiveness*. Anxiety is thought of as abnormal when it occurs to a much greater degree than is typical for most people – when it occurs more often and with greater severity than the stimulus (circumstance) warrants. It is not only high levels of anxiety that are dysfunctional; low levels, such as those postulated in the psychopathic/sociopathic individual that are thought to adversely affect socialization (notably social cognition and moral development), can also be maladaptive.

The meaning of the problems for the child – the sense made of them, the pay-off they provide – and indeed for his or her family, also constitute a vital element of the overall assessment. At its simplest, behaviour is a function of certain contingent stimuli, originating in the person's internal and external environment. Here, the important questions are: 'What triggers (elicits) the phobia?' or 'What reinforcement does the child get for behaving in this way?' At a more interpretative level, the child's behaviour may have the function of solving (or attempting to solve) a developmental or life problem. To make sense of it, one might ask, *inter alia*: 'What immediate "solutions" (even if self-defeating in the longer term) do the child's actions provide for himself or herself?' Also: 'What purpose does the child's behaviour serve in terms of his or her family life and its psychological and social dynamics?'

Phobic Anxiety

At the age of 11, children exhibit an increase in fear. Among 11- and 12-year-olds, worries connected with school are nearly half as many again as worries about home matters. Abnormal fears (phobias) involve an intense dread in the presence of an object or situation often amounting to panic and, although the object may be individual to the adolescent, certain forms are common, for example social fears. Some definitions of phobia emphasize the incapacitating or restrictive effect of a phobia, in contrast to the more common fears which most of us endure.

There are various types of phobia. For example, some teenagers have a persistent fear of, and compelling desire to avoid, a social situation (say, a party) in which they are exposed to possible scrutiny by others and fear that they may act in a manner that will cause embarrassment or humiliation. In the case of agoraphobia, the young person has an intense fear of, and thus avoids, being alone or in public places.

Adolescents are often tormented by low self-esteem, worries about the future, and fears about such matters as attending school or participating in social activities. These problems may give rise to sheer panic attacks of the most distressing kind. There is no doubt about the power of fear to alter and disrupt thought and behaviour. Anxiety (which can be focused or 'free floating') can erode the adolescent's capacity to enjoy life. The condition arises in large part from a subjective appraisal by the person that there is a threat to his or her physical or psychological well-being.

Identifying controlling variables

1. ANTECEDENTS/PRECURSORS OF ANXIETY

Anxiety may be learned or elicited by the following processes:

- The appraisal of threat – e.g. separation in young children, distressing life events, conditions of living or work, family relationships especially during childhood, and physical illnesses manifesting themselves with an anxiety component.
- Classical conditioning – the pairing of a previously neutral stimulus with a situation of pain or fear.
- Modelling – the person perceives others whom he or she perceives as being like him- or herself behaving in an anxious way. This person acts as a model for the acquisition of anxiety.
- Traumatic learning – an experience of intense fear or pain can lead to acute anxiety being experienced in similar subsequent situations e.g. following a road accident.
- Generalization of learned anxiety to other settings – e.g. a person who suffered humiliation at school may experience acute anxiety in any situation involving being tested or judged (e.g. at a driving test).
- Vicarious learning – a person may become fearful through seeing someone else undergoing a fearful event.
- Cognitive processes – the highly individual way in which people perceive situations is crucial in understanding anxiety. Some people typically see danger in situations which are simply stimulating or routine to others, e.g. having an argument or travelling by aeroplane.

The human being's appraisals of threat are essentially personal. S/he responds to perceived danger or threat by:

- Fighting – an aggressive response, to deal by combat with potential threat
- Fleeing – a retreat designed to avoid potential threat
- Freezing – an alert, but immobile, response, in the hope of escaping the attention of the potential threat.

The fact that in modern times it is more often than not the symbols of danger, rather than real life-endangering threat, to which the body's emergency system reacts, means that the physical reactions are inhibited and are not resolved in active, vigorous physical activity. If the stress is repetitive and the physical reactions thus 'chronic', we could get a situation in which previously adaptive reactions become dysfunctional and contribute to psychosomatic illness (e.g. hypertension, ulcers, asthma).

2. COGNITIVE APPRAISAL

The role of cognitive appraisal and attributions are critical in the subjective appraisal of stress (Herbert, 1998a). Cognitive processes are indispensable elements in any causal theory of emotion. Emotional activity results from the child's appraisal of the situation – whether it is dangerous (primary appraisal) – and the evaluation of the coping processes he or she has available (secondary appraisal). One of the determining factors – dispositional conditions – refers to the individual's psychological structure (e.g. beliefs, attitudes). When analysing childhood anxiety and coping strategies, it is vital to remember that children mature cognitively in a manner that changes the way they construe the world they live in and the interpretation they put on people and events. Several authors, noting the developing of statistically 'normal' fears in childhood, have demonstrated how they arise from increasingly sophisticated cognitive structures in the maturing child.

3. AGE

We have already seen the considerable attention given to the developmental features of anxiety in childhood. There is undoubtedly a patterning in the type of fears present at various ages (Ollendick and King, 1991). Simple phobias seem to date back to early childhood, whereas social phobias tend to have their onset in adolescence or later. Separation anxiety occurs at about 8 months of age and is related to attachment developments. It may also contribute to the raised incidence of school phobias at age 11.

One can only speculate about the reasons for these age-related patterns: the notion of developmental and life tasks and the crises to which they give rise may throw some light on this conundrum. Certainly cognitive factors are significant.

4. SEX

The findings regarding sex are not consistent, although some investigations suggest that girls are somewhat more tearful than boys and are more vulnerable to neurotic disorder (Herbert, 1974). Whether this is a true organismic variable or a social artefact of willingness to admit to fears on the part of girls is a moot point.

5. GENETIC VARIABLES

The background to the question of a genetic aetiology in anxiety conditions, in particular, and emotional disorders, in general, is that in no example of a psychological condition that has been investigated is the heritability of psychological attributes so high that there is no room for environmental effects. In fact, this statement can be reversed in the case of emotional disorders to a question: Is there any room for a genetic component?

Family resemblances provide an important datum: that is to say, the extent to which influences operate within or between families may be significant. Emotional disorders commonly affect just one child in the family, whereas conduct disorders usually affect several. In examining the nature–nurture issue from another angle (familial concordance in anxious children), studies of parents of anxious children and studies of the children of adults with anxiety disorders produce some ambiguous findings, but on balance indicate a familial predisposition. These findings are not of the order that allows one to be precise about the relative contribution of inherited influences as compared with environmental influences, except to say that the former have a minor role.

6. LIFE STRUCTURE

The term 'life structure' has been used to tackle the interface of the internal and external worlds of the individual and to reflect the fact that despite great complexity at any particular time, there is some structure to life – some regularity. The term refers to the current psychosocial totality of the child, to the transition and change in his or her family life, and encompasses not only behaviour, but also unexpressed longings, moods, regrets and attitudes about one's life as well as all referents to these activities and feelings. This significant aspect of the child's life moves the assessment on from a consideration of current antecedent influences to an inquiry into distal (historical) antecedents.

Very early environmental influences, even those going back to the child's uterine environment, are thought by some to sensitize the child to overreact to stimuli. The philosopher Locke believed that knowledge and memory are built on experience alone, and that fear is learned. In an uncanny anticipation of contemporary behaviour therapy he described a version of systematic desensitization: 'If your child shrieks and runs away at the sight of a frog, let another catch it and lay it down at a good distance from him; at first accustom him to look upon it; when he can do that, to come nearer to it and see it leap without emotion; then to touch it lightly, when it is held fast in another's hand, and so on, until he can come to handle it as confidently as a butterfly or sparrow.'

Traumatic antecedents

It has been suggested that if the mother is under considerable stress during pregnancy, the child may be more reactive and highly strung than he or she would otherwise be. Many postnatal life events have been studied for their adverse consequences on children's psychological well-being: separation from parents (hospitalization, reception into care, divorce, bereavement), trauma (disaster, abuse), and family violence.

There is a range of separation anxieties shown by children – from the normal protests they make when parents go out to the morbidly fearful preoccupation at all times with mother's whereabouts. The sort of child who fits into the latter category is often referred to as 'clinging' or 'over-dependent'. Theorists (Herbert, Sluckin and Sluckin, 1982) have long been interested in the development of bonds or attachments (secure v. insecure) between children and their parents (notably mothers). They have also studied the weakening of these bonds – the period of psychological weaning from the parents – whereby children become persons in their own right. Another area of research concerns the fear of separation that, when it persists, is thought to be central in many neurotic anxiety conditions. From the clinical point of view, the evidence suggests that psychological distress of a kind commonly termed neurotic results (at least in part) from the early disruption of bonds.

Panic Attacks

Panic disorders usually start suddenly with the most common age of onset being in the late-teenage years. They also occur in childhood. Some persons suffer both panic disorder and generalized anxiety. Panic disorder is characterized by recurrent panic attacks, which usually occur unpredictably. Adolescents with panic disorder experience recurrent, unexpected panic attacks followed by at least 1 month of persistent concern about having additional attacks, worry about the implications or consequences of the attacks, or a significant change in behaviour related to the attacks (Mattis and Ollendick, 2002).

Symptoms

A panic attack consists of an intense feeling of apprehension or impending doom that is of sudden onset and is associated with a wide variety of distressing physical symptoms. Some types of panic reaction are preceded by a period or heightened anxiety, others appear to come 'out of the blue' when an individual is not anxious. The characteristic symptoms are as follows:

- Breathlessness
- Palpitations
- Chest pains
- Choking

- Dizziness
- Tingling in the hands and feet.

A panic attack as defined by the DSM-IV (APA, 1994) is a sudden episode of intense fear, apprehension, or discomfort which is accompanied by at least four of the following physical or cognitive symptoms:

- Chest pain or discomfort
- Nausea or abdominal distress palpitations / pounding heart
- Sweating
- Trembling or shaking
- Sensations of shortness of breath or smothering
- Feeling of choking
- Dizziness or light-headedness
- Derealization or depersonalization
- Numbness or tingling sensations
- Chills or hot flushes
- Fear of losing control or going crazy
- Fear of dying.

Mattis and Ollendick (2002) describe three types of panic attacks:

1. Unexpected (or uncued) panic attacks are not associated with a situational trigger and thus occur spontaneously or 'out of the blue'.
2. Situationally bound (or cued) panic attacks almost always occur immediately upon exposure to, or in anticipation of, a situational trigger (e.g. a teenager experiences a panic attack every time s/he is required to sit an examination).
3. Situationally predisposed panic attacks. Panic attacks do not always occur immediately upon exposure to a trigger factor. For instance, a teenager with panic disorder may worry that s/he is losing control or 'going mad'. S/he may believe that the panic attacks are the result of a terminal illness.

There is much individual variability in the age at onset for panic disorder, although it typically begins between late adolescence and the mid-30s (although several cases have their onset in childhood).

Agoraphobia

This is a condition that involves anxiety about being in situations from which escape might be difficult (or embarrassing) or help might not be readily available if a panic attack comes on. It is a common accompaniment of adolescent panic disorder. Teenagers with agoraphobia typically avoid such situations, or will enter them only with a 'safe person', such as a parent. Indeed, many adolescents with panic disorder begin to avoid a variety of situations, such as classrooms, cinemas, shops, public transportation, and being alone, because they anticipate and fear having a panic attack.

For a detailed account of panic disorder, its assessment, treatment and causation, see Mattis and Ollendick (2002). They cite a causal model to explain panic attacks, in which several vulnerabilities or risk factors are required in order for panic to develop:

- An individual must have the tendency to be neurobiologically over-reactive to stress. In other words, some people seem to react to negative life events with a 'false alarm', in which the fight or flight response is triggered unnecessarily. Since this tendency is rooted in genetics, we would expect an adolescent with this vulnerability to possibly have a parent or other family member who also shows the tendency to be over-reactive to stress.
- The initial vulnerability described above will only lead to the development of panic under certain conditions. Specifically, it is through a process of learning over time to associate false alarms with bodily sensations, that panic disorder begins to occur. As a person experiences repeated false alarms (i.e. feelings of great apprehension associated with distressing physical sensations), he may begin to associate the alarm reaction with the actual physical sensations (e.g. rapid heartbeat, dizziness) through the process of conditioning.
- It is through conditioning that a neutral stimulus (i.e. physical sensations) gains the ability to trigger fear after being paired with a fear-arousing stimulus (i.e. a false alarm).
- Once this has occurred, the individual will become extremely sensitive to somatic sensations so that even slight bodily changes (e.g. in response to exercise, temperature fluctuations, etc.) may trigger an alarm reaction or panic attack.

According to this model of panic disorder the individual must also develop anxious apprehension over the possibility that future false alarms or panic attacks will occur. For instance, a teenager with panic disorder will typically worry a great deal about his or her next panic attack and when it might occur, possibly even avoiding situations where s/he fears one might happen.

S/he views the tendency to develop anxious apprehension as a psychological vulnerability that arises from developmental experiences with predictability and control. Finally, avoidance behaviour may develop depending on the person's coping skills and perceptions of safety. Here the issue is whether a person or place exists with whom or where it is relatively safe to have a panic attack.

Obsessive–Compulsive Disorder (OCD)

OCD is one of the more intractable anxiety disorders – a potentially disabling condition that can persist throughout a person's life. The child or adult who suffers from the disorder becomes embedded in a pattern of unwanted, repetitive thoughts and actions that are senseless, repugnant, and distressing, but extremely difficult to control or banish. Most individuals suffering from OCD have both obsessions and compulsions. OCD is estimated to affect 1 to 3 per cent of the population, although this is something of a 'guesstimate' and cannot be claimed to be a true prevalence figure (see Antony, Downe and Swinson et al., 1998).

The disorder occurs over a spectrum from mild to severe. If it remains untreated, and is severe, it can impair (indeed destroy) an individual's capacity to function satisfactorily at work, at school, or even at home. The common obsessive themes (sexual, blasphemous or aggressive) horrify the individual who knows the images and impulses are products of his or her own mind. Repetitive washing or checking are common compulsions.

The general misery caused to children and adolescents with the disorder, their parents and others who teach and care for them, makes an understanding of the condition, and an early intervention, a matter of urgent concern. The ramifications for adult sufferers and their families are also likely to be distressing in various ways that reduce the quality of their lives.

The course of OCD

The average age of onset for childhood OCD is around 10 years, boys tending to develop OCD earlier than girls (see Zohar, 1999). The everyday, isolated obsessions and rituals so common in child development are discontinuous with OCD, and are not predictive of the acquisition of the condition.

There may be long intervals when the symptoms are mild, but for many individuals when once established, they continue (if untreated) throughout life. The reasons for these fluctuations in severity in this condition are not understood. Remission, even after years of illness, occurs in something like a third of patients.

Fortunately, fairly recent discoveries in the areas of pharmacological and behaviour therapy have made what was once considered an irretrievably chronic condition a somewhat less formidable clinical problem (Shafran, 2001). Nevertheless, about 10 per cent of patients suffer a continuous deteriorating course. With regard to familial predispositions, the majority of sufferers do not have affected first degree relatives who also have OCD. Most studies report a 3:2 male–female ratio in those who have the condition.

Anxiety plays an important role in the maintenance of OCD, obsessions eliciting anxiety and compulsions temporarily alleviating it. The cognitive-behavioural theory of OCD suggests that the disorder is maintained when normal intrusive thoughts are appraised in terms of responsibility for harm. The individual is *driven* to take corrective action to reduce the probability of the feared event occurring, to reduce personal responsibility, and to alleviate distress (see Rachman, 1997). Certainly, the evidence suggests that cognitive-behavioural therapy is an effective treatment for the disorder (ibid.).

Depression (Affective Disorder)

Depression is a condition that ranges from the mild to the very severe and disabling. Associated suicide rates rise sharply during adolescence so that it comes to rank among the half-dozen most common causes of death among older adolescents. The incidence statistics fall well below those for adults, and well below the suicide rate in old age.

Several organizations, including the World Health Organization, have produced classifications of the major forms of depression (e.g. the classification in the *International Classification of Diseases* (ICD-10)). The earlier, popular distinction between 'reactive' and 'endogenous' depression seems to be used less today. Moderate forms of depression are occasionally termed 'reactive' when the depression suffered by the individual appears to be reactive to a particular distressing event: for example, a bereavement, a disintegrating relationship, financial difficulties, school failure, and redundancy.

The main dimensions considered in contemporary practice are:

type:	depressive, manic, mixed
special features:	with neurotic symptoms
	with psychotic symptoms
	with agitation
	with retardation or stupor
the course:	unipolar (depression only) or
	bipolar (manic-depression)

Depressive disorders are marked by disturbances of:

* Affect (emotions of sadness and misery)
* Behaviour, marked by slowness and inertia
* Cognitions (thoughts of hopelessness, despair and sometimes suicide)
* Motivation, indexed by apathy, disinterest, everything seeming an effort, little in life seeming worth while
* Biological function, as seen from reductions in sleeping, eating, sexual and other activities.

The checklist below should alert caregivers and professionals to the possible presence of a depressive disorder:

- A demeanour of unhappiness (e.g. weepiness) and misery (more persistent, intense and pervasive than 'the blues' that afflict everyone now and then)
- A marked change in eating and/or sleeping patterns
- Reduced sexual drive
- A feeling of helplessness, hopelessness and self-dislike
- An inability to concentrate and apply him/herself to anything
- Everything (even talking and dressing) is seen as an effort
- Irritability and/or aggressive behaviour (on a 'short fuse')
- A fairly sudden change in ability to work
- Friends being dropped or ignored.

A depressive disorder may be 'masked', particularly in adolescence, by diversions such as drinking, drug-taking, risky and sometimes delinquent activities that act as a temporary 'antidote' to the depression. The problem with the list above is that almost everyone seems to experience these 'symptoms' at times and to some degree. While most people are spared the more severe forms of depression, few of us are not familiar with the milder forms. These often accompany loss, failure or disappointment in one or many areas of life, such as achievements, relationships, employment and status. Many people know only too well the depression that accompanies bereavement. This often lasts, where the attachment was close, for at least 1 to 2 years, but frequently for longer.

It is now recognized that children can suffer from clinical depression; it is certainly one of the more notable disorders to beset adolescents. The disorder is more common in adolescent girls than boys and frequently occurs in conjunction with conduct disorder, anxiety disorder and ADHD (10–17 co-morbidity rates).

The following questions may help in screening the youngster's condition. Mental alarm bells should be ringing if the answers are in the affirmative:

- Are several of the signs (listed above) present?
- Do they occur frequently/intensely?
- Have they persisted for a long time?
- Do they cause extensive suffering to him or her?
- Do they stand in the way of his or her ongoing life-tasks (e.g. working efficiently, enjoying leisure activities)?
- Do they get in the way of his or her relationships with others?
- Do they cause distress in others?

Causal theories

The causation of depression is best understood in terms of interacting variables, rather than in terms of a unitary influence (see Kazdin, 1990):

BIOLOGICAL FACTORS

Heredity:

- In adults heritability for bipolar disorder is estimated to be about 80 per cent.
- The genetic component in unipolar depression is estimated at between 20 and 45 per cent.
- Depressive disorders in children show a marked tendency to run in families. There have been no major twin studies.
- Childhood-onset depression has a strong genetic component.

Circadian and seasonal rhythms are hypothesized to be contributory causes of depressive states:

- When there is desynchrony in the circadian rhythm which governs the sleep–waking cycle. Temporary relief is possible following sleep-deprivation methods.
- When the reduced daylight of winter leads to increased secretion of melatonin by the pineal gland, the result is hibernation-like features of fatigue, oversleeping, an increase in appetite, and weight-gain.

The following physiological stressors are also thought to contribute to depression:

- Premenstrual hormonal changes (Dalton, 1977)
- Viral infections
- Major hormonal changes linked with childbirth.

Other biological factors are listed in table 11 (adapted from Carr, 1999).

PSYCHOLOGICAL STRESS

There is evidence that stressful life-experiences can precipitate a depressive episode. Stressful life events such as loss of employment, the impact of accidents, changes in important relationships, particularly bereavement and divorce, all make great demands upon a person's capacity for coping.

Table 11   Theories regarding biological causes of depression

Hereditary factors	A polygenetic mechanism making for a vulnerability to abnormalities in the neurophysiological or endocrine systems which are dysfunctional in mood disorders
Immune system dysfunction	Chronic stress or acute trauma lead to both immune system functioning and depressive symptoms
Endocrine dysregulation	Depression results from (i) a reduction of thyroxine levels associated with dysregulation of the hypothalamic-pituitary-thyroid axis, and (ii) raised cortisol levels associated with dysregulation of the hypothalamic-pituitary-adrenal axis following chronic stress
Amine dysregulation	Dysregulation of the amine systems in those centres of the brain which subserve reward- and punishment-related experiences. Noradrenaline and serotonin are the main neurotransmitters involved

While many variables may contribute to a depressive disorder, it may well be that the most apparent influence has been 'the final straw' for a person who was already coping with many demands and difficulties. Burke (1986) has shown that racism and discrimination are major triggers of depression in black people. This situation is often compounded by poverty, poor housing, lack of jobs and opportunities. Researchers have highlighted the vulnerability to depression that may be induced by the early loss of important relationships and its associated feelings of helplessness. Akiskal and McKinney (1975) have integrated the many variables (physiological, biological, developmental and psychosocial) that appear to be involved in depressive disorders into a multifactorial model. The emphasis is upon interacting variables which converge into a 'final common pathway', reflecting changes in brain biochemistry, and experienced by the person as depression.

Depression, as we have seen, ranges in intensity from very severe or less severe, with major depression at one end of a continuum, and at the other end, mild depression merging with the anxiety disorders. Anxiety and depression – which both come under the 'internalizing problems' category – have been treated generally as separate disorders in young people. They can, and do, occur together. Depression is more likely to be manifested in children or adolescents with severe symptoms of anxiety (Bernstein and Garfinkel, 1986).

Vulnerability to depression

Some groups of people may be particularly vulnerable to depression. Brown and Harris (1978) investigated variables associated with women's experience of depression in an inner London borough. Several vulnerability factors were reported:

- Loss of mother before the age of 11 years
- Three or more children under the age of 14 years
- The lack of a partner in whom to confide
- The lack of paid employment.

Many females are socialized into roles of dependency and submissiveness. This may predispose them to blame themselves for situations in which they find themselves and to feel that they may be responsible for sexual exploitation and abuse, for example. From such experiences depression is all too likely to develop, particularly where the females concerned feel trapped, unable to see any way out of their predicament.

> People from minority communities may be deeply depressed because of a range of stresses: including racism, isolation, frustration with language difficulties, housing problems, and unemployment. They may miss the support of their close communities acutely (see Littlewood and Lipsedge, 1989).

Suicide and parasuicide

Depression is a common feature of suicide and attempted suicide.

> **Definitions**
> *Suicide*: contains two main components: that the person brought about his or her own death, and that this was done knowingly.
> *Parasuicide*: attempted suicide involves any non-fatal act of self-injury or taking of substance in excess of the generally recognized or prescribed therapeutic dose. By convention, alcohol intoxication alone is excluded.

There has been a tenfold increase in suicide-related incidents since the 1960s among adolescent boys and a fivefold rise for girls. They rank among the half-dozen most common causes of death among older adolescents. The figures are still well below those for adults, and only a minute fraction of the suicide rate in old age. No theorist seems able to explain convincingly the surge in the statistics. There is a relative paucity of research on suicide. There are many unanswered questions: for example, the role of depression in the motivation to commit or attempt to commit suicide.

Attempted suicide is very much a late adolescent phenomenon – the peak being among 15- to 19-year-olds. The rate of attempted suicides for adolescent girls far exceeds that for boys. All studies in industrialized countries report a ratio of females to males of 2:1. For women, there is a peak in the late teens and early twenties; for men, the rate is highest between 20 and 35. Frequently the action is unplanned, impulsive and undertaken in a manner that is likely to be discovered. Teenagers sometimes have fantasies about their own death which involve their 'ending it all' and yet surviving the event by 'attending' their own funeral where they are able to savour the grief and guilt displayed by errant parents or boyfriends/girlfriends. These fantasies indicate how, in some adolescents, the finality of death is not fully appreciated, or at least not while in a depressed or hysterical state, and not at the time when the gesture (and, often, more than a gesture) of suicide is contemplated. The cliché that suicide is often a cry for help is true despite its banality. Threats of suicide should not be treated lightly and not dismissed with the words 'If she really meant it she would do it, not threaten to do it'. Many individuals who have threatened to commit suicide do in the end carry out their threat. In cases of adolescent depression the disorder may require careful analysis because (as we have seen) sometimes the outward and visible sign of the problem takes the form of 'acting out' delinquent activity.

We do know that suicide rates are positively correlated with the following factors:

- Male sex
- Increasing age
- High density of population
- Residence in big towns
- A high standard of living
- Economic crisis
- Alcohol and addictive drug consumption
- A broken home in childhood
- Mental disorder and physical illness.

Among factors inversely related to the suicide rate are female sex, youth, low density of population (though it must not be too low), rural occupation, religious devoutness, being married, large families, lower socioeconomic class and war.

There are several significant factors that are related to current parasuicidal episodes:

- Depression, which may be accompanied by suicidal thoughts
- Persistent insomnia and social withdrawal
- Feelings of hopelessness and worthlessness
- Use of violent methods of self-harm, or serious overdose.

Kreitman (1983) indicates the following risk factors of suicide following a parasuicide:

- Age – risk increases with age
- Sex – males are more at risk than females
- Social isolation – especially after loss of an important relationship
- Unemployment
- Alcohol and drug abuse – especially with recent loss of job
- Sociopathic personality
- History of multiple previous suicide attempts.

Paykel, Prusoff and Myers (1975) compared stressful life events among 53 people who attempted suicide, and a matched control group. The former reported four times as many such events as the control group, and many of these events had occurred in the month preceding the attempt. Paykel and colleagues categorized people who attempted suicide (and who attended an emergency treatment centre) into the following groups:

- Those who took an overdose of minor drugs, with less risk to life and mainly interpersonal motivations
- A smaller group who employed more violent methods, and who were greatly at risk
- A group of recurrent attempters, who had made many previous attempts, and who were overtly hostile.

The issue of motivation is often difficult to assess, but commonly includes both a 'cry for help' and the seeking of a period of oblivion to relieve stress, an intent to die is often absent (see Kreitman, 1983).

Schizophrenia

Probably the most disabling mental health problem associated with late adolescence, where it often has its onset, is schizophrenia. In about half the cases there have been non-psychotic abnormalities in childhood or early adolescence. Schizophrenia is a severe and disabling psychosis in which there is a fundamental disturbance of personality, one that has a profound effect on academic and social development. The symptoms include delusions (e.g. false beliefs), hallucinations (usually auditory – hearing voices), false perceptions, difficulties of thinking, feeling and behaviour. Thought disorder may involve a sense of being controlled by alien forces. The person with schizophrenia manifests abnormal affect, emotional responses out of keeping with context.

Wing (1978) states that schizophrenia has, on average, a lifetime risk rate of about one per cent in all the populations so far investigated throughout the world. The illness most commonly has its onset during the early twenties for men, and a little later for women.

At present the cause or causes of schizophrenia are not clearly understood. We do know that:

- Stress and tension appear to exacerbate the illness, making the symptoms more severe.
- People who develop schizophrenia possibly have a familial predisposition that increases their risk of suffering from the mental illness.
- Some people recover from schizophrenia completely, but most continue to experience some difficulties and may suffer relapses.
- Although complete cures are not available, relapses can be reduced or prevented, and life difficulties overcome.
- Family members and friends can be most helpful by encouraging the patient to strive, gradually, to regain former skills.

Course of the illness

The acute episode is characterized by delusions and/or hallucinations based upon them. Affected persons report that they:

- hear their thoughts spoken aloud
- hear voices commenting on their behaviour
- believe that their behaviour, thinking and bodily functions are influenced by external agents, and
- explain these experiences in terms of physical or supernatural forces.

In about a quarter of cases, the disorder is limited to one or two acute episodes and the prognosis is good. In about another quarter, the course is marked by severe negative symptoms from the outset, and the prognosis is poor. The negative symptoms (making for a chronic syndrome) are characterized by:

- Flattening of affect (loss of emotional liveliness)
- Loosening of associations in thinking (i.e. making remarks which don't make sense)
- Slowness, under-activity, lack of motivation.

Prevalence

Estimates of the frequency of schizophrenia, using rigorous diagnostic criteria, indicate (see Gottesman, 1991; Wing, 1978):

- A fairly even distribution among nationalities
- A fairly even distribution among social classes
- A prevalence of 3.4 per 1000 in the UK, higher among unskilled and homeless people.

Causal influences

HEREDITY (SEE GOTTESMAN, 1991; RUTTER ET AL., 1999A,B)

The influence of hereditary factors is assessed, *inter alia*, by examining the rates of disorder among the relatives of sufferers. The lifetime risk of developing schizophrenia is proportional to the amount of shared genes, as indicated in table 12.

The precise nature of the genetic mechanisms in schizophrenia is unknown. Clearly, hereditary factors alone cannot fully account for schizophrenia or, for that matter, other psychological disorders. People of Afro-Carribbean origin living in the UK, to take one example of environmental risk, experience increased rates of schizophrenia compared to those living in the West Indies, and compared with other ethnic groups living in the UK. Even among the identical twins of schizophrenics, many do not develop the disorder. The majority of persons who develop schizophrenia have no relatives who suffer from the condition, and many persons who have a possible genetic predisposition do not develop the illness. It therefore seems probable that intrauterine, social or physical environmental factors contribute to the genesis of schizophrenia. How they *interact* is a critical and continuing research question.

Table 12   Life-time risk among relatives of schizophrenically ill people of developing the disorder

	% risk of developing schizophrenia
Monozygotic (identical) twins	48.0
Children of two affected parents	46.0
Dizygotic twins or children with one affected parent	17.0
Brothers and sisters	8.7
Grandchildren	5.0
Parents	3.8
First cousins	2.9
Uncles and aunts	2.0
General population	1.0

BIOLOGICAL CAUSATION

Two syndromes are postulated with different aetiologies:

Type1: The dopamine hypothesis

This theory suggests that one type of schizophrenia is caused by a dysfunction of the mesolymbic dopaminergic system. Neuroleptic medication blocks dopamine activity in people with schizophrenia.

Type 2: Atypical neuroanatomy

Neurodevelopmental factors in the intrauterine environment (e.g. maternal flu virus) and perinatal insults are hypothesized to lead to atypical neuroanatomical development which, in turn, produces schizophrenic symptoms. Three of the neuroanatomical disabilities are:

1. Reduced size of the frontal lobes and reduced neurological functioning there
2. Enlargement of the cerebral ventricles (notably left ventricle) associated with atrophy of the brain
3. Neuronal degeneration of the cortex.

The notion of two syndromes is probably an oversimplification, as there is some overlap in the appearance of these signs and symptoms in schizophrenic individuals.

BIOCHEMICAL INFLUENCES

There can be little doubt, as we have seen, that biological (e.g. genetic factors) as well as psychosocial factors, contribute to the onset and course of schizophrenia, as well as disorders such as major depression. Biological factors also play a part, albeit a more minor role, in antisocial disorders, anxiety states and social inhibitions. Nevertheless, behavioural disorders are reported to reveal a larger genetic influence than common medical disorders such as breast cancer or heart disease.

A succession of biochemical factors has been suggested as causes for different forms of psychopathology. Unfortunately, the evidence is not conclusive, as biochemical factors found in sufferers may be consequences rather than causes. Hospital diets, activity patterns or characteristic emotional responses may influence the brain biochemistry of disordered individuals.

COGNITIVE DEFICITS

Cognitive psychologists suggest that psychotic experience is on a continuum with normal experience, but distorted by a variety of deficits (see Chadwick,

Birchwood and Trower, 1996). Family theorists have inculpated distortions of interpersonal and intrafamilial relationships in the causation of disordered thinking and behaviour (e.g. Laing and Esterson, 1964). A favoured 'explanatory mechanism' for causing thought disorder has been the notion of the so-called 'double bind'. The schizophrenic is bombarded frequently with confusing and contradictory emotional and cognitive 'messages' which leads to thought disorder. This concept has not been validated by experimental investigation.

ENVIRONMENTAL STRESS

Many of the stresses associated with schizophrenia are those associated with poor quality housing, poverty, unemployment, isolation, and other deprivations and pressures of an urban environment.

part vi

Atypical Development
Children with Special Needs

Children are travellers in a strange country of which they know nothing.

John Locke (1632–1704)

Defining Need

With regard to outcomes, children are thought to be 'in need' (in today's legislation) if:

1. they are unlikely to achieve or maintain, or have the opportunity of achieving, or maintaining, a reasonable standard of health or development, without the provision for him/her of specified services by a local authority (Part III of the UK Children Act); or
2. they are likely to be significantly impaired, or further impaired, without provision of such services; or
3. they are developmentally disabled.

Development means physical, intellectual, emotional, social or behavioural development; and *health* means physical or mental health. Concepts of maltreatment are linked to knowledge of a child's developmental needs and attainments. There is a wealth of evidence from various studies that psychological maltreatment affects children's development or leads to psychological disturbance (e.g. Cicchetti, 1990). Chapter 17 deals with this subject.

Developmental Disability

Chapter 15 includes a discussion of intellectual disability and the autistic continuum: the former involving pervasive deficits of development in its severe forms, the latter being a member of the diagnostic category known in the DSM-IV and ICD-10 as a 'pervasive developmental disorder'.

Intellectual disability is the chosen synonym for 'mental retardation', the term used in DSM-IV and ICD-10. This subject is so vast in its rapidly changing theoretical framework and practical applications, and so controversial in its sociopolitical ramifications, that there is no possibility of doing it justice in a general text of this kind.

Over the past two decades, according to the review by Dykens (2000), intellectual impairment research converges on the following three general themes.

1. Co-occurring learning disability and psychopathology

One of the most robust findings to date (ibid.) is that, relative to the general population persons with learning disability are at increased risk (approximately 25 per cent) for psychiatric illness, and an even higher rate for severe behavioural or emotional dysfunction.

2. Families with a learning disabled child

Knowledge of child development enables professionals to be sensitive to the timetable of achievements – walking, talking, and others – about which parents are so proud or, conversely in the circumstances under discussion, intensely worried. When an infant has a learning disability there is usually a dawning realization that something is 'not right'. It is often so gradual that parents cannot say when they began to get concerned. Intellectual impairments, unless of a profound and obvious type (e.g. trisomy 13, kernicterus, Prader-Willi syndrome and tuberous sclerosis), may not lend themselves to reliable diagnosis until the child is older. Adjustment to the fact of handicap may continue over many years, depending to some extent on whether the problem was apparent at birth, or only became clear later, and whether the parents were told clearly and several times about nature of their child's impairment.

Parents' reactions to their handicapped child are frequently formulated in terms of a series of stages:

- shock or denial, followed by
- guilt
- despair
- depression
- disappointment, and
- eventual acceptance or adjustment.

By no means all parents experience this ordered sequence of emotional reactions to the birth of an atypical (handicapped) child; nor are they necessarily affected adversely over the longer term. There have been marked changes over time in the description of parental reactions to a child with learning disabilities, ranging from a pathology (mourning and melancholy) model, to a more heterogeneous and optimistic perspective. Whatever the outcome over the medium or longer term, the early period of adapting to the arrival of (or revelation about) an atypical child is fraught with difficulty. After all, adapting one's lifestyle to the advent of a 'normal' baby can of itself be difficult for parents. This, then, is a time when an expert and sensitive psychological intervention could make a lot of difference to that outcome, one that attends the needs of the parents and their child.

3. Developmental approaches to learning disability sequences and profiles

Researchers have taken an increasing interest in the way in which persons with different genetic influences develop across cognitive, linguistic and behavioural domains. As a result, we know more about these disorders themselves, as well as how developmental processes might be organized in persons without learning disabilities. Dykens (2000) believes that this line of work confirms the dictum stated in the introduction to the present book in relation to disability in general, namely that we can learn more about the normal functioning of an organism by studying its pathology, more about its pathology by studying its normal condition.

The Child Who is Ill

Chapter 16 describes the needs of the chronically ill child, and the child who has to be admitted to hospital with a serious illness or degenerative disorder, perhaps never to return home. A major influence on the psychological well-being of young patients is the recognition of their need for information regarding their illness, hospitalization, and likely interventions; also their right (where old enough) to be actively involved in decisions about their care. There is evidence that the provision of information is linked to a reduction in fear, stress, and post-operative pain. Children's potential to understand complex health and illness concepts is now known to be greater than was once thought possible (see Davis, 1993). Family bereavement is discussed.

It is perhaps appropriate to introduce the following chapters that deal with children in need, by quoting from the 'Ten Child Care Commandments' in Mia Kellmer Pringle's *The Needs of Children* (1975).

1. Give continuous, consistent, loving care – it's as essential for the mind's health as food is for the body.
2. Give generously of your time and understanding – playing with and reading to your child matters more than a tidy, smooth-running home.

3. Provide new experiences and bathe your child in language from birth onwards – they enrich a child's growing mind.
4. Encourage a child to play in every way both by him/herself and with other children – exploring, imitating, constructing, pretending and creating.
5. Give more praise for effort than for achievement.
6. Give a child ever-increasing responsibility – like all skills, it needs to be practised.
7. Remember that every child is unique – so suitable handling for one may not be right for another.
8. Make the way you show disapproval fit your child's temperament, age and understanding.
9. Never threaten that you will stop loving your child or give him/her away; you may reject the child's behaviour but never suggest that you might reject him/her.
10. Don't expect gratitude; your child did not ask to be born – the choice was yours.

Child Protection

Chapter 17 deals with a tragic group of needy children, those who are abused emotionally, physically, and sexually. Emotional abuse (to take the condition that, in a sense, pervades the other two) is sign-posted by parental indifference, the outward and visible sign of a deep-seated emotional rejection of the child, which is often accompanied by hostility and highly inappropriate, abusive actions. Maltreatment and neglect during infancy produce misery and insecurity that defy the language of science. Something of the plight of abused children reveals itself in the imagery of George Eliot's verse:

> *A child forsaken, awakening suddenly,*
> *When gaze affeared on all things round doth rove,*
> *And seeth only that it cannot see*
> *The meeting eyes of love.*

Insecure attachments, over time, adversely affect children's intellectual and socioemotional development (Belsky, 1993). The same parental acts of rejecting, terrorizing, ignoring, isolating and corrupting do have different effects on their victims depending on the child's stage of development: infancy, early childhood, school age or adolescence. Older children may find help emotionally by having access to supportive friends, school teachers, or youth leaders. Younger children, however, have limited opportunities to receive emotional nurturing outside the home unless there is extended family support from grandparents or uncles and aunts. Being so vulnerable to rejection and neglect, they are in particular in need of protection.

Pervasive Developmental Difficulties

Early to Late Childhood and Adolescence

We do not understand ourselves because
We do not know what we have been,
And hence what we may be

Peter Laslett (1915–2001)

The term 'pervasive developmental difficulties' is used here, not in its narrow DSM/ICD diagnostic sense, but rather as a description of the wide-ranging *developmental* ramifications of three very different atypical disorders: learning disability, autistic impairments, and anorexia nervosa.

Intellectual (Learning) Disability

The estimated number of children under 16 in Britain with a learning/ intellectual disability (a preferred synonym for 'mental retardation' as defined by DSM-IV/ICD-10) in the late 1980s was 97,000 or 9 per 1000 population (*Office of Population and Census Surveys*, 1989). The population is diverse, with a wide range of disabilities. The range of severe types of learning disability is illustrated in table 13 while table 14 shows some distinctive cognitive profiles in three forms of intellectual disability.

Children who are intellectually impaired, no matter what specific syndrome they suffer from, or what the causes may be, learn more slowly than the average child and to a degree that ranges from moderate to severe difficulties in learning. Severely impaired children have difficulty in abstracting the general principles that describe their environment and which help them to plan, organize actions and solve problems of everyday life. Prevalence data suggest that the presence of *challenging behaviours* (notably attention-seeking,

Table 13 Intellectual impairment and its implications

Impairment	Features	Prevention	Implications
Cri du chat syndrome (anom. 5)	Autosomal abnormalities present at conception (deletion of part of short arm of chromosome 4 or 5)	None	Mild to moderate intellectual impairment; occasionally severe intellectual disability.
Down's syndrome Subtypes: (i) trisomy 21 (94%) (ii) trisomy mosaics (3%) (iii) translocation (3%)	Extra or added 21st chromosome (94% of cases) Present at conception Physical anomalies and learning disabilities	Amniocentesis can indicate affected fetus Chorionic villus test (CVT) Alpha-fetoprotein test (AFP)	Intellectual impairment most probable; a majority severely so Most variability in trisomy mosaics subtype
Edward's syndrome (tri 17 or 18)	Autosomal abnormalities present at conception	Primary disorder 1 in 5000 Not preventable	Mild to moderate intellectual impairment; occasionally severe intellectual disability Many congenital problems Early death
Epiloia (tuberous sclerosis)	1 in 1000 births Causal mechanisms uncertain	No treatment available	Many are impaired intellectually
Galactosaemia	Defect of carbohydrate mechanism Prevalence at birth: 0.02/1000	Screening programme after birth Special diet prescribed	Extreme intellectual impairment if not treated

Syndrome	Description	Tests / screening	Effects
Klinefelter's syndrome	An extra X chromosome XXY (XXXY, XXXXY, XXYY, XXXYY variations) Sex chromosome disorder affecting 1 in 500 male births	Amniocentesis Chorionic villus test (CVT)	For XXY mild to moderate intellectual impairment; occasionally severe intellectual disabilities Physical anomalies Phenotypically male with some secondary female characteristics
Patau's syndrome (tri 13)	Autosomal abnormalities present at conception Prevalence at birth 2/1000	None	Mild to moderate intellectual impairment; occasionally severe intellectual disability Tall Social development problems
Phenylketonuria (PKU) (mode of inheritance a recessive gene)	Metabolic disorder; a defect of protein metabolism 1 in 100 European-Americans is a carrier	Amniocentesis Chorionic villus test (CVT) Screening after birth	Extreme intellectual impairment if not treated by special diet Hyperactivity
Tay-Sachs Disease (mode of inheritance a recessive gene)	Enzyme disease Accumulation of lipoids in the nervous system 1 in 4000 births 1 in 30 USA is a carrier	Amniocentesis CVT Genetic counselling	Extreme intellectual impairment Apparently healthy infancy becoming progressively worse Usually death before 5 years
Turner's syndrome (XO) (missing chromosome)	1 in 2500 female births Normal sexual development lacking at puberty	None Female hormone oestrogen can produce a more 'womanly' appearance	Fertility sterile Normal verbal intelligence Below average on some spatial tests (impairment level) Some physical stigmata

overactivity, temper tantrums, aggression, screaming, wandering, destructive-ness and self-injury, night-waking and settling difficulties) is high. Such children may have as many as seven or eight behaviour problems on average. Children and adolescents with intellectual disabilities are at much greater risk of developing psychopathology than children who are not impaired (see Dykens, 2000, for a review).

Classification of Intellectual Impairment

The classification of intellectual and functional impairment has been operationalized by using measures of the intelligence quotient (IQ) (see below). The IQ has for a long time been the foundation of most classifica-tions of intellectual impairment. In spite of doubts about comparability it has been applied widely for purposes of research and policy decisions. The *Diagnostic Statistical Manual* IV system of classification suggests the following categories with their prevalence figures:

Profound handicap   IQ 0–19   1 in 2000 population
Severe handicap   IQ 20–34   1 in 300 population
Moderate handicap   IQ 35–49   1 in 300 population
Mild handicap   IQ 50–70   1 in 70 population

In practice, IQ 50 has been the most widely used convention for defining 'where handicap' begins, in the epidemiological literature. The profound

Table 14 Distinctive cognitive profiles in three forms of intellectual disability (strengths)

	Down's syndrome	Fragile X syndrome	Williams syndrome
visual-spatial processing and memory	+		
visual gestures	+		
receptive language	+		
verbal skills		+	
vocabulary		+	
acquired knowledge		+	
contextual learning		+	
simultaneous processing		+	
lexicon, linguistic affect			+
syntax, grammar			+
facial recognition and memory			+
mentalizing abilities, music			+
auditory-verbal processing and short-term memory			+

category has achieved poorer agreement, coming into play for IQs of under 25 or 20.

The IQ

An exclusively IQ based classification has severe limitations. Many critics of this restrictive means of classification highlight the uncertain validity and reliability of tests, also their lack of 'culture fairness' (see Aman, 1991). In any event, the cognitive features of an individual are not static, unchanging, or undifferentiated. There is abundant evidence that people with learning disabilities have much potential (sadly too often hidden or unsought) for the kind of development and learning that can greatly enhance their lives. The means of assessing the IQ is discussed in appendix II.

One of the issues in the simplistic classifying of people with learning disabilities is the failure to take account of their distinctive cognitive profiles. The raised incidence of psychopathology in children with learning disabilities tends also to be presented in a form that glosses over the distinctive differences in vulnerability patterns to be found in the various syndromes (see table 14).

Fryers (1984) is of the opinion that no set of categories and no single system of classification is satisfactory, nor can it ever be, however defined. The group of people with whom we are concerned suffer from a ragbag of disorders, difficulties, and needs, and a varying ragbag at that. They have been brought together almost by historical accident of educational development. They do not, and cannot, constitute an entity except we make it so. He adds that service planners should try to understand the conceptual problems before applying simple criteria. To study and to plan clearly defined standard categories is essential, but whatever system of classification is satisfying to the epidemiologist or convenient to the planner or administrator should not be allowed to determine the lifestyle and lifetime services for any individual. Taxonomies are for groups, categories serve the needs of professionals; individual clients require thorough, multidisciplinary assessment of their individual situation, constantly updated, and a service delivery system that can respond to their changing needs and those of the family.

The most useful objectives of an assessment process will be concerned with decisions about future intervention in terms of management and resource allocation. The most accurate assessment is likely to emerge from multiple sources of information on how the child functions at home, at school and in the community. The criteria are about *adaptive behaviour* which includes the individual's effectiveness (relative to his age) in areas such as social responsibility, communication, daily living skills, coping with schooling demands, personal independence and self-sufficiency. The developmental context is yet another criterion. A brain trauma suffered in an accident in childhood may result in learning disability. The same injury in an adult would be classified as organic brain damage.

Table 15 Causes and distribution of intellectual disability

Cause	Distribution (%)
Intrauterine influences	10
Perinatal trauma	10
Postnatal trauma	6
Teratogens/toxins	3
Infections	6
Congenital abnormalities	20
Genetic abnormalities	45

Causation

Up to 75 per cent of cases of profound learning (intellectual) disability are due to identifiable organic causes. A summary of causes contributing to disability and their distribution is exhibited in tables 13 and 15.

Of the genetic abnormalities, 15 per cent of learning disability is attributed to Down's syndrome, 10 per cent to fragile X syndrome. The remaining 20 per cent is accounted for by conditions such as hydrocephaly, microcephaly and other brain disorders. Among the other conditions with serious impairment are the following:

- Kernicterus: Due to accumulation of excessive bilirubin in Rh incompatibility between fetus and mother, it results in athetoid cerebral palsy, with stained teeth, upward-gaze paralysis, high-frequency hearing loss and mental retardation. Its incidence has decreased significantly due to postnatal therapy.
- Hypothyroidism (congenital cretinism): These infants are noted to be large for gestational age, with low muscle tone, a large tongue and a hoarse cry. If thyroid supplementation is initiated before 6 weeks, developmental delays can be averted. However, such delays are inevitable if treatment has not occurred beyond the first year of life; these include mental retardation and delayed bone and dental maturation.
- Congenital rubella syndrome is attributed to the mother's contraction of rubella prior to the seventeenth week of pregnancy; affected children suffer intrauterine growth retardation, microcephaly, cataracts, sensorineural hearing loss and congenital heart disease. Intellectual impairment, deafness and cerebral palsy are common developmental problems.
- The Noonan syndrome is characterized by short stature, congenital heart defects, widely spaced downward-slanting eyes, low-set ears and chest deformity; the affected children also show mild mental retardation, motor delays, hearing deficits and articulation defects.

- The Prader-Willi syndrome: As infants these children show poor muscle tone, feeding and temperature control. Tone improves with age, but a disproportionate appetite and severe obesity follows. Other characteristics include small hands and feet, small genitalia and short stature. Associated with the deletion of chromosome 15, children develop serious behavioural problems (with food as the focus) and mental retardation.
- Trisomy 13 is associated with microcephaly, brain malformations, cleft lip and palate, congenital heart defects, multifingers, and eye, kidney and digestive system malformations. Affected children also show profound mental retardation and cerebral palsy.
- Trisomy 21 is better known as Down's syndrome.
- Tuberous sclerosis is associated with under-pigmented areas and acne-like facial lesions in young children, other characteristics include infantile spasms and calcium deposits on the brain. Malignancies, hydrocephalus, and tumours of the heart are common. Children may have mild to moderate intellectual disability.

Whereas, as we saw earlier, some 75 per cent of cases of profound intellectual disability are due to identifiable organic causes, only 10 per cent of cases of mild intellectual disability are the result of discrete organic factors. Polygenetic and sociocultural factors (e.g. family disorganization, poverty, limited parental education, lack of intellectual stimulation in the home, parental privation and deprivation) are the predominant contributory determinants (Guralnick, 1998). (See Bathshaw and Perret, 1992; Kerr, 2002; Moser, 1985; and Rutter et al., 1999a,b, for discussions of these and other disabilities).

Developmental progress

The likelihood that a child will be suffering from additional physical and sensory handicaps increases with the severity of the intellectual impairment; however, the presence of physical or sensory handicaps does not necessarily imply a learning disability. The generalized learning difficulty, and consequent slow cognitive development of intellectually atypical children, does mean that they remain dependent on parents, or parental substitutes, for longer than normal. They move from stage to stage in child development more slowly and scholastic achievement will be lower, and less rapid, than average. Just as a large proportion of the typical child's behavioural, social and emotional development is dependent on learning, so it is the case for the disabled child. The difference mainly lies in the rate of what is learned, not primarily (there are some exceptions) in how it is learned. Development may be slow, but every child is capable of learning, provided that the all-important teaching (e.g. playing with, talking to, and instructing) is appropriate to the child's level of comprehension.

Diagnosis

Diagnosis, in terms of aetiology, is concerned largely with specific patterns of structural impairment of chromosomes, tissues, or organs and their causal processes (Scott, 1994; Simonoff, Bolton and Rutter, 1996). This is of importance for primary prevention and for helping parents to come to terms with their child's disorder without guilt or shame (Fryers, 1984). Although biochemical and neurological diagnosis is also concerned with structure, the principal clinical focus is impairment of function. This is important for secondary prevention, limiting consequent disability, and controlling concurrent impairments such as cerebral palsy and epilepsy. For all of this, accurate and early assessment by a multidisciplinary paediatric team is a necessity. This should lead to a programme (e.g. facilitated in large part by portage workers) geared to the special needs and positive qualities of the individual child.

Challenging behaviour associated with learning disability includes (Emerson, 1995):

- Aggression towards others (e.g. biting, hitting)
- Aggression towards self – especially in profoundly handicapped people (e.g. head-banging, self-scratching)
- Screaming or shouting
- Hoarding of food
- Disorders of thought or cognition: a firm diagnosis is very difficult in this client group
- Emotional distress common to all people (e.g. bereavement)
- Organic disorders (e.g. dementia).

Intellectually impaired children learn maladaptive behaviours in the same way as children who are not handicapped, but there are some important differences:

- Parents may consider the child to be 'ill' on a long-term basis, and so not expect more reasonable behaviour from their child – 'After all, he is mentally handicapped; we can't expect him to stop banging his head on the walls.'
- Because children with learning disabilities take longer to learn, procedures that would have been successful in modifying challenging behaviour if continued, tend to be abandoned because there is so little improvement in the short term (i.e. the parallel situation to teaching new developmental skills).

Teaching the child new ways of behaving requires a more structured approach than is necessary with the unimpaired child. This structure, understandably, seems to go against the grain for many parents, who quite understandably prefer to rely on a less formal more intuitive approach to their normal children.

For most parents, the idea of the expert handing out advice on child-rearing 'ex cathedra' was always doomed to increase the likelihood of failure. It is now recognized that all parents have a considerable expertise that needs to be mobilized in cooperation with specialists so that a jointly agreed programme may be evolved (see Herbert and Wookey, 1998).

Pervasive Developmental Disorders

The ICD-10 defines a number of separable categories under the general heading of pervasive developmental disorders:

- Childhood autism: Impaired or abnormal development must be present *before* 3 years of age, manifesting the *full triad* of impairments:
  1. in reciprocal social interaction
  2. in communication, and
  3. in restricted, stereotyped, repetitive behaviour.
- Atypical autism: Onset of impaired or abnormal development is seen after 3 years of age, and is shown in one or two of the above triad of impairments.
- Rett's syndrome: A syndrome limited to previously normal girls with decelerating head growth in infancy, early autistic behaviours, severe mental handicap, hand wringing, clapping, licking or other stereotyped hand movements. Most are non-verbal, many develop epilepsy, episodic hyperventilation, muscular hypotonia, and scoliosis. Although indefinite survival occurs, there is an excess of early deaths (see Kerr, 2002).
- Childhood disintegrative disorder: There is the appearance of autistic behaviours following completely normal development until at least the age of 2 years. It may be associated with loss of motor and cognitive skills and with epilepsy. It must not be attributable to a defined progressive degenerative disease of the brain.
- Overactive disorder associated with learning disability and stereotyped movements: This diagnosis is used to identify individuals who show pre-pubertal hyperactivity, stereotyped movements and problems with attention in association with severe mental retardation.

For Asperger's disorder, see the section that follows later.

The Autistic Continuum

Lorna Wing (1978) is of the view that research and clinical experience point to the existence of what she calls an 'autistic continuum' of impairments in certain children. They involve serious aberrations in the development of social interaction, communication and imagination and consequent rigid, repetitive behaviour. She states that the continuum ranges from the most profoundly physically and mentally impaired person, who has social impairment as one item among a multitude of problems, to the most able, highly intelligent person with social impairment in its subtlest form as his only disability. It overlaps with learning disabilities and shades into eccentricity. It is approximately equivalent to 'pervasive developmental disorder' as defined in the psychiatric manuals.

- Prevalence: The prevalence of the syndrome varies according to how it is defined: estimates vary from 4.0 to 13.8 per 10,000 population.
- Social class: There appears to be little or no effect related to class.
- Sex ratio: In the same way as the prevalence varies with the diagnostic criteria used, so does the sex ratio. It is generally quoted as 4 male:1 female. Estimates range from 16:1 to 1:1 (for low IQs).

Wing and Gould (1979) describe a triad of impairments in autism and say that all three must be evident:

1. Impairment of social relationships
2. Impairment of social communication
3. Impairment of imagination.

Rutter (1978b) stated that classification should take a 'multiaxial' approach in which the following are described on separate independent axes:

- the behavioural 'syndrome'
- the intellectual level
- the medical conditions, and
- the psychosocial situation.

A further criterion involves disturbances of response to sensory stimuli. This includes disturbances of motility – a wider definition of stereotypic (beyond play) behaviour (e.g. imitation, hand clapping or oscillating, body rocking, head banging or rolling and twirling objects).

Whereas 'schizophrenia' is the name given to a group of mental illnesses that usually develop after the age of puberty, and which have a characteristic pattern of clinical symptoms, and a characteristic course and outcome, there is no justification for finding analogies between it and between autism. Autism is a condition of maldevelopment in childhood – which simply has as one of its features (like schizophrenia) social withdrawal. This characteristic is shared with many other psychotic conditions (see chapter 14). It is thought to be secondary in childhood autism to difficulties in language and communication.

A detailed assessment of the clinical characteristics of the twins from the *British Twin Study of Autism* by Le Courteur et al. (1996) led to the conclusion that:

- phenotypic expression extends more broadly than autism as currently defined by either ICD-10 or DSM-IV, and
- the wide range of clinical manifestations reflects considerable variable expression of the same genotype.

This suggests that a broader range of communication and social impairment (in particular) should be included as part of the concept of autism, notably for research and intervention purposes. For example, consider the following three points.

1. PRESERVATION OF SAMENESS

Autistic children become very disturbed over changes in their surroundings and alterations in their routines. Temper tantrums may greet the apparently most trivial change, for example, their 'regimented' toys accidentally pushed out of place. Obsessional attributes may be even more pronounced at adolescence.

2. EXTREME TENDENCY TO AUTISTIC ALONENESS

From early in life the infants' preference to be alone – his or her inability to relate to persons and situations – becomes noticeable. This self-absorption, the physical repudiation (drawing away) of cuddling, the lack of concern about the comings and goings of people, and the preoccupation with things soon begin to disturb his or her caregivers. This rejection of social interaction has its corollary in a retardation of development.

3. ATTACHMENTS/SOCIAL BEHAVIOUR

There is a general agreement that it is the distinctive anomalies in social development that are most specific within the triad of impairments and most handicapping across the range of children with autism. Reports of autistic children indicate differences in the sorts of attachment behaviour which are characteristic of normal children. They do respond to others' emotions and they are able to form affectionate attachments (Capps, Sigman and Mundy, 1994), but they do not show an intense eagerness to share, and in play they do not pretend to act like other people, except in a ritual, echolalic manner.

Autistic children (to the concern of their parents) tend not to keep close by them and may not even show any acknowledgement of their return after an absence, let alone any sign of greeting. They do not seem to use their parents for comfort, although they will enjoy a game of rough and tumble. Another characteristic of autistic children's social behaviour is their failure to seek bodily contact to gain comfort or security (see Rutter, 1978b).

A marked lack of social relatedness is reflected in the child's later social development. Many autistic children do not develop appropriate play skills. Most autistic children also do not form normal friendships with other children. They can truly be called social isolates.

Research into the social behaviour of autism has primarily focused on *eye contact* and gaze aversion, the approach and avoidance of autistic children, play skills, and social skills training. Hutt and Ounsted (1966) measured the amount of time autistic and non-autistic children spent looking at either room fixtures or faces drawn on the wall. The autistic children spent significantly more time looking at the room fixtures than at any of the drawn faces. The face most avoided by these children was a smiling human face with eyes. This is in marked contrast to the fascination with faces shown by infants (see p. 65).

Autistic children may imitate, but they do so self-centredly or like an echo, without the creativity, humour and companionship that is so charming in ordinary toddlers' play. They seem not to be aware of how one normally negotiates meanings, intentions and beliefs with language.

Rutter (1983) stated that we are forced to the conclusion that autistic children's social abnormalities do stem from some kind of 'cognitive' deficit if by that one means a deficit in dealing with social and emotional cues. It appears that the stimuli that pose difficulties for autistic children are those that carry emotional or social 'meaning'.

Intelligence

The majority of autistic children are intellectually impaired as measured by standard intelligence tests. Among autistic children tested in the pre-school years, 74 per cent had IQs below 52. When these same children were tested six years later, the majority still scored in the impaired range. Even the majority of the children who had shown the most social improvement and who had received several years of treatment and special education scored in the handicapped range. Intelligence appears to remain stable over time, irrespective of current treatment or educational input. The intellectual impairments appear to be independent of disturbances in social relationships and of motivational factors (Rutter, 1983).

Speech and language

A defining characteristic of autistic children is their extreme deficits in speech and language. Some 50 per cent are non-verbal and emit only a few sounds.

They may acquire some appropriate speech but this depends on receiving intensive therapy. Those children who do learn to speak, before special training, usually manifest speech that is non-communicative. Sixty-five per cent of the autistic children in one study who had not developed language by age 5 remained mute all of their lives.

The deficits of autistic children who have speech are characterized by adequate phonology and syntax, but deficits at the level of semantics and pragmatics. Impaired pragmatics is the most significant characteristic of autistic communication. (For a detailed discussion of clinical pragmatics see Smith and Leinonen, 1992.)

Stimulus over-selectivity

This is a perceptual disability in which a child responds only to part of a relevant cue, or even to a minor, often irrelevant feature of the environment. It has been studied mostly in autistic children and has been found to occur, particularly in those with lower IQs. It has been suggested that stimulus over-selectivity greatly hinders autistic children in learning complex discriminations in language and social skills. It may also help explain the common need among autistic children to keep their environments the same or unchanging.

Self-stimulatory behaviour

An autistic child may spend hours switching on and off, or gazing at, lights, rocking, twirling, or flapping hands. All of these activities have a social and educational cost for autistic children. The problems associated with self-stimulation and self-injury include ostracism because other people are frightened or put off by them. A promising approach to the treatment of self-injurious behaviour (SIB) is first performing a functional analysis of what sets the stage for, or reinforces, the behaviour, and then changing the environment in accordance with contingencies. For example, Carr and Durand (1985) performed a functional analysis of SIB that revealed that some children were using their SIB as a means of communication. The treatment consisted of teaching appropriate forms of communication, which resulted in a decrease in SIB. Self-stimulatory activity may interfere with an autistic child's attention and learning new tasks. It may disrupt previous learning and interfere with observational learning. It may displace socially acceptable play. Studies have shown that the kinesthetic, visual, and auditory feedback received from engaging in the self-stimulatory behaviour is reinforcing. For example, when the sound associated with spinning objects (auditory feedback) is blocked (sensory extinction), the frequency of object spinning decreases. Some studies have shown that autistic children will work at one task to earn the opportunity to self-stimulate.

Autistic children engage in more self-stimulation in an unstimulating or unfamiliar environment. When tasks are failed, self-stimulation increases with ensuing frustration, and it decreases when there is a correct response. These findings indicate that autistic children do use self-stimulatory activities to maintain environmental regularity by avoiding boring or unfamiliar situations, or those in which failure is probable.

Self-injurious behaviour (SIB)

A long-standing definition of SIB is that it is behaviour which leads immediately or cumulatively to self-inflicted tissue damage. The child inflicts physical damage on his or her own body by means of a wide variety of actions such as hair pulling, face scratching, slapping, eye gouging, and arm and leg banging. The most common forms of SIB are head banging and self-biting, usually on the hands or wrists. The sensory feedback received from self-inflicting a wound may be reinforcing. Self-injurious behaviour is similar to self-stimulation, but much more destructive and frightening.

There is a difference of opinion whether to include conditions such as the following as part of the SIB category:

- Pica (ingestion of inedible objects)
- Self-induced vomiting and rumination
- Polydipsia (excessive drinking)
- Aerophagia (swallowing air)
- Teeth grinding.

SIB occurs in intellectual disability, autism, schizophrenia and also other conditions. There are significant but not particularly high correlations between the various SIB stereotopies.

The present evidence (see Rojahn, Tasse and Morin, 1998) suggests that SIB and stereotyped behaviours are determined by multiple independent biological and environmental factors, and that these factors have a strong developmental component (e.g. neurobiological irregularities).

Differential diagnosis

Autism can be differentiated from at least five major categories of disability, including pervasive developmental disorder, childhood schizophrenia, developmental aphasia, mental handicap, and environmental deprivation.

1. PERVASIVE DEVELOPMENTAL DISORDER

Within this category fall children who in the past have been labelled as having atypical development, symbiotic psychosis, childhood psychosis, and childhood schizophrenia.

2. CHILDHOOD SCHIZOPHRENIA

Schizophrenic and autistic children share sustained impairment in social relations, resistance to change in the environment, speech abnormalities, and inappropriate affect. Nevertheless, there are features that can be used to distinguish them, notably the age of onset of the disorder. Children develop psychoses in two waves. The first wave begins to show symptoms before the age of 3, and the second between ages 5 and 15. The children who typically show the characteristics associated with autism are members of the first wave, with onset of the disorder before the age of 30 months. Children of the second wave, those who have some period of normal development before the onset of the full syndrome between the ages of 30 months and 15 years more closely resemble schizophrenic adults in symptomatology. These children may be diagnosed as childhood schizophrenics.

3. DEVELOPMENTAL APHASIA

In developmental aphasia children either fail to develop, or are delayed in the development of, receptive and expressive language. These children share with autistic youngsters speech patterns such as echolalia, pronoun reversal, sequencing problems, and difficulties in comprehension. However, the language deficits of autistic children are more severe and more widespread than those typically seen in aphasic children.

Unlike autistic children aphasic children generally make eye contact, achieve meaningful communication through the use of gestures, exhibit emotional intent, and engage in imaginative play.

Language-disordered children are more likely to be of normal intelligence than are autistic children. These children may also develop problems in social relationships; they are seen as secondary to the primary language handicap.

4. LEARNING DISABILITY (INTELLECTUAL IMPAIRMENT)

Both autistic children and children who would receive a primary diagnosis of mental handicap share poor intellectual ability that persists through the life span. Other similarities may include echolalic speech, self-stimulation, self-injury, and attentional deficits. What differentiates the two conditions is communication. Although the ability to communicate in mentally handicapped children may be limited, their intent and motivation are apparent. Whereas intellectually impaired children are typically characterized by slow physical development, autistic children are not.

The pattern of intellectual impairments differs. Whereas it is common for children with severe learning disability to show impairments over a wide range of functioning, autistic youngsters usually display a more variable pattern. Thus, autistic children tend to score poorly in assessments of the use of language meaning and concepts, and higher on performance assessments such as visual-spatial and mechanical abilities.

Autistic children are more likely to show some isolated areas of outstanding functioning in the areas of music, mechanical ability, rote memory, and mathematics. As we have seen it is the case that the majority of autistic youngsters are also intellectually impaired. When both syndromes are present, the child typically receives both diagnoses.

5. ENVIRONMENTAL DEPRIVATION

Features of autism have been likened to the characteristics of children suffering from maternal deprivation, anaclitic depression and hospitalism, which are all characterized by developmental delays resulting from abuse, neglect, and/or institutionalization. Bettelheim (1967) and Kanner (1943) have even speculated that deprivation in the form of parental emotional abuse or neglect is a contributory causative factor in the development of autism.

There is now general agreement that autism is not caused by neglect and that the behavioural similarities of austistic children and children suffering from extreme deprivation are not as marked as was once thought.

Causation

BIOLOGICAL INFLUENCES

Twin studies (see Folstein and Rutter, 1977) indicate that environmental causes are unlikely to have more than a minor role in the causation of autism. There is a growing consensus that the autistic spectrum is ultimately caused by some biological fault occurring well before birth. Autism and its variants are now recognized as but one of the developmental disorders of brain function, with a variety of different aetiologies and widely differing degrees of severity. As a developmental problem it is a consequence of interactions of biological influences, some of which stem from genetic influences, others from the environment that stimulates and transforms the brain as it is developing.

Biological theories have sought causes of autism in the following areas:

- Birth trauma – no single birth trauma is clearly associated with autism but there is a raised incidence of such difficulties.
- Viral infections – rubella (German measles) in the mother shows a raised incidence.
- Neurophysiology – EEG abnormality estimates range from 10 to 83 per cent. There is an increased incidence of epilepsy (particularly in adolescence).
- Neuropsychology – there is a lack of replicable neuroanatomical findings in this area of research. Neuropsychological deficits are described later.
- Neurochemistry – findings here have been inconclusive.

GENETIC FACTORS

Autism probably originates in the genes or from a pathogenic influence that affects brain organization in early embryo or fetal development before birth. There is compelling evidence from a range of independent studies for a strong genetic component in the underlying liability for autism – a heritability of above 90 per cent (see Le Courteur et al., 1996; Rutter et al., 1999). The very size of the disparity between the monozygotic twin-pair concordance rate (60–90 per cent) and the dizygotic rate (less than 5 per cent) indicates the likelihood that the genetic predisposition is due to several genes acting synergistically in combination (ibid.).

The effects do not appear until the brain has attained a certain level of maturity and certain psychological functions emerge. Autism may be a *spectrum condition*. The full expression of the autistic condition may be found in one child in a family, but the siblings may also be affected, although less severely.

There are rare cases in which families have three or more autistic children (Ritvo et al., 1990). Genetic studies suggest a polygenic recessive gene model (involving many genes from both parents) as a cause for some of the cases.

ASSOCIATED CONDITIONS

Depending on the nature and extent of the damage, autism may occur as a very 'pure' disorder, but may also occur together with other impairments. It would seem that genetic heterogeneity is a feature of autism as it is in other disorders. For example:

- The rate of fragile X in autism is estimated at about 2.5 per cent (Bailey et al., 1993) with occasional cases being associated with other chromosomal anomalies.
- Tuberous sclerosis, a single gene Mendelian disorder (chromosomes 9 or 16), is often associated with autism, epilepsy and intellectual impairment.

- In a few cases, autism has been found to be associated with (and presumably due to) some medical condition giving rise to brain pathology. For example, infantile spasms with congenital rubella have been linked with autism (Rutter, 1983). Of course, there are medical syndromes that are also associated with general learning disability. But it should be noted that the medical conditions that give rise to intellectual impairment differ strikingly in their links with autism.

Frith (1989) states that if different handicaps can be superimposed on autism, then the immense individual variation in children diagnosed as autistic would be less puzzling. This logic fits in well with the concept of the autistic continuum, a concept based on the empirical finding that all autistic children show all three of Wing's criteria:

- Social incompetence
- Communicative impairment
- Imaginative impairment (no spontaneous pretend play).

These impairments give rise to different kinds of behaviour at different ages and at different levels of ability.

NEUROPSYCHOLOGICAL DEFICITS

Clinical neuropsychology is defined as an applied science concerned with the behavioural expression of brain dysfunction. The presence of some form of organic brain dysfunction in autistic children was first indicated in follow-up studies. About a quarter to a third of cases of epileptic seizures in autistic youngsters occurred during adolescence (Rutter, 1970b). Subsequent epidemiological research (Deykin and MacMahon, 1979) confirmed both the increased incidence of epilepsy in autism, and the oddity that it has its onset during the teenage years. Most intellectually impaired children with epilepsy first have seizures during early childhood.

Evidence seems to support the theory that there is some brain anomoly that can be linked to the Wing triad, but not to any other handicaps. Whatever the primary cause, autism cannot be regarded as a haphazard collection of symptoms. Rather it is a distinct and definable disorder, despite considerable individual variation and despite inconsistencies in diagnostic practice across different centres. From this point of view it becomes an important aim – according to Frith (1989) – to identify a single cognitive deficit. Such a deficit would eventually need to be mapped onto the brain system. Frith states that although the nature and origin of any brain abnormality is unknown, it can be assumed that it involves a 'final common pathway'. The concept of the final common pathway allows one to leave open the question of primary cause while earmarking a particular brain system that, when damaged by whatever means, will always lead to a particular disorder. If there were several independent dysfunctions, then presumably researchers would not have discovered such a strong common denominator as is implied by the triad.

COMPETING THEORIES

There has been considerable debate among practitioners and theoreticians over the extent to which the primary disorder in autism is emotional, social, cognitive or 'metacognitive' (Trevarthen et al., 1996). The fact is that many aspects of the causation of autism remain a mystery, but many theorists relate much of the bizarre symptomatology to deficits and/or abnormalities of cognition. This applies particularly to the autistic child's problems of communication. Frith (1989) observes that from the beginning, evident even in the earliest descriptions of autism, there was the idea that by studying their language we should come nearer to understanding autistic children. We have seen how autistic children have peculiar problems of speech and language and this has attracted the attention of linguists and psychologists alike. As a result there is now an impressive number of published investigations from which, in Frith's opinion, a surprising conclusion has emerged. It is the notion that the speech and language problems that can be so freely observed in autistic children are not actually at the core of the disorder, but rather, the consequences of a broader communication failure.

COMMUNICATION AND INFORMATION PROCESSING

Autistic children display deficits and abnormalities in communication prior to the period when language is normally acquired. Babbling is infrequent and conveys less information than that of non-autistic infants. However, they often cry and scream to indicate need. They do not use gestures (as deaf children try to do) as a substitute for speech and it has proved difficult to train them to do so.

It is significant that the autistic child's apparent insensitivity to other persons' feelings and overtures appears before the child is 3 years old. The point is made that the development of the child's mind fails at the time when most children begin to be extremely sensitive to and interested in other people's ideas and actions, and when speech is beginning. Nine to 12 months is a stage in development when a baby is normally changing rapidly; it is a time of the most intense communication and sharing of different ways of doing things, when children are expected to be insatiably curious and full of imagination about meanings in their play. They want to put these ideas into language. They demonstrate increases in alertness, in intelligence and curiosity, in purposeful, constructive handling of objects, in memory, and in willingness to share experiences and actions with companions.

By way of contrast the autistic child is handicapped in his/her communicating with others in several significant ways connected with language and information-processing.

LANGUAGE: PRAGMATICS AND SEMANTICS

'Pragmatics' is at the interface of language and sociability while 'semantics' is at the interface of language and cognition. Both are in deficit in autistic children.

Severely delayed, and often very deviant language, is regularly the presenting complaint of parents of pre-school children on the autistic continuum. The one exception is the subgroup referred to as Asperger's disorder (see below). Many autistic children who can answer concrete questions appropriately answer open-ended questions such as why, when and how in a manner that is quite beside the point.

Seriously impaired comprehension and persistent lack of expressive language are associated with poor cognitive outcome in autism. Indeed, the ability to acquire speech appears to be a crucial prediction of later adjustment in autistic children (Eisenberg and Kanner, 1956). Like the child with developmental aphasia, the autistic child has not only a fundamental difficulty in the comprehension of language, but in addition a disturbance in the organization of perception.

Luria (1961) proposed that the 'second signalling system' concerned with meaning and language comes to dominate and direct the first, which is concerned with the organization of direct sensory input. The hierarchical organization of sensory systems therefore functions to a very large extent to determine which aspects of the environment constitute figure and which aspects constitute background. One would expect that the organization of behaviour would depend on whether and how such a hierarchical structure of sensory systems has developed. Experiments performed by Hermelin and O'Connor (1970a,b) demonstrated that this development is relatively orderly in most non-psychotic intellectually impaired children. At a mental age of about 4 to 5 years visual dominance is established in the sensory hierarchy of the first signalling system. In autistic children, even within this system, the structural hierarchy seems to be insufficiently developed. Variables such as intensity or reinforcement schedules, rather than sensory modality seem to determine response behaviour. Their behaviour appears more random and less predictable than learning disability controls.

In short, the authors demonstrated that less intellectually impaired children respond most often to words, Down's children to light and autistic children most often to the most intense signal regardless of its modality or meaning. Hermelin proposed that the failure to achieve auditory dominance may be a factor in the impaired speech of autistic children. A child's failure to achieve order and meaningful structure from the incoming messages from the environment would explain his or her obsession with sameness, social withdrawal, limited span of attention, and intensely violent emotional reactions when receiving certain forms of stimulation. (The 30 year old research by Hermelin and O'Connor remains relevant today (Hobson, 1991).)

There have been many brave efforts (see Kiernan's 1983 review) to teach autistic children non-vocal means of communicating. There is some evidence that even some of the most handicapped children can learn to communicate needs using signs and symbols that may assist the development of their spoken language.

INFORMATION PROCESSING ('METACOGNITION')

The theory that autism is basically a cognitive disorder that interferes with social functioning has been re-formulated by Baron-Cohen, Leslie and Frith (1985) who describe the condition as arising from a primary disorder of metacognition or 'interpersonal perspective taking', notably thinking on other persons' thinking. For a person to possess metacognition or a 'theory of mind' s/he must (it is assumed) have a higher order cognitive-perceptual processing system, i.e. certain crucial inner language processes (Hobson, 1993a,b). (See p. 72.)

COGNITIVE DEFICIT THEORY

Wing's triad has been explained in terms of a single cognitive deficit (Baron-Cohen, Leslie and Frith, 1985; Leslie, 1987). This deficit has important consequences for language and communication development. The infant comes into the world with cognitive abilities that have as their aim the representation of what things and people are like – building up considerable knowledge about his/her relationships to the outside world. The child forms representations of their physical appearance, properties and function with impressive efficiency. Intellectual impairment in such first-order representations in children caused by pervasive brain damage does not provide an explanation for Wing's triad of impairments; rather it is due to a fault in second-order representations.

PSYCHOLOGICAL INFLUENCES

The earliest literature on the psychological causes of autism was mainly psychoanalytic in orientation. The best known exponent was Bruno Bettelheim who directed the Orthogenic School at the University of Chicago. Bettelheim (1967) believed that there were three basic types of autistic children, differing in the degree of withdrawal brought about by the severity of early neglect by their parents, notably their mothers:

1. The mute children who have totally severed communication and contact with the real world. They treat other humans as objects and constitute the most disturbed type.
2. The children who have some language and display occasional anger outbursts. They have some contact with reality, but still do not act independently.
3. The children commonly labelled as schizophrenic. They have fairly good language skills and form limited social relationships; however, they have rich fantasy lives that interfere with normal functioning.

Autism, in his view, represents a fixation at the first stage of 'primary narcissism', a failure to shift to object relations (physical and social). The autistic child tries to blot out stimuli in order to avoid psychological pain. The source of this pain, he suggests, is the mother who fails to nurture the child emotionally although her care at the physical level is adequate.

These mothers of autistic or schizophrenic children were harshly labelled 'refrigerated' or 'schizophrenogenic' and depicted as cold, detached and rejecting with little interest in people and little human warmth. They were also described as highly intellectual (Bettelheim, 1967; Eisenberg and Kanner, 1956). It has also been suggested that autism is caused by a 'double bind' attitude of mothers who superficially give the appearance of being warm but are in reality cold and indifferent to their children.

This kind of speculation has been conclusively refuted by painstaking research (see Gelfand, Jensen and Drew, 1985). For example, when parents of autistic children are compared to parents of children with other forms of handicap, no differences have been found on personality or interaction measures. Gelfand et al. (ibid.) make the point that psychoanalysts were never able to answer satisfactorily the question why a child would regress or become fixated in sexual development to such a cataclysmic degree. It is not difficult to imagine the demoralization of families and the damage to mothers' reputations and self-esteem that resulted from this stigmatizing theory of psychogenic autism.

The therapeutic methods that flowed from this psychoanalytic theory involved reducing, indeed minimizing all parental contact while the autistic child was at the Orthogenic School. Children were regressed to relive earlier experiences in an ethos of total acceptance; treatment could last several years. There is no objective evidence that the method produced real and positive changes in the autistic problems of the children exposed to this regime.

Interestingly it was not only the psychoanalysts who proposed a retreat by the autistic child in early development brought about by failures of parenting. The behaviourist theory of Charles Ferster (1961) postulated a kind of retreat into a self-stimulatory world because the parents do not provide enough consistent reinforcement. The severe behavioural deficits of autism are attributed to a faulty conditioning history. This theory has not been confirmed; the behaviour patterns described by Ferster have never been objectively observed in the parents of autistic children. It does not explain other symptoms of autism such as the profound cognitive deficits.

Any idea that autistic children might come from dysfunctional families has to deal with the finding that the marital stability of the families of autistic children has been found to be greater than for other disturbed children. It has been reported that 11 per cent came from broken homes as compared with 50 per cent for other types of emotionally disturbed children. Other studies have found similar results or rates of divorce equal to those of families who do not have handicapped children.

Asperger Syndrome/Disorder (AD)

The relationship of AD to autism is controversial. There is an overlap in their problems, and some theorists maintain that AD is simply high ability autism. Hans Asperger published a paper *Autistic Psychopathy in Childhood* in 1944 (translated and annotated by Uta Frith in *Autism and Asperger Syndrome*), in which he described 'a particularly interesting and highly recognisable type of child'. The type had in common what he called 'a fundamental disturbance that manifests itself in their physical appearance, impressive functions and, indeed, their whole behaviour'. After a period of neglect, his identification of a syndrome closely related to autism has become a matter of theoretical and practical clinical concern and debate.

Features of Asperger's disorder

Children with AD suffer, in Frith's view (1989), from a particular form of autism; they belong to the autistic spectrum (some theorists prefer the term 'high functioning' or 'mild' autism).

- A notable feature of the syndrome is their ability to speak fluently by the age of 5; the language development may have been slow to begin with and also very odd in the way it is used for communication.
- They often become quite interested in other people as they grow older. However, they are socially inept and inappropriate.
- They show abnormalities of social imagination.
- They tend to be extremely egocentric.
- The knowledge they accumulate is fragmented, lacking in 'common sense'; they fail to learn from their experience in a manner that provides social meaning and useful guidelines for living.
- They develop obsessive interests.
- They manifest abnormal sensory responses.

Whether or not autism and AD should be considered as distinct and mutually exclusive diagnostic categories, or the latter as a subcategory of the former, cannot yet be given a definitive scientific answer. In both autistic and Asperger conditions the following difficulties are common:

- Non-verbal pragmatics includes the interpretation and display of facial expressions, body postures, gestures, and acoustic aspects of speech (prosody) that clarify the intent of verbal communications. (Autistic children are likely not to look at the person they are speaking to, not to use gestures to supplement speech, to speak in a monotonous voice with an odd robotic rhythm or in a high pitched sing-song that may make affirmative sentences sound like questions.) They tend not to notice threatening facial expressions or a raised tone of voice. An early sign of impaired non-verbal pragmatics is their failure to look up when called by name, or to point out things they want.
- Verbal pragmatics involve initiating communication, staying on topic, engaging in meaningful dialogue, using language as a tool to comment or fulfil needs, providing appropriate turn-taking. In AD these are seriously impaired (Bishop and Adams, 1990). (Verbal autistic children may engage in long monologues that have no discernible communicative intent, or ignore signs of impatience from the recipient of the boring; non-stop talk.)
- Semantic deficits refer to aberrations in the organization of word meanings (lexicon) and the retrieval of words, spontaneous speech, the comprehension of verbal utterances and the ability to put together coherent discourse.

Anorexia Nervosa

The word 'anorexia' means loss of appetite. Anorexia nervosa is a problem particularly (but not only) associated with adolescent girls. It also affects pre-pubescent children. This disorder is essentially about weight rather than eating. A girl who is anorexic deliberately restricts her food intake. Indeed, she does not want to eat at all, because she believes she is fat and wishes to lose weight. However, the presence or absence of hunger or appetite is not a crucial feature of anorexia nervosa. Some anorexic individuals do suffer from pangs of hunger and these can be intense (Garfinkel, 1974). Others commonly deny that they experience hunger, even when emaciated. Nevertheless, the teenager will characteristically act as if she had lost her appetite.

The central feature of the disorder is a body weight that is abnormally low for the age, height and sex of the person accompanied by a distorted perception by the sufferer of her body. There is a further crucial feature: the individual's attitude to her weight. What makes life difficult for parents and other would-be helpers is that someone with anorexia nervosa will not always be open or truthful about her feelings and will frequently resist help. If she is, she is likely to say that she is ashamed of her body and very frightened of the thoughts of being heavier. She may suffer in various ways through being thin, but compared with putting on weight it seems to her the lesser evil.

The term anorexia nervosa was coined in the late 1880s by the English physician William Gull, but was vividly depicted under the name 'nervosa phthisis' by Richard Morton in 1694 as follows:

> ... I do not remember that I did ever in all my practice see one, that was conversant with the living, as much wasted with the greatest degree of a consumption (like a skeleton only clad with skin); yet there was no fever but on the contrary a coldness of the whole body ... only her appetite was diminished, and her digestion uneasy.

This girl was 18 years old; she appears to have suffered an eating disturbance that occurs primarily in adolescent females.

Leon and Dinklage (1989) state that the consistent feature of this condition is 'the relentless pursuit of thinness, that is the phenomenon of continual dieting or food restriction to the point of self-starvation and sometimes death'. Actually, few have a history of being overweight. The obsession with avoiding becoming fat results in a sharp reduction in food intake, and is often accompanied by an almost frantic, indeed compulsive, regime of exercising. Despite a striking resemblance among anorexic patients, there is convincing evidence that anorexia nervosa is a heterogeneous syndrome.

There is a large area of agreement between the ICD-10 and DSM-IV diagnostic criteria for anorexia nervosa, with regard to:

- criteria of weight loss (15 per cent below that expected for age and height)
- body-image distortion
- weight phobia (self-induced loss of weight/fear of becoming obese), and
- amenorrhoea (absence of at least three consecutive menstrual cycles when otherwise expected to occur).

Behavioural characteristics

The typical progression is:

- Dieting (as many other adolescents do), sometimes as a result of teasing about being fat
- An increasing range of items to reduce or cut out; also an increasing expertise regarding the calorie content of foods

- Loss of control of dieting (it may be months before the thinness and/or the severity/abnormality of the dieting is noticed)
- There is sometimes a distortion of body image (e.g. emaciation is not seen as thinness or as being repellant)
- Parents feel helpless in the face of the single-mindedness and drivenness of their adolescent
- There may be rigorous exercising and abuse of laxatives/diuretics and self-induced vomiting
- There is a powerful need to be *in control* of all aspects of food intake
- For some young people there are episodes of bingeing, followed by fasting or purging (bulimic features within the spectrum of anorexia nervosa tend to be infrequent in adolescence)
- Extreme hyperactivity of a highly ritualized nature is common (e.g. complex daily rituals of rigorous exercise)
- A restriction of interests (e.g. preoccupation with topics such as diet and food)
- Loss of social contacts
- Reduction of sexual interest
- Mood swings/irritability/insomnia/depression
- Low self-esteem
- Obsessional behaviour (e.g. peculiar eating rituals).

PHYSICAL CHARACTERISTICS

These might involve:

- Emaciation
- Anaemia
- Autonomic nervous system regulation (e.g. hypotension, hypothermia, bradycardia)
- Primary or secondary amenorrhoea
- In males a significant decrease in plasma testosterone levels is found at maximum weight loss, with an increase during weight restoration.

Complications from the eating disorder can affect almost every organ. There are medical illnesses to be checked out (e.g. acquired immune deficiency disease, inflammatory bowel disease, diabetes mellitus) as they can cause weight loss.

PSYCHOLOGICAL CORRELATES

A distinctive set of psychological correlates of anorexia have been reported (e.g. Crisp, Palmer and Kalucy, 1976; Garfinkel and Garner, 1982). The anorexic individual is often described as:

- Withdrawn
- Isolated
- Introverted
- Stubborn
- Selfish
- Manipulative
- Perfectionist
- Hyperactive and controlling.

There appear to be three subtypes among the feeding disorders with regard to the patterns of food consumption and elimination:

1. Restricters, who are characterized by a dieting pattern in which there is a consistently extreme limitation on the amount of food ingested. They exclusively starve themselves and indulge in excessive exercise.
2. Purgers, who are those who starve and purge but do not binge.
3. Bingers, who are notable for a severe dieting regime which is interspersed with episodes of bingeing followed by vomiting or other means of purgation.

In bulimia nervosa – the bingeing subgroup – the pre-morbid weight level is generally higher than is the case in anorexia nervosa.

Whether the distinctions between anorexia nervosa and bulimia and the typologies mentioned earlier (restricters, purgers and bingers) simply represent different indices of severity or are valid clinical entities, remains unresolved. However, it is the opinion of many clinicians that they have pragmatic value as the bulimic features of anorexia nervosa require different management. In the final analysis, what constitutes the consistent feature in persons suffering from this disorder, irrespective of subtype, is a phobia of gaining weight and of taking in food.

Prevalence

Epidemiological reports estimating the prevalence of anorexia nervosa are fraught with methodological problems, inconsistent diagnostic criteria and inadequate archival records. Certainly we can say that the presence of anorexia nervosa before the age of 14 or before the menarche is rare. When it does occur before puberty its features are, in essence, similar to the later onset disorder (Lask and Bryant-Waugh, 1992). The process of puberty tends to be arrested. The prevalence rates of anorexia nervosa in males are low although it may not always be recognized/diagnosed. Estimates of the prevalence rates for females tend to vary but the figure of below 1 per cent for the adolescent population may be close to being accurate. When taking the entire anorexic population into consideration, it appears that males account for between 5 and 15 per cent of the total. There are consistent findings to suggest that anorexia nervosa is probably becoming more frequent; however, whether the rise in numbers is a true increase or due to better identification remains a moot point (see Lucas et al., 1991).

Social classes I and II (the highest socioeconomic strata) appear to manifest more cases of anorexia nervosa than other sections of society (e.g. Crisp, Palmer and Kalucy, 1976). This selectivity is paralleled in the higher socioeconomic status of countries. Severe eating disorders, particularly food restriction, appear to be a mark of an affluent society. In those parts of the world where food is scarce, most persons do not have the luxury of refusing to eat or of getting fat because of having too much to eat. In countries such as India and Sri Lanka, obesity has traditionally been valued as a sign of wealth, but where, for many, food is scarce, extremely low rates of anorexia nervosa are found.

The epidemiology of childhood-onset anorexia nervosa and related eating disorders is as yet relatively unexplored (see Lask and Bryant-Waugh, 1992). There is a case for dealing with *anorexia* and *bulimia nervosa* separately because of differences in:

- clinical symptoms
- their pattern of age at onset, and
- heritability (high in anorexia; low in bulimia).

Steinhausen (1994) makes the point that anorexia nervosa is typically associated with the transition from childhood to adolescence and, in most cases, bulimia nervosa reflects the transition from adolescence to young adulthood. The onset of the former peaks at 14 years of age, the latter at 18 or 19.

The search for a single all-embracing cause has been abandoned by most theorists. Multifactorial causation is what one would expect with problems as complex and many-sided as anorexia and bulimia nervosa. The aetiological factors include individual, family, sociocultural and biological influences, invariably functioning in an interactive fashion.

Individual influences

PSYCHOANALYTIC THEORIES

It is hardly surprising that anorexia nervosa, with its strong age-related (pubertal) association, should be explained in terms of extreme sexual conflicts entailing symbolism of fear of pregnancy, incestuous impregnation, the denial of femininity. These highly speculative notions have failed to gain empirical support. Nevertheless, the hypothesized intense fear of the anorexic youth of becoming physically and emotionally mature has proved a popular formulation by developmental theorists from differing theoretical orientations.

Hilde Bruch who is widely known for her book *The Golden Cage: The Enigma of Anorexia Nervosa* (1978) was of the opinion that anorexia is the result of a very early and profound disturbance in mother–child interactions. (One has to say that there is a lack of specificity in such theorizing in the sense that a similar psychodynamic script has been written for autism, schizophrenia and bronchial asthma, to mention but a few problems of childhood.) According to Bruch the young person's *ego development* is deficient, manifesting itself by a disturbance in body identity that includes a lack of a sense of owning one's body. The refusal to eat gives many anorexic patients a sense of 'specialness' and superiority and a feeling of being a better person, more worth while, through the self-control of losing weight in such a disciplined manner.

The anorexic male or female, in Bruch's view, is continually fearful of not being fully acknowledged and loved within the family; also – as a consequence of pubertal changes in their bodies – anxious about expectations that they assume more independence. There is a sense of life-events removing their control over life, forcing them to be autonomous. The anorexic individual's desire for specialness becomes confused with the pursuit of thinness. The implication of this notion for treatment is to help him or her to develop a sense of competence in areas of activity in which they feel inadequate.

BEHAVIOURAL THEORIES

In the case of behavioural and social learning theories, there has been less concern with formulating all-embracing causal theories of anorexia nervosa and its development (as occurs in psychodynamic aetiologies) than with tackling specific aspects of the problem with behavioural techniques. One such aspect – food refusal – is considered a manifestation of avoidance behaviour. A functional analysis would be considered vital in understanding the development of the eating disturbance for the particular individual.

Leon (1979) proposed that, in anorexia nervosa, a learned association develops between negative thoughts and images about weight-gain and eating. Gradually this learning process becomes strengthened and generalizes to an association between thoughts or images of food and feelings of revulsion. This aversive affect then also occurs in association with the actual eating of food. A conditioned aversion to food intake becomes established, and a judgement is made that eating will lead to weight gain. The reinforcer (see p. 125) maintaining this sequence is the anxiety reduction associated with the affirmation of self-control and control over one's life through food restriction.

THE NEED TO BE IN CONTROL

The striving for, and maintenance of thinness, may serve as an affirmation of control over life in general. Support for this hypothesis came from a study by Leon, Bemis and Lucas (1980) on 18 newly hospitalized anorexic patients who indicated that dieting and weight loss resulted in a feeling of self-control and willpower, and in a generally greater feeling of control over their lives.

SEXUAL TRAUMA

Several studies have indicated a correlation between the experience of sexual abuse and eating disorders (Lask and Bryant-Waugh, 1992). The pathway from childhood sexual trauma to an eating disorder is unclear and a reminder to us of the fact that anorexia nervosa is a *heterogeneous* condition. There is little hard evidence of psychosexual problems as complicating factors in the causation of eating disorders (Scott, 1987).

PRE-MORBID PERSONALITY PROFILE

A common pre-morbid pattern described in the literature is one of compliance, perfectionism and dependence in the child.

Familial factors

In studying the family process in anorexia nervosa, one should beware of developing stereotypes about anorexic families. Families (in general) undergoing intensive treatment may be different on a number of factors from families not involved in therapy. Further, wide differences between families of anorexic patients are also evident. Hypotheses about typical familial styles of interacting, constellations, or dynamics, for anorexic individuals have found no empirical support.

Reports do, however, suggest a raised incidence of emotional and weight problems and disturbed interactions and communications

Biological factors

Various biological influences – hormonal and endocrine factors, malfunctioning of the hypothalamus – have been considered as causal in anorexia nervosa. The physical consequences of under-nutrition must be a priority consideration.

Severe restriction of food intake

Duker and Slade (1988) point out that increasing under-nutrition and low weight can create or contribute to:

- Dependence
- Restlessness and hyperactivity
- A preoccupation with food
- Personality change
- Disturbances of thinking (reduction of complex thought, extremeness, lowered capacity for abstract thinking, reduced coping strategies, poor concentration, deteriorating memory)
- Clumsiness
- Disorientation
- Diminished sexuality
- Attenuation of mood and feeling (leading to detachment)
- Euphoria/elation.

Starvation and rigorous exercise produce a 'cocktail' of chemicals in the anorexic person's body. Duker and Slade state that this is how an individual can come to derive a particular pleasure, or sense of well being, from strenuous exercise. It is also how, by further stimulating the body's production of endormorphins, hyperactivity itself acts as its own spur in the anorexic, as it does in any person who is excessively dedicated to running, gymnastics or other activity. It is thus that chronic low-weight anorexia nervosa can be viewed as an addiction to starvation. Occasionally anorexics refer to themselves as starvation junkies, and some psychiatrists now have come to see the low-weight anorexic as being dependent on the biological states that result from starvation, as 'hooked' on recurrent fixes of internally generated brain chemicals.

Genetic factors

There is a genetic influence at work (see Garfinkel and Garner, 1982). Twin studies suggests that 44–50 per cent of monozygotic twins are concordant for anorexia nervosa. Holland, Sicotte and Treasure (1988) found 56 per cent of monozygotic twins to be concordant for the disorder and only 5 per cent concordant in the case of dizygotic twins. It would seem that a genetic predisposition for anorexia and adverse environmental influences interact to bring about the condition.

Pre-morbid obesity

Many patients who become anorexic have had problems with regulating their food intake before the development of this self-starvation regime. Crisp et al. (1977) found a high proportion of pre-morbid obesity, including massive obesity, in the anorexic patients they treated. Many have a history of being overweight before the age of 12.

Food regulation

Outcome studies indicate food regulation problems. Hsu (1990) noted that bulimia was present at follow-up evaluation in 14 to 50 per cent of patients in the studies he reviewed, and that 10–28 per cent reported vomiting after food intake. It is clear that a normalization of eating patterns does not necessarily parallel a normalization of weight. At follow-up, many patients continue to express an inordinate concern with food and eating. The issue of self-control, particularly in relation to food intake, continues to be a concern of many anorexic individuals, including those individuals whose weight has been restored to a normal or near-normal level.

Summary

Hsu (1990) suggests that adolescent dieting provides the entree into an eating disorder if such dieting is intensified 'by adolescent turmoil, low self- and body-concept, and poor identity formation'. In his opinion the dangers are further exacerbated if there is a family history of affective or eating disorders or alcohol or substance abuse. There could be other risk factors to do with personality and psychological attributes described earlier. Biological factors have also been implicated (e.g. a hypothalamic disorder). Biological and psychological factors become inextricably intertwined and the question of what comes first, or what is primary, remains a chicken-and-egg conundrum.

chapter sixteen

When a Child is Ill

A child can live through anything so long as he or she is told the truth and is allowed to share with loved ones the natural feelings people have when they are suffering
Eda le Shan: *The Compassionate Friends Newsletter*, 1987

Chronic Illness

It is estimated that 10 to 20 per cent of children suffer from some form of chronic illness; and 10 to 15 per cent of these have severe conditions that constitute a major daily challenge. Boys are more at risk than girls, and children from poor socio-economic backgrounds are particularly vulnerable. Chronically ill children are at risk of developing a variety of cognitive, behavioural, social and emotional problems. Illness of itself cannot be held responsible for creating psychopathology. It is generally the secondary effects of chronicity on a child's care at home, status at school, relationships with peers, the disruption of his or her play and other leisure pursuits, and self-esteem, that must be assessed most carefully by health and educational professionals. Up to 30 per cent are calculated to have secondary psychosocial dysfunctions (Coleman et al., 1987).

In the introduction to the atypical section of the book I mentioned various serious illnesses, some potentially fatal, all to a degree chronic. Five of them are described below.

1. Eczema (atopic dermatitis: neurodermatitis)

The term 'atopy' indicates an inherited tendency to develop one or more of a related group of conditions (eczema of atopic type, bronchial asthma, acute urticaria of atopic type, and allergic rhinitis) that are subject to environmental influences. Ten per cent of the British population is atopic.

Three per cent of children under 5 years of age suffer (and this is the relevant verb) from atopic eczema. It is a chronic skin disorder of childhood brought about by an allergic reaction to a wide variety of foods, clothing fabrics, weather conditions, inhalants, and cosmetic substances. It is affected by stress. The eczema causes itching, sometimes so severe the child is 'beside itself' with frustration, pain and general misery. It is most common between the ages of 3 months and 2 years. It may begin between 1 month and 1 year. It usually subsides at around 3 years of age, but it may flare up at ages 10 to 12 and continue through to puberty. It is frequently associated with, or followed by another largely allergic condition: bronchial asthma.

2. Bronchial asthma

The most common chronic illnesses of childhood involve pulmonary functions and it is bronchial asthma that is the most common respiratory ailment. It can be very serious in its implications, sometimes leading to death. Bronchial asthma illustrates general principles which are (or have been) thought to apply to psycho-physiological conditions in general. The emphasis on the personality of the sick individual (in systematic clinical studies) was very much a post-World War II phenomenon. The revolutionary advances made in the early part of this century in medical technology, particularly in physical methods of diagnosis and treatment and the uncovering of hitherto unseen physical agents (micro-organisms) which cause certain illnesses, tended to reinforce a one-sided organic approach to disease. For a long time, in keeping with the prevailing medical bias, asthma was considered almost solely as a physical (an allergic and infective) illness, and physical desensitization and the use of drugs became the main methods of treatment. However, an analysis of the literature of the 1940s and 1950s in particular reveals a considerable shift in orientation.

Crucial to this approach was the assumption that some illnesses represent, in certain circumstances, an individual's specific reaction to his or her life-situation – almost what one might call a mode of behaviour. Patients were no longer regarded simply as collections of separate bodily organ systems, each of which is subject to breakdown, but rather as unique individuals living in certain types of environment, subject to a variety of physical and psychological stresses to which they react as *whole* persons. Thus, in disease, causation is sought both in the nature of the individual and his or her environment; it is the child who has a particular illness; not just a disease that 'has' the child (Herbert, 1974).

It has been found that particular attacks or phases of the illness can be precipitated or prolonged by psychological stresses, such as conflict, anxiety and anger, as well as physical stresses (e.g. dietary factors, allergies, infections, pungent olfactory stimuli, etc.). Treatment of the symptoms by physical means alone is often ineffective. The advance brought about by a psychophysiological perspective in medicine is due to the reinstatement of the person into the consideration of his or her illness.

3. Diabetes mellitus (type 1 diabetes)

Although this disease, 'invisible' to anyone other than the sufferer, cannot be cured, it can be controlled in what will involve a daily, life-long commitment. Diabetes results from a failure of the pancreas to produce sufficient insulin to metabolise glucose that then appears in the patient's urine. Normally it would be absent. If this abnormally high level of blood glucose (hyperglycaemia) continues untreated the person experiences excessive hunger and thirst and output of urine. Children may wet the bed. A marked loss of weight and lassitude are also characteristic. The illness, if unchecked, leads to widespread destruction of body tissue producing heart disease and circulatory problems that may result in the amputation of limbs. Neurological impairment and blindness may also occur. Although diabetes is a chronic disease for which there is no cure, it is eminently treatable, by painless injections of insulin and a strictly managed diet.

The neglect of self-care may lead to patients manifesting frustration, anger, fear and other intense and negative emotions. Compliance, particularly during adolescence, can be a problematic issue, given the youngster's forgetfulness, unreliability, or refusal to medicate her/himself. This is especially the case when insulin injections are required regularly, alongside dietary discipline.

4. Childhood cancer

Advances in the treatment of cancer have transformed an acute disease that usually proved fatal, into a chronic condition in which the majority are cured or survive for longer periods of time. The improved prognosis is brought about by aggressive therapy that may continue for years, and by the technology that allows for more accurate differentiation and treatment of tumours.

Cancer is a relatively rare disease. In fact it is a generic term for a heterogeneous group of disorders. The most common forms for children under 15, accounting for almost half of the cases, are leukaemia and tumours of the brain and nervous system. The precise causes of this group of diseases are poorly understood. They appear to be the result of a complex interaction of environmental, genetic and viral factors.

The diagnosis of cancer in a child, given the dread that still accompanies the disclosure despite the improved prognosis, is quite likely to disrupt the family's peace of mind. The physical problems may be added to by a wide range of non-disease related stresses and strains, thus adversely affecting the child's development. Across all areas of paediatric psychology, the child's adjustment may be mediated or moderated by the parents' adaptation to their child's diagnosis (Lavigne and Faier-Routman, 1993). However, in the case of the next of the chronic, life-threatening illnesses (HIV), the parents, as Lwin and Melvin (2001) point out, may also be adjusting to their own identical illness and the circumstances by which they became infected.

5. HIV and AIDS

HIV

Human immunodeficiency virus (HIV) constitutes a global health threat to children (UN AIDS, 1998). HIV is a complex retrovirus that attacks and weakens the human immune system and, thus, multiple systems of the body. The most common type is Type 1 or HIV-1, although other variants exist. It wreaks havoc by infecting and destroying T4 (or 'helper' T) cells which, in a normally functioning immune system, activate the 'killer T cells' that defend the body from viruses entering it. Once HIV has infected the T4 cells it may remain latent for a time. Even without medical treatment, a small number of HIV-infected children may remain asymptomatic for as long as a decade.

AIDS

The first report of AIDS (acquired immune deficiency syndrome) in children came from the USA in 1982. It is not a separate infection, but refers to a spectrum of illnesses, any of which can occur in a child with symptomatic HIV infection. It indicates that the virus has depleted the immune system, leaving him or her vulnerable to more serious illnesses. It is thus thought of as the severe, often terminal, end of the medical sequelae of HIV infection. The duration between HIV infection and the onset of AIDS is variable. As the infection proceeds, the child's immune system is unable to defend itself against other infections, the ultimate outcome being death (see Brown, Lourie and Pao, 2000). Lwin and Melvin (2001) comment that the 'death sentence', so often associated with HIV infection 15 years ago, is no longer applicable in populations where adequate treatment is available. This still means a shorter life for countless children and their infected parents, in large parts of the world.

Advances in medical treatment methods (e.g. antiretroviral drugs) mean that infected children are living longer, often into school age, adolescence and beyond. Despite international trends of increasing infection, more than 65 per cent of children with HIV are living past 5 years of age. Such is the physical and psychological stress of living with AIDS, many of these children will become involved with mental health professionals, where they are available.

Many children and adolescents come from backgrounds of risk and lack protective influences. Routes of transmission are several:

- Sexual intercourse (the majority of new AIDS cases among adolescents)
- Same-sex contact is the main risk for young males
- Heterosexual contact is the main risk for young females
- Sexual abuse (a relatively small proportion of cases)
- Vertical transmission from HIV-infected mother to her unborn child
- Vertical transmission from childhood-HIV survivors to sexual partners, now grown up and sexually active
- Breast milk
- Blood products
- Intravenous drug use.

In cases of vertically transmitted paediatric AIDS from mother to child, the most common mode of transmission, the mother, being infected with the virus, is likely to die before her child reaches adulthood.

Neurocognitive aspects of HIV infection may involve progressive encephalopathy (PE) (prevalence of 13 to 23 per cent) characterized by the following symptoms:

1. Impaired brain growth
2. Progressive motor dysfunction
3. Loss or plateauing of developmental milestones
4. Cognitive and language delays.

Neurological complications caused by HIV infection most often occur during development of the CNS (central nervous system), and can thus have an extremely adverse impact on the child's development. Among the many physical symptoms of AIDS is a failure to thrive, and other developmental delays such as learning disabilities. Behaviour problems and mental health disorders, notably psychosocial difficulties, are common (Thompson, Westwell and Viney, 1994). There are many difficulties for the child or adolescent to bear on top of poor health, for example, the response of others when they hear of the diagnosis, the resulting social ostracism, and the inevitable aggressive medical treatment.

A detailed account of the potential of this condition (not always realized) to hinder or devastate development is provided by Thompson, Westwell and Viney (ibid.).

Implications of Acute and Chronic Illness

The new life-extending combined therapies available for HIV present parents and children with a far more optimistic outlook than was once possible, for a life lies ahead. Nevertheless, there remain many of the common concerns (notably about adherence, quality of life, and adolescent sexual activity) reported in other chronic conditions. A multifactorial assessment of direct and indirect influences is required when attempting to link behavioural and developmental factors to progression of the disease (Lwin and Melvin, 2001). HIV may be a medical condition, but it is also one that is compounded by a wide range of social, cultural and economic circumstances.

Another important implication of serious illnesses is the separation from loved ones they so often bring about. Separations tend to disrupt children's attachment to their parents, notably when they or their parents have to go to hospital. Even studies of healthy children (let alone ill children) separated from their parents in the second and third years of life, have demonstrated their disruptive potential (see Robertson and Bowlby, 1952). Observations of their behaviour tend to show a predictable sequence of behaviour:

- In the first or 'protest' stage children react to the separation – brought about by (for example) their mother's hospitalization – with tears and anger. They demand their mother's return and seem hopeful that they will succeed in getting her back. This stage may last several days.
- Later they become quieter, but it is clear that they are just as preoccupied with their absent mother and still yearn for her return. However, their hopes may have faded. This is called the phase of 'despair'.
- Often the stages alternate: hope turns to despair, and despair to renewed hope. Eventually a greater change occurs; children seem to forget their mother so that, when they see her again, they remain curiously uninterested in her and may seem not to recognize her. This is the so-called stage of 'detachment'.

In each of these phases children are prone to tantrums and episodes of destructive behaviour. After reunion with their parents, they may be unresponsive and undemanding – to what degree and for how long depends on the length of the separation and whether or not they have been visited. If not it is likely that unresponsiveness will persist for varying periods, ranging from a few hours to several days. When at last this unresponsiveness subsides, the intense ambivalence of their feelings for their mother is made manifest. There is a storm of feeling, intense clinging, and whenever mother leaves them even for a moment, acute anxiety and rage.

Here is the mother of a 4-year-old speaking:

'Ever since I left her that time I had to go into hospital (two periods, 17 days each, child aged 2 years), she doesn't trust me any more. I can't go anywhere – over to the neighbours' or to the shops – I've always got to take her. She wouldn't leave me. She went down to the school gates at dinner time today. She ran like mad home. She said, "Oh Mum, I thought you was gone!" She can't forget it. She's still round me all the time. I just sit down and put her on my knee and love her. If I don't do it, she says "Mum, you don't love me any more"; I've *got* to sit down.'

Serious Illness (Hospitalization)

But what of the child who has to go to hospital with a serious illness or life-threatening illness or degenerative disability – perhaps never to return home? How much greater must be the intimations, the fears, of separation! The suffering, particularly the unspoken, uncomprehending distress, of children is difficult to bear.

The parents, too, are badly affected. A diagnosis of serious (perhaps terminal) illness brings about a radical shift in the way parents perceive or construe their child – in other words, the 'stories' they tell themselves about her/him. The previous story of a well child must be reconstructed as a story about an ill child. This requires a huge adjustment in parents' thinking about their child, a process that arouses fear and anxiety. Uncertainty prevails; parents cannot anticipate what will happen to their child. The days, months and years that were taken for granted can no longer be counted on. Children also have to adapt to the disease, perhaps the dawning awareness of death, and re-order their thoughts (constructs) and feelings. Parents will need to overcome their own difficulties so as to nurture and communicate openly with the child.

Davis believes that the skills of doing this are essentially similar to those used by professionals to communicate with parents, so that it becomes appropriate that professionals should explicitly share these skills with parents where necessary (see Davis, 1993).

Development of the Concept of Death

The way in which children make sense of (or fail to comprehend) death and grief is related, *inter alia*, to their cognitive, emotional and physical stages of development. It is necessary to remember that it is based upon generalizations to which there are exceptions, especially with regard to differences in life-experience, and individual differences in the rate of development.

The information below is based on empirical studies (see Kane, 1979):

Children under 4 years of age

COGNITIVE FACTORS

The 'pre-conceptual stage' of cognitive development lasts from about 2 to 4 years of age (Piaget, 1929). At this stage children's concepts are not fully formed. They don't understand, for example, the permanence of death. Because their thinking is prelogical and often 'magical' (the notion that some things and people have power over others; also the child experiencing him/ herself as at the centre of things), misconceptions and misinterpretations of the 'world' they live in can be a problem. Another source of worry to the child is their misinterpretation of causality. The immature kind of thinking called 'psychological causality' refers to the tendency in young children to attribute a psychological motive as the cause of events. For example, children may think that a parent has gone to hospital because he or she is angry with them, rather than due to illness.

- Distress on separation implies attachment to the person. The mean age of the onset of attachment is in the third quarter of the first year (notably 6 to 8 months).
- Very young children (most 3-year-olds and even younger children) are aware of death and are familiar with the word 'death' before they enter school.
- Their ability to conceptualize death and its implications is very limited. For example, because they do not understand that death is final, they may search for the departed parent and pester the surviving one ('When is Mummy/Daddy coming back?').

Children develop a realistic concept of death gradually; new components of comprehending are 'added in' so as eventually to bring about a full grasp of its realities (Kane, 1979). Hopefully, much of this learning occurs as children encounter 'small bereavements' such as a pet's death. Truthful, factual explanations of death, given in a calm manner, provide them with a grasp of reality, which will help their adjustment to later, more personal, losses such as the death of a grandparent.

EMOTIONAL FACTORS

At this early stage, children's emotional reactions to the disappearance of a parent – for whatever cause – tends to be similar. Children of barely 4 years of age can yearn for departed parents, and wait for their return. John Bowlby makes the point that children older than a few weeks or months display the same separation anxiety whether the parent is away for a few hours or for considerably longer.

Young children cannot sustain a sad mood for prolonged periods of time. They cannot differentiate feelings as finely as older children.

PHYSICAL FACTORS

Children who are too young to make themselves understood through speech may react physically to the bereavement by:

- Wetting
- Loss of appetite
- Disturbed sleep
- Clinging behaviour
- Catching infections.

Children aged 5 to 10 years

COGNITIVE FACTORS

The intuitive stage of thinking (4 to 7 years) moves the child on from the pre-conceptual stage (2 to 4) mentioned earlier, and they develop the ability to classify, order and quantify things, but they are still unaware of the principles which underlie these abilities. It is only in the next stage of concrete operations (7 plus) that these principles become more explicit, so that children can explain their logical reasoning in a satisfactory way.

Before 6 or 7, children often attribute life to inanimate objects. It is between the age of 7 and 9 that there appears to be a nodal point in children's development of concepts about life and death. By about 7 most children have a fairly clear idea of 'life' and a more or less complete concept of 'death'. It shouldn't be forgotten that many 5-year-olds have a fairly full concept. When children are about 8 to 9 they realize that dying can apply to themselves.

Kane (1979) describes the child's understanding of death between the ages of 5 and 10 in terms of the components he or she is cognitively capable of comprehending, as follows:

- Separation (understood by most 5-year-olds): Young children can be very aware that death means separation from their parents, friends or brothers and sisters. This may be the main concept they focus on, and they may be concerned that they will feel lonely or that their parents will be lonely without them.
- Immobility (understood by most 5-year-olds): The awareness that dead people cannot move can concern some children who are not also aware that dead people cannot feel, see or hear.
- Irrevocability (understood by most 6-year-olds): The fact that once people die they cannot come back to life again is essential in understanding death. Many children younger than 5 or 6 may not realize the finality of the process. Children play games at being shot and dying, but then leap to life the next minute. 'Pretend' death and 'real' death need to be made clear, so that the child realizes that 'real' death means never living again.
- Causality (understood by most 6-year-olds): There is always a physical cause of death. Young children, however, often have unusual or 'magical'

ideas about what causes death. For example, a nasty wish, saying something horrible or being naughty can sometimes be perceived as having
caused illness or death. Children need to understand that it is not such
imaginary events that cause death, but that something is wrong with the
body which is causing people to die.

- Dysfunctionality (understood by most 6-year-olds): Explanations about
death to children should include the cessation of bodily functions, for
example, that the body stops breathing, growing, seeing, hearing, thinking and feeling, and the heart stops beating. Some children worry that
they might be able to hear what is happening to themselves but not be
able to tell anyone.
- Universality (understood by most 7-year-olds): Knowledge that every living
organism dies at some time is important in understanding that everyone
must die eventually. This idea can comfort some children who may believe
that everyone lives forever and that it is unfair that they, or someone
they are close to, are dying.
- Insensitivity (understood by most 8-year-olds): That a dead person cannot feel anything is often difficult for young children to understand. For
example, if they walk on a grave they may wonder if they are 'hurting'
the person under the ground. One possible way of helping a child who is
dying in great pain is to help him or her to realize that death will relieve
them of this torment.

The conceptual development of children with a serious illness like leukaemia is
not significantly different overall from that of healthy children (Clunies-Ross
and Lansdowne, 1988).

EMOTIONAL FACTORS

Disturbances of emotion and behaviour are common. In one study, 50 per
cent manifested problems such as school refusal, stealing and poor concentration 1 year after the loss of a parent; 30 per cent displayed problems after
2 years.

Adolescents

COGNITIVE FACTORS

- Appearance of the dead is understood by most 12-year-olds. A dead body
looks different to a living body, and children may be very interested in
the physical characteristics of death. They can seem ghoulish sometimes
in their desire for detailed descriptions of what a dead person looks like.
- Adolescents, like adults, realize the permanence of death and therefore
tend to look for meanings: the big 'why?' questions.

- The adolescent's thinking is flexible. He or she is capable of abstract thought, can hypothesize and work things out (principles etc.) for themselves. Thus, they may have their own theories about death and question cherished beliefs about, say, the afterlife, in a way that dismays the surviving parent.

EMOTIONAL FACTORS

- Adolescents express their grief more like adults.
- The developmental task of separating from parents may be delayed (particularly for eldest children or those who are the same sex as the deceased parent). The adolescent's search for identity may be influenced by his/her answers to the 'why' questions referred to above.
- Some adolescents display an apparent lack of feeling or indifference owing (it is postulated) to conflicts between the drives toward independence and continuing dependence (referred to above).

Family bereavement: Potential problems

- Although some very young children have an almost complete concept of death, the individual differences, especially for the under-eights, are very large.
- Children have difficulty in calling up memories when very young. (Photograph albums are helpful here in recalling family events.)
- They find it difficult to imagine that they will miss the dying sibling or parent at times (e.g. anniversaries, holidays) and are thus unprepared for the distress when these occasions come around.
- Their egocentricity and literal-mindedness might cause them to blame themselves for the death and departure.
- They may have fantasies about being reunited with the loved person.
- They may wish to 'die' in order to be reunited with the loved person.
- Illusions or hallucinations of seeing the parent (a common experience in adults too) may be taken to be real.
- Children's 'playing out' of dying and death may seem callous and inappropriate to the adult observer who is unaware of the function of play.
- Children may have difficulties of concentration and other learning difficulties at school following a bereavement.
- They only gradually develop the capacity to sustain feelings of sadness over a period of time, and may be misinterpreted as being unfeeling.
- They may feel embarrassed at being 'different' (having lost a parent) at school.
- They may feel anxious about losing the other parent.

- They may worry about who is going to feed them and, in other ways, look after them.

The difficulty with assessing children's knowledge of the concept of death is the dependence on verbal expression. Children who are more verbally competent have a more complete concept of death than those who are not. It may be that children are aware of the concept of death before they are able to express it adequately. Stages in the concept of illness that contribute to an awareness of death have been outlined as follows:

Stage 1: 'I am very ill.'
Stage 2: 'I have an illness that can kill people.'
Stage 3: 'I have an illness that can kill children.'
Stage 4: 'I may not get better.'
Stage 5: 'I am dying.'

Researchers have found that when children of different ages were asked 'Do you believe that some day you will die?', the following percentages said 'yes', at different ages:

- age 5   50 per cent
- age 6   73 per cent
- age 7   82 per cent
- ages 8 to 10   100 per cent.

Meadows (1993) is of the opinion that children need to be approximately 9 years of age for death to be a reality, and adolescent before a mature view is possible, one in which the consequences for the family are appreciated. As in all these matters, individual children will progress at different rates. Among the criticisms of stage theory (e.g. proponents such as Piaget) is the assumption that children's confusion about, or understanding of health and illness, are inevitable outcomes of intellectual immaturity, and can only be overcome by advancement in maturation and chronological age (Meadows, 1993; Wood, 1988). Children are often (perhaps wrongly) assumed to be incapable of comprehending information about their situation on these grounds. A problem with stage theory is the temptation to identify what children are unable to do rather than what they can do.

Ethical Issues

There are many ethical questions raised by the caring for a terminally ill child. They involve issues that, by definition, are not susceptible to dogmatic 'right' v. 'wrong' prescriptive answers. Thus the following discussion is one based on my personal opinions and professional experience, rather than empirical evidence.

Being kept in the dark

Children aware of secrecy may feel isolated, abandoned by the people they depend on and trust, at a time when they are most vulnerable. They are not 'blind' or 'deaf' to non-verbal signals, tones of voice, and 'special' expressions from staff and family. They notice their parents showing extreme worry and sadness, hear their ambiguous, guarded, stilted conversations. And they wish to know what is happening. Children often choose a particular person who they want to talk to about death and dying. Although some children may not be asking questions, it does not necessarily mean they are not preoccupied with concerns about death. After all, they may see the death of other children on the ward, or they may know of other children with the same illness that proved to be fatal.

The parents may be unable to face the reality that their child is dying and so will not talk about it, even though the nearness of the end is obvious. Although some parents need to deny the reality of their child's impending death in order to survive emotionally, it is important that this is not foisted on the child as an extra burden. If healthcare professionals wish to get permission to talk with the child about the subject parents cannot face, they might make the point that in giving such a 'go ahead' parents are recognizing that their child has needs which deserve priority.

If parents can be persuaded – and depending on policies of 'whether', 'who' and 'how' on a particular ward – children who are questioning and demonstrating that they know they might be dying, surely have the right to have their questions answered clearly and openly. They may be struggling with terrifying fantasies about death, and talking about dying allows such fantasies to be disclosed and (hopefully) defused. Having said that, Elisabeth Kubler-Ross (1983) makes the point that although all patients have the right to know, not all patients have the need to know.

What do I say to the child?

The child may ask questions about death suddenly, out of the blue, catching staff and parents unprepared and off guard. The resulting consternation may lead to precipitate, ill-judged responses. The generally held view at present is that parents' wishes should be respected as to whether the child should be told that he or she is dying. Healthcare professionals are likely to seek permission from parents who are often reluctant to talk about these issues, or encourage them to talk with the child. It is an emotionally fraught situation for everyone concerned when parents refuse to talk openly with their dying child, especially when he or she is asking for information or reassurance.

It is important to be prepared, to be thoughtful and to find out from the child what she or he already knows, what they think or suspect, and what they really want to know. The latter is crucial. Seriously ill children may disclose something that has been on their mind for some time, or an event on the ward may precipitate the worried enquiry. They may have seen or heard that another child on the ward has died. This may be the first time the question has been asked. Questions about death might occur in the context of discussions about their illness and treatments. Reflecting a child's questions back to them is a way of encouraging the expression of feelings. For example, if a child suddenly asks, 'Am I going to die?' the response could be 'What is it that makes you think you are going to die?' Children may demonstrate a sophisticated understanding about the severity of their illness, or they may simply conclude that something is serious because they saw someone crying or whispering about them. They may not actually be asking about death, but about why their parents are so distressed. Children who do not understand the answers they are given, or do not get the answers they need, are likely to return repeatedly to the issue that is worrying them. A child's previous experience of death – a relative or pet animal that has died – can be used to introduce the topic of his or her own illness.

Hilton Davis (1993) counsels parents on the wide variety of situations requiring the care of seriously ill and disabled children. It is also a guide to the literature on preparing children for hospitalization, their competence to give informed consent, their understanding of their illness and its implications, and their views of pain and death. There is much to learn from the hospice movement about the provision of care and compassion for dying children, and emotional support for their families.

chapter seventeen

Child Abuse and Maltreatment

But what am I?
An infant crying in the night:
An infant crying for the light:
And with no language but a cry.

Tennyson: *In Memoriam*

Child abuse is defined in terms of three of the categories for placing children on the protection register, as defined by the UK Department of Health and Social Security in 1986. They are:

1. *Physical abuse* involves physical injury to a child. This might be due to excessive corporal punishment. It also includes deliberate poisoning where there is definite knowledge or a reasonable suspicion that the injury was inflicted, or knowingly not prevented.
2. *Sexual abuse* refers to the involvement of dependent, developmentally immature children and adolescents in sexual activities they do not truly comprehend, to which they are unable to give informed consent, or which violate social taboos concerning family roles.
3. *Emotional abuse/neglect* refers to the severely adverse effect on the behaviour and emotional development of a child caused by persistent or severe emotional ill-treatment or rejection. As all abuse involves some emotional ill-treatment, this category is used where it is the main or sole form of abuse. Neglect involves the persistent or severe neglect of a child (for example, exposure to dangers such as cold and starvation that results in serious impairment of the child's health or development, including non-organic failure to thrive). There are several types:
   - *Physical neglect* is the failure to provide a safe and nurturing home for a child and may include a failure to feed, shelter, clothe and protect from harm. Failure to thrive may be due to physical and/or emotional neglect.
   - *Emotional neglect* is the failure to nurture the psychological, social and emotional aspects of a child's life and may involve an absence of

love, affection, attention, intellectual and emotional stimulation, social interaction, and warmth related to a lack of cuddling and demonstrative caring.

- *Supervisory neglect* is the failure to provide supervision to assure safety and/or protection; the child should not be left alone for periods of time inappropriate for age and development, and not be abandoned.
- *Medical neglect* is the failure to provide medical care, including immediate and appropriate care for critical injuries or illnesses, immunizations and medical treatment when needed.
- *Educational neglect* is the failure to provide school enrolment and attendance on a regular and timely basis so that the child is appropriately on time, in school when not ill, and provided with necessary clothing and materials for school.

Physical Abuse

Research indicates that maltreatment and witnessing parental aggression during early childhood predispose children to develop conduct problems (Moffitt and Caspi, 1998). Conduct problems, in turn, predict later partner violence, which first emerges in adolescent dating experiences. Rates of partner violence double among young couples who move from dating into cohabiting, and who bear children at a young age. Thus aggressive behaviour becomes highly stable across the life-course of individuals, and is transmitted from generation to generation within families.

The picture that emerges from a plethora of studies of the different forms of aggression expressed between family members is that family violence is a many-sided phenomenon, caused and maintained by a wide range of influences (Azar, Ferrarro and Breton, 1998; Browne and Herbert, 1997). (See also figure 25 on p. 297.) Nevertheless, there are certain characteristics that are common to individuals who abuse. They tend to have low self-esteem, a sense of personal incompetence (low self-efficacy) and a sense of being unsupported and helpless. Other features include, *inter alia*, depression, social isolation, a tendency to be aggressive and little evidence of warmth or empathy. Their predisposition to violence is exacerbated by their impulsivity and poor self-control. Many experience difficulties in their marriages or cohabitations. Such perpetrators may have been as children themselves the victims of abuse.

The early clinical and research interest in maltreatment of children focused on the physical abuse (the 'battered child' syndrome) and neglect (e.g. Kempe et al., 1962). Unfortunately, the welcome raising of consciousness about the need to protect abused children was biased adversely by the almost exclusive media attention given to the relatively few parents who sadistically torture their children. There is a risk of stigmatizing all parents involved in non-accidental injury as 'monsters' and 'a race apart', a travesty of the real situation. It is likely to lead to the withdrawal of understanding for, and sympathy towards, the majority of parents whose excesses of discipline are impulsive, but not necessarily malicious. They are involved, in many instances, and this is not to excuse them, in situations that can go wrong for *any* parents in the course of rearing children. A majority of physically abusive incidents involve relatively minor injuries, occurring during what most parents perceive to be 'disciplinary encounters'. Fortunately, there is a great deal that can be done to reduce these caregivers' disciplinary difficulties with children they regard as 'unmanageable' (Herbert, 1993; Herbert and Wookey, 1998; Patterson, 1982; Webster-Stratton and Herbert, 1994).

Emotional Abuse

Assessment of emotional abuse is complicated by vague criteria that resist rigorous operational definition. The concept of emotional abuse is thus in danger of being over-inclusive. It includes both acts of omission and commission. Clearly, it is an advantage to have tangible indicators to pinpoint its presence (Garbarino, Goffmann and Seeley, 1986). Emotional abuse:

- entails punishment of positive operant behaviour such as smiling, mobility, manipulation
- is behaviour which results in discouragement of parent–infant bonding (for example, pushing children away every time they seek proximity, comfort and affection)
- involves the punishment of self-esteem as when parents endlessly criticize their child
- is parental behaviour leading to the punishing of those interpersonal skills (for example, friendliness) which are vital for acceptance in environments outside the home (for example, school and peer groups).

Different types of child abuse often co-occur, and their interactive effect is not well understood. There is a growing consensus among professionals that emotional abuse (perhaps better named maltreatment) is at the core of all major forms of abuse. It requires particular attention to disentangle emotional from physical acts of maltreatment.

Child Sexual Abuse (CSA)

Many childhood sexual experiences of different kinds come about through largely unwanted contact with adults, and for countless young people such experiences are likely to have been repetitive and damaging. CSA has short-

and long-term consequences for the child's psychological functioning. They involve, *inter alia*, emotional and conduct problems, attainment and behaviour difficulties at school, precocious sexualized behaviour and post-traumatic stress disorder (PTSD). The outlook for the children who are victims of this secretive and intimidatory form of abuse, if not detected early, is serious. They are likely to be repetitively abused for many years with the result that personal relationships may be blighted and psychosexual and personality development distorted. The estimates of the numbers who suffer long-term psychosocial problems through to later life vary considerably from study to study. About 20 per cent suffer long-term problems that persist into adulthood. About two-thirds of CSA cases suffer psychological symptoms in the 18 months following the cessation of the abuse (Edgeworth and Carr, 2000).

Definition

The most widely used definition of sexual abuse describes it as the involvement of dependent developmentally immature children or adolescents in sexual activities they do not truly comprehend, to which they are unable to give informed consent and that violate the sexual taboos of family roles. The last part of this definition clearly does not fit reconstituted families or extrafamilial abuse. Age differentials between abuser and victim are put as low as 2 years these days, in the light of child-to-child sexual abuse.

Not until the late 1970s was CSA 'discovered' by the public at large, and by policy makers. When, eventually, clinicians and researchers came to address themselves systematically to the issue of sexual maltreatment of children, the focus was mainly on what was still thought of, despite masses of historical material on sexual mores through the ages, as rarely occurring incest. Sigmund Freud's writings on the origins of the 'incest taboo', and the psychosexual development of children, acknowledged the sexuality of children and the existence (his 'seduction theory') of widespread sexual abuse of children (Freud, 1896/1961, 1939/1974). Later, he appeared to retreat from his acceptance of the reality of patients' reports of traumatizing sexual seductions within the family, by positing the distorting role of their fantasies, then weaving them into the theory of the Oedipus Complex. (See Masson, 1992 and Ferris, 1998, for an account of these contentious issues.)

Undoubtedly there was in Freud's time an even more powerful cultural reluctance than there is today to believe children's accounts of abuse. Such a mind-set persists despite incontrovertible evidence that children and adolescents continue to be sexually assaulted by adults (mothers, fathers, relatives, cohabitees, caregivers in day centres and residential homes) and by other children (e.g. siblings). The incidence of abuse remains unacceptably high. A great deal is at stake: the short- and long-term prognosis is a grave one (see below).

Gorey and Leslie (1997) published a review of 16 North American surveys and reported adjusted prevalence rates of between 12 and 17 per cent for females and 5 and 8 per cent for males. A Mori Poll conducted by female interviewers on a nationally representative UK sample of 2019 men and women is of interest (Baker and Duncan, 1985). Ten per cent of participants reported being sexually abused before the age of 16 years (12 per cent of females, 8 per cent of males) with no special risks in specific social class categories. While 63 per cent reported only a single experience, 23 per cent were repeatedly abused by the same person, and 14 per cent subjected to multiple abuse by a number of people. Of the perpetrators, 49 per cent were known to the victims and 14 per cent of all abuse took place within the family. Fifty-one per cent of the experiences reported as abusive involved no physical contact, 44 per cent involved physical contact but not sexual inter-course, and 5 per cent full sexual intercourse.

Assessment

Assessment may serve several purposes, a priority being the investigation of whether a child is being sexually abused or not. There may be a need to assess the nature and ramifications of the abuse for the planning of an inter-vention and the allocation of resources. It may also be about the estimate of risk, the attempt to identify those who are vulnerable to maltreatment with a view to introducing remedial or preventive programmes. CSA needs to be considered as occurring in the context of a more general breakdown in caregiver behaviour that negatively influences both children's self-system and the social system in which they are reared.

Background to sexual maltreatment

1. The term CSA includes the following acts: rape, sexual intercourse, buggery (and penetration), masturbation, digital (finger) penetration, fondling, exhibitionism or flashing, involvement in pornographic activity.
2. The female:male rates for victims of CSA are around 2.5:1 in community research samples, and about 5:1 in clinical populations.
3. Disabled children are sexually abused more frequently than non-disabled children (Westcott and Jones, 1999).
4. No significant difference in prevalence rates for social class or ethnic membership has been found.
5. Male perpetrators predominate (under 20 per cent are female).
6. CSA occurs at all ages. Almost 40 per cent are initially abused before the age of 10, though abuse may continue beyond this age. CSA peaks for girls at 6 to 7 years of age and at the onset of puberty.

8. Intrafamilial cases are over-represented in clinical investigations.
9. They are most commonly perpetrated by fathers, stepfathers and siblings.
10. Extrafamilial abuse is most commonly perpetrated by people known to, and trusted by, the family (e.g. friends, relatives, neighbours, babysitters, teachers, caregivers and club-leaders).
11. Boys are more commonly victims of extrafamilial abuse, girls of intra-familial abuse.
12. Co-morbidity of CSA with physical child abuse is about 20 per cent; one might speculate that emotional abuse is likely to be linked to CSA in a high proportion of cases.
13. Presence of a stepfather may double a girl's risk of being sexually abused (Finkelhor and Baron, 1986).

The CSA formulation

The grouping of abuse into types – physical, emotional (psychological) and sexual abuse, plus neglect – carried, at one time, the assumption that each type of maltreatment could be distinguished (in the manner of syndromes) on the basis of their causes. It is now recognized that the different types of child abuse often co-occur. The reality that emerges from research is that there are many common precursors and contributory determinants of abuse. It has not been possible to isolate causal pathways specific to the different categories (Horowitz et al., 1997; Farmer and Owens, 1995). Emotional abuse or maltreatment is thought to be at the core of all major forms of abuse (e.g. Garbarino, Goffmann and Seeley, 1986).

CSA is something of a minefield. The decision to initiate a child protection enquiry into whether abuse is taking place is not an easy one given the intrusive and potentially disruptive nature of the process. Clearly, in the light of the heterogeneity of contributory influences on CSA, the diverse consequences for the child, a single agency or assessment strategy is unrealistic. A multidisciplinary approach is recommended by Azar, Ferraro and Breton (1998), one that includes medical, behavioural and educational evaluations of children, as well as assessments of parents' behaviour, attitudes and history. They describe four goals for assessment:

1. Immediate dangers to the child, and procedures to ensure his/her safety
2. Functioning of individual family members and the family as a system within a larger community
3. Parental responses to child-rearing needs (Sluckin, Herbert and Sluckin, 1983)
4. Children's special needs (see Herbert, 1993).

Medical assessment

This approach concerns itself with physical evidence of CSA in the individual; it involves a paediatric examination of the allegedly abused child by a physician who is familiar with normal genital and anal appearances in childhood. When physical abnormalities are suggested from the history, a forensic physician is likely to be invited to attend the examination (see Bamford and Roberts, 1989; Hanks, Hobbs and Wynne, 1988). Problems of physical diagnosis have been recognized by the 1991 Royal College of Physicians report in the UK, of a working party on Physical Signs of Sexual Abuse in Children which concluded that there was a clear overlap between abused and non-abused populations with regard to physical signs. This conclusion highlighted the need for adequate data on the range and variation in appearance of normal genitalia in children.

Psychological assessment

Identification of sexual abuse depends mainly upon the child's accounts of her/his experiences. The interviews with the child, when a case comes to the notice of agencies, are of prime importance, and must mesh with other parts of the multidisciplinary assessment process. Unfortunately, there does not appear to be a body of scientific research currently that helps the practitioner to differentiate *bona fide* cases from those that are at fault. Babiker and Herbert (1998) observe that sexual abuse takes place within a sociocultural context, and diagnostic decisions are greatly influenced by the estimated cost of a false diagnosis. This cost is determined to a large extent by decisions about the trade-off between the two types of error:

1. the risk of misclassifying children who are being abused and possibly subjecting them to further trauma, versus
2. the risk of misclassifying children who are not being abused, and possibly subjecting them and their family to the distress of an unnecessary intervention.

Observation

It is important to be alert to possible warning 'signs'. Many of these signs in children and adolescents are open to alternative explanations, and are thus vulnerable to misinterpretation as sexual abuse. The lists below present (respectively) some of the physical and behavioural signs of possible sexual abuse (see Herbert, 1993). Physical warning signs of possible child sexual abuse might be:

- Sleeplessness, nightmares and fear of the dark
- Bruises, scratches, bite marks
- Depression, suicide attempts
- Anorexia nervosa
- Eating disorders or change in eating habits
- Difficulty in walking or sitting
- Pregnancy (particularly with reluctance to name the father)
- Recurring urinary tract problems
- Vaginal infections or genital/anal damage
- Venereal disease
- Bed-wetting
- Vague pains and aches
- Itching or soreness.

Behavioural warning signs of possible child sexual abuse are:

- Lack of trust in adults
- Fear of a particular individual
- Withdrawal and introversion
- Running away from home
- Girl takes over the mothering role
- Sudden school problems, truanting and falling standards
- Low self-esteem and low expectations of others
- Stealing
- Drug, alcohol or solvent abuse
- Display of sexual knowledge beyond the child's years
- Sexual drawing
- Prostitution
- Vulnerability to sexual and emotional exploitation
- Revulsion towards sex
- Fears of school medical examinations.

The interview

The following categories of information have been recommended by MacFarlene and Krebs (1986) as areas of enquiry during an interview to help establish a context for the abuse and to aid in the child's recounting of essential details:

1. Who abused the child? Were others present? Where were significant others when the abuse occurred? Is the child aware of any sexual activities between the abuser and other children? Has the child been abused by anyone else?

2. What happened? The interviewer needs to ask for specific details of the abuse and cover all areas of possible abusive activities.
3. Where did this occur? (For each incident, the interviewer should ask where the abuse occurred.)
4. When did this occur? How often did this occur? (Here children need to be oriented and the interviewer should refer to significant events in time. For example, 'What class were you in?'; 'Was it hot or cold out?'. Often it is helpful to begin with the first abusive event which may be less traumatizing and then move on to more recent events.)
5. How did the abuser engage the child? Was the child threatened, or asked to keep the abuse a secret? Did the child ever try to tell someone what happened? What made the child decide to tell now? How does the child feel about what happened?

The child in CSA cases

Interviews and the impediments for data-gathering (e.g. video-taping, video-linking) require careful and sensitive structuring and implementing respectively, so as not to lead or mislead children, and particularly not to abuse them further (Bentovim, 1987; Herbert, 2000). Children may be reluctant to reveal sexual abuse because they have tried before to tell someone, but were not believed. The possibility that children may fabricate evidence or be coached (perhaps coerced, bullied or bribed) into making false accusations has been investigated, particularly within the context of custody disputes. Young children are thought unlikely to lie about sexual abuse unless coerced. Features indicative of fictitious reports include lack of emotion, an absence of emotion and threat in the child's account, lack of detail, the presence of a custody access dispute, and pre-existing post-traumatic stress disorder (PTSD) (see Jones and McGraw, 1987).

The perpetrator in CSA cases

Many adult males convicted of sexual offences against children began their offending in their teenage years. Although it is a widespread belief among practitioners, there is little evidence to support the notion that offenders themselves were usually child victims of sexual offences. Finkelhor (1984) posited among the four preconditions that must operate in order for abuse to occur:

1. The abuser must be motivated to abuse the child.
2. The abuser must satisfy some emotional need.
3. The abuser must find children particularly sexually arousing.
4. The abuser may have access to adult sexual relationships blocked.

It would be helpful if we possessed some personality and motivational specificities to guide an assessment. However there seems to be no 'typical' child sex perpetrator. There is also no evidence that sex abusers can be categorized according to their preferences of victim (e.g. boy or girl, intrafamilial or extrafamilial). Abel et al., (1988) reported that 23 per cent of perpetrators committed offences against both family and non-family members, and a similar percentage offended against both boys and girls.

One of the most pervasive disturbances of parenting, apart from the deviant abuse itself, has a bearing on the second precondition, and involves the perpetrator's cognitive distortions about children (e.g. seeing them as 'wanting the sexual contact', seeing themselves as 'educating' children) (Stermac and Segal, 1989). They typically rely on such cognitions to trivialize their actions, and minimize the impact on their victims.

Epilogue

At the end of this account of the typical and atypical development of children and adolescents, I am conscious of a paradox for the reader. These pages contain so much about children, their parents and families, and yet so little. The subject is so vast that a book like this can only scratch the surface. What it can do is indicate not only the wide range of individual differences between children as they develop, as well as the universal aspects of their maturation, but also the common humanity and potential of children no matter how disabled or socially disadvantaged. Margaret Mead in her 1949 book *Male and Female*, encapsulates this belief with these words: 'We need every human gift and cannot afford to neglect any gift because of artificial barriers of sex or race or class or national origin.'

We have observed children on two of their journeys: first through prenatal intrauterine life, and second the postnatal years – from infancy, early childhood, the school years, to young adulthood. I can think of no better way of ending this book about childhood, than by quoting the following fragment of poetry from Kahil Gibran's *The Prophet*:

> *Your children are not your children*
> *They are the sons and daughters of*
> *Life's longing for itself.*
> *They come through you but not from you*
> *And though they are with you, yet they belong not to you.*
> *You may give them your love but not your thoughts,*
> *For they have their own thoughts.*
> *You may house their bodies but not their souls,*

For their souls dwell in the house of tomorrow which you cannot visit, not even in your dreams.
You may strive to be like them, but seek not to make them like you.
For life goes not backward nor tarries with yesterday.

False and True Beliefs

Given that a theory of mind encompasses the understanding of one's own and other people's state of mind, including wanting, believing, pretending, we need measures of this concept. There are vignettes that attempt this. For instance:

> Sally has a marble. She puts it in a basket to keep and then goes away.
> Anne takes the marble out of the basket and puts it in a box.
> When Sally returns where will she look for her marble?

To predict this it doesn't matter where the marble really is. It is where Sally thinks it is that is important.

A 3-year-old child predicts according to where the marble really is. Most 4-year-olds can predict Sally's mental state. Understanding mental states begins with very young children. Two-year-olds can be engaged in pretending, e.g. pretend drinking or pouring from an empty glass. This is not like having a false belief; 2-year-olds understand 'just pretending'. From about 18 months children react to imaginary situations.

A research project used three groups of children:

- Autistic children, mean age 12 years
- Down's syndrome children, mean age 10 years
- Normal children, mean age 4 years.

It produced the following results for the 'Sally' problem:

- Normal children achieved over 80 per cent correct
- Down's syndrome children achieved over 80 per cent correct
- Autistic children achieved 20 per cent correct.

The children with Down's syndrome responded in line with their mental ages but the autistic children did not.

Another study acted out the 'Sally' situation using real people. Autistic children were just as unsuccessful at this. Language-impaired children with a language age of 7 had 100 per cent passes, whereas only 25 per cent of the autistic group passed.

Several examples of 'false-belief tasks' (and their test/re-test reliability) are described by Hughes, Adlam et al. (2000).

The Measurement of Intelligence

We have seen how learning disability is defined, in part, by intellectual status. Intellectual disability is a particularly common deficit in autistic disorders. So perhaps this is the appropriate time to ask how intelligence is measured.

- It is possible to arrange problems in order of their difficulty for children of various ages, and to divide them into sets appropriate for children of 4, of 5, of 6, and so on.
- When a child is tested, the examiner puts increasingly difficult tests to him or her until s/he cannot answer any of the questions for a given age level.
- From these results the examiner works out the child's mental age.
- In this way, a child's performance can be assessed in comparison to that of a 'normal' or 'typical' child of a particular age.
- The child could then be said to have a mental age (or the intelligence) of a 5-year-old or a 6-year-old, or whatever it may be.

If, for example, a child passed all tests for age 4, half those for age 5 and none for age 6, his or her mental age would be $4^{1}/_{2}$. Intelligence can be described as a ratio between mental age and chronological age. This ratio is called the 'intelligence quotient' (IQ) and shows how quickly a child's mental abilities are developing in relation to his or her age in years. It also has the advantage of making it possible to compare the 'intelligence' of children of different ages. For example, if two children, one aged 5 and one aged 4, score a mental age of 5 on the test, then the younger child is (in the narrow meaning of an IQ) the more intelligent, and the actual difference can be worked out quite precisely.

The following figures give a general idea of the number of young people found at each intelligence level. They are based on the bell shaped *normal curve*, a statistical concept that reflects the fact that intelligence as measured by IQ tests is normally distributed in the general population.

- An IQ of 100 represents the midpoint of the population's intelligence.
- About 2.5 per cent of children lie below IQ 70.
- Another 2.5 per cent lie above IQ 130.
- IQs of 70–85 and 115–130 are each found in 10 per cent of the population.
- Seventy-five per cent of the people are in the 'average' intelligence range of 85–115.

As we can see, the number of children who are intellectually above this level decreases as their level of ability rises. The same applies to children who fall below the average.

Probably the most commonly used psychometric instrument in use for testing a child's IQ is the Wechsler Intelligence Scale for Children (WISC-III) (1992). The categories it operationalizes are given below:

IQ	Classification	Theoretical normal curve (% included)	
130 and above	Exceptionally high	2.2	98th percentile
120–129	High	6.7	91–98
110–119	High average	16.1	75–91
90–109	Average	50	25–75
80–89	Low average	16.1	9–25
70–79	Low	6.7	2–9
69 and below	Exceptionally low	2.2	Below 0.1 percentile

The IQ

The trouble with the IQ is that it is a summary score. It obscures some of the underlying differences *between* people, and also some of the unique qualities of intellect *within* the individual. It doesn't always tell us whether the child is persistent, quick, or accurate in his or her intellectual endeavours, or whether s/he has a creative type of intelligence. Berger (1986) puts forward two main reasons for the negative ethos surrounding the measurement of IQ:

- First, there is the now well-documented historical and contemporary association between IQ testing and allegations of discrimination, racial, educational, or otherwise.

- Second, philosophers, many psychologists – especially those in the developmental and cognitive fields – as well as others are, to say the least, sceptical if not dismissive of IQ tests being paraded as devices that can generate a measure that in turn encompasses something as remarkable, complex, and subtle as human intelligence.

Berger argues, on the basis of the evidence, that IQ tests do not index intelligence, or at least 'not the type of intelligence that any self-respecting person would like to lay claim to'. Furthermore, he argues that IQ tests do not *measure* in any meaningful sense of the term measurement. You might well ask what is left? What remains is that they provide a numerical expression of performances; and tests, in his view, are useful insofar as they provide data that can be interpreted in ways that are relevant to clinical (and presumably educational) problems. Psychological tests are administered not because psychologists wish to produce a score, but because knowledge of the score enables certain clinically relevant statements to be made or hypotheses to be formulated or validated. And, of course, it is useful to have instruments that produce reasonably robust scores. The question of the suitability of a test for indexing performance and interpreting scores can usually be decided on the basis of expectancy tables or regression equations.

What kind of performance, then, is indexed by some of the popular tests? There is sufficient evidence that IQs have non-chance (i.e. statistically reliable) associations, concurrent and predictive, with a wide range of behavioural phenomena that are important in clinical practice for elucidating developmental, academic and behaviour problems. We know that IQs are quite good predictors of school achievement for *older* children. There are high correlations between academic deficits and the conduct disorders. There is a direct association between a child's IQ score and later adjustment (prognosis) for infantile autism (Babiker and Herbert, 1998; Rutter, 1970a,b) and learning disability. When combined with other variables such as socioeconomic status, family conditions and the presence of learning disabilities, IQ is an important factor in predicting academic success and adult outcome, for children with attention deficit disorder. For very young children, intelligence tests are helpful in uncovering developmental delays but have little predictive validity for school performance or the likelihood of behaviour problems. Berger (1986) acknowledges these advantages. The question for him is not *whether* to use IQ tests but *how* to do so.

For the author, intelligence is more than the ability to get a good score on a certain kind of test, even more than the ability to do well in school; these are at best only the outward and visible indicators of something far more important. Intelligence is about a style of life, a way of behaving in various situations; not simply about how much we know, but how we behave when we don't know.

References and Bibliography

Abel, G.G., Becker, J.V., Cunningham-Rather, J., Mittelman, M.S. and Rouleau, J.L. 1988: Multiple paraphilic diagnoses among sex offenders. *Bulletin of the American Academy of Psychiatry and the Law*, 16, 153–68.

Adorno, T.W., Frenkel-Brunswik, E., Levinson, D. and Sanford, R. 1950: *The Authoritarian Personality*. New York: Harper & Row.

Aggleton, P., Hurry, J. and Warwick, I. 1999: *Young People and Mental Health*. Chichester: John Wiley.

Ainsworth, M.D.S., Behar, M., Waters, E. and Wall, S. 1978: *Patterns of Attachment: A Psychological Study of the Strange Situation*. Hillsdale, NJ: Lawrence Erlbaum.

Akiskal, H.S. and McKinney, W.T. 1975: Overview of recent research in depression. *Archives of General Psychiatry*, 32, 285–305.

Allport, G.W. 1937: *Personality: A Psychological Interpretation*. London: Constable.

Allport, G. 1954: *The Nature of Prejudice*. New York: Doubleday.

Anastasi, A. 1987: *Psychological Tasting*. New York: Collier Macmillan.

Andre, T. and Phye, G.D. 1986: Cognition, learning and education. In G.D. Phye and T. Andre (eds) *Cognitive Classroom Learning: Understanding, Thinking and Problem Solving*. Orlando, FL: Academic Press.

Andrews, G. and Harris, M. 1964: The syndrome of stuttering. *Clinics in Developmental Medicine*, vol. 17. London: Heinemann Medical Books.

Anhall, K. and Morris, I.L. 1998: Developmental and adjustment issues of gay, lesbian and bisexual adolescence: A review of the empirical literature. *Clinical Child and Family Review*, 1, 215–30.

Anthony, E.J. 1957: An experimental approach to the psychopathology of childhood: Encopresis. *British Journal of Medical Psychology*, 30, 146–75.

APA, 1994: DSM-IV: *Diagnostic and Statistical Manual of the Mental Disorders* (4th edn). Washington, DC: American Psychiatric Association; Beverly Hills, CA: Sage Publications.

Apgar, V. 1953: A proposal for a new method of evaluation of the newborn infant. *Current Research in Anesthesia and Analgesia*, 32, 260–67.

Apgar, V. and Beck, J. 1974: *Is My Baby All Right?* New York: Pocket Books.

Aslin, R.N. 1981a: Development of smooth pursuit in human infants. In D.F. Fisher, R.A. Monty and J.W. Senders (eds) *Eye-movements: Cognition and Visual Perception.* Hillsdale, NJ: Erlbaum.

Aslin, R.N. 1981b: Experimental influences and sensitive periods in perceptual development: A unified model. In R.N. Aslin, A.J. Alberts and M.R. Peterson (eds) *Development of Perception: Psychological Perspectives. Vol. 2, The Visual System.* New York: Oxford University Press.

Asperger, H. 1944: Die aunstisehen im kindersalter. *Archiv fur Psychiatrie und Nerven Krankheiten*, 17, 76–136.

Ausubel, D.P. and Sullivan, E.V. 1970: *Theory and Problems of Child Development*, 2nd edn, London: Grune and Stratton.

Axline, V. 1947a: *Dibs: In Search of Self.* Boston MA: Houghton Mifflin.

Axline, V.M. 1947b: *Play therapy: The inner dynamics of childhood.* Boston, MA: Houghton Mifflin.

Azar, S.T., Ferraro, M.H. and Breton, S.J. 1998: Intrafamilial child maltreatment. In T.H. Ollendick and M. Hersen (eds) *Handbook of Child Psychopathology* (3rd edn). New York: Plenum Press.

Babiker, G. and Herbert, M. 1998: Critical issues in the assessment of child sexual abuse. *Clinical Child and Family Psychology Review*, 1, 231–52.

Bailey, J.M., Pillard, R.C., Neale, M.C. and Agyei, Y. 1993: Heritable factors influence sexual orientation in women. *Archives of General Psychiatry*, 50, 217–23.

Baillargeon, R. and De Vos, J. 1991: Object permanence in young infants: Further evidence. *Child Development*, 62, 1227–46.

Baker, A.W. and Duncan, S.P. 1985: Child sexual abuse: a study of prevalence in Great Britain. *Child Abuse and Neglect*, 9, 33–47.

Baker, R.L. and Mednick, B.R. 1984: *Influences on Human Development: A Longitudinal Perspective.* Boston: Klawer Nijhoff.

Balaban, M.T. 1995: Affective influences on startle in five-month-old infants: Reactions to facial expressions of emotion. *Child Development*, 66, 28–36.

Baldwin, S. 1985: No silence please. *Times Educational Supplement*, 679, 8 November, p. 25.

Baltes, P.B., Reese, H.W. and Lipsitt, L.P. 1980: Life-span developmental psychology. *Annual Review of Psychology*, 31, 65–110.

Bamford, F. and Roberts, R. 1989: Child sexual abuse: II. In R. Meadow (ed.) *ABC of Child Abuse.* London: British Medical Journal.

Bandura, A. 1969: *Principles of Behavior Modification.* New York: Holt, Rinehart and Winston.

Bandura, A. 1977: *Social Learning Theory.* Englewood Cliffs, NJ: Prentice-Hall.

Barber, J.G., Delfabbro, P.H. and Cooper, I.L. 2001: The predictors of unsuccessful transition to foster care. *Journal of Child Psychology and Psychiatry*, 42, 785–90.

Barkley, R. 1990: *Attention Deficit Hyperactivity Disorder: A Handbook for Diagnosis and Treatment* (2nd edn). New York: Guilford Press.

Barkley, R. 1996: *Taking Charge of ADHD.* New York: Guilford Press.

Barnett, B. and Parker, G. 1998: The parentified child: Early competence or childhood deprivation? *Child Psychology and Psychiatry Review*, 3, 146–55.

Baron, J.S., Fennell, E.B. and Voeller, K.K.S. 1995: *Pediatric Neuropsychology in the Medical Setting.* New York: Oxford University Press.

Baron-Cohen, S., Leslie, A.M. and Frith, U. 1985: Does the autistic child have a theory of mind? *Cognition*, 21, 37–46.

Bathshaw, M.L. and Perret, Y.M. 1992: *Children with Disabilities: A Medical Primer* (3rd edn). Baltimore, MD: Brookes.

Battro A.M. 2001: *Half a Brain is Enough: The story of Nico*. Cambridge: Cambridge University Press.

Baumrind, D. 1971: Current patterns of parental authority. *Developmental Psychology Monographs*, 1, 1–102.

Beard, R. and Chapple, J. 1995: An evaluation of maternity services. In B.F. Sachs, R. Beard, E. Papiernik and C. Russell (eds) *Reproductive Health Care for Women and Babies*. New York: Oxford University Press.

Beekman, D. 1977: *The Mechanical Baby*. New York: Meridan.

Beilin, H. 1992: Piaget's enduring contribution to developmental psychology. *Developmental Psychology*, 28, 191–204.

Bell, R.Q. 1968: A reinterpretation of the direction of effects in socialization. *Psychological Review*, 75, 81–95.

Bell, R.Q. and Waldrop, M.F. 1982: Temperament and minor physical anomalies. In Ciba Foundation Symposium No. 89, *Temperamental Differences in Infants and Young Children*. London: Pitman.

Bellman, M. 1966: Studies on encopresis. *Acta Paediatrica Scandanavia* (supplement), 170, 7–132.

Belsky, J. 1988: The effects of day care reconsidered. *Early Childhood Research Quarterly*, 3, 235–72.

Belsky, J. 1990: Parental and nonparental childcare and children's socioemotional development: A decade of research. *Journal of Marriage and the Family*, 52, 885–903.

Belsky, J. 1993: Etiology of child maltreatment: A developmental-ecological analysis. *Psychological Bulletin*, 114, 413–34.

Belsky, J. 2001: Developmental risks (still) associated with early child care. *Journal of Child Psychology and Psychiatry*, 42, 845–59.

Benoit, D., Parker, K.C.H. and Zeanah, C.H. 1997: Mothers' representations of their infants assessed prenatally: stability and association with infants' attachment classification. *Journal of Child Psychology and Psychiatry*, 38, 307–14.

Bentovim, A. 1987: The diagnosis of child sexual abuse. *Bulletin of the Royal College of Psychiatrists*, 11, 295–9.

Berger, M. 1986: Toward an educated use of IQ tests: A reappraisal of intelligence testing. In B.B. Lahey and A.E. Kazdin (eds) *Advances in Clinical Child Psychology*, vol. 19. New York: Plenum Press.

Berger, K.S. 2000: *The Developing Person: Through Childhood* (2nd edn). New York: Worth Publishers.

Bernstein, G.A. and Garfinkel, B.D. 1986: School phobia: The overlap of affective and anxiety disorders. *Journal of the American Academy of Child and Adolescent Psychiatry*, 25, 235–41.

Berry, J.W., Poortinga, T.H., Segall, M.H. and Dasin, P.R. 1992: *Cross-Cultural Psychology: Theory, Method and Applications*. Cambridge: Cambridge University Press.

Besag, F.M.C. 1988: Cognitive deterioration in children with epilepsy. In M.R. Trimble and E.H. Reynolds (eds) *Epilepsy, Behaviour and Cognitive Function*. Chichester: John Wiley.

Bettelheim, B. 1967: *The Empty Fortress: Infantile Autism and the Birth of the Self*. New York: The Free Press.

Bingham, C.R. and Crockett, L.J. 1996: Longitudinal adjustment patterns of boys and girls experiencing early, middle and later sexual intercourse. *Developmental Psychology*, 32, 647–58.

Bishop, D.V.M. 1992: The underlying nature of specific language impairment. *Journal of Child Psychology and Psychiatry*, 33, 3–66.

Biswas, M.K. and Craigo, S.D. 1994: The course and conduct of normal labor and delivery. In A.H. De Cherney and M.L. Pernoll (eds) *Current Obstetric and Gynecological Diagnosis and Treatment*. Norwalk, CT: Appleton and Lang.

Bjorklund, D.E. 1995: *Children's Thinking: Developmental Function and Individual Differences* (2nd edn). Pacific Grove, CA: Brookes/Cole.

Blake, H. and Lile, B. 1995: The impact of type of school-based programs on self-efficacy development of teen-aged parents. *Dissertation Abstracts International Section A: Humanities and Social Sciences*, 55, 30–78.

Blanz, B., Schmidt, M.H. and Esser, G. 1991: Family adversities and child psychiatric disorder. *Journal of Child Psychology and Psychiatry*, 32, 393–450.

Bloom, L. 1991: *Language Development from Two to Three*. Cambridge: Cambridge University Press.

Bower, T.G.R. 1966: The visual world of infants. *Scientific American*, 215, 80–92.

Bower, T.G.R., Broughton, J.M. and Moore, M.K. 1970: Infant responses to moving objects: an indicator of response to distal variables. *Perception and Psychophysics*, 8, 51–3.

Bowlby, J. 1951: *Maternal Care and Mental Health*. Geneva: World Health Organization.

Bowlby, J. 1969: *Attachment and Loss. Vol. 1, Attachment*. New York: Basic Books.

Bowlby, J. 1973: *Attachment and Loss. Vol. 2, Separation, Anxiety and Anger*. New York: Basic Books.

Bowlby, J. 1988: *Attachment and Loss. Vol. 3, A Secure Base: Clinical Applications of Attachment Theory*. London: Routledge.

Brackbill, Y. 1958: Extinction of the smiling response in infants as a function of reinforcement. *Child Development*, 29, 115–24.

Brazelton, T.B. 1984: *Neonatal Behavioural Assessment Scale*. Philadelphia: Lippincott.

Brockington, I. 1996: *Motherhood and Mental Health*. Oxford: Oxford University Press.

Bronfenbrenner, U. 1989: Ecological systems theory. In R. Vasta (ed.) *Annals of Child Development: Theories of Child Development: Revised Formulation and Current Issues*, vol. 6. Greenwich, CT: JAI Press.

Brown, G.W. and Harris, T. 1978: *Social Origins of Depression: A Study of Psychiatric Disorders in Women*. London: Tavistock.

Brown, L., Louri, K.J. and Pao, M. 2000: Children and adolescents living with HIV and AIDS. *Journal of Child Psychology and Psychiatry*, 41, 81–96.

Browne, K. and Herbert, M. 1997: *Preventing Family Violence*. Chichester: John Wiley.

Bruch, H. 1954: Parent education or the illusion of omnipotence. *American Journal of Orthopsychiatry*, 24, 123.

Bruch, H. 1978: *The Golden Cage: The Enigma of Anorexia Nervosa*. Cambridge: Harvard University Press.

Bruner, J.S. 1975: *Beyond the Information Given*. London: Allen & Unwin.

Burke, A. 1986: Racism, prejudice and mental illness. In J. Cox (ed.) *Transcultural Psychiatry*. London: Croom Helm.

Burlingham, D. 1979: To be blind in a sighted world. *Psychoanalytic Study of the Child*, 34, 5–30.

Bushnell, I.W.R., Sai, F. and Mullin, J.T. 1989: Neonatal recognition of the mother's face. *Journal of Developmental Psychology*, 17, 3–13.

Butler, N. and Golding, M. 1986: *From Birth to Five: A study of the Health and Behaviour of British Five Year Olds*. Oxford: Pergamon Press.

Buys, M.L. (ed.) 1990: *Birth Defects Encyclopedia*. Denver: Center for Birth Defects Information Services.

Calapinto, J. 2000: *As Nature Made Him*. New York: Harper Collins.

Caldwell, B.M. 1964: The effects of child care. In M.L. Hoffman and L.W. Hoffman, (eds) *Review of Child Development Research*, vol. I. New York: Russell Sage Foundation.

Call, J.D. 1985: *Practice of Pediatrics*. Philadelphia, PA: Harper & Row.

Cameron, J.R. 1978: Parental treatment, children's temperament and risk of childhood behavior problems. *American Journal of Orthopsychiatry*, 48, 140–47.

Capaldi, D.M. and Patterson, G.R. 1991: Relation of parental transitions to boys' adjustment problems. *Developmental Psychology*, 27, 489–504.

Capps, L., Sigman, M. and Mundy, 1994: Attachment security in children with autism. *Development and Psychopathology*, 6, 249–61.

Caron, R.F. and Carlson, V.R. 1979: Infant perception of the invariant shape of objects varying in slant. *Child Development*, 50, 716–21.

Carr, A. 1999: *The Handbook of Child and Adolescent Clinical Psychology*. London, Routledge.

Carr, A. 2002: *Risky sexual behaviour in adolescence*. Oxford: BPS/Blackwell. (M. Herbert (ed.) PACT Series.)

Carr, E.G. and Durand, V.M. 1985: Reducing behaviour problems through communication training. *Journal of Applied Behaviour Analysis*, 18, 111–26.

Case, R. and Okamoto, Y. 1996: The role of central conceptual structures in the development of children's thought. *Monographs of the Society for Research in Child Development*, 61, nos. 1–2, serial no. 246.

Caughy, M.O. 1996: Health and environmental effects on the academic readiness of school-age children. *Developmental Psychology*, 32, 515–22.

Chadwick, P., Birchwood, H. and Trower, P. 1996: *Cognitive Therapy for Delusions, Voices and Paranoia*. Chichester: Wiley.

Chavira, V., Lopez, S.R., Blacher, J. and Shapiro, J. 2000: Latina mothers' attributions, emotions, and reactions to the problem behaviors of their children with developmental disabilities. *Journal of Child Psychology and Psychiatry*, 41, 245–52

Chen, C. and Stevenson, H.W. 1995: Motivation and mathematics achievement: a comparative study of Asian-American, Caucasian-American and East Asian high school students. *Child Development*, 66, 1215–34.

Chess, S. 1964: Editorial, 'Mal de Mere'. *American Journal of Orthopsychiatry*, 34, 613–14.

Chomsky, N. 1968: *The Acquisition of Syntax in Children from 5 to 10*. Cambridge, MA: MIT Press.

Chomsky, N. 1976: *Reflections on Language*. London: Fontana.

Cicchetti, D. 1990: The organization and coherence of socioemotional, cognitive and representational development. Illustration through a developmental psychopathology perspective on Down's syndrome and child maltreatment. In R.A. Thompson (ed.) *Nebraska symposium on motivation. Vol. 36, Socioemotional development*. Lincoln: University of Nebraska Press.

Cicchetti, D., Toth, S. and Bush, M. 1983: Developmental psychopathology and incompetence in childhood: suggestions for intervention. In B.B. Lahey and A.E. Kazdin). *Advances in Clinical Child Psychology*, vol. 11 (eds) New York: Plenum Press.

Clayden, G.S. 1988: Is constipation in childhood a neurodevelopmental abnormality? In P.J. Mills (ed.) *Disorders of Gastrointestinal Motility in Childhood*. Chichester: John Wiley.

Clayden, G.S. and Agnarsson, U. 1991: *Constipation in Childhood*. Oxford: Oxford University Press.

Cleckley, H. 1944/1976: *The Mask of Sanity*. London: Henry Kimpton.

Clunies-Ross, C. and Lansdowne, R. 1988: Concepts of death: illness and isolation found in children with leukaemia. *Child Care, Health and Development*, 14, 373–86.

Cody, H. and Hynde, G.W. 1999: Neurological advances in child and adolescent mental health: The decade of the brain. *Journal of Child Psychology and Psychiatry*, Review 4, 103–8.

Cohen, S. and Williams, G.M. 1991: Stress and infectious disease in humans. *Psychological Bulletin*, 109, 5–24.

Coleman, J. and Hendry, L. 1999: *The Nature of Adolescence* (3rd edn). London: Routledge.

Cooke, J. and Williams, D. 1987: *Working With Children's Language*. Tucson, AZ: Communication Skill Builders.

Crain, W.C. 1985: *Theories of Development: Concepts and Applications*. Englewood Cliffs, NJ: Prentice-Hall.

Crisp, A.H., Palmer, R.L. and Kalucy, R.S. 1976: How common is anorexia? A prevalence study. *British Journal of Psychiatry*, 128, 549–54.

Crisp, A.H. et al. 1977: The long-term prognosis in anorexia nervosa: Some factors predictive of outcome. In R.A. Vigersky (ed.) *Anorexia Nervosa*. New York: Raven Press.

Crittenden, P.M. 1988: Distorted patterns of relationship in maltreating families: The role of internal representation models. *Journal of Reproductive and Infant Psychology*, 6, 183–99.

Dalton, K 1977: *The Premenstrual Syndrome and Progesterone Therapy*. London: Heinemann Medical Books.

Danziger, K. 1971: *Socialization*. Harmondsworth: Penguin.

Darwin, C. 1859: *On the origin of species*. London: Macmillan, John Murray.

Davids, A., DeVault, S. and Talmadge, M. 1963: Anxiety, pregnancy and childbirth abnormalities. *Journal of Consulting Psychology*, 25, 74–7.

Davis, H. 1993: *Counselling Parents of Children With Chronic Illness or Disability*. Leicester: BPS Books.

Dawkins, R. 1978: *The Selfish Gene* (2nd edn). Oxford: Oxford University Press.

Deater-Deckard, K. 2001: Recent research examining the role of peer relationships in the development of psychopathology. *Journal of Child Psychology and Psychiatry*, 42, 565–80.

De Casper, A.J. and Fifer, W.P. 1980: Of human bonding: Newborns prefer their mothers' voices. *Science*, 208, 1174–6.

Denney, C.B. 2001: Stimulant effects in attention deficit hyperactivity disorder: Theoretical and empirical issues. *Journal of Clinical Child Psychology*, 30, 98–109.

Dennis, W. 1960: Causes of retardation among institutional children: Iran. *Journal of Genetic Psychology*, 96, 47–59.

Diamond, M.C. 1990: *Enriching Heredity: The Impact of the Environment on the Anatomy of the Brain*. New York: Free Press.

Dick-Read, G. 1942: *Childbirth Without Fear*. London: Macmillan.

Dollard, J. and Miller, N.E. 1950: *Personality and Psychotherapy*. New York: McGraw-Hill.

Donaldson, M. 1978: *Children's Minds*. London: Fontana.

Drillien, C. 1964: *The Growth and Development of the Prematurely Born Infant*. Edinburgh: E. & S. Livingston.

Duker, M. and Slade, R. 1988: *Anorexia Nervosa: How to Help*. Milton Keynes: Open University Press.

Dunn, J.B. 1975: Consistency and change in styles of mothering. In *Parent–Infant Interactions. CIBA Foundation Symposium*, 33, 155–76.

Dunn, J. 1984: *Sisters and Brothers*. London: Fontana.

Dunn, J. 2000: Siblings. *The Psychologist*, 13, 244–8.

Dunn, J. and Kendrick, C. 1982: *Siblings: Love, Envy and Understanding*. Cambridge, MA: Harvard University Press.

Durkin, K. 1995: *Developmental Social Psychology: From infancy to old age*. Oxford: Basil Blackwell.

Dworetzky, J.P. 1981: *Introduction to Child Development*. St Paul, MO: West Publishing.

Dykens, E.M. 2000: Annotation: Psychopathology in children with intellectual disability. *Journal of Child Psychology and Psychiatry*, 41, 407–17.

East, P.L. 1992. Pregnancy risk among the younger sisters of pregnant and childbearing adolescents. *Journal of Developmental and Behavioral Pediatrics*, 13, 128–36.

Edelstein, J. and Herbert, M. 1998: *Separation and Divorce: A Collaborative Training and Counselling Course*. Exeter: Impact Publications, PO Box 342, Exeter EX6 7ZD, UK.

Edgeworth, J. and Carr, A. 2000: Child abuse. In A. Carr (ed.) *What Works with Children and Adolescents?* London: Routledge.

Eisenberg, L. and Kanner, L. 1956: Early infantile autism. *American Journal of Orthopsychiatry*, 26, 556–66.

Eliot, George, 1929: *Silas Marner*. New York: Macmillan.

Elkind, D. 1967: Egocentrism in adolescence. *Child Development*, 38, 1025–34.

Ellis, A.W. 1993: *Reading, Writing and Dyslexia* (2nd edn). Hove: Psychology Press.

Erikson, E. 1965: *Childhood and Society* Harmondsworth, Penguin.

Erikson, E. 1968. *Identity: Youth and Crisis*. New York: Norton.

Erickson, M.F., Sroufe, L.A. and Egeland, B. 1985: The relationship between quality of attachment and behaviour problems in preschool in a high-risk sample. In I. Bretherton and E. Waters (eds) *Growing Points in Attachment Theory and Research*. Monographs of the Society for Research in Child Development, 50, (1–2), 147–66.

Etchegoyan, A. 2000: Perinatal mental health: psychodynamic and psychiatric perspectives. In P. Reder, M. McClure and A. Jolley (eds) *Family Matters: Interfaces Between Child and Adult Mental Health*. London: Routledge.

Eysenck, H.J. 1967: *The Biological Basis of Personality*. Springfield, IL: C.C. Thomas.

Falloon, L.R., Boyd, J.L. and McGill, C.W. 1984: *Family Care of Schizophrenia*. London: Guildford.

Farmer, E. and Owens, M. 1995: *Child Protection Practice: Private Risk and Public Remedies: Decision Making, Intervention and Outcomes: Protection Work*. London: HMSO.

Farrell, M. and Taylor, E. 1994: Drug and alcohol use and misuse. In M. Rutter, L. Hersov and E. Taylor (eds) *Child and Adolescent Psychiatry: Modern Approaches*. Oxford: Blackwell Scientific.

Farrington, D.P. 1991: Childhood aggression and adult violence: Early precursors and later life outcomes. In D.I. Pepler and K.H. Rubin (eds) *The Development of Childhood Aggression*. Hillsdale, NJ: Erlbaum.

Farrington, D.P. 1995: The development of offending and anti-social behaviours from childhood: Key findings from the Cambridge study of delinquent development. *Journal of Child Psychology and Psychiatry*, 360, 929–1064.

Farrington, D.P. 2002: Developmental Criminology and Risk-focussed Prevention. In M. Maguire, R. Morgan and R. Reiner (eds) *The Oxford Handbook of Criminology* (3rd edn). Oxford: Clarendon Press.

Ferreira, A.J. 1960: Emotional factors in the prenatal environment. *Review of Medicine and Psychosomatics*, 4, 16–17.

Ferris, P. 1998: *Dr. Freud: A Life*. London: Pimlico/Random House.

Ferster, C.B. 1961: Positive reinforcement and behavioural deficits of autistic children. *Child Development*, 32, 437–56.

Finkelhor, D. 1984: *Child Sexual Abuse: New Theory and Research*. New York: Free Press.

Finkelhor, D. and Baron, L. 1986: High risk children. In D. Finkelhor et al. (eds) *Sourcebook on Child Sexual Abuse*. Beverly Hills, CA: Sage.

Flavell, J.H. 1992: Cognitive development: Past, present and future. *Developmental Psychology*, 28, 998–1005.

Fletcher, J.C. and Evans, M.I. 1983: Maternal bonding in early fetal ultra-sound examination. *New England Journal of Medicine*, 305, 392–3.

Folstein, S. and Rutter, M. 1977: A twin study of individuals with infantile autism. In M. Rutter and E. Schopler (eds) *Autism: A Reappraisal of Concepts and Treatment*. New York: Plenum Press.

Fonagy, P., Steele, H. and Steele, M. 1991: Maternal representations of attachment during pregnancy predict the organisation of infant–mother attachment at one year of age. *Child Development*, 62, 891–905.

Fonagy, P., Moran, G.S. and Higgitt, A.C. 1989: Insulin dependent diabetes mellitus in children and adolescents. In S. Pearce and J. Wardle (eds) *The Practice of Behavioural Medicine*. Leicester: The British Psychological Society/Oxford University Press.

Fordham, K. and Stevenson-Hinde, J. 1999: Shyness, friendship quality and adjustment during middle childhood. *Journal of Child Psychology and Psychiatry*, 40, 757–68.

Francis, G. and Gragg, R. 1996: *Obsessive Compulsive Disorder*. Thousand Oaks, CA: Sage.

Freud, A. 1946: *The Psychoanalytic Treatment of Children*. London: Imago.

Freud A. 1958: *Adolescence: Psychoanalytic Study of the Child*. New York: International Universities Press.

Freud, S. 1896/1961: The aetiology of hysteria. In J. Strachey (ed. and trans.) *The Standard Edition of the Complete Psychological Works of Sigmund Freud*, vol. 3. London: Hogarth Press. (Original work published 1896.)

Freud, S. 1939/1974: *Introductory Lectures on Psychoanalysis*. Harmondsworth: Penguin Books.

Frick, P.J. 1998: Conduct disorder. In: T. Ollendick and M. Hersen (eds) *Handbook of Child Psychopathology* (3rd edn). New York: Plenum.

Frick, P.J. et al. 1993: Oppositional defiant disorder and conduct disorder: A meta-analytic review of factor analysis and cross-validation in a clinic sample. *Clinical Psychology Review*, 13, 319–40.

Frith, U. 1989: *Autism: Explaining the Enigma*. Oxford: Basil Blackwell.

Frith, U. (ed.) 1992: *Autism and Asperger Syndrome*. Cambridge: Cambridge University Press.

Fryers, T. 1984: *The Epidemiology of Intellectual Impairment*. London: Academic Press.

Gaines, R. et al. 1978: Etiological factors in child maltreatment: A multivariate study of abusing, neglecting, and normal mothers. *Journal of Abnormal Psychology*, 87, 531–40.

Garbarino, J. and Binn, J.L. 1992: The ecology of childbearing and childrearing. In J. Garbarino (ed.) *Children and Families in the Social Environment* (2nd edn). New York: Aldine de Gruyter.

Garbarino, J., Goffmann, E. and Seeley, J.W. 1986: *The Psychologically Battered Child*. San Francisco, CA: Jossey-Bass.

Garfinkel, P.E. 1974: Perception of hunger and satiety in anorexia nervosa. *Psychological Medicine*, 4, 309–15.

Garfinkel, P.E. and Garner, D.M. 1982: *Anorexia Nervosa: A Multi-Dimensional Perspective*. New York: Brunner/Mazel.

Geary, D.C., Bow-Thomas, C.C., Liu, F. and Siegler, R.S. 1996: Development of arithmetic competencies in Chinese and American children: Influences of age, language, and schooling. *Child Development*, 67, 2022–44.

Gelfand, D.M., Jenson, W.R. and Drew, C.J. 1985. *Understanding Child Behavior Disorders*. New York: Holt, Rinehart and Winstone.

Gelman, R. 1972: Logical capacity of very young children. Number invariant rules. *Child Development*, 43, 75–90.

Gerber, A. 1993: *Language-Related Learning Disabilities: Their Nature and Treatment*. Baltimore, MD: Brookes.

Gerrard, N. 2000: Feature article. *Observer Review*, 15 October, 1–2.

Gesell, A. et al. 1940: *The First Five Years of Life*. New York: Harper & Row.

Goldberg, G.L. and Craig, C.L. 1983: Obstetric complications in adolescent pregnancies. *South African Medical Journal*, 64, 863–4.

Goldenberg, R.L. 1995: Small for gestational age infants. In B.P. Sachs et al. (eds) *Reproductive Health Care for Women and Babies*. New York: Oxford University Press.

Goldstein, S. (ed.) 1995: *Understanding and Managing Children's Classroom Behavior*. New York: John Wiley.

Goodman, B.R. 1994: Brain disorders. In M. Rutter, E. Taylor and L. Hersov (eds) *Child and Adolescent Psychiatry* (3rd edn). Oxford: Blackwell Scientific Publications.

Goodman, R. 1999: *Office of National Statistics Survey of the Mental Health of Children and Adolescents in Great Britain*. London: HMSO.

Goodnow, J.J. 1969: Problems in research on culture and thought. In D. Elkind and J. Flavell (eds) *Studies in Cognitive Development: Essays in Honour of Jean Piaget*. Oxford: Oxford University Press.

Goodnow, J.J. and Collins, A.W. 1990: *Development According to Parents: The Nature, Sources and Consequences of Parents' Ideas*. Hillsdale, NJ: Erlbaum.

Gorey, K.M. and Leslie, D.R. 1997: The prevalence of child sexual abuse: Integrative review adjustment for potential response and measurement biases. *Child Abuse and Neglect*, 21, 391–8.

Gottesman, J. 1991: *Schizophrenia Genetics: The Origin of Madness*. New York: Freeman.

Graziani, L.J., Pasto, M. and Stanley, C. 1986: Neonatal neurosonography correlation of cerebral palsy in preterm infants. *Pediatrics*, 78, 88–95.

Greenacre, Y. 1945: The biological ecology of birth. In *The Psychoanalytic Study of the Child* (pp. 31–51). International University Press.

Greenberg, M.T. and Speltz, M.L. 1988: Attachment and the ontogeny of conduct problems. In J. Belsky and T. Nezworski (eds) *Clinical Interventions of Attachment*. Hillsdale, NJ: Erlbaum.

Groos, K. 1901: *The play of man*. London: Heinemann.

Guerin, S. and Hennessy, E. 2002: *Aggression and Bullying*. Oxford: BPS/Blackwell. (M. Herbert (ed.) PACT Series.)

Gustafson, G.E. and Harris, K.L. 1990: Women's responses to young infants' cries. *Developmental Psychology*, 26, 144–52.

Hainline, L. 1985: Oculomotor control in human infants. In R. Groner, G.W. McConkie and C. Menz (eds) *Eye Movements and Human Information Processing*. Amsterdam: Elsevier.

Haith, M.M. 1990: Progress in the understanding of sensory and perceptual processes in early infancy. *Merrill-Palmer Quarterly*, 36, 1–26.

Hall, G. Stanley, 1904: *Adolescence: Its Psychology and its Relation to Physiology, Anthropology, Sociology, Sex, Crime, Religion and Education*, vols I and II. New York: D. Appleton.

Hamer, D. and Copeland, P. 1998: *Living With Our Genes*. New York: Doubleday.

Hanks, H., Hobbs, G. and Wynne, J. 1988: Early signs and recognition of sexual abuse in the pre-school child. In K. Browne, C. Davies and P. Stratton (eds) *Early Prediction and Prevention of Child Abuse* (see rev. edn, 2002). Chichester: Wiley.

Harkness, S. and Super, C.M. 1995: Culture and parenting. In M.H. Burnstein (ed.) *Handbook of parenting. Vol. 2, Biology and Ecology of Parenting*. Mahwah, NJ: Erlbaum.

Harlow, H.F. 1971: *Learning to Love*. San Francisco, CA: Albion.

Henderson, S.E. 1985: Motor skill development. In D. Lane and B. Stratford (eds) *Current Approaches to Down's Syndome*. London: Cassell.

Herbert, M. 1964: The concept and testing of brain damage in children. *Journal of Child Psychology and Psychiatry*, 5, 197–216.

Herbert, M. 1974: *Emotional Problems of Development in Children*. London: Academic Press.

Herbert, M. 1987a: *Behavioural Treatment of Children with Problems: A Practice Manual* (2nd edn). London: Academic Press.

Herbert, M. 1987b: *Conduct Disorders of Childhood and Adolescence* (2nd edn). Chichester: Wiley.

Herbert, M. 1987c: *Living With Teenagers*. Oxford: Basil Blackwell.

Herbert, M. 1990: *Planning a Research Project*. London: Cassell.

Herbert, M. 1991: *Clinical Child Psychology: Behaviour, Social Learning and Development*. Chichester: John Wiley.

Herbert, M. 1993: *Working with Children and the Children Act*. Leicester: BPS Books (The British Psychological Society).

Herbert, M. 1994: Behavioural methods. In M. Rutter, E. Taylor and L. Hersov (eds) *Child and Adolescent Psychiatry: Modern Approaches* (3rd edn). Oxford: Blackwell Science.

Herbert, M. 1998a: *Clinical Child Psychology: Social Learning, Development and Behaviour.* (2nd edn). Chichester: Wiley.

Herbert, M. 1998b: Clinical formulation. In M. Hersen (ed.) *Comprehensive Clinical Psychology.* New York: Plenum Press.

Herbert, M. 2000: Assessment of child sexual abuse: Behaviour change. *Behaviour Change,* 17, 15–27.

Herbert, M. 2002: Behavioural therapies. In M. Rutter and E. Taylor (eds) *Child and Adolescent Psychiatry,* vol. 4. Oxford: Blackwell.

Herbert, M. and Kemp, M. 1969: The reliability of the brain. *Science Journal,* 5a, 47–52.

Herbert, M., Sluckin, W. and Sluckin, A. 1982: Mother-to-infant bonding. *Journal of Child Psychology and Psychiatry,* 23, 205–21.

Herbert, M. and Wookey, J. 1998: *Childwise Parenting Skills Manual.* Exeter: Impact Publications, PO Box 342, Exeter, EX6 7ZD, UK.

Hermelin, B. and O'Connor, N. 1970a: *Psychological Experiments With Autistic Children.* Oxford: Pergamon Press.

Hermelin, B. and O'Connor, N. 1970b: Crossmodal transfer in normal, subnormal and autistic children. *Neuropsychologica,* 2, 229–32.

Hersov, L.A. 1960: Persistent nonattendance at school./Refusal to go to school. *Journal of Child Psychology and Psychiatry,* 1, 130–36/137–45.

Hetherington, E.M., Cox, M. and Cox, R. 1982: Effects of divorce on parents and children. In M. Lamb (ed.) *Nontraditional Families.* Hillsdale, NJ: Erlbaum.

Hetherington, E.M. and Stanley-Hagan, M. 1999: Adjustment of children with divorced parents: A risk and resiliency perspective. *Journal of Child Psychology and Psychiatry,* 40, 120–40.

Hewitt, K., Powell, I. and Tait, V. 1989: The behaviour of 9-month- and 2-year-olds as assessed by health visitors and parents. *Health Visitor,* 62, 52–4.

Heyne, D. and Rollings, S. (with King, N. J. and Tonge, B.) 2002: *School refusal.* Oxford: BPS/Blackwell. (M. Herbert (ed.) PACT Series.)

Hinde, R.A. 1979: Family influences. In M. Rutter (ed.) *Scientific Foundations of Developmental Psychiatry.* London: Heinemann.

Hobson, R.P. 1991: Against the theory of 'theory of mind'. *British Journal of Developmental Psychology,* 9, 33–51.

Hobson, R.P. 1993a: *Autism and the Development of Mind.* Hove/Hillsdale: Laurence Erlbaum.

Hobson, R.P. 1993b: Through feeling and sight to self and symbol. In U. Neisser (ed.) *The Perceived Self: Ecological and Interpersonal Sources of Self-Knowledge.* New York: Cambridge University Press.

Holland, A.J., Sicotte, N. and Treasure, J. 1988: Anorexia nervosa: Evidence for a genetic basis. *Journal of Psychosomatic Research,* 32, 561–72.

Holzman, M. 1997: *The Language of Children* (2nd edn). Oxford: Blackwell.

Hopkins, B. 1991: Facilitating early motor development: An intracultural study of Indian mothers and their infants living in Britain. In J.K. Nugent, B.M. Lester and T.B. Brazelton (eds) *The Cultural Context of Infancy. Vol. 2, Multicultural and Interdisciplinary Approaches to Parent–Infant Relations.* Norwood, NJ: Ablex.

Horne, J. 1988: *Why We Sleep: The Function of Sleep in Humans and Other Mammals*. Oxford: Oxford University Press.

Horne, J. 2001: State of the art: Sleep. *The Psychologist*, 14, 302–6.

Horowitz, F.D. 1990: Developmental models of individual differences. In J. Colombo and J. Fagen (eds) *Individual Differences in Infancy: Reliability, Stability, Prediction*. Hillsdale, NJ: Erlbaum.

Horowitz, L.A., Putnam, F.W., Noll, J.G. and Trickett, P.K. 1997: Factors affecting utilization of treatment services by sexually abused girls. *Child Abuse and Neglect*, 21, 35–48.

Howe, D. 1995: *Attachment Theory for Social Work Practice*. Basingstoke: Macmillan.

Howe, D., Brandon, M., Hinings, D. and Schofield, G. 1999: *Attachment Theory, Child Maltreatment and Family Support*. London: Macmillan.

Hsu, L.K.G. 1990: *Eating Disorders*. New York: Guilford Press.

Hubert, J. 1974: Belief and reality: Social factors in pregnancy and childbirth. In M.P. M. Richards (ed.) *The Integration of a Child into a Social World*. Cambridge: Cambridge University Press.

Hughes, C., Adlam, A., Happe, F., Jackson, J., Taylor, A. and Caspi, A. 2000: Good test-retest reliability for standard and advanced false–belief tasks across a wide range of abilities. *Journal of Child Psychology and Psychiatry*, 41, 483–90.

Hughes, P., Turton, P., Hopper, E., McGauley, G.A. and Fonagy, P. 2001: Disorganized attachment behaviour among infants born subsequent to stillbirth. *Journal of Child Psychology and Psychiatry*, 42, 795–801.

Hutt, C. and Ounsted, C. 1966: The Biological significance of gaze aversion with particular reference to the syndrome of infantile autism. *Behavioral Science*, 11, 346–56.

Huttenlocher, F.H. 1991: Early vocabulary growth: Relationship to language input and gender. *Developmental Psychology*, 27, 236–48.

Isabella, R.A., Belsky, J.H. and von Eye, A. 1989: Origins of infant–mother attachment: An examination of interactional synchrony during the infant's first year. *Developmental Psychology*, 25, 12–21.

Iwaniec, D., Herbert, M. and Sluckin, A. 1988: Helping emotionally abused children who fail to thrive. In K. Browne, C. Davies and P. Stratton (eds) *Early Prediction and Prevention of Child Abuse*. Chichester: Wiley.

Jahoda, M. 1958: *Current Concepts of Positive Mental Health*. New York: Basic Books.

James, W. 1890/1950: *The Principles of Psychology* (2 volumes). New York: Dover/Holt.

Jeffrey, R. and Jeffrey, P.M. 1993: Traditional birth attendants in rural northern India: The social organization of childbearing. In S. Lindenbaum and M. Lock (eds) *Knowledge, Power and Practice: The Anthropology of Medicine and Every Day Life*. Berkley, CA: University of California Press.

Johns, N. 1971: Family reactions to the birth of a child with a congenital abnormality. *Medical Journal of Australia*, 7, 277–82.

Jones, C. 1994: *Attention Deficit Disorder: Strategies for School-Age Children*. Tucson, AZ: Communication Skill Builders.

Jones, D. and McGraw, J.M. 1987: Reliable and fictitious accounts of sexual abuse to children. *Journal of Interpersonal Violence*, 2, 27–45.

Kagan, J. 1984: *The Nature of the Child*. New York: Basic Books, Inc.

Kagan, J. 1989: *Unstable ideas: Temperament, Cognition and Self*. Cambridge, MA: Harvard University Press.

Kagan, J., Arcus, D., Snidman, N., Feng, W.Y. and Greene, S. 1994: Reactivity in infants: A cross-national comparison. *Developmental Psychology*, 30, 342–5.

Kane, B. 1979: Children's concepts of death. *Journal of Genetic Psychology*, 134, 141–5.

Kanner, L. 1943: Autistic disturbances of affective contact. *Nervous Child*, 2, 217–50.

Kazdin, A.E. 1990: Childhood depression. *Journal of Child Psychology and Psychiatry*, 31 121–60.

Keith, J. 1985: Age in anthropological research. In R.H. Binstock and E. Shanus (eds) *Handbook of Aging and the Social Sciences* (2nd edn). New York: Van Nostrand Reinhold.

Kellmer Pringle, M.L. 1975: The Needs of Children. London: Hutchinson.

Kelly, G.A. 1955: *The Psychology of Personal Constructs*. New York: Norton.

Kempe, C.H., Silverman, E.N. and Steele, B.B., 1962: The battered child syndrome. *Journal of the American Medical Association*, 187, 17–24.

Kendall, P.C. and Gosch, E.A. 1994: Cognitive-behavioral interventions. In T. H. Ollendick et al. (eds) *International Handbook of Phobic and Anxiety Disorders in Children and Adolescents*. New York: Plenum Press.

Kerr, A. 2002: Annotation: Rett syndrome: recent progress and implications for research and clinical practice. *Journal of Child Psychology and Psychiatry*, 43, 277–88.

Kiernan, C.C. 1983: The exploration of sign and symbol effects. In J.J. Hogg and P.J. Mittler (eds) *Advances in Mental Handicap Research. Vol. 2: Aspects of Competence in Mentally Handicapped*. Chichester: Wiley.

King, P.M. 1985: Formal reasoning in adults: A review and critique. In R.A. Mines and K.S. Kitchener (eds) *Adult Cognitive Development*. New York: Praeger.

King, N.J., Hamilton, D.I. and Ollendick, T.H. 1998: *Children's Phobias: A Behavioral Perspective*. Chichester: Wiley.

King, N.J., Ollendick, T.H. and Tonge, B. 1995: *School refusal: Assessment and treatment*. Boston: Allyn and Bacon.

Klaus, M.H. and Kennell, J.H. 1976: *Maternal–Infant Bonding*. St Louis, MO: Mosby

Kluckhohn, C., Murray, H.A. and Schneider, D.M. (eds) 1953: *Personality in Nature, Society and Culture*. New York: Knopf.

Kohlberg, L. 1963: The development of children's orientations toward a moral order: 1. Sequence in the development of moral thought. *Vita Humana*, 6, 11–33.

Kohlberg, L. 1976: Moral stages and moralization: The cognitive-developmental approach. In T. Lickona (ed.) *Moral Development and Behavior: Theory, Research and Social Issues*. New York: Holt, Rinehart and Winston.

Kopp, C.B. and Kaler, S.R. 1989: Risk in infancy. *American Psychologist*, 44, 224–30.

Kopp, S. and Gillberg, C. 1992: Girls with social deficits and learning problems: Autism. Asperger syndrome or a variant of these conditions. *European Child and Adolescent Psychiatry*, 1, 89–99.

Korkman, M., Liikanen, A. and Fellman, V. 1996: Neuropsychological consequences of very low birth weight and asphyxia at term: Follow-up until school-age. *Journal of Clinical Neuropsychology*, 18, 220–33.

Krebs, J.R. and Davies, N.B. 1993: *An Introduction to Behavioural Ecology* (3rd edn). Oxford: Blackwell.

Kreitman, N. 1983: Suicide and parasuicide. In R.E. Kendall and A.K. Zealey (eds) *Companion to Psychiatry Studies* (3rd edn). Edinburgh: Churchill Livingstone.

Kubler-Ross, E. 1983: *On Children and Death*. New York: Macmillan.

Laing, R.D. and Esterson, A. 1964: *Sanity, Madness and the Family*. Harmondsworth: Penguin.

Laird, J. and Green, R. 1996: *Lesbians and Gays in Couples and Families: A Handbook for Therapists*. San Francisco, CA: Jossey-Bass.

Lask, B. and Bryant-Waugh, R. 1992: Early onset anorexia nervosa and related eating disorders. *Journal of Child Psychology and Psychiatry*, 33, 281–300.

Leboyer, F. 1975: *Birth Without Violence*. New York: Knopf.

Le Courteur, A. et al. 1996: A broader phenotype of autism: The clinical spectrum in twins. *Journal of Child Psychology and Psychiatry*, 37, 785–802.

Lee, S.G. and Herbert, M. (eds) 1970: *Freud and Psychology*. Harmondsworth: Penguin Books

Leifer, A.D. 1972: Effects of mother–infant separation on maternal attachment behaviour. *Child Development*, 43, 1203–18.

Lejeune, J., Gautier, M. and Turpin R. 1959: Le mongolisme: Premer example d'aberrationautosomique humaine. *Annals de Geneteque*, 1, 41.

Leon, G. 1979: Cognitive–behaviour therapy for eating disturbances. In P. Kendall and S. Hollon (eds) *Cognitive Behavioral Interventions: Theory, Research and Procedures*. New York: Academic Press.

Leon, G.R., Bemis, K.M. and Lucas, A.R. 1980: Family interaction, control and other interpersonal factors as issues in the treatment of anorexia nervosa. *Paper read at World Congress in Behavior Therapy*, Jerusalem, Israel.

Leon, G.R. and Dinklage, D. 1989: Childhood obesity and anorexia nervosa. In T. H. Ollendick and M. Hersen (eds) *Handbook of Child Psychopathology*. New York: Plenum Press.

Leslie, A.M. 1987: Pretence and representation: The origins of "theory of mind". *Psychological Review*, 94, 412–26.

Levy, G.D. and Fivush, R. 1993: Scripts and gender: A new approach for examining gender-role development. *Developmental Review*, 13, 126–46.

Lewis, V. 1987: *Development and Handicap*. Oxford: Basil Blackwell.

Lin, C. 1993: Breech presentation. In C. Lin, M.S.V. Verp and R.J. Sabbagha (eds) *The High-Risk Fetus: Pathophysiology, Diagnosis, Management*. New York: Springer-Verlag.

Littlewood, R. and Lipsedge, M. 1989: *Aliens and Alienists: Ethnic Minorities and Psychiatry* (2nd edn). London: Hyman.

Locke, J. 1690: *Some Thoughts Concerning Education*, Sections 38 and 40. London: Cambridge University Press, 1913.

Loeber, R. 1991: Antisocial behavior: more enduring than changeable. *Journal of the American Academy of Child and Adolescent Psychiatry*, 30, 393–7.

Loeber, R., Green, S.M., Lahey, B.B., Christ, M.A.G. and Frick, P.J. 1992: Developmental sequences in the age of onset of disruptive child behaviors. *Journal of Child and Family Studies*, 1, 21–41.

Loeber, R. and Hay, D.F. 1997: Key issues in the development of aggression and violence from childhood to early adulthood. *Annual Review of Psychology*, 48, 371–410.

Loehlin, J.C. 1992: *Genes and Environment in Personality Development*. Newbury Park, CA: Sage.

Lotter, V. 1978: *Autism: A Reappraisal of Concepts and Treatment*. New York: Plenum Press.

Lucas, A.R. et al. 1991: Fifty-year trends in the incidence of anorexia nervosa in Rochester, Minnesota: A population based study. *American Journal of Psychiatry*, 148, 917–22.

Luria, A.R. 1961: *The Role of Speech in the Regulation of Normal and Abnormal Behavior*. New York: Liveright Publishing.

Lwin, R. and Melvin, D. 2001: Paediatric HIV infection. *Journal of Child Psychology and Psychiatry*, 42, 427–38.

Lynch, M.A., Roberts, J. and Gordon, M. 1976: Predicting child abuse: Signs of bonding failure in the maternity hospital. *British Medical Journal*, 1, 624–6.

McClelland, D. 1961: *The Achieving Society*. Princeton: Van Nostrand.

Maccoby, E.E. 1980: *Social Development: Psychological Growth and the Parent–Child Relationship*. San Diego, CA: Harcourt Brace Jovanovich.

McDonald, K. 1991: Rites of Passage. In R.M. Lerner, A.C. Peterson and J. Brooks-Gunn (eds) *Encyclopedia of Adolescence*, vol. 2. New York: Garland.

MacFarlane, A. 1975: Olfaction in the development of social preferences in the human neonate. In *Parent–Infant Interaction Ciba Foundation Symposium 33*. New York: Elsevier.

MacFarlane, J.W. 1977: *Psychology of Childbirth*. Cambridge, MA: Fontana.

MacFarlene, K. and Krebs, S. 1986: Techniques for interviewing and evidence-gathering. In K. MacFarlene and J. Waterman (eds) *Sexual Abuse of Young Children*. New York: Guilford.

McKenzie, B.E., Tootell, H.E. and Day, R.H. 1980: Development of visual size constancy during the first year of human infancy. *Developmental Psychology*, 16, 163–74.

McMichael, J.K. 1971: *Handicap: A Study of Physically Handicapped Children and their Families*. London: Staples.

Main, M. and Weston, D.R. 1981: The quality of the toddler's relationship to mother and father: Related to conflict and the readiness to establish new relationships. *Child Development*, 52, 932–40.

Marcia, J.E. 1980: Identity in adolescence. In J. Adelson (ed.) *Handbook of Adolescent Psychology*. New York: Wiley.

Marschark, M. 1993: *Psychological Development of Deaf Children*. Oxford: Oxford University Press.

Martin, G.B. and Clark, R.D. 1982: Distress crying in neonates: Species and peer specificity. *Developmental Psychology*, 18, 3–9.

Martorano, S.C.A. 1977: A developmental analysis of performance on Piaget's formal operations tasks. *Developmental Psychology*, 13, 666–72.

Masson, J.N. 1992: *The Assault of Truth: Freud's Suppression of the Seduction Theory*. New York: Farrar, Strauss and Giroux.

Mattis, S.G. and Ollendick, T.H. 2002: *Panic Disorder and Anxiety*. Oxford: BPS/Blackwell. (M. Herbert (ed.) PACT Series.)

Maughan, B. and Yule, W. 1994: Reading and other learning difficulties. In Rutter, M., Hersov, L. and Taylor, E. (eds) *Child and Adolescent Psychiatry: A Modern Approach*. Oxford: Blackwell Scientific.

Maurer, D. 1985: Infant's perception of facedness. In T. Fields and N. Fox (eds) *Social perception in infants*. Norwood, NJ: Ablex.

Mead, M. 1928/1988: *Coming of age in Samoa: A Psychological Study of Primitive Youth for Western Civilization*. New York: William Morrow.

Mead, M. 1935/1988: *Sex and Temperament in Three Primitive Societies*. New York: William Morrow.

Mead, M. 1949/1996: *Male and Female: A Study of the Sexes in a Changing World*. New York: William Morrow.

Meadow, K.P. 1980: *Deafness and Child Development*. London: Edward Arnold.

Meadows, S. 1993: *The Child as Thinker*. London: Routledge.

Meltzoff, A.N. and Moore, M.K. 1977: Imitation of facial and manual gestures by human neonates. *Science*, 198, 75–8.

Middleton, J.A. 2001: Practitioner review: Psychological sequelae of head injury in children and adolescents. *Journal of Child Psychology and Psychiatry*, 42, 165–80.

Miles, T.R. 1990: Developmental dyslexia. In M.W. Eysenck (ed.) *The Blackwell Dictionary of Cognitive Psychology*. Oxford: Blackwell.

Milner, D. 1997: Racism and childhood identity. *The Psychologist*, 10, 123–5.

Moffit, T.E. and Caspi, A. 1998: Implications of violence between intimate partners for child psychologists and psychiatrists. *Journal of Child Psychology and Psychiatry*, 39, 137–44.

Money, J. 1993: *The Adam Principle*. New York: Prometheus Press.

Montagu, M.F.A. 1964: *Life Before Birth*. New York: The New English Library.

Moore, T. 1966: Difficulties of the ordinary child in adjusting to primary school. *Journal of Child Psychology and Psychiatry*, 7, 299.

Moore, K.L. and Persaud, T.V.N. 1993: *Before We Are Born: Essentials of Embryology and Birth Defects* (4th edn). Philadelphia: Saunders.

Morelli, G.A., Rogoff, B., Oppenheim, D. and Goldsmith, D. 1992: Cultural variations in infants' sleeping arrangements: Questions of independence. *Developmental Psychology*, 28, 604–13.

Moser, II.M. 1985: *Prenatal/Perinatal Factors Associated With Brain Disorders*. NIH publication T5-1149, Washington, DC: US Government Publishing Office.

Mount, F. 1983: *The Subversive Family: An Alternative History of Love and Marriage*. London: Unwin.

Murray, L. and Trevarthen, C.B. 1985: Emotional regulation of interaction between two-months-olds and their mothers. In T.M. Field and N.A. Fox (eds) *Social Perception in Infants*. Norwood, NJ: Ablex.

Mussen, P.H., Conger, J.J. and Kagan, 1984: *Child Development and Personality* (6th edn). London: Harper & Row.

Nation, K. 2001: Reading and language in children: Exposing hidden deficits. *The Psychologist*, 14, 238–43.

Needleman, R.D. 1996: Growth and development. In R.E. Behrman, R.M. Kliegman and A.M. Arvin (eds) *Nelson Textbook of Pediatrics* (15th edn). Philadelphia: W.B. Saunders.

Nelson, K. 1973: Structure and strategy in learning to talk. *Monographs of the Society for Research in Child Development*, 38, no. 149, 1–2.

NICHD, 1997: Early child care research network: The effects of infant child care on infant–mother attachment security. *Child Development*, 68, 861–79.

O'Brien, P.J. and Hay, D.A. 1987: Birthweight differences, the transfusion syndrome and the cognitive development of monozygotic twins. *Acta Genet Med Gemellol*, 36, 181–96.

O'Connor, T.G., Thorpe, K., Dunn, J. and Golding, J. 1999: Parental divorce and adjustment in adulthood: Findings from a community sample. *Journal of Child Psychology and Psychiatry*, 40, 777–89.

O'Dempsey, T.J.D. 1988: Traditional belief and practice among the Pokot people of Kenya with particular reference to mother and child health. 2. Mother and child health. *Annals of Tropical Paediatrics*, 8, 125.

Odent, M. 1984: *Birth Reborn*. New York: Pantheon.

Okagaki, L. and Sternberg, R.J. 1993: Parental beliefs and children's school performance. *Child Development*, 64, 36–56.

Ollendick, T.H. and King, N.J. 1991: Fears and phobias of childhood. In M. Herbert, *Clinical Child Psychology: Social Learning, Development and Behaviour*. Chichester: John Wiley.

Ollendick, T.H. and King, N.J. 1998: Assessment practices and issues with school-refusing children. *Behaviour Change*, 15, 16–30.

Olweus, D. 1974: Bullying at school. Basic facts and effects of a school based intervention programme. *Journal of Child Psychology and Psychiatry*, 35, 1171–90.

Orme, N. 2000: *Mediaeval Children*. New Haven: Yale University Press.

Parten, M.B. 1932: Social participation among preschool children. *Journal of Abnormal Social Psychology*, 27, 243–69.

Pasamanick, B. and Knobloch, H. 1961: Epidemiological studies on the complications of pregnancy and the birth process. In G. Caplan (ed.) *Prevention of Mental Disorders in Childhood*. New York: Basic Books.

Patterson, G.R 1982: *Coercive Family Process*. Eugene, OR: Castalia.

Pavlov, I.P. 1927: *Conditioned Reflexes*, G.V. Anrep (trans. and ed.). Oxford: Oxford University Press.

Paykel, E., Prosoff, B.A. and Myers, J.K. 1975: Suicide attempts and recent life events. *Archives of General Psychiatry*, 32, 327–33.

Penfield, W. and Roberts, L. 1959: *Speech and Brain Mechanisms*. New Jersey: Princetown University Press.

Phatak, J.P. 1969: Motor and mental development of Indian babies from one month to thirty months. *Indian Paediatrics*, 6, 18–23.

Philpott, R.H. 1995: Maternal health care in the developing world. In B.P. Sachs et al. (eds) *Reproductive health care for women and babies*. New York: Oxford University Press.

Piaget, J. 1929: *The Child's Conception of the World*. London: Routledge and Kegan Paul.

Piaget, J. 1932: *The Moral Judgement of the Child*. New York: Harcourt.

Piaget, J. 1950: *The Psychology of Intelligence*. San Diego, CA: Harcourt Brace Jovanovich.

Piaget, J. 1954: *The Construction of Reality in the Child*. New York: Basic Books.

Piers, Maria, 1978: *Infanticide: Past and Present*. New York: Norton.

Pinker, S. 1994: *The Language Instinct*. New York: Morrow.

Pinker, S. 1997: *How the Mind Works*. London: W.W. Norton.

Plomin, R. 1990: *Nature and Nurture: An Introduction to Behaviour Genetics*. Pacific Grove, CA: Sage.

Plomin, R. 2001a: Genetics and behaviour. *The Psychologist*, 14, 134–9.

Plomin, R. 2001b: Human genome project. *The Psychologist*, 14, no. 4, 174.

Plomin, R. and Bergaman, C.S. 1991: The nature of nurture: Genetic influence on 'environmental' measures. *Behavioural and Brain Sciences*, 14, 373–427.

Plomin, R. and McClearn, G.E. (eds) 1993: *Nature, Nurture and Psychology*. Washington: APA Books.

Polka, L. and Werker, J.F. 1994: Developmental changes in perception of nonnative vowel contrasts. *Journal of Experimental Psychology: Human Perception and Performance*, 20, 421–35.

Premack, D. and Woodruff, G. 1978: Does a chimpanzee have a theory of mind? *Behavioral and Brain Sciences*, 1, 512–26.

Purpura, D.P. 1974: Dendrite spine dysgenesis and mental retardation. *Science*, 186, 1126–8.

Pushkin, L. and Veness, T. 1973: The development of racial awareness and prejudice in children. In P. Watson (ed.) *Psychology and Race*. Harmondsworth: Penguin.

Rachman, S. 1997: A cognitive theory of obsessions. *Behaviour Research and Therapy*, 35, 793–802.

Rapin, I. 1996: Practitioner review: Developmental language disorders – A clinical update. *Journal of Child Psychology and Psychiatry*, 37, 643–55.

Reason, R. 2001: Educational practice and dyslexia. *The Psychologist*, 14, 298–301.

Reed, G.F. 1963: Elective mutism in children: a reappraisal. *Journal of Child Psychology and Psychiatry*, 4, 99–107.

Reynell, J. 1978: Developmental patterns of visually handicapped children. *Child Care, Health and Development*, 4, 291–303.

Reynolds, E.H. 1988: Historical aspects. In M.R. Trimble and E.H. Reynolds (eds) *Epilepsy, Behaviour and Cognitive Function*. Chichester: John Wiley.

Richards, M.P.M. and Bernal, J.F. 1971: Social interaction in the first days of life. In H.R. Schaffer (ed.) *The Origins of Human Social Relations*. London: Academic Press.

Richman, N., Stevenson, J. and Graham, P. 1975: Prevalence and patterns of psychological disturbance in children of primary age. *Journal of Child and Adolescent Psychology and Psychiatry*, 16, 101–3.

Ridley, M. 1995: *Animal behaviour* (2nd edn). Oxford: Blackwell.

Rieffe, C. and Terwogt, M.M. 2000: Deaf children's understanding of emotions: Desires take precedence. *Journal of Child Psychology and Psychiatry*, 41, 601–8.

Ritvo, E.R. et al. 1990: The UCLA University of Utah epidemiologic survey of autism – the etiologic of rare diseases. *American Journal of Psychiatry*, 147, 1614–21.

Robertson, J. and Bowlby, J. 1952: Responses of young children to separation from their mothers. *Courrier de la Centre Internationale de l'enfance*, 2, 131–42.

Robson, K.S. and Kumar, H.A. 1980: Delayed onset of maternal affection after childbirth. *British Journal of Psychiatry*, 136, 347–53.

Rojahn, J., Tasse, M.J. and Marin, D. 1998: Self-injurious behavior and stereotypes. In T.H. Ollendick and M. Hersen (eds) *Handbook of Child Psychopathology* (3rd edn). New York: Plenum Press.

Roland, A. 1988: *Search of Self in India and Japan: Towards a Cross-Cultural Psychology*. Princeton University Press.

Rosenblith, J. 1992: *In the Beginning: Development from Conception to Age Two* (2nd edn). Newbury Park: Sage.

Rousseau, J.J. 1762/1932: *Emile, or Concerning Education*, book 2. New York: Dutten.

Rutter, M. 1970a: Psychological development – predictions from infancy. *Journal of Child Psychology and Psychiatry*, 10, 49–62.

Rutter, M. 1970b: Autistic children: Infancy to adulthood. *Seminars in Psychiatry*, 2, 435–50.

Rutter, M. 1971: Normal psychosexual development. *Journal of Child Psychology and Psychiatry*, 11, 259–83.

Rutter, M. 1972: *Maternal Deprivation Reassessed*. Harmondsworth: Penguin Books

Rutter, M. 1978a: Early sources of security and competence. In J.S. Bruner and A. Garton (eds) *Human Growth and Development*. London: Oxford University Press.

Rutter, M. 1978b: Diagnosis and definition of childhood autism. *Journal of Autism and Developmental Disorder*, 8, 139–61.

Rutter, M. 1979: *Changing youth in a changing society*. The Nuffield Provincial Hospitals Trust.

Rutter, M. 1983: Cognitive deficits in the pathogenesis of autism. *Journal of Child Psychology and Psychiatry*, 24, 513–31.

Rutter, M. 1990: Psychological resilience and protective mechanisms. In J. Rolf et al. (eds) *Risk and Protective Factors in the Development of Psychopathology*. New York: Cambridge University Press.

Rutter, M. 1995: Clinical implications of attachment theory, retrospect and prospect. *Journal of Child Psychology and Psychiatry*, 36, 549–71.

Rutter, M., Maughan, B., Mortimore, P., Ousten, J. and Smith, A. 1979: *Fifteen Thousand Hours: Secondary Schools and their Effects on Children*. Cambridge, MA: Harvard University Press.

Rutter, M. and Quinton, D. 1977: Psychiatric disorder – ecological factors and resistance to psychiatric disorder. *British Journal of Psychiatry*, 147, 598–611.

Rutter, M., Silberg, J., O'Connor, T. and Simonoff, E. 1999a: Genetics and psychiatry: I Advances in quantitative and molecular genetics (pp. 3–18); II Empirical research findings (pp. 19–36). *Journal of Child Psychology and Psychiatry*, 40, 3–18.

Rutter, M., Silberg, J., O'Connor, T. and Simonoff, E. 1999b: Genetics and child psychiatry: II Empirical research findings. (37–55) *Journal of Child Psychology and Psychiatry*, 40.

Rutter, M., Tizard, J. and Whitmore, K. (eds) 1970: *Education, Health and Behaviour*. Harlow: Longman. (Reprinted 1981, Krieger, Melbourne, FC.)

St James-Roberts, I., Bowyer, J. et al. 1994: Infant crying patterns in Manali and London. *Child Care, Health and Development*, 20, 323–37.

St James-Roberts, L. and Plewis, I. 1996: Individual differences, daily fluctuations, and developmental changes in amounts of infant waking, fussing, feeding and sleeping. *Child Development*, 67, 2527–40.

Sameroff, A.S. and Chandler, M.J. 1975: Reproductive risk and the continuum of caretaking casualty. In F.D. Horowitz et al. (eds) *Review of Child Development Research*, vol. 4. Chicago: Chicago University Press.

Schaffer, H.R. 1977: *Mothering*. London: Open Books/Fontana.

Schaffer, H.R. 1990: *Making Decisions About Children: Psychological Questions and Answers*. Oxford: Basil Blackwell.

Scott, D.W. 1987: The involvement of psychosexual factors in the causality of eating disorder: Time for a re-appraisal. *International Journal of Eating Disorders*, 6, 119–213.

Sears, R.R., Maccoby, E.E. and Lewin, H. 1957: *Patterns of Childrearing*. London: Harper & Row.

Seligman, M.E.P. 1975: *Helplessness: On Depression, Development, and Death*. San Francisco, CA: Freeman.

Selman, R.L. 1980: *The Growth of Interpersonal Understanding*. Orlando, FL: Academic Press.

Shaffer, D.R. 1999: *Developmental psychology: Childhood and Adolescence*. Pacific Grove, CA: Brooks/Cole.

Shafran, R. 2001: Obsessive–compulsive disorder in childhood and adolescence. *Journal of Child Psychology and Psychiatry*, 6, 50–58.

Shahidullah, S. and Hepper, P.G. 1993: Prenatal learning tests? *Journal of Reproductive and Infant Psychology*, 11, 143–6.

Shaw, M. 1986: Substitute parenting. In W. Sluckin and M. Herbert (eds) *Parental Behaviour*. Chichester: Wiley.

Shaywitz, B.A. 1987: *Yale Children's Inventory*. New Haven, CT: Yale University Medical School.

Shaywitz, S.E. 1996: Dyslexia. *Scientific American*, 276, 78–84.

Sheridan, M. 1989: *Protecting Children: A Guide for Social Workers Undertaking a Comprehensive Assessment*. London: Department of Health, HMSO.

Shirley, M.M. 1938: Development of immature babies during their first two years. *Child Development*, 9, 347–60.

Simeonsson, R.L. and Rosenthal, S.L. (eds) 2001: *Psychological and Developmental Assessment: Children with Disabilities and Chronic Conditions*. New York: The Guilford Press.

Siminoff, E., Bolton, P. and Rutter, M. 1996: Mental Retardation: Genetic findings, clinical implications and research agenda. *Journal of Child Psychology and Psychiatry*, 37, 259–80.

Sinha, D. and Sinha, M. 1997: Orientation to psychology: Asian and Western. In S.R. Kao and D. Sinha (eds) *Asian perspectives on psychology*. Princeton University Press.

Skinner, B.F. 1953: *Science and Human Behavior*. New York: Free Press.

Slater, A. 1990: Infant development: The origins of competence. *The Psychologist*, 3, 109–13.

Slobin, D.I. 1985: Crosslinguistic evidence for the language making capacity. In D.I. Slobin (ed.) *The Crosslinguistic Study of Language Acquisition. Vol. 2, Theoretical issues*. Hillsdale, NJ: Erlbaum.

Sluckin, W. and Herbert, M. 1986: *Parental Behaviour*. Chichester: Wiley.

Sluckin, W., Herbert, M. and Sluckin, A. 1983: *Maternal bonding*. Oxford: Basil Blackwell.

Sluckin, A., Foreman, N. and Herbert, M. 1990: Behavioural treatment programmes and selectivity of speaking at follow-up to a sample of 25 selective mutes. *Australian Psychologist*, 26, 132–7.

Smith, B.R. and Leinonen, E. 1992: *Clinical Pragmatics: Unravelling the Complexities of Communicative Failure*. London: Chapman Hall.

Snowling, M.J. 2000: *Dyslexia*. Oxford: Blackwell.

Sontag, L.W. 1941: The significance of fetal environmental differences. *American Journal of Obstetrics and Gynecology*, 42, 996–1003.

Sontag, L.W. 1944: Differences in modifiability of fetal behaviour and physiology. *Psychosomatic Medicine*, 6, 151–4.

Spelke, F.S. and Owsley, C.J. 1979: Intermodal exploration and knowledge in infancy. *Infant Behaviour and Development*, 2, 12–29.

Spencer, H. 1978/1898: *The Principles of Psychology*. New York: Appleton.

Spock, B. 1945: *The Commonsense Book of Baby and Child Care*. New York: Duell, Sloan and Peane.

Sroufe, L.A. 1990: Considering normal and abnormal together: The essence of developmental psychopathology. Development and Psychopathology, 2, 335–47.

Standish, L. 1982: The loss of a baby. *The Lancet*, i, 611–12.

Stayton, D.J., Hogan, R. and Ainsworth, M.D.S. 1971: Infant obedience and maternal behaviour: The origins of socialisation reconsidered. *Child Development*, 42, 1057–69.

Steinhausen, H.C. 1994: Anorexia and bulimia nervosa. In M. Rutter, E. Taylor and L. Hersov (eds) *Child and Adolescent Psychiatry* (3rd edn). Oxford: Blackwell Scientific.

Stermac, L.E. and Segal, Z.V. 1989: Adult sexual contact with children: an examination of cognitive factors. *Behaviour Therapy*, 20, 573–84.

Stern, E. 1977: *The First Relationship: Infant and Mother*. London: Fontana/Open Books.

Stevenson, H.W., Chen, C. and Lee, S. 1993: Mathematics achievement of Chinese, Japanese and American children: ten years later. *Science*, 259, 53–8.

Stigler, J.W., Lee, S.V. and Stevenson, H.W. 1987: Mathematics classrooms in Japan, Taiwan and the United States. *Child Development*, 58, 1272–85.

Stopes, Marie, 1920/2001: *Radiant Motherhood: A Book for Creating the Future* (3rd edn). London: G.P. Putnam.

Stoppard, M. 2000: *Conception, Pregnancy and Birth* (rev. edn). London: Dorling Kindersley.

Stott, D.H. 1966: *Studies of Troublesome Children*. London: Tavistock.

Sullivan, H.S. 1953: *The Interpersonal Theory of Psychiatry*. New York: Norton.

Super, C.H. 1980: Cross-cultural research on infancy. In H.C. Triandis and A. Heron (eds) *Handbook of Cross-Cultural Psychology; Developmental Psychology*, vol. 4. Boston: Allyn and Bacon.

Szasz, T.S. 1960: *The Myth of Mental Illness: Foundations of a Theory of Personal Conduct*. New York: Hoeber-Harper.

Tanner, J.M. 1990: *Foetus Into Man: Physical Growth From Conception to Maturity* (2nd edn). Cambridge, MA: Harvard University Press.

Thelen, E. 1984: Learning to walk: Ecological demands and phylogenetic constraints. In L.P. Lipsitt and C. Rover-Collier (eds) *Advances in infancy research*, vol. 3. Norwood, NJ: Ablex.

Thelen, E. and Ulrich, B.D. 1991: Hidden skills: A dynamic systems analysis of treadmill stepping during the first year. *Monographs of the Society for Researching Child Development*, 56, Serial No. 223.

Thomas, A. and Chess, S. 1986: The New York longitudinal study: From infancy to early adult life. In R. Plomin and J. Dunn (eds) *The Study of Temperament: Changes, Continuities and Challenges*. Hillsdale, NJ: Erlbaum.

Thomas, A., Chess, S. and Birch, H.G. 1968: *Temperament and Behaviour Disorders in Children*. London: University of London Press.

Thompson, A.A. 1991: Construction and reconstruction of early attachments: Taking perspective in attachment theory and research. In D.P. Keating and H.G. Rosen (eds) *Constructivist Perspectives in Atypical Development*. Hillsdale, NJ: Erlbaum.

Thompson, C., Westwell, P. and Viney, P. 1994: Psychiatric aspects of human immune deficiency virus in childhood and adolescence. In M. Rutter, E. Taylor and M. Hersov (eds) *Child and Adolescent Psychiatry: Modern Approaches* (3rd edn). Oxford: Blackwell Scientific.

Thurman, S. 1997: LSD on the playground? Teen drug trends: Users get younger, substances harder. *Christian Science Monitor*, 89, 3.

Torgerson, A.M. and Kringlen, E. 1978: Genetic aspects of temperament differences in infants. *Journal of the Academy of Child Psychiatry*, 17, 433–44.

Trevarthen, C. and Aitken, K.J. 2001: Infant intersubjectivity: Research, Theory and Clinical Applications. *Journal of Child Psychology and Psychiatry*, 42, 3–48.

Trevarthen, C. et al. 1996: *Children with Autism: Diagnosis and Interventions to Meet Their Needs*. London: Jessica Kingsley.

Tubman, J.G., Windle, M. and Windle, R.C. 1996: The onset and cross-temporal patterning of sexual intercourse in middle adolescence: Prospective relations with behavioural and emotional problems. *Child Development*, 67, 327–43.

Ucko, L.E. 1965: A comparative study of asphyxiated and non-asphyxiated boys from birth to 5 years. *Developmental Medicine and Child Neurology*, 7, 643–57.

Vaughan, B.E., Kopp, C.B. and Krakow, J.B. 1984: The emergence and consolidation of self-control from eighteen to thirty months of age: Normative trends and individual differences. *Child Development*, 55, 990–1004.

Vesterdal, J. 1976: Psychological mechanisms in child-abusing parents. In J.V. Cook and R.T. Bowles (eds) *Child Abuse: Commission and Omission*. Toronto: Butterworth.

Vygotsky, L.S. 1962: *Thought and Language*. Cambridge, MA: MIT Press.

Wallach, M.A. and Wallach, L. 1983: *Psychology's Sanction for Selfishness*. San Francisco, CA: Freeman.

Wallerstein, J. and Blakeslee, S. 1989: *Second chances*. New York: Ticknor and Fields.

Wallerstein, J. and Kelly, J. 1980: *Surviving the Breakup: How Children and Parents Cope with Divorce*. New York: Basic Books.

Waters, E., Wippman, J. and Sroufe, L.A. 1979: Attachment, positive affect and competence in the peer group: Two studies in construct validation. *Child Development*, 50, 821–9.

Watson, J.B. 1928: *Psychological Care of Infant and Child*. New York: Norton.

Watson, J.D. and Crick, F.H.C. 1953: Molecular structure of nucleic acids: A structure for deoxyribose nucleic acid. *Nature*, 171, 737–8.

Webster-Stratton, C. 1991: Annotation: Strategies for working with families and conduct-disordered children. *Journal of Child Psychology and Psychiatry*, 32, 1047–68.

Webster-Stratton, C. and Herbert, M. 1994: *Troubled families: Problem children. Working with Parents: A Collaborative Process*. Chichester: Wiley.

Weiner, B. 1986: *An Attributional Theory of Motivation and Emotion*. New York: Springer-Verlag.

Weiner, B. 1995: *Judgements of Responsibility: A Foundation for a Theory of Human Conduct*. New York: Guilford Press.

Weir, K. 1982: Night and day wetting among a population of three year olds. *Developmental Medicine and Child Neurology*, 24, 479–84.

Weisner, T.S. and Gallimore, R. 1977: My brother's keeper: Child and sibling caretaking. *Current Anthropology*, 18, 169–90.

Weisner, L.A. and Gillenwater, J.M. 1990: Pure tone sensitivity of two five-week old infants. *Infant Behaviour and Development*, 13, 355–75.

Wellings, K., Field, J., Johnson, A. and Wadsworth, J. 1994: *Sexual behaviour in Britain*. Harmondsworth: Penguin.

Wellman, H.M. 1990: *The Child's Theory of Mind*. Cambridge, MA: MIT Press.

Werner, E.E. 1972: Infants around the world: Cross-cultural studies of psychomotor development from birth to two years. *Journal of Cross-cultural Psychology*, 3, 111–34.

Werner, E.E. 1979: *Crosscultural Child Development: A View from Planet Earth*. Monterey, CA: Brooks/Cole.

Werner, E. and Smith, R.S. 1982: *Vulnerable But Invincible: A Longitudinal Study of Resilient Children and Youth*. New York: McGraw-Hill.

Westcott, H. and Jones, D.P.H. 1999: Annotation: The abuse of disabled children. *Journal of Child Psychology and Psychiatry*, 40, 497–506.

Whiting, B.B. and Edwards, O.P. 1988: *Children of Different Worlds: The Formation of Social Behaviour*. Cambridge, MA: Harvard University Press.

Williams, A. and Carmichael, A. 1985: Depression in mothers in a multiethnic industrial municipality in Melbourne. *Journal of Child Psychology and Psychiatry*, 26, 277–88.

Wing, J.K. (ed.) 1978: *Schizophrenia: Towards a New Synthesis*. London: Academic Press.

Wing, L. and Gould, J. 1979: Severe impairment of social interaction and associated abnormalities in children: Epidemiology and classification. *Journal of Autism and Developmental Disorders*, 9, 11–29.

Winnicott, D. 1958: *Collected papers*. London: Tavistock.

Winters, K. 1998: Treatment recognizes link between delinquency and substance abuse. *Corrections Today*, 60, 118–23.

Wood, D. 1988: *How Children Think and Learn*. Oxford: Blackwell.

World Health Organization (WHO) 1992: *International Classification of Impairments, Disabilities and Handicaps*. Geneva: WHO.

World Health Organization, 1996: *Multi-axial Classification of Child and Adolescent Psychiatric Disorders. ICD-10: Classification of Mental and Behavioural Disorders in Children and Adolescents*. Cambridge: Cambridge University Press.

Wright, D. 1971: *The Psychology of Moral Behaviour*. Harmondsworth: Penguin.

Yarrow, M.R., Campbell, J.D. and Burton, R.V. 1968: *Child Rearing: An Inquiry into Research and Methods*. San Francisco: Jossey-Bass.

Yonas, A. and Owsley, C. 1987: Development of Visual Space Perception. In P. Salapatek and L. Cohen (eds) *Handbook of Infant Perception*, vol. 2.

Zmetkin, A.J. and Rapoport, J.L. 1986: The pathophysiology of attention deficit disorder with hyperactivity: A review. In B.B. Lahey and A.E. Kazden (eds) *Advances in Clinical Child Psychology*, vol. 9. New York: Plenum.

Zeanor, C.H. and Emde, R.N. 1994: Attachment Disorders in Infancy and Childhood. In M. Rutter, E. Taylor and L. Hersov (eds) *Child and Adolescent Psychiatry: Modern Approaches*. Oxford: Blackwell Scientific.

Zippay, A. 1995: Expanding employment skills and social networks among teen mothers: Case study of a mentor program. *Child and Adolescent Social Work Journal*, 12, 51–69.

Zohar, A.H. 1999: The epidemiology of obsessive–compulsive disorder in children and adolescents. *Psychiatric Clinic of North America*, 8, 445–60.

Index

Printed in Poland
by Amazon Fulfillment
Poland Sp. z o.o., Wrocław